西北政法大学国际法研究中心
西北政法大学郑斌航空与空间法研究所 主办

本书获陕西省哲学社会科学重点研究基地——
西北政法大学国际法研究中心专项基金、陕西省国际法学科
“三秦学者”科研创新团队专项资金资助

CHINA AVIATION LAW
REVIEW

中国航空法评论

（第三卷）

王瀚/主编

法律出版社
LAW PRESS·CHINA

《中国航空法评论》编委会

《中国航空法评论》主编及编委简介

主　编

王　瀚:武汉大学法学博士,中国社会科学院法学博士后。原西北政法大学党委委员、副校长,二级教授,丝绸之路区域合作与发展法律研究院院长,陕西省哲学社会科学重点学科(国际法学科)带头人,陕西省哲学社会科学重点研究基地——西北政法大学国际法研究中心主任,航空法治现代化协同创新中心负责人、首席专家,郑斌航空与空间法研究所所长,陕西省"三秦学者"特聘教授,中国社会科学院首届"十大杰出法学博士后"。

兼任吉林大学、西南政法大学、大连海事大学和华东政法大学兼职教授和博士生导师、广东外语外贸大学云山讲座教授、中国国际私法学会副会长、中国国际法学会常务理事、陕西省法学会国际法研究会会长、最高人民法院首批涉外商事海事审判专家库专家、最高人民法院"一带一路"司法研究中心研究员、中国国际经济贸易仲裁委员会仲裁员。曾任陕西省人大常委会内务司法委员会法律咨询专家、陕西省人民政府法律顾问。

主持和完成国家社科基金、司法部、中国法学会、外交部等9项课题研究工作,独著《华沙国际航空运输责任体制法律问题研究》《国际私法之程序法比较研究》《国际航空运输责任法研究》3部,合著或主编《当代国际法专题研究》《现代国际法学》《国际航空私法各论》等学术著作20余部,在《中国法学》《比较法研究》《法律科学》《现代法学》《中国国际法年刊》等期刊发表学术论文60余篇。先后获得陕西省人民政府哲学社会科学优秀成果一等奖2项、三等奖2项;司法部优秀成果三等奖1项;陕西省高校人文社会科学优秀成果一等奖和二等奖各1项、三等奖2项;西安市人民政府优秀社会科学成果一等奖1项、二等奖2项。荣获"陕西省师德先进个人""陕西省师德标兵""陕西省劳动模范""陕西省高校优秀教师"等称号,并获得中国法学会1999年和2002年"全国杰出中青年法学家"提名奖。

编　委

程家瑞:希腊雅典大学法学博士,我国台湾地区著名法学家。亚洲国际航空暨太空法研究所董事会主席、中华比较法学会会长、亚洲厦门国际法高等研究院理事会秘书长。

董念清:北京师范大学经济学博士,中国民航干部管理学院教授,北京市法学会航空法学研究会会长,中国航空运输协会特聘专家。

郭仁刚:中国民用航空局政策法规司副司长。

黄解放:荷兰莱顿大学航空法学博士,武汉大学国际法研究所教授,国际民用航空组织法律事务与对外关系局局长,中国法学会航空法学研究会顾问。

韩　钧:中国人民大学法学博士,中国民用航空局华北地区管理局党委书记、副局长。

柳　芳:武汉大学法学博士,联合国国际民用航空组织秘书长。

刘亚军:西安交通大学经济学博士,西北政法大学国际法学院院长,教授。

刘　萍:大连海事大学法学博士,重庆大学法学博士后。西北政法大学国际法学院教授。

聂　颖:原中国航空集团公司办公厅巡视员、总法律顾问。

吴建端:荷兰莱顿大学航空法学博士,原中国东方航空集团公司政策研究室主任。

赵　云:荷兰鹿特丹伊拉斯莫斯大学法学博士,香港大学法律学院教授,香港国际仲裁中心仲裁员,国际空间法学会会员。

张　炎:西安阎良国家航空高技术产业基地党工委副书记、纪委书记、西北通用航空协会会长、国家特级飞行员。

[美]保罗·史蒂芬·邓普西(Paul Stephen Dempsey):佐治亚大学法学博士(J. D.),麦吉尔大学民法博士(D. C. L.),原加拿大麦吉尔大学航空与空间法研究所所长。

[荷]帕布罗·门德斯·戴莱·昂(Pablo Mendes De Leon):荷兰莱顿大学航空与空间法国际研究所所长、欧盟航空法协会主席、荷兰地区法院荣誉法官、国际商会航空运输委员会委员。

[韩]金斗焕(Doo Hwan Kim):韩国航空宇宙政策法学会名誉会长。

执行主编

张超汉:吉林大学法学博士,上海交通大学法学博士后,国家公派加拿大蒙特利尔大学联合培养博士。西北政法大学国际法学院副教授、郑斌航空与空间法研究所副所长,陕西省首批"千人计划"青年学者。

西北政法大学郑斌航空与空间法研究所简介

郑斌航空与空间法研究所是西北政法大学依托陕西省哲学社会科学重点研究基地（国际法研究中心）和陕西省哲学社会科学重点学科（国际法学科）成立的专门从事航空法与空间法学术研究、人才培养、科研服务的综合性、专业化高校智库平台，原为成立于2009年的西北政法大学航空与空间法研究所，2017年8月更名为“郑斌航空与空间法研究所”。为服务于我国航空强国战略和陕西航空领域军民融合的战略发展，2014年7月西北政法大学与西安阎良国家航空高技术产业基地、西部机场集团合作共同成立了全国首个航空法领域协同创新研究中心——航空法治现代化协同创新中心。为适应我国通用航空事业的发展需要、推进通用航空法学术研究、促进通用航空法治建设，2013年10月西北政法大学与西安阎良国家航空高技术产业基地合作设立和共建了全国首家通用航空法研究所。郑斌航空与空间法研究所现拥有独立的办公场所和资料信息中心，并拥有郑斌航空法图书馆，收藏有国际上享有盛誉的杰出航空法学家郑斌先生捐赠的国际航空法和空间法图书、期刊、国际组织报告等3000余种、册。

郑斌航空与空间法研究所所长由我国航空法专家、原西北政法大学副校长,二级教授、博士研究生导师、陕西省"三秦学者"特聘教授,中国社会科学院首届"十大杰出法学博士后"王瀚教授担任。目前,郑斌航空与空间法研究所共有专职研究人员10人,其中教授3人、副教授4人,研究人员均具有博士学位。为开展国际航空法学术合作和交流,增强航空法研究力量,研究所聘请了国内外一流航空法与空间法学者加盟,开展合作研究。著名航空法专家、新西兰奥克兰大学保罗·史蒂芬·邓普西(Paul Stephen Dempsey)教授(曾任加拿大麦吉尔大学航空与空间法研究所所长),荷兰莱顿大学航空与空间法国际研究所所长、欧盟航空法协会主席帕布罗·门德斯·戴莱·昂(Pablo Mendes De Leon)教授,美国乔治·华盛顿大学艾略特国际关系学院外层空间法专家、韩国航空宇宙政策法学会名誉会长金斗焕(Doo Hwan Kim)教授和我国台湾地区著名法学家、亚太航空法协会主席程家瑞先生先后受聘担任研究所的学术顾问和客座教授。已故我国著名航空法专家刘伟民教授曾于2010~2016年受聘研究所的客座教授和执行所长。研究所对推动航空法学术研究、人才培养、学科发展和智库建设做出了重要贡献。

为传承"航空法之父"、杰出航空法专家、英国伦敦大学华裔终身教授郑斌先生的航空法学术思想和学术精神,弘扬航空法治思想、崇尚航空法治学术创造、增强航空法的国际学术交流,研究所自2017年起设立"郑斌航空法与空间法讲习教授"岗位,从全球招聘航空法与空间法的顶尖学者专家担纲国际航空法与空间法前沿问题的研究和专题讲座。

郑斌航空与空间法研究所始终注重国际学术合作与交流,先后与国际民航组织法律局、中国驻国际民航组织代表处、加拿大麦吉尔大学航空与空间法研究所、荷兰莱顿大学航空与空间法国际研究所等重要国际机构和航空法学术研究机构建立合作关系,开展实质性的合作交流活动,先后接待了莫桑比克民航局长伊曼琼斯凯文先生、中国驻国际民航组织副代表丁春宇等航空领域官员。研究所目前已形成包括本科、硕士、博士、博士后在内的完备的航空法人才培养体系。其中,已为超过1000名本科生开设航空法课程(全国为数不多的为本科生开设航空法课程的高校之一),已培养航空法专业硕士研究生30余人、博士研究生近10人、博士后2人。

郑斌航空与空间法研究所目前已承担各类航空法课题(国家级、省部级及横向课题)20余项,承担行业、地方重大委托科研任务10余项,发表学术论文80余篇;出版《国际航空运输责任法研究》《国际航空产品责任法研究》《国际航空运输垄断行为法律规制研究》《国际航空法专论》《航权开放与西安国际直接通航法律问题》等系列研究成果,主办《中国航空法评论》,创办"中国航空法文库",获得省部级以上奖励12项,厅局级奖励11项,其他科研获奖7项。

郑斌航空与空间法研究所的智库建设已取得显著成效,研究人员以专家身份多次受邀参加国务院法制办、国家空管委、中国民用航空局、中国法学会关于《民用航空法》立法修订和航空法起草的咨询论证工作;研究所出具的咨询报告——《关于完善航空立法,加强空域管理的咨询意见》被教育部采纳,已上报至中共中央办公厅,供中央领导参阅;研究所为国际民航组织理事会第211届第9次会议审议的巴西与美国争端的程序问题提供了智力支持,获得中国驻国际民航组织代表处专函致谢;研究所积极投身和服务于陕西省空港经济建设和航空产业发展,提供航空法研究智力支持,先后参加了陕西省空港新城自贸区政策创新方案论证、西咸新区空港新城航空物流发展扶持实施办法专家评审、西安至首尔航空货运航线开通论证等航空法咨政服务活动。

研究所先后主办了"中加航空法论坛"、"中美航空法论坛"、"纪念《蒙特利尔公约》实施10周年学术论坛"、"纪念《国际民用航空公约》签署70周年暨世界商业航空运营100周年法治论坛"(与加拿大麦吉尔大学航空与空间法研究所联合主办)等重大国际学术论坛,举办了"面向'一带一路'的中国民航法治创新学术论坛",在全国产生了重大影响。为适应我国低空开放和通用航空事业的发展,与西安阎良国家航空高技术产业基地合作,先后3次承办“中国国际通用航空大会通用航空法治论坛”,该论坛已经被列入国务院批准的“中国国际通用航空大会”专业论坛,成为中国首个通用航空法治的专业论坛和通用航空法治实践和学术研究的品牌交流平台。

目　录

特　稿

The Principle of Non-discrimination in International Air Law
…………………………………………………… Pablo Mendes de Leon　3
打造“空中丝绸之路”　推进“一带一路”倡议的法律思考
…………………………………………………………… 吴建端　25

航空立法

我国航空立法路径争议述评…………………………………… 王立志　47
中国示范法:“一带一路”区域民航法的建立………………… 李亚凝　64

航空器融资租赁

飞机融资租赁的法律适用
——以《开普敦公约》为视角 ……………………………… 陈　胜　89

"一带一路"视野下中国航空器融资租赁登记制度的完善
…………………………………………………… 李毅阳 丁达人 101
Legal Market for Aircraft Financing in China ………… Luping Zhang 114

航空法前沿

上海国际航空仲裁院仲裁程序之完善 …………………… 张婉露 137
亚太民航委员会的构建问题:国际组织法的视角 …………… 赵劲松 152
民用无人机国际立法的新近发展与反思 ………………… 张雪莹 162
论航空运送人之责任限制 ……………………………… 吴光平 183
美国对国际航空运输法律自由化的影响论析 ……………… 周亚光 225

资 讯

著名国际法学家、英国伦敦大学终身名誉教授郑斌先生向
西北政法大学捐赠图书 ………………………………………………… 257
"一带一路"民航法治实践与创新
——2017年中国法学会航空法学研究会年会综述 ……… 时杜娟 262
西北政法大学郑斌航空与空间法研究所2017年学术活动大事记 …… 274

《中国航空法评论》稿约 ……………………………………………… 302

Contents

Leading Articles

The Principle of Non-discrimination in International Air Law
…………………………………… by Pablo Mendes de Leon(3)
Legal Aspects Concerning the Building of "Silk Road in the Air" to Promote China's Belt and Road Initiative …… by Wu Jian-duan(25)

Aviation Legislation

A Review of the Controversies in Making Chinese Aviation Law
…………………………………………………… by Wang Li-zhi(47)
Chinese Model Law on Civil Aviation for the Belt and Road Region: Theory and Practice ……………………………… by Li Ya-ning(64)

Aircraft Finance & Leasing

The Application of the Law of Aircraft Leasing
—in the Context of the Cape Town Convention …… by Chen Sheng(89)

Improving the Aircraft Finance Lease Registration System of China under the Belt and Road Initiative ······································ by Li Yi-yang and Ding Da-ren (101)

Legal Market for Aircraft Financing in China ······ by Luping Zhang(114)

Aviation Law Frontier

Enhancing the Effectiveness of Procedures of Shanghai International Aviation Court of Arbitration ····················· by Zhang Wan-lu(137)

Construction of Asia-Pacific Civil Aviation Commission: A Perspective of International Organization Law ··············· by Zhao Jin-song(152)

A Review of ICAO's Recent Rulemaking on Unmanned Aircraft System ·· by Zhang Xue-ying(162)

A Study on the Limitation of Liability of Air Carrier ·· by Wu Guang-ping(183)

The Impact of U. S. on the Liberalization of International Air Transport Law ···································· by Zhou Ya-guang(225)

News & Events

Eminent International Jurist Mr. Bin Cheng, Emeritus Professor of University College London, Donated Books to Northwest University of Political Science and Law ··· (257)

Practice and Innovation of the Belt and Road Aviation Rule of Law —A Summary of the Annual Meeting of Aviation Law Research Society of China Law Society in 2017 ····················· by Shi Du-juan(262)

Academic Events of Bin Cheng Institute of Air and Space Law of Northwest University of Political Science and Law(2017) ············ (274)

Call for Papers for China Aviation Law Review ·························· (302)

特　　稿

The Principle of Non-discrimination in International Air Law

Pablo Mendes de Leon [*]

This contribution to the China Air Law Review discusses the principle of non-discrimination against the background of international law and international air law. There is a need to define, and thus understand it, because it is often used without clearly interpreting it.

Section 1 contextualises the subject under international law, where it has a prominent place, while explaining the complexity of its scope. This is also true for international air law, but I believe that it is essential to place the principle in the correct context, and define it in light of the applicable regime. Hence, section 2 will analyse this principle in the light of the history and most relevant legal provisions of aviation treaties and international agreements, whereas section 3

* Professor of Air and Space Law, Leiden University, the Netherlands.

will serve as an illustration in practice. The last section 4 will provide a summary and conclusions.

1. Discrimination under International Law: A Complex Discussion

1.1 Origins

The prohibition of discrimination has become an essential principle in international and national law, and international and domestic relations between States or the State and related bodies, undertakings and private persons. It is laid own in a number of areas of international law, including but not limited to human rights law, labour law, foreign investment and international trade agreements and international criminal law. One of its origins lies in the Fourteenth Amendment to the United States Constitution that has been adopted as early as 9 July, 1868. ① In it, citizenship rights and equal protection of the laws has been guaranteed pursuant to the previous history, and related following the enhanced status of slaves after the American Civil War.

The principle found its way into the United Nations (UN) Charter of 1945. In its very first provision, the need for international cooperation among the peoples of the world, without distinction as to race, sex, language, or religion has been emphasized as one of the main purposes of this organisation. ② Meanwhile, the arguments for non-discrimination are evolving from race,

---

① See "The US Constitution: 14th Amendment", Accessed www. 14thamendment. us/amendment/14th_amendment. html, October 2, 2017.

② See Art. 1 (3) of the UN Charter (1945): "The Purposes of the United Nations are: To achieve international co-operation in solving international problems of an economic, social, cultural, or humanitarian character, and in promoting and encouraging respect for human rights and for fundamental freedoms for all*without distinction* as to race, sex, language, or religion".

language, and religion to colour and political opinion, whereas international and regional treaties added additional grounds, interpretations, and applications. In treaties and international agreements applying to undertakings including airlines non-discrimination on the basis of nationality of the undertaking, or the principal asset it uses, that is, aircraft, is predominant as to which see section 2.2.

1.2 Definitions

It follows from the above patchwork based pattern that an unequivocal definition of non-discrimination does not exist. Its meaning depends on the context, that is, the international or domestic regulation, in which it is used.

In human rights law, it has beenexplained as "fairness in treating people without prejudice". But what is fair? To determine fairness regards must be had to the applicable rules, policies and prevailing circumstances. The term "without prejudice" is not so easy to understand either-for instance, prejudice as to what? The religion of the people, their beliefs and orientation?

More relevant for the present discussion is international trade law, as it will be illustrated in the history of international civil aviation (section 2.1), provisions of the Chicago Convention (section 2.2), market access in international air transport (section 2.3) and case law (section 3). For instance, non-discrimination is a fundamental principle of the world trading system.① The Preamble of the Marrakesh Agreement Establishing the World Trade Organization, also known as the WTO Agreement, proclaims "the elimination of discriminatory treatment in international trade relations" as one of the chief objectives of the World Trade Organization (WTO).② This principle has been

---

① As to which see, for instance, Julia Ya Qin, "Defining Nondiscrimination under the Law of the World Trade Organization", *Boston University International Law Journal* 23, 2005, p. 216.

② See Marrakesh Agreement Establishing the World Trade Organization, pmbl., cl. 3, Apr. 15, 1994, 1867 U.N.T.S. 154, 33 I.L.M. 1144 (1994) [hereinafter WTO Agreement].

drawn up in many other provisions of the WTO related Agreements, including "General exceptions"① thereto, and in the General Agreement on Tariffs and Trade (GATT). The various modalities of non-discrimination will be discussed in the next section.

1.3 Related Concepts

Discrimination must be distinguished from *differentiation*. This distinction helps to fine tune the definition of non-discrimination, and is also relevant for the practice of the operation of international air services. Thus, in France, attention has been paid to "traitement différentiel", that is, differential treatment, which has been widely discussed in the area of environmental law. ② It is very often hard to determine whether differential treatment is allowed, and where the boundaries of the prohibition of discrimination are crossed. Instances can also be found in labour relations where employers treat their employees differently depending on their attitude and personality, and sometimes age.

Courts play an instrumental role in refining these distinctions. For instance, in one of the first judgments assessing the scope of non-discrimination, the European Court for Human Rights (ECHR) determined that not all types of differential treatment in the provision of rights and freedoms constitute prohibited discrimination under the European Human Rights Convention. ③

---

① See Art. XX.

② See for instance, Philippe Cullet, *Differential Treatment in International Environmental Law*, Routledge, 2002.

③ In the judgements of 23 July 1968 of the cases *Relating to Certain Aspects of the Laws on the Use of Languages in Education in Belgium*, Nos. 1474/62, 1677/62, 1691/62, 1769/63, 1994/63, 2126/64, the ECHR explained the following criteria for the distinction between differential treatment and non-discrimination: "a. the facts disclose a differential treatment; b. the distinction does not have an aim, that is, it has no objective and reasonable justification having regard to the aim and effects of the measure under consideration; and c. there is no reasonable proportionality between the means employed and the aim sought to be realised..."

"Positive" discrimination can be considered as the reverse of discrimination. Inlabour law, women sometimes receive preferential attention when they apply for certain professions. In international trade law, it means that foreign companies are more favourably treated than domestic companies which is not forbidden by international trade law. I shall revert to this in section 2.

Under the WTO regimereferred to in the previous section, two "modalities" of the non-discrimination principle have been shaped, namely, the Most Favoured Nation (MFN) treatment obligation and the national treatment obligation. The MFN treatment obligation prohibits a country from discriminating between countries; the national treatment obligation prohibits a country from discriminating against other countries. ①

International air transport is practically the only activity which is not subject to the WTO/GATS (General Agreement on Trade in Services). Hence, with the exception of three ancillary services, ② the above principles do not apply to the operation of "core" elements of international air services, that is, the performance of traffic rights, pricing of air services and the use of capacity of aircraft. ③

The above subtle distinctions may also be made to apply in international air law. Various provisions in the Chicago Convention on international civil aviation of 1944 pertain or allude to non-discrimination, MFN and national treatment as to which see the next section.

---

① See Julia Ya Qin, "Defining Nondiscrimination under the Law of the World Trade Organization", *Boston University International Law Journal* 23, 2005, pp. 217 – 220.

② In the General Agreement on Tariffs in Services (GATS), the Annex on Air Transport explicitly limits coverage of air services to only (1) aircraft repair and maintenance, (2) Computer Reservation Systems (CRSs), now also referred to as Global Distribution Services (GDS), and (3) selling and marketing of air transportation.

③ See section 2.3.

2. The Non-discrimination Principle under International Air Law

2.1 Background of Non-discrimination in International Civil Aviation

The above UN Charter of 1945[①] was preceded by the Chicago Conference preparing for the Convention on international civil aviation. The move thereto had been initiated by the United States. Traditionally, American foreign policy had protested against the discrimination inherent in the British, Portuguese and Spanish colonial systems. These systems were based on monopoly, exclusion and the *closed door*, that is, closed for foreign powers and their undertakings. Overseas territories were regarded by the mercantilist statesmen as a means of enriching the national State. That is also why navigation and trade between mother State and overseas territories were monopolised.[②] At the same time, international air transport came to be viewed as trade rather than as an instrument of political and military power, at least by the United States. The relative strength of the United States at the end of this period contributed to initiating a liberal system of regulations governing world trade.

---

① See section 1.1.

② Cf. S. Metzger, "1960 Proceedings of the American Society of International Law", in *The Law of International Trade*, Lerner Law Book Company, 1996, pp. 656 - 657, argues: "Prior to 1948... no customary rule of international law ... precluded trade discrimination ... As can be seen, there were two principal characteristics of the preferential arrangements which had persisted until the mid-twentieth century. They were either relics of relationships which had earlier existed among the participants as in the case of British 'Empire' preference, U.S. Philippine and Cuban arrangements, and the French Union, or they were preferences among neighbouring countries which individually were relatively small markets and which, even when they were more or less united so far as customs duties were concerned, remained relatively small with a consequentially relatively slight impact on the trade of those third countries which were discriminated against as a result of the preference."

As to international civil aviation, monopolies in large parts of theworld inherited from the past era would stand in the way of American aspirations to become a dominant aviation power and to exploit the commercial benefits of aviation. To achieve this objective, landing rights were needed in all parts of the world. The American position in historical perspective was outlined by A. Berle:

"The American position at the International Civil Aviation Conference has been: (1) This is the Twentieth Century. (2) In theair there is no excuse for an attempt to revive the Sixteenth and Seventeenth Century conceptions by which transportation pioneers first got *exclusive concessions*, widened those by *political influence to great blocs of territory*, and then negotiated with each other for *advantageous arrangements*, to the *exclusion* of a great part of the world. In other words, there is no excuse for a modern air British East India Company or Portuguese Trading Monopoly or 'Spanish Main' conception. Instead, we propose a *system of mutualized permissions* to use the air *without prejudice to sovereignty*, like the mutualized permissions to use coastal waters and seaports, and permitting to all countries the chance to get into the air."①

Preferential and exclusive arrangements made by former world powerswith their overseas territories which were under their *sphere of influence* would hamper these aspirations. That is why the American government insisted from the beginning of the discussions on the application of *non-exclusivity* of international operating rights, in order words, avoidance of discriminatory treatment with respect of the operation of international air services which should be opened up to all States and their airlines.

---

① Cf. B. Berle, "Navigating the Rapids, 1918 - 1971" in Berle, Beatrice Bishop and Travis Beal Jacobs, eds., *From the Papers of Adolf A. Berle*, New York, Harcourt Brace Jovanovich, Inc., 1973, pp. 501 - 502.

In relation to the relatively liberal American ideas, the United Kingdom adopteda protectionist attitude. The position of the United Kingdom was, of course, quite different from that of the United States: its economic situation was deplorable, it had devoted its aviation efforts to military purposes during the Second World War and was anxious to maintain its interests as a world power.

The Chicago Convention (1944) reflect the above positions and viewpoints in its Preamble and substantive provisions as to which see the next section.

2.2 Provisions on Non-discrimination in the Chicago Convention

The Preamble of the Chicago Convention dictates thatinternational air transport services ought "to be established on the basis of equality of opportunity" and this is the principle which is closest to "non-discrimination" and related concepts. However, it can also mean that "no country left behind"① as prescribed by the International Civil Aviation Organization (ICAO) which has been set up by this convention. Each country should be enabled to participate in international air transport, whether on a discriminatory basis or not when it comes to the operation of international air services as to which see section 2.3 below. Moreover, this proclamation is a matter of principle rather than of "hard" law.

Other than that proclamation, the term "discrimination" occurs only once in the "hard law" treaty provisions of this convention, namely when it prescribes "avoid discrimination between contracting States".② This provision is formulated in a prudent manner: it encourages avoiding, rather than forbids discrimination. Moreover, its meaning has never been tested in case law, has not

① See "No Country Left Behind", Accessed www.icao.int/about-icao/NCLB/Pages/default.aspx, July 5, 2018.

② See Art. 44(g).

or hardly been analysed in publications, and not been used in practice, that is, in negotiations between States.

A number of provisions directly or indirect refer to equality of treatment, uniformity of regulation, or even national treatment, and, in an isolated case, even to the MFN clause. Thelast mentioned reference is briefly alluded to in the next section. In such instances, the Chicago Convention has opted for the expression "uniformity" of regulations which must be applied without distinction as to nationality of the aircraft, rather than of the airline, which comes under economic regulation as to which see the following section. Because the Chicago Convention is primarily a *safety* convention, it focuses on the application of uniform regulation on the navigation and use of *aircraft*.

Those references can be found in the field of safety and security, environmental protection and access to airports. Among them are the following:

(1) The establishment of *prohibited and restricted areas* in national air space. ①

(2) The *application of domestic air regulations* pertaining to the admission to or departure from national airspace to aircraft engaged in international air navigation② which was subject of discussion in the EU ETS case. ③

---

① Article 9 – *Prohibited areas.* "Each contracting State may, for reasons of military necessity or public safety, restrict or prohibit uniformly the aircraft of other States from flying over certain areas of its territory, provided that *no distinction* in this respect is made between the aircraft of the State whose territory is involved, engaged in international scheduled airline services, and the aircraft of the other contracting States likewise engaged."

② Article 11 – *Applicability of air regulations.* "Subject to the provisions of this Convention, the laws and regulations of a contracting State relating to the admission to or departure from its territory of aircraft engaged in international air navigation, or to the operation and navigation of such aircraft while within its territory, shall be applied *to the aircraft of all contracting States without distinction as to nationality*, and shall be complied with by such aircraft upon entering or departing from or while within the territory of that State."

③ See Pablo Mendes de Leon, "Enforcement of the EU ETS: The EU's Conclusive Efforts to Export its Environmental Values", *Air & Space Law* 37(4/5), 2012, pp. 287–306.

(3) The establishment of *airport and other charges*. ①

(4) *Recognition of certificates and licenses* complying with minimum ICAO norms forming the basis for the admission of operators of foreign aircraft to national airspace. ② Certificates of airworthiness, confirming the safety of the aircraft, and licenses, on the competencies of the crew, meeting these minimum norms must be accepted by *all* ICAO States.

The provision of airport charges hints, to begin with, at "the aircraft of *all the other* contracting States", but continues to state that "The like *uniform* conditions shall apply to the use, by aircraft of *every* contracting State, of all air navigation facilities..." implying that national treatment must be respected when it comes to access to airports. The other provisions, in particular those pertaining to the establishment of prohibited areas and the applicability of air navigation regulations, are founded on the national treatment principle. This principle has been further explained in case law as to which see section 3, below.

If the strength of ICAO regulations lies in their potentially global acceptance, its weaknesses follow from this strength: they are *minimum* standards, which are designed to be accepted *as such* by all countries of the

① Article 15 – *Airport and similar charges*. "Every airport in a contracting State which is open to public use by its national aircraft shall likewise... be open *under uniform conditions to* the aircraft of all the other contracting States. The like uniform conditions shall apply to the use, by aircraft of every contracting State, of all air navigation facilities, including radio and meteorological services, which may be provided for public use for the safety and expedition of air navigation."

② Article 33 – *Recognition of certificates and licenses*. "Certificates of airworthiness and certificates of competency and licenses issued or rendered valid by the contracting State in which the aircraft is registered, shall be *recognized as valid by the other contracting States*, provided that the requirements under which such certificates or licenses were issued or rendered valid are *equal to or above the minimum standards* which may be established from time to time pursuant to this Convention."

world.① However, there are still States that do not follow the minimum standards, while an increasing number of States and jurisdictions including the US and the EU is not satisfied with this minimum level for safety, security and environmental matters drawing up higher standards.

2.3 The Differentiated Nature of Market Access in International Air Transport

Lack of common understanding on the operation of international scheduled air services during the Chicago Conference led to the adoption of Article 6 of this convention, pursuant to which States agree among themselves on the terms and conditions of such operations.② In practice, this position resulted in the adoption of over 3000 bilateral air services agreements worldwide which differ, and differentiate as to treatment of the undertakings, that is, the airlines, in terms of traffic rights, capacity, pricing and other elements of economic regulation of international air services.

Traffic rights form the essence of international air transport. They have been

---

① Article 37 – *Adoption of international standards and procedures.* "Each contracting State undertakes to collaborate in securing*the highest practicable degree of uniformity* in regulations, standards, procedures, and organization in relation to aircraft, personnel, airways and auxiliary services in all matters in which such *uniformity will facilitate and improve air navigation.*"

② Article 6 – *Scheduled air services.* "No scheduled international air service may be operated over or into the territory of a contracting State, except with the special permission or other authorization of that State, and in accordance with the terms of such permission or authorization."

divided into "Freedoms of the Air"① which actually are not freedoms but un-Freedoms of the Air which can be turned into Freedoms of the Air in the context of a bilateral or multilateral air services agreement.

For instance, if China grants so called fifth Freedom traffic rights on the footing of its bilateral air services agreements with Singapore and Tokyo for the operation of air services by Singapore Airlines on the Beijing-Tokyo route, it does not have to accord similar rights to Thailand, or to Australia, for the benefit of their carriers, that is, Thai Airways and Qantas.

Consequently, market access in international air transport is arranged on the basis of agreements which do not foresee in the application of non-discrimination principle, neither in the form of nationaltreatment, nor MFN. This is the principal reason why the operation of air services remains outside of the WTO/GATS

---

① First freedom: The right to fly across foreign territory without landing; e. g. Air China flies through the airspace of the Russian Federation to Germany without landing. Second freedom: The right to land in foreign territory for non-traffic purposes; e. g. China Southern flies from Guangzhou to Tokyo and makes a stop for refuelling purposes in Seoul. Thirdfreedom: The right to carry traffic either from the territory of the State whose nationality the airlines possesses or where the airline is established, into a foreign territory; e. g. Air France carries traffic from Paris to Dublin. Forth freedom: The right to carry traffic from the territory into the territory of the State whose nationality the airlines possesses or where the airline is established; e. g. China Eastern carries traffic from New York to Shanghai. Fifth freedom: The right to carry traffic from one point in a foreign territory into a point in another foreign territory and vice versa, which carriage is linked with a third and fourth freedom traffic right respectively; e. g. Singapore Airlines carries traffic from Beijing to Tokyo, connecting to its service from Singapore to Beijing. SixthFreedom: The right to carry traffic from one point in a foreign territory into a point in another foreign territory via the State whose nationality the airlines possesses or where the airline is established; e. g. Etihad Airlines carries traffic from Vienna to Hong Kong via Abu Dhabi. Seventhfreedom: The right to carry traffic from one point in a foreign territory into a point in another foreign territory and vice versa, which carriage is not linked with a third and fourth freedom traffic right respectively; e. g. FedEx carries traffic between Bangkok and Jakarta. Eighthfreedom: The right to carry traffic between two points in a foreign territory, which carriage is linked with third or fourth freedom carriage; e. g. Xiamen Airlines carries traffic between Milan to Rome in Italy, connecting to its service between Beijing and Milan. ninth freedom: The right to carry traffic between two points in a foreign territory, which carriage is not linked with third or fourth freedom carriage; e. g. British Airways flies and carries traffic between Paris and Toulouse, France.

regime, which is not expected to change soon.

The above picture applies to all traffic rights, with the exception perhaps of the operation of domestic services by a foreign airline. Article 7 (2) of the Chicago Convention① has been interpreted as an MFN clause but it is unlikely to have that meaning. ②

Neither the application of the national treatment principle, nor of the non-discrimination principle appear to prevent contracting States of the Chicago Convention in practice from engaging into "positive discrimination", that is, by granting foreign carriers a more favourable treatment than national carriers. This state of affairs is evidenced the rules and practices applied by the United States in the 1990s, under which foreign carriers operating international air services received certain priority rights in the process of slot allocation at the so called "High Density Airports" in the US as compared with US carriers. To grant national carriers a better treatment in respect of, for instance, slot allocation, may be allowed under the non-discrimination principle which merely forbids discrimination *as between foreign carriers* but not under the national treatment principle which is designed to give *all* carriers, whether national or foreign, the same treatment, subject to the option of granting foreign carriers a better treatment than national carriers.

---

① Article 7 - *Cabotage.* "Each contracting State shall have the right to refuse permission to the aircraft of other contracting States to take on in its territory passengers, mail and cargo carried for remuneration or hire and destined for another point within its territory. *Each contracting State undertakes not to enter into any arrangements which specifically grant any such privilege on an exclusive basis to any other State or an airline of any other State, and not to obtain any such exclusive privilege from any other State.*"

② See Pablo Mendes de Leon, *Cabotage in International Air Transport Regulation*, Dordrecht, Martinus Nijhoff Publishers, 1992, pp. 41 -52.

2.4 Concluding Remarks

Matters related to safety, immigration and facilitation, infrastructure and security are regulated at a world-wide level, namely, in the Chicago Convention, the 19 Annexes thereto, and related ICAO policies. Global regulation makes sense because this central rule making effort fosters uniformity of the measures and thus enhances the "safe and orderly" operation of international air transport services. It also assures that such services are established "on the basis of equality of opportunity and operated soundly and economically". ①

Differentiated treatment of airlines when it comes to market access and market behaviour does not infringe non-discrimination or national or equal treatment principles, or MFN clauses which dominate the WTO regime, for the simple reason that those principles do not apply to the operation of air services. This state of affairs is not likely to change in the near future.

---

① See the Preamble of the Chicago Convention.

3. Cases on Non-discrimination

3.1 Settlement of Disagreements and Disputes in International Civil Aviation

The Chicago Convention,[①] and bilateral air services agreements,[②] encompass procedures for dispute settlement. However, little use little use has been made of the dispute settlement devices provided by these instruments because disagreements are resolved by bilateral consultations and negotiations. This state of affairs is a reflection of the rich history of aerial diplomacy.

---

① Article 84 – *Settlement of disputes.* "If any disagreement between two or more contracting States relating to the interpretation or application of this Convention and its Annexes cannot be settled by negotiation, it shall, on the application of any State concerned in the disagreement, be decided by the Council. No member of the Council shall vote in the consideration by the Council of any dispute to which it is a party. Any contracting State may, subject to Article 85, appeal from the decision of the Council to an ad hoc arbitral tribunal agreed upon with the other parties to the dispute or to the Permanent Court of International Justice. Any such appeal shall be notified to the Council within sixty days of receipt of notification of the decision of the Council."

② For instance, see the following bilateral provision on *Settlement of Disputes* 1. "If any dispute arises between the Contracting Parties relating to the interpretation or application of this Agreement, the Contracting Parties shall in the first place endeavour to settle their dispute by bilateral negotiations. 2. If the Contracting Parties fail to reach a settlement by negotiation, the dispute may at the request of either Contracting Party be submitted for decision to a tribunal of three arbitrators, one to be named by each Contracting Party and the third to be agreed upon by the two arbitrators so chosen, provided that such third arbitrator shall not be a national of either Contracting Party. Each of the Contracting Parties shall designate an arbitrator within a period of sixty (60) days from the date of receipt by either Contracting Party from the other Contracting Party of a diplomatic note requesting arbitration of the dispute and the third arbitrator shall be agreed upon within a further period of sixty (60) days. If either of the Contracting Parties fails to designate its own arbitrator within the period of sixty (60) days or if the third arbitrator is not agreed upon within the period indicated, the President of the Council of the International Civil Aviation Organization may be requested by either Contracting Party to appoint an arbitrator or arbitrators. 3. The Contracting Parties undertake to comply with any decision given under paragraph 2 of this Article." See also: ICAO Assembly Resolution, *Authorization to the Council to Act as an Arbitral Body*, ICAO Do 9848; P. M. J. Mendes de Leon, "Settlement of Disputes in Air and Space Law", in Chia-Jui Cheng, ed., *Proceedings of the International Conference on Air Transport and Space Applications in a New World*, Tokyo, 1995, pp. 329–339.

Disagreement is not the same as dispute. Infact and in law, a disagreement precedes the dispute. A dispute exists when a disagreement reaches a degree of definition and clarity where negotiations and consultations have failed to achieve consensus. Consequently, the views of the two sides concerning the performance of international obligations are clearly opposed, necessitating methods of dispute settlement including arbitration and adjudication. ①

If the two parties do not succeed in resolving their disagreement through consultations, it becomes a dispute. A dispute must be resolved pursuant to the proceedings laid down in the legal regime, that is, the provisions of the Chicago Convention or the applicable air services agreement, whose substantive provisions have given rise to the disagreement.

The following section briefly describes disputes in the field of international civil aviation, with special reference to the involvement of the non-discrimination and related principles.

3.2 Aviationdisputes Explaining Non-discrimination

3.2.1 India-Pakistan on the Establishment of Prohibited and Restricted Area(1952)

In this case India claimed that Pakistan was denying its aircraft the right to fly over certain parts of its(Pakistan's) territory in violation of certain provisions of the Chicago Convention , including its Article 9 of the Chicago Convention. This provision formed the chore of the disagreement obligates States to respect for the *non-discrimination* principle as to which see section 2.2 above. In short, if a State party to the Chicago Convention decides to close its national airspace for the reasons set out in the mentioned Article 9, it must do so for the aircraft of

① See ICJ, Interpretation *of the Peace Treaties with Bulgaria*, *Hungary and Romania*, Advisory opinion of 30 March 1950(first phase), 1950 IC7 Reports 65, p.74.

all States, that is, registered in those States, which are parties to the Chicago Convention.

Pakistan had declared a certain part of its territory a "prohibited area" under Article 9 of the Chicago Convention. This area was located under anair route from India to Pakistan. According to India, the "prohibited area" was unreasonable and unnecessary, and a non-uniformly supervised prohibition. Moreover, an Iranian air carrier was allowed to fly through what was declared a "prohibited area". This was in violation of the non-discrimination provision which was contained in the mentioned Article 9.

The ICAO Council invited parties to enter into direct negotiations. A few months later, representatives of the two countries announced that the dispute had been settled by agreement in an amicable atmosphere of cordiality, and that the decision was a triumph of reason and goodwill to see the other's point of view.[①] The dispute was resolved upon negotiations between the parties, helped by an intervention on the part of a Working Group of the ICAO Council.[②]

3.2.2 International Recognition of Certificates of Airworthiness(1981)

As stated in section 2.2 above, ICAO rules, especially the Standards and Recommended Practices(SARPs) must be *uniformly* applied. Article 37 of the Chicago Convention stresses, be it indirectly, in this respect the *safety* of international air navigation.

In this rather old case, the US court argued that the minimum requirements set forth by ICAO, in particular the Standards contained in Annex 8 on the Operation of Aircraft, had been satisfied by the applicant. Consequently, the US aviation authorities, more specifically the federal Aviation Authority were not

---

① ICAO Bulletin of January/February 1953 at 26 and R. T. Dicker, "The Use of Arbitration in the Settlement of Bilateral Air Rights Disputes", *The Vanderbilt International*, 1967, pp. 131 – 132; see also B. Cheng, *The Law of International Air Transport*, London, Stevens, 1962, pp. 101 – 103.

② ICAO Doc. 7367(A7 – P1), (1953) at 74 – 76.

allowed to require higher standards. ①

3.2.3 Airport Charges: The London Heathrow Arbitration Case(1992)

In November 1979, the British Airport Authority announced very large increases in user charges for the year 1980/81. The increase had the effect of raising charges to the US carriers operating at London Heathrow Airport, especially Pan Am and TWA, but also Flying Tigers, by some 60 to 70 per cent. According to the charging system which was set up by the British Airport Authority in 1979, a rather sharp differentiation was made between aircraft movements in *peak* hours and in *off-peak* hours. As a result, American carriers were particularly affected by the new charging system. Of course, in law, no distinction was made between UK and non-UK carriers. The American carriers contended that the British Airport Authority was bound to make Heathrow Airport available to all operators or all aircraft of other States party to the Chicago Convention on equal terms. Also, they relied on a provision of the Bermuda 2 Agreement that the charges must be *cost related*. ②

The arbitration tribunal found that the UK government had failed to monitor the pricing system of the British Airport Authority. Its sharply differentiated peak/off-peak chargingsystem was in practice working " inequitably " to the detriment of the US airlines. It was argued that British Airways was enjoying

---

① See *British Caledonian Airways Ltd.* v. *Langhorne Bond*, *Federal Aviation Administration and others*, United States Court of Appeals, District of Colombia, Decision of 2 September 1981; 665 F.2d 1153(*British Caledonian* v. *Bond*, C.A.D.C. 1981).

② See Art. 10 of Bermuda 2:"User charges may reflect, but shall not exceed, the full cost to the competent charging authorities of providing appropriate airport and air navigation facilities, and may provide for a reasonable rate of return on assets, after depreciation. In the provision of facilities and services, the competent authorities shall have regard to such factors as efficiency, economy, environmental impact and safety of operations. User charges shall be based on sound economic principles and on the generally accepted accounting practices within the territory of the appropriate Contracting Party." See also, ICAO, *Statement by the Council to contracting States on Charges for Airports and Air Navigation Services*, 1992, ICAO Doc 9082/4 at 3:"The cost basis for airport charges."

some advantages that were denied to US airlines, in relation to rescheduling flights out of peak hours, amounting to infringement of national treatment. The UK government was required to pay the US government about US $ 30 million, passing the compensation to the US airlines involved.

3.2.4 The Noise Restrictions at European Airports (2000)

In the *Hushkit*① dispute between the 15 EU states and the US in 2000, the US sued these 15 EU states regarding the imposition of noise measures at European airports which went beyond those established by ICAO. The US relied on arguments coming from international aviation law, that is, provisions of the Chicago Convention and ICAO policies and resolutions, including those pertaining to the applicability of *uniform* ICAO regulations.

The EU had to withdraw its regulation designed to impose stricter noise standards addressing all (whether EU based or not) airlines when landing at airports in the EU.② This argument pertains to the above discussed national treatment principle in relation to access to airports.

3.2.5 The EU ETS Case (2008 - 2012)

In this case the question arose, among others, whether the imposition of an Emission Trading Scheme (ETS) amounts to payment of a charge as referred to in the above Article 15 of the Chicago Convention. It prescribes the "national treatment" of aircraft, irrespective of their nationality. Again, there is no international law problem if only EU air carriers are affected by the measure, as "positive discrimination" or "reversed discrimination" are not forbidden by

① "Hushkit" refers to a devise placed on aircraft engines in order to reduce the produce of noise.

② See ICAO Council, Report of the 161st Session held on 25 November 2000, Accessed http://www.icao.int/Applications/Hyperlink2/display.cfm? Name = C-MIN%20161%2F4&Lang = E, July 5, 2018.

international air or trade law. ①

The EU, on its side, ② preferred to rely on a provision which gives contracting States of the Chicago Convention to regulate air navigation in their national airspaces as they deem fit, as long as air navigation rules are applied *without discrimination to the aircraft of all other contracting States*. ③

This case has caused international and vehement repercussions which were unprecedented in the history of international civil aviation. The lack of respect for the principle that international air navigation must be uniformly regulated was only a facet of this case in which the extra-territoriality of the EU measure created sharp frictions between EU States and most non-EU States. ④

3.3 Concluding Remarks

The above cases demonstrate, among others, that civil aviation is a trade affair conducted by States. A disagreement between private parties relating to charges is solved as an inter-State dispute. Again, the interpretation of the non-discrimination principle must be assessed in relation to its context.

---

① See section 1.3, above.

② See, for instance, Common Position 13/2008 adopted by the Council on 18 April 2008, *with a view to adopting a Directive so as to include aviation activities in the scheme for greenhouse gas emission allowance trading within the Community*, O. J. 2008 C 122E/19, at Consideration(8).

③ Art. 11 *Applicability of air regulations*. "Subject to the provisions of this Convention, the laws and regulations of a contracting State relating to the admission to or departure from its territory of aircraft engaged in international air navigation, or to the operation and navigation of such aircraft *while within its territory*, shall be applied to the aircraft of all contracting States without distinction as to nationality, and shall be complied with by such aircraft upon entering or departing from or while within the territory of that State."

④ See Pablo Mendes de Leon, "Enforcement of the EU ETS: The EU's Convulsive Efforts to Export its Environmental Values", *Air & Space Law* 37 (4/5), 2012, pp. 287 – 306. and B. F. Havel & J. Q. Mulligan, "The Triumph of Politics: Reflections on Judgment of the Court of Justice of the European Union Validating the Inclusion of Non-EU Airlines in the Emissions Trading Scheme", *Air & Space Law* 37(1), 2012, pp. 3 – 33.

4. Concluding Remarks

Non-discrimination generally is not an easy concept to understand. It has to be defined in order to give it a meaning. This is not always the case, in which contextualisation of the regime in which it is used most give an answer to questions pertaining to its implementation and application.

Non-discrimination as a principle is used in many areas of law. It underwent a strong development in the 20th century which continues in the current one. It has links with related concepts such as national treatment, equal treatment and the MFN clause in international trade law.

International aviation law has also adopted this principle, be it more "disguised" under the cloak of uniformity. Uniformity of regulations and policies is a mantra in international aviation law as States, and especially operates such as airlines, operators of airports and air traffic controllers must understand the global rules and measures applying globally. This mantra has this supported the principal objective of the Chicago Convention which is the promotion of safety.

With the exception of the establishment of airport charges, non-discrimination and related concepts do not necessarily apply to the economic regulation of international air transport. Access to the air transport market is regulated on a differentiated basis, but it may go too far to identify that differentiated treatment as discriminatory because non-discrimination is not mandated by the international air law regime, contrasting it sharply against the international trade regime.

If disagreements on this subject arise, they will be solved in most cases by aerial diplomacy, that is, consultations and negotiations. The few cases involving non-discrimination have shed a light on its meaning in practice, but, in fact, not more than that.

It is anticipated that the above approach towards the application of the non-discrimination principle and related concepts in international civil aviation will not change in the near future. States keep a predominant interest in maintaining it for policy and trade reasons, and will not easily proceed to, for instance, the WTO regime. China's trade oriented policy of the past years may yield a more fine-tuned view on the present state of law and affairs. I hope that this brief essay makes a fruitful contribution to legal thinking on this subject.

打造“空中丝绸之路”推进“一带一路”倡议的法律思考

吴建端*

自2013年我国政府提出“一带一路”倡议以来，围绕“一带一路”倡议的建设包括“空中丝绸之路”建设稳步推进，互联互通网络逐步成型，贸易投资大幅增长，重要项目合作稳步实施，取得了一批重要的早期成果。随着“一带一路”倡议的进一步落实，潜在法律风险和法律问题特别是民航法律问题，值得我们去探讨。本文结合各种案例，通过分析“一带一路”面临的法律问题包括民航法律问题，从国际法、区域法和冲突法角度，阐述了法律意识提高的必要性，法律风险防范的必要性和依法经营的重要性，剖析了我国民航建设“空中丝绸之路”中的法律风险和潜在问题，提出了把握机遇，提高合意识，加强法律制度建设，队伍建设和研究重点内容的看法与建议，以保障“空中丝绸之路”建设的顺利进行。

---

* 法学博士，上海社会科学院研究生院兼职教授，上海璞燕信息科技有限公司总经理。

一、前　　言

2013年9~10月,我国国家主席习近平在出访中亚和东南亚国家期间,先后提出共建"丝绸之路经济带"和"21世纪海上丝绸之路"的重大倡议,得到国际社会高度关注和响应。据2016年的数据,"一带一路"包含60多个沿线国家,覆盖44亿人口,占全球的63%;①经济规模达21万亿美元,占全球国民生产总值的55%。

由中国首倡的"一带一路"的建设从无到有、由点及面,进度和成果超出预期。目前,已有全球100多个国家和国际组织共同参与,40多个国家和国际组织与中国签署合作协议,形成了广泛国际合作共识。经济走廊建设稳步推进,互联互通网络逐步成型,贸易投资大幅增长,重要项目合作稳步实施,取得了一批重要的早期收获。我国民航充分发挥其独特优势,走在"一带一路"建设的前端。到2017年年底,我国有26家航空公司从国内的47个城市口岸通航35个"一带一路"参与国家的80个城市。航班量比"一带一路"倡议提出的2013年年底增长120%,②其他的各类合作也同步展开。随着"一带一路"倡议的进一步落实,随之而来的许多法律风险和潜在的法律问题特别是民航法律问题,值得我们去探讨。

二、"一带一路"面临法律问题广泛而且复杂

(一)法律问题具有世界性、普遍性和复杂性

"一带一路"倡议,就是要打通世界经济航路,联结全球经济海洋,构筑"空中丝绸之路",为全球化注入新的生机与活力,成为引领全球化新时代的

① 参见《"一带一路":国家战略的重大创新》,载新华网:http://news.xinhuanet.com/world/2016-09/07/c_129272136.htm,最后访问日期:2017年8月12日。

② 参见《中国与"一带一路"参与国家通航量四年翻番　空中丝绸之路初现雏形》,载丝路网:http://newslu.sxdaily.com.cn/2018/0122/55956.shtml,最后访问日期:2018年3月10日。

宏大实践。① “一带一路”倡议着眼推动我国新一轮对外开放、着力推动沿线国家共同发展,成为打造人类命运共同体的主动作为,②就是以共商、共建、共享为原则,以开放包容为特征,以互利共赢为追求。

“一带一路”合作所产生的辐射效应,已经不单单是对沿线60多个国家,也不是某一特定区域,而是对世界经济、政治、文化和法律等多个方面造成深刻影响。

国内外普遍认同我国的“一带一路”倡议。英国牛津大学《国际事务》杂志③2018年第1期发表的文章中,有学者认为,中国主导的“一带一路”和亚投行,中国倡导的全球化对各国都有利(ipso facto, beneficial for all)。④

美国加利福尼亚州官员表示,洛杉矶港可作为对接“一带一路”的“海上枢纽”。⑤ 澳大利亚维多利州州长丹尼尔·安德鲁表示,“一带一路”合作为澳大利亚企业提供了一个更广阔的发展平台,希望澳大利亚企业积极参与“一带一路”建设。⑥

新西兰新中关系促进委员会2018年5月1日发布了一份关于“一带一路”倡议的专题研究报告,指出“一带一路”倡议堪称“世纪工程”,包容性强,覆盖面广,带来的机遇难以限量。⑦ 2017年8月14日新西兰首个“一带一

---

① 参见《“一带一路”赋予全球化新内涵》,载新华网:http://news.xinhuanet.com/2017-01/23/c_1120370146.htm,最后访问日期:2018年4月1日。

② 参见《“一带一路”是打造人类命运共同体的重要桥梁》,载新浪网:http://finance.sina.com.cn/wm/2017-05-11/doc-ifyfekhi7258295.shtml,最后访问日期:2017年12月10日。

③ 《国际事务》由位于伦敦的英国皇家国际事务研究所——查塔姆研究所(Chatham House)创办和编辑。它是全球领先的国际关系期刊之一,也是为数不多的内容覆盖整个学科的期刊之一。该期刊内容生动活泼,为读者提供最新的、对影响当今世界格局的关键问题的批判性思考。

④ “China's challenge to the Pax Americana: The AIIB, and 'One Belt, One Road'”.

⑤ 参见《洛杉矶港可做美国对接“一带一路”的“海上枢纽”》,载观察者网:http://www.guancha.cn/economy/2017_05_18_409037.shtml,最后访问日期:2018年3月9日。

⑥ 参见《希望澳大利亚企业积极参与“一带一路”建设》,载新华网:http://news.xinhuanet.com/2017-05/30/c_1121058678.htm,最后访问日期:2018年3月21日。

⑦ 参见《新西兰力挺“一带一路”:如不及时参与,会错失良机》,载海外网:http://kan.china.com/news/socom/249960.html,最后访问日期:2018年5月3日。

路”产业园就与中国检验认证集团新西兰公司签署了战略合作协议。①

事实上,“一带一路”也已经成为全球化进程,构建人类命运共同体的重要组成部分。2016 年第 71 届联合国大会通过决议,首次写入“一带一路”倡议,得到会员国一致赞同,这充分表明,倡议已转化为国际共识。有外媒对此评论道,联合国与中国携手推进全球化。②

由此,在实施“一带一路”倡议的进程中所产生的影响和参与建设的众多国家涉及的法律问题(包括民航)就可能是世界性、普遍性的,不会局限于“一带一路”沿线国家的法律制度,而是涵盖了世界上各主要法律体系和国际法律制度。牛津大学法学院“一带一路”研究项目组认为,推进“一带一路”建设需要构建法律和制度结构,来解决跨国界、国际性行动所产生的复杂的、前所未有的问题。③

第一,我们面临的法律问题不仅是平面的,而且是立体的。例如,中国对“一带一路”沿线国家的投资融资相当一部分来自域外,而投资额中,近 1/3 是经由新加坡投向这些沿线国家的项目,很有可能需要借助新加坡比较完善的司法制度,包括解决跨境商业纠纷的调解、仲裁和诉讼机制,而伦敦、我国香港特别行政区等地也提供解决争端的可能性。④

第二,我们必须逐步熟悉投资目标国的法律体系和相关的制度,结合我国的对外投资的法律规定,持续深化同沿线国家和企业在法规、技术、标准、管理等各领域的交流合作,才能扎实推动重大项目的落实落地,在“一带一

---

① 参见《这个发达国家表示:不参加“一带一路”就亏了》,载新浪网:http://news.sina.com.cn/c/zj/2018-05-03/doc-ifzyqqiq5628536.shtml,最后访问日期:2018 年 5 月 4 日。

② “UN Joins Beijing to Advance Globalism With‘One Belt, One Road’”, Accessed https://www.thenewamerican.com/world-news/asia/item/26050-un-joins-beijing-to-advance-globalism-with-one-belt-one-road, May 17, 2017.

③ “One Belt One Road”,载牛津大学法学院网:https://www.law.ox.ac.uk/one-belt-one-road,最后访问日期:2017 年 12 月 7 日。

④ 参见《新加坡总理:将为“一带一路”新中企业提供融资支持》,载新浪财经头条网:http://cj.sina.com.cn/articles/view/1923970420/72ad7574020008415?cre=tianyi&mod=pcpager_focus&loc=3&r=9&doct=0&rfunc=81&tj=none&tr=9,最后访问日期:2018 年 4 月 12 日。

路”建设中实现资源的高水平跨国配置。

第三,我们面临的法律不仅是“一带一路”沿线国家,而且延伸至域外。2015 年 7 月中俄两国元首商定,将“一带一路”建设与欧亚经济联盟建设对接,中俄共同建立欧亚伙伴关系亦是其延续,①在经济对接的实践中,必然也要面临“一带一路”沿线国家之外的法律问题。我国与阿根廷、巴西、智利正在加快“一带一路”战略与拉美区域一体化倡议的融合对接,推动多个领域的合作,涉及复杂的法律关系。

第四,推进“一带一路”倡议有利于世界进一步了解中国的法制建设和忠实地履行遵循国际义务。国外有些学者,对我国法治建设仍然停留在过往的印象当中。例如,美国普林斯顿大学学者玛丽亚·阿黛尔(Maria Adele Carrai)就认为,尽管中国与世界的一体化令人吃惊,但中国对于现有的国际制度和法律秩序的态度还比较模糊,甚至还有某种程度的例外(exceptionalism)或背离(divergence)。②这实质上也反映了有些西方国家的官员、学者等对中国致力于法律体制现代化有些误解,③需要更多沟通与理解。

第五,“一带一路”倡议实施过程中产生的争议具有多样性和复杂性。俄罗斯律师叶夫根尼·拉舍夫斯基(Evgeny Raschevsky)就认为,至少有三种很有特点的潜在争议,一是国与国之间的贸易争端;二是投资者和国家间的投资争议;三是“纯粹”产生于运输、贷款、公司融资、股权协议和货物供应等

---

① 参见《供给侧改革促消费、“一带一路”引领对外开放情况发布会》,载国务院新闻办公室网:http://www. scio. gov. cn/video/33836/Document/1543673/1543673. htm,最后访问日期:2018 年 3 月 16 日。

② “Is There A Chinese International Model? The Belt and Road Initiative as A Case Study. -Cwo Fellow Maria Adele Carrai”,载普林斯顿大学网:http://wws. princeton. edu/news-and-events/events/item/there-chinese-international-model-belt-and-road-initiative-case-study,最后访问日期:2017 年 11 月 29 日。

③ Despite all the possible security and financial obstacles, the BRI might have serious implications not only for the international economic legal order, but also for international politics, and it can reveal aspects of a Chinese international model that is likely to re-emerge.

过程中的“单纯”的商业争议。①这些争议的解决,既涉及世界贸易组织的规则适用问题,也涉及成员国与非成员国之间的法律适用,还牵涉不同法律制度和文化背景的争议方协调和对法律法规的理解与适用的问题。

由此看来,在实施“一带一路”的倡议过程中,我们不仅要了解把握世界各国的法律体系和我国法律体系的对接问题,我们还要未雨绸缪地深入研究各种法律问题和法律体系的融合和交汇问题。以我国民航为例,在推进民航强国和参与“一带一路”建设的进程中,不仅要瞄准全方位提升国际竞争力目标,熟悉沿线国家的法律体系,加快与国际先进的法律体系接轨,着力增强国际民航规则标准参与度,保障航空业全产业链发展,而且要研究互联网时代下,民航整个生态圈的法律问题、跨界的法律问题和全球民航业面临的新的法律问题。②

(二)“一带一路”倡议的法律意义

共建“一带一路”倡议源于中国,但机会和成果属于世界。只要各方秉持和遵循共商共建共享原则,就一定能把“一带一路”打造成为顺应经济全球化潮流的最广泛国际合作平台。坚持开放共赢,勇于变革创新,向着构建人类命运共同体的目标不断迈进,共创亚洲和世界的美好未来。③ “一带一路”倡议提出来之后,我国各地政府、企事业单位纷纷表态,支持国家“一带一路”倡议,但也有部分媒体和个人将“一带一路”倡议表述为“一带一路”战略。“倡议”与“战略”的不同表示,从法律意义上来讲,可能不仅涉及国际关系,更涉及国家主权原则的尊重。

我们知道,国家主权原则是当代国际关系的依据,更是国际法的基石。

---

① Evgeny Raschevsky, “When ‘One Belt One Road’ Project Disputes Arise, Who will Resolve Them?”,载汤森路透网:http://arbitrationblog. practicallaw. com/when-one-belt-one-road-project-disputes-arise-who-will-resolve-them,最后访问日期:2017 年 12 月 20 日。

② 参见冯正霖:《开启新时代民航强国建设新征程》,载《人民论坛》2018 年第 5 期。

③ 参见《习近平主席出席博鳌亚洲论坛 2018 年年会开幕式并发表主旨演讲》,载人民网:http://cpc. people. com. cn/n1/2018/0411/c64094 - 29918032. html,最后访问日期:2018 年 5 月 4 日。

当代国际法对主权原则的确认主要体现在1945年通过的《联合国宪章》中。宪章的序言申述了“大小各国平等权利”的信念。具体而言，为了避免两次世界大战带来的战祸重演，重申基本人权，人格尊严与价值，以及男女与大小各国平等权利之信念。[①]《联合国宪章》第2条第1款明确规定，“本组织系基于各会员国主权平等之原则”。1970年的《国际法原则宣言》[②]将各国主权平等之原则列为国际法7项基本原则中的第6项，并对主权原则的内容作出详细说明：“其具体规定是：各国一律享有主权平等，各国不问经济、社会、政治或其他性质有何不同，均有平等权利与责任，并为国际社会之平等会员国。”

世界著名国际法学家奥本海[③]给主权的定义是：“主权是最高权威，即一个独立于世界上任何其他权威之外的权威。因此，依照最严格和最狭隘的意义，主权含有全面独立的意思，无论在国土以内或在国土以外都是独立的。”[④]在国家政治制度、经济发展模式方面拥有独立自主权。在国际法层面，各个国家无论大小、强弱，其主权都是平等的。

（三）航空业面临的法律问题牵涉面大

民航业是国民经济的重要基础产业，其发达程度体现了当代世界经济的现代化水平，加快“空中丝绸之路”是推进“一带一路”的重要组成部分，也有

① 我联合国人民同兹决心欲免后世再遭今代人类两度身历惨不堪言之战祸，重申基本人权，人格尊严与价值，以及男女与大小各国平等权利之信念，创造适当环境，俾克维持正义，尊重由条约与国际法其他渊源而起之义务，久而弗懈，促成大自由中之社会进步及较善之民生。参见《联合国宪章》序言部分。

② 全称为《关于各国依联合国宪章建立友好关系及合作之国际法原则之宣言》。

③ 拉沙·法朗西斯·劳伦斯·奥本海（Lassa Francis Lawrence Oppenheim），1858年3月30日出生于德国法兰克福附近的温德肯，先后求学于柏林洪堡大学、哥廷根大学、海德堡大学和莱比锡大学，攻读哲学、医学、神学和法律。奥本海是国际法学实证主义学派的代表人物。他主张国际法是由国际条约和习惯构成的，而不是一套传统的自然法理论，并强调国内法和国家主权要高于国际法。

④ 沈春光：《全球化浪潮对国家主权的挑战及其对策》，载《中国特色社会主义研究》2003年第2期。

许多法律问题值得关注。

目前,中国民航已与“一带一路”上43个沿线国家实现空中直航,每周有超过4000多个航班。国内航空公司已在“一带一路”沿线的24个国家设立了境外营业部。[①] 2017~2018年冬春季,我国航空公司新开“一带一路”沿线国家国际航线95条,主要集中在东欧、中亚、东南亚、南亚及南太平洋地区国家。国外航空公司新开18条“一带一路”沿线国家的国际航线,主要集中在菲律宾、马来西亚、泰国、越南、柬埔寨、哈萨克斯坦等国家。[②] 但同时,我国与沿线国家的双边航空关系也有需要加强的地方。例如,我国与一些国家的航权还未充分利用,尚未通航或航班稀少;与一些国家间的运力额度很紧,继续扩大航权等;有些国家的政府部门利用两国尚未签订避免双重征税协定,[③]要求中方空运企业补交税款,都需要研究双边或多边的相关条款的解读与执行的问题。

2018年2月26日中国商飞公司与华融金融租赁在北京签署30架C919大型客机和20架ARJ21新支线飞机购机协议。C919大型客机国内外用户达到28家,订单总数达到815架,ARJ21新支线飞机客户达到21家,订单总数达到453架。[④] 2016年范堡罗航展上印度尼西亚一家航空公司签下了60架ARJ21飞机的订单。国产新舟系列飞机、运-12已经成功出口多个国家运营。截至2018年4月20日,我国向“一带一路”沿线国家已经交付50架运12系列飞机,运-12飞机还获得了美国适航证,并成功出口美国。可见,在我国民航不断推动民航产品、管理、技术、标准和服务“走出去”的同时,需

---

① 参见《中国民航鼎力支持“一带一路”》,载民航资源网:http://news.carnoc.com/list/403/403323.html,最后访问日期:2017年5月17日。

② 参见《民航执行冬春航季航班计划 新开“一带一路”航线95条》,载中国发展网:http://www.chinadevelopment.com.cn/news/zj/2017/10/1186429.shtml,最后访问日期:2017年12月25日。

③ 参见《我国签订的避免双重征税协定一览表》,载国家税务总局网:http://www.chinatax.gov.cn/n810341/n810770/index.html,最后访问日期:2018年4月2日。

④ 参见《中国商飞与华融金融租赁签署30架C919大型客机和20架ARJ21新支线飞机购机协议》,载中国科技网:http://www.stdaily.com/cgzspt/0231/2018-04/16/content_659628.shtml,最后访问日期:2018年4月16日。

要研究好法律合同文本,国际化的适航要求和产品责任问题[①]等。

刚果(布)民航局已经向 ARJ21 飞机颁发了型号合格证,这意味着该飞机已经可以出口到刚果(布)共和国了,也期望我国飞机制造商以此为起点,进一步扩大在非洲乃至其他国家民航部门获得更多的型号合格证认可。我们还应当研究、分析、总结和借鉴国际领先的实践、国际规范和惯例,研究航空产品目标国的法律环境,全面制定涉及航空产品责任、售后服务的法律规范、服务标准合同文本,为我国航空产品更多地走向世界早作准备,打好基础。

近年来,我国公司展开了多次关于航空发动机、飞机制造、机场、航空公司和相关产业的海外收购,提升了我国民航的实力,也推动了我国民航不仅参与"一带一路"建设,更是进一步融入全球化当中去。在此背景下,我国民航面临法律适用和值得研究涉及面越来越广泛,越来越多涉外的航空企业并购、消费者权益保护和其他涉外商事法律问题等。

2018 年 2 月首届亚太地区民航部长级会议日前在北京举行。会议讨论通过了《北京宣言》,旨在促进亚太地区"一带一路"沿线国家民航发展,从航空安全、空中航行服务、事故调查和人力资源等方面表达了亚太民航各成员国的共同关切、共同立场、共同愿景,[②]其中的航空安全、空中航行服务和事故调查等,涉及广泛的国际国内法律制度的建立与协同。

三、"一带一路"建设中民航热点法律问题

我国民航业秉持政策沟通、设施联通、贸易畅通、资金融通、民心相通的"五通"指导思路,以航空的通达性、便捷性、竞争力提升为目标,通过"空中丝绸之路"建设,推动人流、物流、资金流、信息流,助力"一带一路"建设,同

---

① 参见张超汉:《国际航空产品责任研究》,法律出版社 2017 年版,第 11 页。

② 参见《促进亚太"一带一路"民航发展》,载新浪网:http://news.sina.com.cn/c/2018-02-04/doc-ifyreuzn2471597.shtml,最后访问日期:2018 年 2 月 4 日。

时也面临一系列法律热点,需要我国去解决。

(一)双边、多边的航空协定的法律问题

目前,我国已与120个国家和地区签署了双边政府航空运输协定。其中,我国与“一带一路”沿线62个国家签订了双边政府航空运输协定,并与东盟签订了首个区域性的航空运输协定。[①] 这些协定有的是天空开放协定,有的是形式上的天空开放实际上并未开放,也有的是形式上未天空开放实质上开放度很高。

我国与“一带一路”沿线国家基本均已有航权安排,东盟10国的三四业务权已放开,给航空公司拓展拓深航线网络提供了有力的资源保障。但南亚部分重要国家如印度、孟加拉的航权已用完,至俄罗斯和中东欧部分国家如捷克的航权也所剩不多,造成航空公司新开加密航线困难。

2003年我国民航局代表在加拿大蒙特利尔召开的国际民航组织世界范围航空运输会议上,提出了“积极、渐进、有序、有保障”地开放国际航空运输市场的政策,标志着中国民航对外开放迈入了一个崭新的阶段,而相应的国家政策也发生了调整。[②]从2015年开始,多年来推进中国国际航空运输市场开放的美国,不再坚持其一贯秉持的开放立场,甚至不愿意与中方探讨适度扩大运力安排,而是将注意力和重点转为美方企业在中国获得航班时刻的问题。[③]近年来,我们空运企业在国外面临外国政府要求补交所得税的问题以及与欧盟的平行协定。

我国应当全盘思考我国民航在新的历史条件国际航空政策的走向问题,在坚持“积极、渐进、有序、有保障”的原则前提下,梳理我国与“一带一路”沿

---

① 参见《中国航企当好“一带一路”建设的“先行军”》,载中国民航网:http://www.caacnews.com.cn/1/6/201705/t20170524_1215126.html,最后访问日期:2018年1月19日。

② 参见《中国民航参与国际合作 提高竞争力实现双赢》,载民航资源网:http://news.carnoc.com/list/121/121689.html,最后访问日期:2018年1月19日。

③ 参见《中国民航以积极、渐进、有序、有保障方式扩大中美航权安排》,载新华网:http://www.xinhuanet.com/politics/2015-08/27/c_128173218.htm,最后访问日期:2018年1月27日。

线国家和其他国家的双边和多边航空运输协定,根据不同国家分类制定航空协定模板并定期更新,同时要及时解决空运企业在建设“空中丝绸之路”和国际化的进程中面临的新旧问题,争取达到“双赢”的目的。

(二)联盟合作问题

通过航空联盟将我国航空公司的国际航线网络和航空服务延伸至“一带一路”各地区和国家的更多其他城市。[①] 传统意义上航空公司之间的联盟主要是通过三大航空联盟来进行。例如,传统上航空联盟,已经从联程、常旅客计划、代码共享,发展到全面航班时刻、航线协调,联合经营的收入及收益共享以及更高级别的股权合作(见图1)。通过更高层面的合作共赢,其经营风险要比单纯的航线开辟和运力投入要小很多,也有许多的法律问题值得深入研究。未来可能需要航空公司开展其他方面的合作,新近的一些大型航空公司之间的合作不但有参股,而且是跨联盟间的合作。在此情况下,原有的合作纽带如何维持,法律关系如何界定,值得法律工作者和学者的仔细探究。

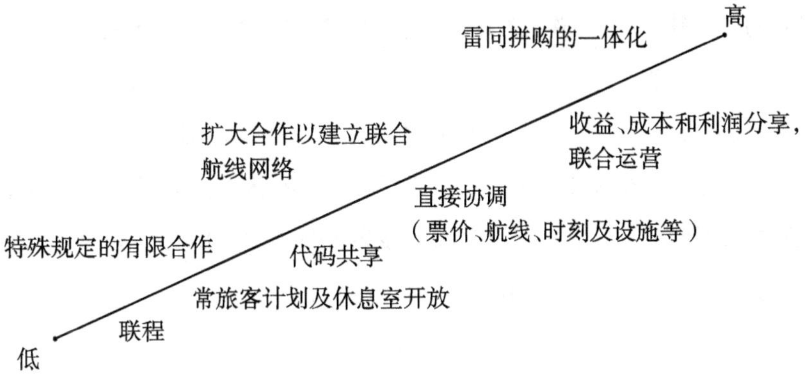

图1

① 参见《“一带一路”背景下我国民航运输业的发展对策研究》,载参考网:http://www.fx361.com/page/2017/0712/2054026.shtml,最后访问日期:2017年12月23日。

(三)加强反垄断等问题研究

在反垄断领域和金融领域,[①]美国法院的手就伸得比较长,有时候会适用"长臂管辖"(Long Arm Statute)原则。例如,根据美国《外贸反托拉斯促进法》(Foreign Trade Antitrust Improvement Act),如果外国贸易主体的行为对美国国内商事行为或美国的进出口贸易产生"直接、显著、合理可预期"的影响,则美国的反垄断法可以得到适用。这一做法,确保美国可以更好地在本国公司面临他国公司所谓的不正当竞争行为威胁时提供保护。又如,在有些航空空难索赔案中,美国法院利用长臂管辖和最低联系原则,行使了管辖权,虽然后来美国初裁不管辖空难赔偿诉讼,但已经给企业造成很大的困扰和信誉损失。[②]

此外,为落实国家"一带一路"倡议,各家航空公司都在调整布局新开通"一带一路"的航线,但毕竟这一地区大部分处在相对欠发达阶段,长期运营可能面临困难。如果能将"一带一路"航线纳入补贴范围,无疑将鼓励航空公司新开、增开"一带一路"航线,进一步助推航空公司在"一带一路"战略上的步伐,更好地服务国家"一带一路"倡议。在欧美,政府补贴是航空业经常面临并且涉及反垄断问题,也是各相关企业关注的问题。法律问题复杂而且多样化,国家补贴也并非不可为之。美国就有学者认为,政府补贴很正常,[③]问题在于如何在法律上站得住脚,我们也需要从法理上给企业支持,让企业尽可能做到在合法并且有效益地经营。

---

① 2014年年初,美联储开始对外资银行实行新的监管模式,由母国监管转为"东道国监管",要求在美营业的大型银行接受其监管。对于那些在美资产总额超过500亿美元的外资银行,必须在美国各自子公司之上,再建立一家中间控股公司,并享受与美国其他控股公司一样的资本金、风险管理与流动性要求,将其完全置于美联储的监管之下。

② 参见《美初裁不管辖包头空难赔偿诉讼》,载法制网:http://www.legaldaily.com.cn/bm/content/2007-05/28/content_624954.htm,最后访问日期:2018年5月2日。

③ See Kevin Mitchell, "Government Support to the Airline Industry Is Common", Published on April 15, 2015, Accessed https://www.linkedin.com/pulse/government-support-airline-industry-common-kevin-mitchell/, March 15, 2018.

（四）加强通用航空法律问题研究

我国通用航空产业已经进入了一个高速发展期。根据国家发改委发布的数据显示，截至2016年年底，全国通用航空企业达322家，在册通用航空器2088架，全年飞行76.1万小时，同比分别增长14.6%、11.4%、4.0%。全国各类通用航空产业园区达140余个。[①] 我国通航产业未来发展空间较大，至2020年将形成超万亿元的新兴市场，与“一带一路”沿线国家开展合作的前景广阔。

美国的经验表明，通用航空每年对经济的贡献超过2000亿美元，人均接近350美元。[②] 美国通用航空人均GDP贡献最高的州，通常分布在人口稀少且交通运输方式受限于土地面积和地形因素的地区，而这些地区的地理、地貌与“一带一路”所涉及的地区非常相似。[③] 可见，通用航空（包括无人机）未来有很大的发展空间，如商务、旅游和物流投递。在美国联邦航空管理局现在每年发布的航空业发展报告的通航部分包括相当篇幅的无人机内容。

通用航空在商务旅行、航空物流、促进人际交流以及发展当地旅游经济中，均发挥着重要作用。特别值得指出的是，全球无人机产业正进入一个快速发展的阶段，未来潜力不可低估。美国联邦航空管理局2017年的报告认为，到2021年，美国商用无人驾驶航空器系统（俗称无人机系统）将达到42万套，而2016年只有4.2万套。[④] 早在1990年，美国就准许无人机进入国家空域系统（National Airspace System，NAS）。2015年年初，美国联邦航空管理局宣布了针对55磅以下小型无人机系统的规章（107部），[⑤]为小型无人机融

---

① 参见《通用航空产业进入高速发展期 市场空间巨大》，载网易财经网：http://money.163.com/17/0418/02/CI95STJ4002580S6.html，最后访问日期：2018年4月13日。

② 参见《通用航空能助飞中国“一带一路”》，载中国航空新闻网：http://www.cannews.com.cn/2016/0624/155394.shtml，最后访问日期：2018年4月14日。

③ 同上。

④ FAA“Forecast Highlights(2017－2037)”.

⑤ Ultimate Guide to FAA's Part 107(14 CFR Part 107), Accessed https://jrupprechtlaw.com/faas-new-far-part-107-drone-operators-need-know, March 30, 2018.

入美国国家空域道路上铺平道路。近年来,我国无人机市场增长迅速,截至2018年3月23日,无人机实名登记数量已增至18万架以上。与此同时,无人机大有在通用航空和货运航空等诸多领域逐步替代有人驾驶航空器的趋势。预计2022年,农业生产和娱乐航拍领域或将率先初步实现行业普及。[①]民用无人机还保持国际市场的竞争优势,产品出口贸易额实现快速增长。海关监测预警数据显示,2017年前3个季度,我国出口无人机80.5亿元人民币,比2016年同期增长96.4%。[②] 笔者认为,未来我国无人机产业在推进"一带一路"建设进程中,必定会在民航合作中占据一席之地,而相应的法律制度应当尽快地建立起来,尽早出台国际标准,否则既不利于行业的发展也会影响我国无人机产业在"一带一路"沿线国家乃至全球的地位。

(五)全面提高合规意识,防范违规风险

参与"一带一路"建设,我们将面临错综复杂的法律环境,我国在推进"四个全面"部署中,要求将对法治的尊崇、对法律的敬畏转化成思维方式和行为方式,做到在法治之下,而不是法治之外,更不是法治之上想问题、作决策、办事情,非常及时,也很有必要。中兴通讯事件暴露出中国企业管控合规风险的能力滞后、企业合规管理体系存在明显漏洞,法律观念薄弱,有章不守,制度成为摆设。在全球化进入新阶段,企业竞争进入到全球价值链竞争的当今时代,这是一个重大隐患,有很大法律风险。[③] 在美国司法部的多项指控中,认为中兴重复违法甚至对代理律师撒谎,[④]其中很重要的一点原因

---

① 参见《我国民用无人机未来四年将在多领域实现普及》,载中国航空新闻网:http://www.cannews.com.cn/2018/0329/173150.shtml,最后访问日期:2018年3月30日。

② 同上。

③ 参见《中兴通讯,比罚单更沉重的反思》,载凤凰网:http://tech.ifeng.com/a/20180418/44961007_0.shtml,最后访问日期:2018年4月18日。

④ "ZTE Corporation then went to Great Lengths to Devise Elaborate, Corporate-wide Schemes to Hide Its Illegal Conduct, Including Lying to Its Own Lawyers", Accessed https://www.justice.gov/opa/pr/zte-corporation-agrees-plead-guilty-and-pay-over-4304-million-violating-us-sanctions-sending, April 19, 2018.

是高管法律意识比较淡薄。

中兴风波对中国企业来说是一次大范围的冷空气影响,大面积降温,容易引发感冒发烧,但也不见得完全是坏事。对于我国先进大型企业来说,要成就世界品牌,前提就是在全球范围内要做守法合规的表率。① 对于航空企业来说,国际化程度日益提高,企业在全球经营,要大力提升法律意识,适时地建立起卓有成效的法律风险防范机制。

第一,要有合规意识,企业内部规章制度的制订和员工特别是高管代表公司作出的行为既要符合国内法,也要符合相关的国际条约和关联国家的法律规定,还要规避个人的行为给公司造成的负面影响和连带责任。②

第二,要有国际化的、规范化的员工手册。例如,注意避免有种族主义倾向表述,要明确反对性骚扰等内容(笔者曾主持过相关域外案件的处理),要防范发达国家法院通过国内法来介入发生在“一带一路”上的法律纠纷。

第三,要注意研究消费者的权益保护问题。“一带一路”有些航线通达欧盟成员国,而欧盟对于航空消费者的保护措施和法律规定都比较严,需要在经营和服务注意防范法律风险。

第四,要全面推动合规体系建设。通过体系建设,加强合规风险管理,提升合规风险管理掌控能力,围绕企业发展战略和经营目标,以提高合规管理水平和核心竞争力作为合规工作目标。笔者认为,要树立合规管理无小事的思想观念,有效防范经营各环节中的合规风险。

(六)要有违法成本意识

企业在境内外违规的成本越来越高,天文数字的处罚金额案例越来越

---

① 参见《中兴风波是创新中国的一场冷水浴》,载新浪网:http://finance.sina.com.cn/zl/china/2018-04-23/zl-ifznefkh9288145.shtml?cre=zl&r=user&pos=2_2,最后访问日期:2018年4月23日。

② 笔者在1997年曾处理过因员工在海外的个人不良行为引发的诉讼,该个人行为导致公司成为被告。

多,[①]企业付出的是真金白银,对企业损害很大。2016 年年初,荷兰电信巨头 VimpelCom 因其在乌兹别克斯坦向政府官员行贿,受到美国证券交易委员会和美国司法部共计 7.95 亿美元的经济处罚。[②] 2016 年 5 月 19 日美国卡普兰福克斯事务所对外宣布,28 家航企涉嫌航空货运价格垄断民事案件即将结案,法庭文件多达 1800 万页,30 多位目击者,87 份口供,诉讼时间几乎长达 10 年,总赔偿金高达 12.36 亿美元。此案涉及各公司之间的合作协议、来往函电、会议记录和员工的行为等诸多法律漏洞和违法问题。[③]

四、加强航空法学研究,服务“空中丝绸之路”建设

(一)我国民航法学研究的体系问题

航空法学研究是加强我国航空法制建设的基础型和指导性工作。近年来,我国航空法的研究和实践已经从局限在空域、航班延误和航空承运人责任问题等比较有限的范围向更广阔的领域推进,法学研究队伍不断扩大。“一带一路”空中丝绸之路的建设,要求我们航空法律研究更上一层楼。

我国的航空法研究远未形成系统性的优势,首先是研究的深度还不够,在国际上叫得响的法学论文和演讲还屈指可数。例如,在全球顶尖的航空法年刊如 *Annals of Air and Space* 等刊物发表论文的航空与空间法研究者屈指可数。[④] 其次是政府机关和学术机构的研究成果、学术演讲与实际脱节。有些是应景之作,质量不高,仅作为一次性的业绩上报;有些虽然编印了一些国

---

① 参见《企业合规体系建设的法律视角》,载中伦网:http://www.zhonglun.com/Content/2017/11-03/1649523532.html,最后访问日期:2018 年 4 月 11 日。

② 参见《合规九要素:企业全面合规的系统方法》,载德勤网:https://www2.deloitte.com/cn/zh/pages/risk/articles/nine-elements-of-compliance.html,最后访问日期:2018 年 4 月 28 日。

③ 参见《28 家知名航企成被告 国航支付 5000 万美元和解》,载搜狐网:http://business.sohu.com/20160525/n451333255.shtml,最后访问日期:2018 年 4 月 29 日。

④ See Wu Jianduan, “The Carrier's Liability Regimes in China”, *Annals of Air and Space Law*, 2008. The Annals has been publishing original articles, drafted in English or French, covering the entire spectrum of domestic and international air law and the law of space applications. The contributors are academics and leading practitioners from all parts of the world.

家的法律法规手册，却存在操作性差的问题，缺乏及时性，做不到及时跟踪沿线国家的法规修订等。国际航空运输协会就主张，航空法律工作要从四个方面入手：一是分析国际航空法律法规政策对于航空运输业的影响；二是确定构成国际航空公司商业环境的法律要素；三是防范常见的航空法律陷阱；四是及时应对航空法律法规的变化。① 笔者认为，这四个方面也可以说是航空法学研究的价值所在。

希望能够借助民航国际化、全球化和打造“空中丝绸之路”这样的契机，加强航空法学研究队伍的建设，加快航空法律人才的培养，特别是既懂得法学又懂得经济和管理的复合型人才的培养，加深航空法学的研究，特别是航空法学与经济学、管理学和其他法学学科的跨学科交叉研究。我国航空法学研究应当立足中国、借鉴国外、开展合作，②侧重民航“一带一路”“国际化”“全球化”法律问题研究、把握当代、面向未来的思路，来构建中国特色航空法学研究体系。

（二）要全面地梳理民航面临的法律问题

推进“一带一路”倡议，建设“空中丝绸之路”，我国航空法学工作者面临一系列需要认真探索的跨界的法律问题：

既要研究“一带一路”国家的与民航相关的法律法规现状和发展趋势，如当地涉及民航活动税收制度和外汇的管理，又要研究我国与这些国家现有民用航空运输协定的补充、修订和完善。

既要研究与“一带一路”国家发展民航关系的法律问题，也要从构建“人类命运共同”角度出发，研究世界民航普遍面临的进一步健康发展的法律保障问题。

既要研究与“一带一路”民航相关的民商事法律问题，也要重点关注我

---

① See “International Air Law Diploma”, Accessed http://www.iata.org/training/diploma_program/Pages/air-law.aspx, May 4, 2018.

② 要大力同国际民航组织、国际航协、国外研究机构开展多方位多层面的合作，尽快进入国际航空法学研究的前沿。

国民航发展面临的安全法律制度的进一步完善问题。①

既要研究与航空运输相关的各国法律,也要研究"单纯"涉及商业活动的法律问题,包括但不限于涉及投资合作方面的法律问题。

既要积极参与国际规则的制定,也要在建设"一带一路"和民航强国的过程中争取逐步把握制定国际民航规则标准的主导权和话语权。

(三)从法律理念和制度上总结好的经验

我国民航发展迅速,发展质量明显提升,体现中国特色的管理经验,也值得从法律层面进行很好的总结。例如,中国民航坚守飞行安全底线,坚持持续安全发展,安全水平世界领先,百万架次重大事故率均低于世界平均水平。2013~2017年,我国民航运输航空百万小时重大事故率为0,同期世界平均水平约为0.0872,其中美国为0.0220,我国民航百万架次重大事故率为0;同期世界平均水平为0.1745,其中美国为0.0480,我国民航亿客公里死亡人数为0;同期世界平均水平为0.0074。② 这其中既有队伍管理体系、安全责任体系和安全管控举措的效果,也有我国多年来坚持进一步健全安全法规体系的努力。如果能够更多地从法律层面及规章制度建设方面进行分析、判断和总结,通过多边或双边的交流和推广,相信对"一带一路"沿线乃至其他地区的国家都有借鉴作用,也能进一步提升我国民航的话语权。

(四)更多地关注互联网时代涉及的风险问题

随着互联网特别是移动互联网的发展,航空运输已经不是单一的运输活

---

① 按照民航"十三五"规划关于航空运输总周转量的预期增量,即从800多亿吨公里增长到1400多亿吨公里,同样的增长美国用了14年时间,中国计划用5年来实现,所形成的安全压力比以往更大,全行业必须坚持安全第一,切实做到对安全隐患零容忍。中国的航空安全实践所形成的体系化的规则,对于"一带一路"沿线国家乃至世界民航都有很好的参照价值。参见《我国民航业将保持强劲发展态势》,载中国网:http://ydyl.china.com.cn/2018-03/28/content_50759452.htm,最后访问日期:2018年4月3日。

② 参见《民航局:近五年来 我国运输航空百万小时重大事故率为0》,载人民网:http://finance.people.com.cn/n1/2017/1018/c1004-29594488.html,最后访问日期:2018年5月6日。

动。各空运企业致力于提供打造全场景智能化电商平台，实现从单一机票销售向综合出行产品销售的转型，进而构建航空旅行综合生态圈，新型的法律问题也由此产生，特别提及民航网络安全和消费者个人信息的保护问题。

各空运企业网络承载的业务系统急剧上升，访问用户也迅速增加，因此给民航网络的安全运行带来很大挑战。主要有三个方面：一是民航网络安全管理面临的攻击威胁，包括软硬件系统漏洞、不法分子恶意攻击、病毒木马垃圾邮件等。二是各个民航企业的日常运行数据、客户私人信息等以及在航班上浏览微博、网页，通过微信与朋友交流所产生的信息安全。三是IT系统的问题。2017年7月由于网络发展故障，美国西南航空公司取消了2000个航班，损失超过8200万美元。各国和国际民航组织正在探索规则网络安全的方法。在国际航空方面，1944年的《国际民用航空公约》第37条规定，各国承诺“最大限度的在规定、标准、程序和组织方面进行合作”。通过国际民航组织，在《国际民用航空公约》的附件17加入针对网络安全措施，会促使各国为一起制定全球统一的航空网络安全标准而努力。①

关于消费者数据保护问题，欧盟2016年通过的《一般数据保护条例》（以下简称《条例》）规定，②为欧洲居民提供商品和服务的企业，就必须遵守《条例》，而与企业的办公室或服务器在哪里无关。③ 与以往的规定相比，提高了执行力度的同时也大大地提升了惩罚力度，对于一般性的违法，罚款上限是1000万欧元或企业上一年度全球营业收入的2%（两者中取数额大者）；对于严重的违法，罚款上限是2000万欧元或企业上一年度全球营业收入的4%（两者中取数额大者），特别值得我国空运企业的关注。④《条例》对于航空运输活动消费者数据隐私保护的加强具有很强的借鉴意义，有利于提

---

① 参见《欧盟数据隐私保护的新进展》，载中国社会科学网：http://www.cssn.cn/sjxz/gzdt/zxdt/201609/t20160918_3204332.shtml，最后访问日期：2018年5月6日。

② 2016年4月14日，欧洲议会投票通过了商讨4年的《一般数据保护条例》（General Data Protection Regulation，GDPR），该法案将于2018年5月25日正式生效。

③ 参见欧盟的《条例》第2条和第3条的规定。

④ 这一力度已经与欧盟反垄断处罚处于同一量级。

升全球航空业对消费者数据隐私保护的规范化重视程度。我国近期正在征求意见的《民航网络信息安全管理规定》,也将有利于航空运输中的消费者信息的保护。

五、结　语

航空运输是推进我国经济高质量发展的重要内容,建设“空中丝绸之路”也是“一带一路”建设的重要内容。民航不仅仅是一种重要的交通运输方式,作为国家重要的战略产业,服务国家战略、社会经济发展同样是民航高质量发展的重要作用。以航空运输为主要内容的“空中丝绸之路”建设,不仅有助于我国企业参与国际竞争、实现跨越式发展,更有助于搭建连接中国和世界的“空中桥梁”,改变沿线国家和地区交通落后的现状,实现基础设施互联互通,拉动沿线各地经济增长。①

航空运输业是一个高度需要规矩、规则、规章和法律规范的行业。经过几代民航人、法律工作者、政府部门和各利益相关者的共同努力,我国民航业在法律制度、法律意识、依法行政、依法经营上已经取得了很大的成绩,但仍然有很大的提升空间和很多可以改进的地方。

在建设“空中丝绸之路”,推进“一带一路”倡议的过程中,要以国际化和超前的眼光,着力提升法律意识,善用法律思考,依法经营合规运行,在推进“一带一路”倡议,建设“空中丝绸之路”中,②要保障高质量发展,离不开法律制度和体系的保障,更离不开法律意识的提升,自觉依法行政,依法建设,依法经营,依法开展国际合作,堵住安全和信息漏洞,扎紧篱笆,才能保障我国民航事业在“一带一路”建设中发挥重要作用,建设好“空中丝绸之路”。

① 参见《航空产业成为“一带一路”建设的重要内容》,载新华网:http://www.xinhuanet.com/air/2018-01/18/c_1122278767.htm,最后访问日期:2018年2月30日。

② 参见《新时代民航强国建设的本质是高质量发展》,载中国民航局官网:http://www.caac.gov.cn/XWZX/MHYW/201712/t20171228_48227.html,最后访问日期:2017年12月30日。

航空立法

我国航空立法路径争议述评

王立志*

法律在制定之时即已过时。这一立法悖论在我国《民用航空法》(以下简称《民航法》)中体现得尤为明显。其主要原因在于我国航空业发展过于迅速,以至于法律尚未深入人心就发现其规制乏力。在《民航法》制定后不久,人们就开始研究对其进行修改。截至目前,航空法界与航空实务界业已形成共识,[①]即认为现行航空立法不能满足我国日益增长的航空发展需求,空域资源分配不当,导致延误频发,航空公司与消费者之间权益保护不均衡,导致双方矛盾突出。在这种认识下,从21世纪开始,我国进入了新的一轮以修改《民航法》为引领的航空法立法进程。自2003年至今,民用航空局已经组织起草了多

* 中国民航大学航空法律与政策研究中心副教授、法学博士,硕士研究生导师。

① 参见李乾贵、郑囿君、黄炳蓉等:《美国航空法立法模式对中国空法立法的借鉴》,载《管理学家》2010年第8期。

个修改建议稿。[1] 然而随着讨论的深入,有人认为应该制定《航空法》,而不是修改《民航法》。由此导致我国航空立法在修法路径与制法路径之间展开旷日持久的论战。在此过程中,出现了第三种声音,即认为应当双管齐下,一边制定《航空法》,一边修改《民航法》。即使这三种看法内部,也存在立法理念分歧。究竟我国的航空立法应当采取哪种路径,作为上述立法活动的参与者,笔者有幸面对面与各种意见进行交流,[2]深感对我国航空立法的路径选择进行理性的思考刻不容缓。

一、修改《民航法》:保守还是激进

在我国航空立法未来发展的路向上,人们最早的想法是修改《民航法》。这一主张认为,《民航法》是1995年制定的,经过多年的实践,已经显露出其先天不足,存在诸多问题,需要通过修改予以完善。同时,制定《民航法》时的航空实践与今天的实践发生了一定的改变,需要修改《民航法》以更准确地规制实践。在实际修改工作中,逐渐出现了两种不同的声音:一种观点主张对现有《民航法》中不适应航空实践的内容进行修改,并尽力解决法律自

---

① 第一轮航空法立法是新中国成立后到"文化大革命"前,是立法的探索与准备期,很难说那时有真正意义上的航空法,主要是一些飞行管理等制度。第二轮是在"文化大革命"后到2000年之前,在经过"文化大革命"的磨难之后,中国一些学者开始呼吁制定航空法。该轮立法进程中,具有里程碑意义的立法行动是1995年通过的《民航法》。此后不久,人们开始讨论《民航法》存在的问题。可以说,从《民航法》实施后不久,修改《民航法》的呼声一直此起彼伏未曾停歇过。1999年12月民航局曾向国务院法制办上报《关于建议修改〈中华人民共和国民用航空法〉的函》(民航体函〔1999〕928号),建议修改《民航法》,并展开论证研究工作。2003年正式启动了《民航法》修改工作。据我所知,民航局组织下制定了4个《民航法》修订版本,分别是2007年《〈民航法〉修订讨论稿》、2012年《〈民航法〉(修订)讨论稿》和2015年及2016年《〈民航法〉修订征求意见稿》。在此过程中,催生了制定《航空法》的观念。这一过程可视为第三轮航空法立法。

② 本文作者参加了民航局法规司组织的"航空法制定研究小组",也参与了民航局法规司自2015年3月26日以来召开的历次《民航法》修订与《航空法》起草立法论证会、征求意见会,提供过一些意见。同时作者作为国家空管委组织的"航空法起草小组"成员,参与起草《〈航空法〉建议稿》,对其间发生的各类意见和争论均有所了解。此外,作者还从法典化的视角独立起草了《〈中华人民共和国航空法〉建议稿》,达600余条,亦是对各种理论争议进行思考的结果。

身存在的主要问题即可,无须对《民航法》进行大刀阔斧的彻底修改。此观点相对保守,主要为民航局官方及中国民航科学技术研究院的民航法修改课题组所坚持。保守主义的修法路径坚持温和地改良《民航法》,其理由为:《民航法》经过多年的实践,其主要制度是适合航空产业的发展的,对我国航空运输的促进作用非常明显,尽管目前出现了一些新的运输模式和发展方向,但有关研究尚不充分,应当继续研究,仅对于实践证明存在问题的部分进行修改就可以了。全面地修改《民航法》实质上是一次完全的新法制定过程,而制定新的《民航法》并无必要。同时,对《民航法》的全面修改可能导致更多的分歧,影响本次的修法成功。目前民航局召集的多次"《民航法》修改稿征求意见会"以及其牵头起草的2012年《〈民航法〉修订讨论稿》、2015年及2016年《〈民航法〉修订征求意见稿》均以对《民航法》个别条款的调整为主,尤其是强调对1999年《蒙特利尔公约》的衔接。① 修订稿对一些应当增加规定的重要问题,如区际航空问题并未涉及,②基本体现了保守主义的修法思路。

另一种主张是对《民航法》进行彻底的修改,完全剔除不合时宜的制度,衔接国际公约,③并增加一些重要制度,解决现实中无法可依的现象,比如,航班延误赔偿标准、④区际航空制度、对新形态的多式联运的规制、航空领域中的生化反恐等,使《民航法》能够完全适应现代航空产业的发展。这一主张较为激进,其核心主张是对《民航法》进行全面的体检,如赵劲松博士就认为,"民航法的修改及完善涉及到航空运输业的方方面面,是一项庞大的系统

---

① 对此早有学者在理论上提供了支持。参见张晓明、裴敏、赵红:《借鉴新公约修订〈民用航空法〉》,载《中国民用航空》2004年第10期。

② 民航局组织起草的2007年、2012年、2015年和2016年4个《民航法》修改版本在结构上与现行《民航法》一致,仅2015年版增加了"民用航空安全保卫"一章。在内容上主要是对部分不符合现实的内容进行了修改,另外对公共航空运输一章进行了"蒙特利尔式"的改造。可以说,这3个版本均是保守地改良《民航法》观念的产物。

③ 参见朱子勤:《修改我国民用航空法的两点建议》,载《法制日报》2008年11月2日,第10版。

④ 参见杨甫旺:《关于修改〈民用航空法〉,制定航班延误赔偿标准的建议》,载《现代物流报》2014年3月14日,A06版。

工程,应进行长期地跟踪研究”。[①] 激进派认为,《民航法》虽然在过去的实践中对航空产业起到了促进作用,但其重要制度存在很多缺陷,比如,航空器留置权制度没有规定,航空器优先权登记制度不合理,“通用航空法律法规和标准体系存在严重的不完整、不合理性”,[②]等等,需要进行系统的修改,增加缺席的制度,不能只是对个别现有制度进行适应性修改,认为这样的小修小补不利于《民航法》的完善。其理据之一是修法程序启动复杂,《民航法》修改议题已经提出10余年了,但至今无法正式进入人大立法规划,如果不珍惜本次修法机会,对《民航法》进行充分的修订,将在近期丧失《民航法》完善的机会,会对航空实践造成巨大的阻碍。

《民航法》修改的保守与激进之争只是对法律修改程度不同的争议。保守主义的立场以法的稳定性为基础,而激进主义的立场则以法的预见性与理论自足为依据。保持法的相对稳定性是法具有权威性的前提。[③] 我们绝不可能推翻《民航法》的所有制度另外构建一套完全不同的民航法律制度,但同时也不能因此就忽略对实践发展趋势的基本判断,并在此基础上制定相对超前的法律规则。事实上,正是因为法律的预见性,才导致法律在制定之后一个较长时期内仍然能够对现实具有较好的规制作用,才能保证法律相对稳定。如果法律缺乏预判性,在较短时间内被实践所超越,则法律可能成为阻碍实践的规则,而不是促进和保障实践的规则。缺乏预见性的立法必然难以保持其稳定性。故此,对《民航法》以预见性为基础、并继承其成功之处进行修改,实质上比小修小补更能够保持其稳定性。

同时,民航发展的实践需要法律适应其步伐。《民航法》已有10余年的实践过程,其间暴露出的问题不在少数,这些问题的存在表明:《民航法》仅仅是对其制定之前我国的民航发展状况有所把握,但并未预见到在其实施不久后民航实践所发生的多次重要改革,也未预见到我国航空运输周转量的飞

① 赵劲松:《我国民航法修改的几个关键问题》,载《中国民航报》2011年10月18日,第7版。

② 张颖川:《中国航空法立法进程亟待加快》,载《现代物流报》2013年12月3日,第7版。

③ 参见李云龙:《法律要有稳定性》,载《求实》1986年第3期。

跃式上升,当然也未预见到这种飞跃式上升与制度短视之间的尖锐矛盾。因此,对《民航法》进行系统的修订,首先就需要消解民航实践与法律之间的差距和障碍。为此,对《民航法》进行系统的修改,使其符合实践需求,正是《民航法》修改的基本诉求和目标。而对个别制度的小修小改,并不能从根本上改变《民航法》对实践的促进作用越来越小的现实。

在《民航法》应当修改的共识下,珍惜立法机会无疑是立法者不能忽视的问题。法律的修改程序具有非常复杂的影响因素,任何一个因素,如实践中发生的有重要影响的案件、新型业态的发展、各利益共同体的利益诉求、国家的重视程度、民众的呼声等都有可能造成立法程序的加快或者延缓、停滞甚至终止。在如此复杂的情况下,启动多次修改法律的机会并不多。因此,在有机会修改法律的错漏时进行充分的论证,消除其落后于实践的差距,修正其所依赖的理论之不足,实现法律对实践的充分引导与规制,无疑是修改法律的基本任务。《民航法》修改的呼声已有 10 余年,其间多次启动修改研究工作,但多次因为种种原因而暂停修改,最近又一次成为航空界争议的热点,本身就说明了其修改之路充满了不确定因素。因此,《民航法》有机会启动修改程序时,应当高度重视和珍惜,放弃对以后可以适时再修改的想法。尽管《民航法》自制定以来已经经过三次修改,但都是不涉及航空法基本制度的三次小修改:2009 年 8 月 27 日为适应《刑法》的变化修改了《民航法》有关附属刑法的内容,2015 年 4 月 24 日、2016 年 11 月 7 日为适应国务院行政审批制度改革与航空实践的变化,修改了《民航法》有关行政审批与航空人员范围的个别条款。但这些修改并没有对民航实践造成根本性的影响。故此,对于《民航法》的修改不宜保守,而应当在系统的论证与研究后进行充分的修改。

二、统一航空法之原则化路径批判

在推动《民航法》修订工作的过程中,一些学者和部门提出,应当制定我国的《航空法》,而不是修订《民航法》。这一观点以北京航空航天大学的部分学者为代表,其观点集中反映在该学院所开展的"统一航空法立法研究"课题成果之中。张千帆教授、龙卫球教授等指出,"民用航空相对发达、民航法律制度相对完善,但是其他方面相对滞后,如通用航空尤其是私人航空的发展规模仍相当低下"。① "从整体上来看,中国航空法体系的发展存在不平衡现象。"因此,"只有建立军民一体的统一航空法体系,才能同时满足保障空中安全和促进资源利用的发展需要"。该课题组认为,应当"调整目前的航空法律结构,将有关空域管理的飞行规则提升到和民航法同样的法律地位,并将两者融入统一的法律体系……统一航空法将包括空域管理和民航运输两大部分"。② 统一航空法说的核心是中国应当制定一部统一的航空法,其统一的基础是《民航法》与《飞行基本规则》,即将飞行基本规则与民航法整合,形成一部统一的《航空法》,这部法律应当同时调整民航活动与军航活动。

统一航空法的观点一抛出来就受到热捧。特别是被一些航空界的人大代表所认同。"近年来的全国'两会'上,来自航空系统的全国人大代表和政协委员也多次提出了'关于加快航空法立法的建议'。"③比如,中国民航局总飞行师于振发在接受记者采访时就指出,"不论从哪个角度上来讲,制定一部《航空法》都非常有必要。把航空用户的权利、义务、职责通过这部法律明确起来"。④ 全国人大代表张涛认为我国"迫切需要制定航空法处理涉外航空纠纷,维护国家航空权益"。"建议将航空法立法列入国家立法规划,加快立法进程,制定一部具有中国特色、符合国际航空立法规律的航空法,为统一管理航空活动提供基本依据,为实现由航空大国到航空强国的转变提供法律制

---

① 需要说明的是,一般将通用航空作为民用航空的一类来看待,该课题组将通用航空与民航并列的看法并不常见。

② 张千帆等:《建立统一的中国航空法体系——理论初探与立法建议》,载《北京航空航天大学学报》(社会科学版)2008年第2期。

③ 张颖川:《中国航空法立法进程亟待加快》,载《现代物流报》2013年12月3日,第7版。

④ 焦静波、赵继岚:《于振发:应尽快制定出台〈航空法〉》,载《中国航空报》2012年3月10日,第2版。

度保障,为构建中国特色航空法律体系奠定基础。"①

然而,统一航空法究竟应该只是原则化的法律,还是一部规制航空活动的法典?一些学者主张统一航空法应当是一个"'大'航空法",即"规定民航运输和空域管理的一般原则和管理结构,具体的技术性规则可留给单行法律规定,或由职能部门根据《航空法》的精神起草相关法规或规章"。② 这种观点显然是将欲制定的《航空法》作为航空法体系的原则性立法看待,仅制定原则性制度,而不涉及具体操作层面,因而该法也不可能是法典化的航空法。该观点可以称为航空法立法路径中的原则化立法路径。这一立法理念很快被作为制定统一航空法的设计理念,空管委主导下起草的第一版《航空法》就是在该理念指导下起草的。在起草空管委 2015 年版本《〈航空法〉建议稿》时,一开始我们设计的是一个与此不同的法典式版本,尤其是笔者坚持认为原则化立法对于目前的航空实践来说,意义不大。如果一定要制定《航空法》,就应该制定一部航空法典。这一看法可称为法典化路径。③

原则化立法路径在我国具有根深蒂固的影响。我国在新中国成立后到改革开放前的立法基本属于粗线条式的立法。1978 年 12 月鉴于我国长期处于立法匮乏的情况,邓小平同志提出"成熟一条制定一条"的立法指导思想,法律法规的制定开始走"零售"道路。然而,经过多年的航空实践和立法,制定完整的、细化的、具有较强可操作性的航空法典的立法条件逐渐成熟。在这个时候,学者们却突兀地提出制定航空原则性立法,而不是制定具有可操作性、寻法便利性和体系与逻辑自足的航空法典,这令人颇为诧异。与法律法典化相比,原则性立法虽然具有确定法律原则与基本制度的重要作用,但从法律实现的角度来看,原则化立法具有无法避免的缺点。

---

① 贾楠、杰文津:《张涛代表:加快制定航空法促航空由大变强》,载《新华每日电讯》2010 年 3 月 14 日,第 9 版。

② 张千帆、龙卫球、董杜骄、李斌:《建立统一的中国航空法体系——理论初探与立法建议》,载《北京航空航天大学学报》(社会科学版)2008 年第 2 期。

③ 后来该版本被删除了大量民航运输规则,恢复为原则化立法。可见,在当时,制定航空法典还没有得到广泛的认可。

其一,原则化立法缺乏可操作性。原则化立法往往以确立制度框架、原则与基本制度架构为目的,因而其可操作性基本缺失。在具体适用原则性法律时,执法者或者司法者在较大幅度内具有自由裁量权,这种自由裁量权的大量使用必然导致法律实现的差异化,无疑损坏了法律的权威性与确定性。航空法涉及当事人权利与义务的分配、航空市场的调控、国家航权与安全的维护、国际标准的制定、认可与执行、国际合作的开展等诸多问题,这些问题如果缺乏具有可操作性的法律,无疑会因为执法者与司法者的裁量偏差而导致航空市场的失衡,甚至给航空市场造成制度性灾难。可操作性差同时会导致当事人间商谈基础的缺失,进而导致纠纷不止。作为民航活动的基本法律,《民航法》在某些方面缺乏可操作性。如延误作为违约应当承担责任这一原则虽然被《民航法》所确认,但具体如何承担责任《民航法》却毫无规定,承运人认为没有证据证明的损失无须赔偿,而旅客认为延误就应当赔偿,无须证据证明损失的存在。这成为延误索赔的纠纷主因,甚至导致矛盾激化而酿成群体性事件。如果在新一轮航空立法中仍然坚持原则化立法路径,无疑将重蹈《民航法》以及我国诸多原则立法失败的覆辙。正因如此,基于对原则化立法的反思,我国制定了刑法典,并正在制定民法典。航空立法应当借鉴刑事立法与民事立法的经验,制定航空法典。

其二,原则化立法存在寻法不便。原则化立法意味着需要更多的具有可操作性的法律法规以具体化原则性法律所确立的制度。这将导致守法者、执法者与司法者寻法的不便,因为在一部法律中而不是在多部法律中找到具有可操作性的法律规则显然更为便利。就目前而言,旅客在权益受到侵害时往往难以找到法律依据,原因之一就是我国的《民航法》本身就是一部原则化立法,其可操作性并不强,往往需要通过法规和规章甚至航空运行标准才能确定当事人的权利义务。如退票费问题,《民航法》并无明确规则,旅客需要寻找《民用航空旅客、行李国内运输规则》等规章及其他文件才能了解退票规定。对于旅客来说其寻法过程相当不便。

其三,原则化立法不适应我国航空法发展的现实。原则化立法一般是在理论准备不足、实践认识不足但现实需求迫切时进行原则性规定，其要求是符合一般的社会期待即可。对于较为细化的可操作性规则，则因为理论研究的限制，留待将来研究充分时再加以规定，以防止制定出对实践起阻碍作用的法律。因此，原则化立法在一定程度上是立法的无奈，可以看作法典化立法的准备阶段。经过改革开放后的长期发展，我国航空法律已经基本形成了以《民航法》为统领，以行政法规、军事法规与民航规章、地方性航空法规等数百部法规规章为支撑的航空法律体系雏形。同时，我国学者对航空法律理论的研究也不再是《民航法》制定之初的寥落情状，加之我国航空实践的飞速发展，消解了实践不充分的弊端。在这种情形下制定原则性航空法，无疑是落后的立法理念。立法的细化是法律发展的标志之一。在《民航法》制定20多年之后，就应当考虑制定更加细致、精确、具有可操作性的立法——航空法典。航空法的现代化绝不是偷懒可以实现的。

其四，原则化立法不适宜处理航空法律法规和规章之间的相悖之处。众所周知，由于航空法规和规章是在不同时期逐渐制定，并且制定时由于研究不充分，存在各种内部不协调之处，甚至个别术语也存在随意使用的情况，如"航空器经营人"与"航空器运营人"两个概念同时在法律和规章中出现，[①]这二者又均缺乏定义规定，使法律和规章规定的权利义务是否为同一主体的权利义务很难确定。原则化立法很难因为规章使用的术语不同而废除其中一个或全部，特别是原则性法律本身未使用该任一不同术语时就更是如此。原则化立法难以关照法律之间的协调性，通过"与本法不一致的规定作废"之类的方法废除具体的法律法规与规章也存在操作困难的问题。因为其内容太过原则化，而具体法律法规和规章是否与其不一致，尚存在一个艰难的甄别过程，而数百个法律法规与规章的甄别耗时必久，且甄别作废后尚需制定新的规则，这同样不是一朝一夕之功。其结果必然导致航空法律适用的混乱，或出现适用法律的空白期。因此，在存在大量法规与规章的领域，制定原

---

① 《民用航空器事故和飞行事故征候调查规定》使用的是"航空器运营人"一词，而《民航法》《中国民用航空安全检查规则》等则使用了"航空器经营人"的概念。

则性法律并不符合立法规律。而法典化立法过程中,通过保留法律中行之有效的合理规定,并根据立法目标,适当提升法规、规章以及地方性法规中合理的制度为法律,在其编纂过程中可以梳理现行立法,兼之其较详细的规定,便于判断各类规则之间的相悖与相洽之处。

航空立法需要可操作性与体系内、体系间的协调性,原则化立法并不能实现这一点,反而会与上述要求渐行渐远。因此,在航空实践足够充分,理论研究已有起色,法律法规与规章的施行经验丰富,兼之各国立法可资借鉴的情况下,即使不能制定一个大而全的航空法典,也足以完成一部准航空法典。完全没有必要退而求其次,制定原则性航空法。

三、制修并行:双法模式还是单法模式

或许中庸思维永远是国人面临选择困难症时最有效的"救命稻草"。在修订《民航法》与制定《航空法》这两种思路之间,原国务院法制办组织有关部门提出了一种折中方案,即制修并行模式:民航实务急需修改《民航法》中不适宜之处,但《航空法》难以立即出台,基于急用先修原则,一方面继续修订《民航法》,另一方面继续组织研拟《航空法》,二者同时展开,但对于将来是推行一部法律还是两部法律并未明确表态。这就意味着未来可能存在三种模式之一种:《航空法》与《民航法》二法并行模式、统一《航空法》模式或修订后的《民航法》模式。

二法并行模式在 2015 年 3 月底正式被官方提出并开始研究。在《航空法》起草工作一开始,笔者及其他一些起草组的人员就提出,立法之初就应该对《民航法》及未来可能出台之《航空法》之间的关系予以明确,至少涉及三个方面:首先是如何定位两部法律。在制修并行模式下,如果未来真的存在两部航空法律,即《航空法》与《民航法》,那么,其中任何一部法律的定位都会影响另一部法律的定位。二者可能存在的定位是一般法与特别法关系,或者平行的航空一般法律关系,或者上位法与下位法关系。其次是立法目标和

宗旨如何确定。最后是如何切分调整对象。无论未来的《航空法》调整对象是什么,都不可避免地要考虑其是否需要包含《民航法》的调整对象的全部或者部分。这些问题相互关联,但毫无疑问都指向二法的关系。

制修并行思路下的统一《航空法》模式是指修订《民航法》与制定《航空法》同步进行,但在《航空法》通过时废除《民航法》。这与第二种思路中单纯制定统一《航空法》模式中的原则化路径并不相同,但与该模式中的制定航空法典思路殊途同归。在此不予重复讨论。

第三种模式,即修订后的《民航法》模式,是指《民航法》通过修订后能够调整现行航空法律关系,无须制定新的《航空法》。了解《民航法》制定过程的学者认为,《民航法》当初在制定时其名称就是《航空法》,但后来因为一些技术原因加上了"民用"二字,但法律条款本身并不限定于调整纯粹的民用航空法律关系。比如,空域制度、航空工业方面的规定,都表明其对整个航空业的规制意义。现在只需要对《民航法》进行补充扩容并修改一些不适当之处即可,无须另起炉灶制定《航空法》。

上述三种模式争议焦点的实质是《航空法》与《民航法》二者的关系,因为无论是二法并行模式还是单一法律模式,都是以二者是否可以相互包容或者并存为基础。这种包容与并存关系体现在立法目的、法律的调整对象与调整方法上,从法律适用的视角来看,则主要是指二法是否存在一般法与特别法的关系、基本法律与非基本法律之间的关系或者平行法律关系。

第一,立法目的是否存在无法融合之处。耶林指出,"目的是整个法的创造者"。[①] 一部法律的立法目的决定了法律的调整对象与调整方法,也决定了法律之间的关系。《民航法》与《航空法》在未来究竟是一存一废还是二者并立,首先需要考察其立法目的。从目前的《航空法》各版本规定的立法目的条款来看,与《民航法》的目的条款差别较小。比如,根据 2011 年版《航空法》草案第 1 条规定,其立法目的为:"维护国家的领空主权和安全,保障航空

① [德]魏德士:《法理学》,丁晓春、吴越译,法律出版社 2005 年版,第 234 页。

活动安全、顺畅、高效进行,保护航空活动各方当事人的合法权益和社会公众利益,促进航空事业的发展。"可以看出其立法目的完全包容了现行《民航法》的立法目的。这就意味着二法并行缺乏立法目的上的合理性。任何立法都必须有与其他立法不同的立法目的,如果立法目的相同,最具有效率的立法就是修改现行立法,而不是制定新的立法。因此,如果一定要制定新的《航空法》,并且要与《民航法》并存,就必须保证《航空法》与《民航法》在立法目的上的差异性。从目前的各个《航空法》版本来看,这种差异性并不存在。

第二,调整对象与调整方法是否具有差异性。尽管学术界对于航空法的调整对象存在不同的表述,但存在一个近乎一致的看法,即航空法调整的是航空活动。① 这一表述无疑是针对作为一个法律体系的航空法而言,并非是指《民航法》或者《航空法》的调整对象。② 只有法典意义上的《航空法》才具有学术界所界定的航空法的调整对象外延。理论上来说,《民航法》后者的调整对象在外延上更窄一些,仅调整民用航空活动。但事实上,《民航法》第4条规定的航空工业,第七章规定的一切飞行活动均应遵守的飞行规则与空域管理的原则制度,第155条、第166条、第167条规定的航空保险均存在超出民航活动范围的情形。因此,就调整对象而言,《民航法》并不名实相副。而在《民航法》这样一个较为完整的调整对象之外,很难存在新的需要立法调整的其他航空活动。因此,从调整对象来看,二法并行缺乏必要性。目前需要做的是将《民航法》改为《航空法》,并完善和细化其规范。

第三,《航空法》与《民航法》是否存在一般法与特别法的可能。在罗马法时代,就有所谓"个别法"(ius singulare)优于"共同法"(ius commune)的规则,其"个别法"与"共同法"分别为现代法所讲的"特别法"与"一般法"。罗马法学家保罗认为,"个别法是立法当局为某些功利而引入的违背法的一般

---

① 参见贺富永:《航空法学基本理论研究》,科学出版社2014年版,第1~3页。

② 《民航法》在起草之初本来规定了调整对象,但后来被删除了。目前已经提出的《民航法》修改版本与《航空法》草案版本中,均未规定调整对象。

规则的法”,[1]亦即特别法是因特定的立法目的而确立的不同于一般法律规则的规范,是“对某个一般规范加以变通的个别规范,即由于特殊原因而表现为一般规范的例外的个别规范”,一般法律规则是一般情事下通行的规范,是“在狭窄的例外范围之外而被适用的一般规则”[2]的共同法。我国《立法法》第92条以法律的形式确认了“特别法优于一般法”(*lex specialist derogat legi generali*)这一法律适用原则。如果《航空法》与《民航法》均由同一立法主体制定与修改,则二者只能存在《航空法》为一般法、《民航法》为特别法的关系,后者是前者的例外规定。换言之,在所有民航活动中,依据特别法优于一般法的原则,都将适用《民航法》,对于民航活动而言,《航空法》的存在意义不大。而对于所有航空活动均适用的规定,仅存在于空域管理与飞行规则方面,对此《民航法》已有规定。即使将这部分规定在《航空法》中,也仅仅是一种航空活动的通用规则,民航活动并不需要制定不同的空域管理或飞行规则。除此之外,如公共航空运输、航空保险、航空侵权等制度都是《民航法》所特有的制度,作为一般法的《航空法》并不能够规定这些制度的一般法规则,因为《航空法》一旦规定这些制度,将完全替代《民航法》的规定。即使只作原则性规定,《民航法》也不能对其进行具体化,因为特别法的任务是规定不同于一般法的制度,而不是具体化一般法制度。否则《民航法》就变成了《航空法》的实施法,而非特别法。这意味着《民航法》中的公共航空运输、航空保险、航空侵权等制度无法成为《航空法》的例外规则。不例外就不特别,因而也就无法成立所谓特别法与一般法的关系。

第四,基本法律与非基本法律的效力阶层制度能否解决《航空法》与《民航法》的关系问题。既然一般法与特别法关系不适合《航空法》与《民航法》,能否由全国人民代表大会制定《航空法》,而继续由全国人民代表大会常务

---

① [意]彼德罗·彭梵得:《罗马法教科书》,黄风译,中国政法大学出版社1992年版,第10页。

② 孔祥俊:《法律规范冲突的选择适用与漏洞填补》,人民法院出版社2004年版,第267页。

委员会修改《民航法》,使二者成为基本法律与非基本法律的关系?[①] 有学者认为,“中国统一航空法是一部综合性法律,是航空领域的基本法”。[②] 这一看法是上述思路的反映。关于基本法律与非基本法律的效力关系,存在两种不同的观点,即“效力等同说”与“效力阶层说”两种学说。“效力等同说”认为,“我国宪法和立法法规定,全国人大与全国人大常委会都是立法机关,尽管在制定法律的名称上二者有所不同,但是法律文本上并没有规定二者之间在效力关系上有高低优劣之分,因而,全国人大制定的基本法律与全国人大常委会制定的非基本法律在效力上应该是等同的”。[③] 而“效力阶层说”则根据全国人大常委会在地位上从属于全国人大的阶层关系,推定全国人大常委会制定的非基本法律在地位上要低于全国人大制定的基本法律。韩大元教授认为,“‘基本法律’是指由全国人民代表大会制定的仅次于宪法而高于其他法律的对国家政治、经济和社会生活某个领域重大和全局性事项作出规范的法律”。[④] 基本法律作为对国家基本制度的法律化,其效力必然高于一般制度的法律化。如果《航空法》被作为基本法律制度,《民航法》为非基本法律,意味着其效力高于《民航法》。如果这种架构可以存在的话,二法并行模式自无问题。但是这种架构是否合理呢?

从立法规律来看,先确立国家基本制度(基本法律),后依据基本制度制定具体的法律(非基本法律)是立法的客观规律。否则,由于非基本法律缺乏基本法律的制约,可能出现与将来之基本法律相背离的情况。同时,没有基本法律,非基本法律就如无源之水一般,缺乏立法依据。《民航法》作为

① 依据《立法法》,非同一立法主体的立法不存在特别法与一般法的关系,根据韩大元教授的研究结论,“宪法地位的不同决定了全国人大与全国人大常委会是不同性质的机关,不是同一个机关”。故此,全国人大与全国人大常委会制定的法律不存在一般法与特别法关系,依据《立法法》,只能成立基本法律与非基本法律之关系。参见韩大元:《全国人大常委会新法能否优于全国人大旧法》,载《法学》2008 年第 10 期。

② 付翠英:《日本航空法律体系简述:几点启示》,载《北京航空航天大学学报》(社会科学版)2010 年第 5 期。

③ 参见韩大元:《全国人大常委会新法能否优于全国人大旧法》,载《法学》2008 年第 10 期。

④ 韩大元、刘松山:《宪法文本中“基本法律”的实证分析》,载《法学》2003 年第 4 期。

“非基本法”早已施行20余年，而作为“基本法律”的《航空法》尚未产生，这不符合立法规律。

从《民航法》与其他法律的关系来看，由于《民航法》涉及民法、刑法、行政法、国际法等各个不同的部门法，其法律地位需要与其他相关法律相适应。比如我国目前正在制定《民法典》，其中，有关物权编必然要吸收《物权法》的内容，有关债权编要吸收现行《合同法》与《侵权责任法》的内容。《民航法》中大量的制度属于《物权法》《合同法》《侵权责任法》的特别法。一旦《民法典》正式制定，其必然作为国家的基本法律进行规定，而将《民航法》继续作为非基本法律，就必须要遵循非基本法律不得与基本法律相抵触的原则。但《民航法》中的物权登记、交易公示方式、合同赔偿的归责原则等都与一般民事制度不同。如果在《民法典》中采用“民用航空法有规定的，适用其规定”的做法，无疑将《民航法》相关规定视为《民法典》的特别法了，然而作为非基本法律的《民航法》不可能成为作为基本法律的《民法典》的特别法。因而这种做法并不足取。为此，必须将《民航法》中的所有不同于一般民事制度的例外规定原则性地写进《民法典》中，使之成为该法典的特别规定，才可能为《民航法》具体化这些例外规定提供依据。就《航空法》而言，如果其被定位为基本法律，则必然在航空器物权、航空运输合同等领域构成《民法典》的特别法（二者为同一主体制定）。这样一来，作为非基本法律的《民航法》应当不得违背《民法典》与《航空法》，但《民航法》又肩负着具体化《民法典》的特别法《航空法》的任务，就只能与《民法典》作不同的规定，这就陷入了不可救赎的逻辑困境之中。同时，《民航法》只能在《航空法》规定的范围内进行具体化规定，而不能有任何不同（抵触性）的规定。其结果必然使《航空法》成为原则性法律，这又陷入了原则性立法之误区，故而不可行。

从立法的基本内容来看，《民航法》的规定已经涉及整个航空活动，而且其有关制度本身就非常原则，如果在其上再制定更原则性的法律，其必要性何在？比如《民航法》有关飞行的规定本身就不限于民航飞行，该法第76条第1款规定，“在中华人民共和国境内飞行的航空器，必须遵守统一的飞行规则”。这表明无论军事飞行活动还是民用航空飞行活动,均需要依据《民航法》第76条及依其所制定的《飞行基本规则》进行。作为行政法规,《飞行基本规则》是依据《民航法》第76条第1款及第4款而制定的,其调整的不仅包括军事飞行活动,也包括民用飞行活动等各类飞行活动。由此可见,《民航法》的内容并不局限于对民用航空活动的规制,而是对所有航空活动均有规定,且其规定本身已经很原则,并无必要在其上再设置《航空法》。学者们提出制定《航空法》,无非是认为缺乏空域管理规定,且《飞行基本规则》又超出民航活动范围,需要提升至法律层面。[①] 但这种看法忽略了《民航法》第七章的适用范围,即除非明确规定民航活动的,该章适用于所有航空活动。因此,如果仅仅因为空域管理与《飞行基本规则》的适用范围与制定依据的错误理解而提出制定《航空法》,显然缺乏依据。至于《民航法》中空域管理与飞行规则的可操作性缺乏问题,完全可以通过修改法律来实现。

四、结　语

新的一轮航空立法时机已经成熟。当此之时,无论修改《民航法》还是制定《航空法》,均应当仔细考量立法目的、调整对象及不同法律之间的关系,并从立法技术的妥当性出发,以决定修改《民航法》还是制定《航空法》,以及二法是否可能并存。

目前关于领海、陆地领土与领空的法律,均是由全国人大常委会制定的非基本法。空间制度、海洋制度与土地制度均属我国领土主权与安全相关的基本制度,同时也涉及私权与公权的边界与保护问题,依据我国《立法法》第8条的规定,国家主权及基本民事制度等应当制定基本法律或者非基本法律,因而航空活动的规制法律并非必须要制定基本法律。如果《航空法》被作为基本法律制定,则不能同时保留《民航法》,因为这将导致《航空法》成为

① 参见张千帆等:《建立统一的中国航空法体系——理论初探与立法建议》,载《北京航空航天大学学报》(社会科学版)2008年第2期。

不具有可操作性的原则化法律,其实质不过是将《民航法》现有制度进行提炼概括而已,并不比经过修改补充后的《民航法》更便利于守法、执法与司法。当然,为回应完善空域管理、飞行规则、公共航空运输及通用航空等制度的呼声,《民航法》应当在充实其调整对象与完善制度的基础上,以《航空法典》的形式予以颁布。

中国示范法:"一带一路"区域民航法的建立*

李亚凝**

"一带一路"建设充分依靠中国与有关国家既有的双多边机制,借助既有的、行之有效的区域合作平台,传统的国际法在建立国际秩序的同时,存在忽视区域特殊化需求以及先进经验推广的弊端。因此,在"一带一路"建设过程当中,应以采取示范法的形式为宜。中国作为民航大国,民航法规体系一方面充分对接了国际先进经验,另一方面凝结本土安全发展理念,成为连接具有应对性的政策与具有稳固性的法律之间的桥梁,也成为中国民航安全制度体系中最重要的部分之一。因此,有必要将其先进理念汇总成中国民航示范法,供"一带一路"沿线各国参考,助力"一带一路"建设。

---

* 2017 年中国民用航空局安全能力建设项目——"航空法"制定、《民航法》修订中涉及安全管理体系建设研究(172146903070)的阶段性成果。

** 法学博士,中国民航科学技术研究院/中国民航局航空安全技术中心副研究员、中国交通运输协会青工委委员。

一、问题的提出

"一带一路"是"丝绸之路经济带"和"21 世纪海上丝绸之路"的简称。其将充分依靠中国与有关国家既有的双多边机制，借助既有的、行之有效的区域合作平台，"一带一路"旨在借用古代丝绸之路的历史符号，高举和平发展旗帜，积极发展与沿线国家的经济合作伙伴关系，共同打造政治互信、经济融合、文化包容的利益共同体、命运共同体和责任共同体。

交通运输是"一带一路"建设的关键，2016 年中国航空运输业完成客运量和货运量分别达 4.88 亿人次和 668 万吨，同比分别增长 11.9% 和 6.2%。特别是中国国际航线旅客运输量突破 5000 万人次，增速达 22.7%。

中国民航业的发展极大地促进了"一带一路"的建设，民航运行的跨国性对于各国的政策法规的统一性有着较高要求。我国与其他国家或地区签订双边航空运输协定 120 个，比 2017 年年底增加 2 个（萨摩亚、巴布亚新几内亚），其中，亚洲（含东盟）有 44 个，非洲有 24 个，欧洲有 36 个，美洲有 9 个，大洋洲有 7 个。但是"一带一路"沿线国家法律制度各不相同，甚至尚不具备完善的民航政策法规体系，难免对于民航的运行要求会有不一致的地方，而这种不一致存在运行风险。因此，民航业的跨国安全运行以坚实的政策法规为基础。

当然构建多边民航条约是可选途径之一，但是各国国情并不相同，甚至有些国家并不具备完备的民航法律法规政策体系。因此，就当前情势而言，并不具备多边民航条约的条件，这就成为阻碍民航运输业在"一带一路"中作用发挥的"瓶颈"。

笔者将就融合民航安全运行实践与理论的中国示范法在"一带一路"地区推行的可能性进行分析。

二、国际法的不足与示范法的可能

(一)揭开传统国际法的迷雾

传统的国际法具有世界化的趋势,其着眼于将某一类事项在世界范围内达成一致意见,或者形成协商方法。这种方式对于处理国际之间的法律冲突无疑具有相当程度的裨益。但是,国际条约是否真的为各国“平等”地构建了规则?

1. 为什么签订国际公约

大多数人在接触“国际公约”的时候,往往会想到如“国际秩序”这种词汇。这是一种以国内法思维考虑国际法的假象,本质是先设了“超国家”的存在。

第二次世界大战后,鉴于独断性价值体系给人类带来的灾祸,国际社会确立了多元化发展的理念,其本质在于价值的沟通与交互性。简而言之,一种价值观应当是与其他价值观“和而不同”的。《联合国宪章》特别强调了国家主权平等的理念,平等者之间无管辖,如果存在能够统摄一切的“国际秩序”的话,那这一“国际秩序”将是独断性的价值,无疑会造就历史的反复。

因此,“国际秩序”的安全范围是一种价值观,应当与其他价值观“和而不同”,其深刻的含义是国家在主张自身利益的时候,应当与其他国家的利益主张具有兼容性。这就意味着,国家在签署国际公约的时候,至少存在“主张”与“妥协”两种行为,其重点在于“主张”,“妥协”是实现“主张”的方法而已,至于“国际秩序”,在国家以实力和角色的博弈中,并不具有稳定性,似乎只是群体行为的副产品而已。

2. 国家对于国际公约承诺了什么

据上,国家在签署国际公约的时候,所承诺的一切的目的均指向国家利益。国际公约条款的语焉不详为各国按照自身利益进行解释留有充足的空间,而解释的权利由于并没有确切的规定(这实际上也可以看作是国家法的妥协性),因此成为各缔约国所保留的权利。

因此，国际条约中的权利与义务源于各主权国家，而不是相反的关系。一旦这种权利义务的实际施行超出了国家在签署公约的预期，并且可能威胁到国家利益的时候，国家应当考虑推动公约的进一步解释，或者提议修改公约，倘若上述努力失败，为避免沦为获益国的"鱼肉"，退出公约是最明智的选择了。

3. 国际公约在国内适用的规则

首先，对于国际公约内容的解释，需要符合国家利益。实践中，大多数实务界人士与学术界人士特别关注于公约起草者的"立法者原意"，当然从参考的角度无可厚非，但是如果奉为圭臬，则会落入"超国家"的视角。我国在签订诸多国际公约的时候，仍然处于弱国地位，采取公约适用者的地位。改革开放以来，我国已经跃居世界第二大经济体，因此应当积极将中国规则推向世界，或者采取更加有利于我国的公约解释方法，或者提议修改公约甚至推出公约。

其次，我国在国际上在不同的领域所扮演的角色是不同的，或为制造输出国，或为进口大国，或为承租大国。所以对于不同领域的国际公约应当采取不同的解释方法，最大化维护国家利益。

最后，遵循国家利益的解释方法并不意味着不遵守规则，值得注意的是《维也纳条约法公约》提供了丰富的解释方法，但是不同的解释方法极有可能会产生不同的解释结果，对此笔者认为当以国家利益为准绳，权衡不同解释方法。

(二)区域民航示范法何以可能

2013 年至 2017 年，中国与"一带一路"沿线国家货物贸易额累计超过 5 万亿美元，对外直接投资超过 700 亿美元，中国企业在沿线国家推进建设 75 个经贸合作区，上缴东道国的税费 22 亿美元，创造就业岗位 21 万个。

在这之中，交通运输无疑起到了巨大的作用，《推动共建丝绸之路经济带和 21 世纪海上丝绸之路的愿景与行动》中将交通合作表述为"抓住交通基础设施的关键通道、关键节点和重点工程，优先打通缺失路段，畅通"瓶颈"路段，配套完善道路安全防护设施和交通管理设施设备，提升道路通达水平。推进建立统一的全程运输协调机制，促进国际通关、换装、多式联运有机衔接，逐步形成兼容规范的运输规则,实现国际运输便利化。推动口岸基础设施建设,畅通陆水联运通道,推进港口合作建设,增加海上航线和班次,加强海上物流信息化合作。拓展建立民航全面合作的平台和机制,加快提升航空基础设施水平”。

1.“一带一路”建设中民航业的机遇与挑战

交通合作重点中的“拓展建立民航全面合作的平台和机制,加快提升航空基础设施水平”尤为引人注目。实际上,国务院《关于促进民航业发展的若干意见》中也强调“努力增强国际航空竞争力。适应国家对外开放和国际航空运输发展的新趋势,按照合作共赢的原则,统筹研究国际航空运输开放政策。鼓励国内有实力的客、货运航空企业打牢发展基础,提升管理水平,开拓国际市场,增强国际竞争能力,成为能够提供全球化服务的国际航空公司。完善国际航线设置,重点开辟和发展中远程国际航线,加密欧美地区航线航班,增设连接南美、非洲的国际航线。巩固与周边国家的航空运输联系,推进与东盟国家航空一体化进程。加强国际航空交流与合作,积极参与国际民航标准的制定”。

依据产业生命周期理论,民航运输产业发展阶段可划分为形成期、成长期、成熟期与后成熟期。产业不同发展阶段成长驱动因素不同。从产业规模、产业技术与产业组织三方面判断,我国民航运输产业目前处于成长期。① 苏海麟(Soi-Hoi Lam)运用博弈模型对中国和外国航空公司之间的竞争情况进行了博弈分析,研究结果显示,便利性、安全性以及服务质量是影响旅客选在航班的主要影响因素,因此,航空公司应该重点从这几个方面进行考虑,选择适合企业发展的战略,不能仅仅局限在价格营销上。②

中国民航参与“一带一路”战略面临机遇与挑战。一方面,“一带一路”战略横跨亚欧非大陆及附近海洋,多山脉、丘陵、沙漠,涉及诸多国家和地区,从基

---

① 参见李艳伟、郑兴无:《“天空开放”背景下我国民航运输产业成长路径研究》,载《南京航空航天大学学报》(社会科学版)2014年第2期。

② See Soi-Hoi Lam, David A. Hensher, “The Effect of Service Quality and Price on International Airline Competition”, 4 *Transportation Researeh Part E: Logistics and Transportation Review* 44, 2008, pp. 580 – 592.

础设施建设风险来看，就需要能够承担远距离运输的交通工具。根据《2014 年民航行业发展统计公报》，截至 2014 年年底，中国民航国际航线完成运输周转量 240.11 亿吨公里，比 2013 年增长 29.44 亿吨公里，增长 14%，并且我国与其他国家或地区签订双边航空运输协定 116 个，比 2013 年年底增加 1 个。其中，亚洲 43 个国家以及《中华人民共和国政府和东南亚国家联盟各成员国政府航空运输协定》，非洲 23 个国家，欧洲 36 个国家，美洲 9 个国家，大洋洲 4 个国家，应该说中国民航对于"走出去"具有相当的成熟经验与足够的准备。另一方面，从民航业发展的历程来看，民航面临诸多竞争。根据相关研究，770 千米是高铁与民航运输的竞争临界距离，即在 770 千米以下航线高铁对民航影响程度，最大而超过 770 千米民航的优势将越来越明显。① 另外，高速铁路较航空拥有诸多明显优势：一是旅途全程时间短（节省往返机场、候机时间）；二是运送能力大；三是受气候变化影响小，正点率高。

另外，"一带一路"战略作为一项系统性工程，民航除了发挥交通运输的作用之外，如何更加深入地融入国家发展需要中是亟待解决的问题，这就需要树立民航今后一个时期的发展思路。

2. 航空货运方面

1997 年至 2012 年，中国民用航空货运的国内运输量呈现高速递增之势，其中我国香港特别行政区、澳门特别行政区及台湾地区的航空货运较为平稳。但是这比起 2014 年中国快递业务量同比增长 52% 的数字而言，仍然显得有较大提升空间。与此同时，中国民用航空货运的国际运输量无论在总量还是在增幅上远不如国内运输量。甚至在 2010 年之后还出现了总量下滑。

然而这并非是由于国际形势所致，与此相反，国际航空货运市场持续发展，并未出现衰退迹象。到 2017 年，中国民航货运总量达到 23 324 百万吨公里。

通过对欧洲航空货运量（36 672 百万吨公里）、亚太航空货运量（74 001

① 参见南宇峰、杨省贵：《基于旅客出行成本的高铁与民航运输竞争临界距离分析》，载《交通科技与经济》2012 年第 2 期。

百万吨公里)的对比,我们可以发现,亚太地区的航空货运量已经超过欧洲。

从2017年中国与"一带一路"各区域贸易情况来看,中国与其他亚洲、大洋洲地区"一带一路"国家的进出口总额为8178.6亿美元,占中国与"一带一路"国家进出口总额的56.8%,排名第一;其次是西亚地区,进出口额达到2332.4亿美元,占比为16.2%;排在第三的是东欧地区,进出口总额为1611.7亿美元,占比为11.2%;其后分别为南亚、非洲、拉美以及中亚地区,贸易额分别为1271.8亿美元、648.7亿美元、360.0亿美元,占比分别为8.8%、4.5%及2.5%。①

3. 航空客运方面

亚太地区的客运量呈现整体上升的趋势,这表明该地区的航空客运仍然保持相当的活力。

2017年,亚太地区航空客运与世界航空客运相比,增幅仍然存在差距。这至少表明仍然存在较大的可提升空间。克勒赫蒂(Clougherty)运用战略贸易理论提出了政府应该为民航企业积极搭建进军国际航空市场的平台,以提高本国民航企业的国际竞争力。② 而"一带一路"倡议正是为中国民航提供了这样一个平台。

目前,中国已与43个沿线国家实现直航,每周约4200个航班。中国的航空公司已在"一带一路"沿线的24个国家设立了境外营业部。2016年夏秋航季,中国与"一带一路"沿线国家每周往来定期航班达到4232班。中方22家航空公司新增航线92条,运营至36个"一带一路"沿线国家的74个国外城市;37个"一带一路"沿线国家的95家航空公司从101个国外城市运营至48个中国城市。③

---

① 参见《中国与"一带一路"国家 进口增速首超出口》,载新浪网:http://finance.sina.com.cn/roll/2018-05-07/doc-ihacuuvu1922647.shtml,最后访问日期:2018年11月28日。

② Joseph A. Clougherty, "Domestic Airline Concentration: A Positive Strategic Trade Analysis", *Transportation Research Part E: Logistics and Trans portation Review* 38, 2002, pp. 193-203.

③ 参见《数据解读中国航空业的"一带一路"》,载中国民航网:http://news.carnoc.com/list/402/402835.html,最后访问日期:2018年11月28日。

因此,民航示范法更加适合各国国情,使各国能够在借鉴我国先进安全运行理念的同时,充分发挥自身优势,形成“一带一路”区域不依赖或者少依赖国际法的发展模式,符合习近平总书记所提议出的积极发展全球伙伴关系,扩大同各国的利益交汇点,推进大国协调和合作,构建总体稳定、均衡发展的大国关系框架,按照亲诚惠容理念和与邻为善、以邻为伴的周边外交方针深化同周边国家关系,秉持正确义利观和真实亲诚理念加强同发展中国家团结合作的理念。

三、“一带一路”战略中民航业的发展思路

(一)从竞争模式转变为协同模式

民航作为一种交通工具,其与陆上运输、海上运输不可避免地存在竞争关系。但是在“一带一路”建设背景下,需要的是各种资源的“合力”的全局观念,民航业应当从竞争模式转变为协同模式。

1. 替换效率——边际替代率

值得注意的是,协同模式并不意味着放弃竞争,而是形成最佳效率,这就需要借助边际替代率来进行分析。边际替代率(marginal rate of substitution, MRS)在维持效用水平或满足程度不变的前提下,消费者增加 1 单位的某种商品 X 的消费时与所需要放弃的另一种商品 Y 的消费数量的比,被称为商品的边际替代率。在帕累托最优情况下,任意两种商品的边际替代率是相同的。

通过分析不同交通运输方式的优缺点,就可以计算出相互之间的边际替代率。各种交通运输方式之间需要抛弃“单打独斗”的思想,综合分析不同交通工具的效用,树立为大局服务的思想,形成符合“一带一路”实际的协同模式,即在符合现实需要的前提下,将各种交通工具的效率最大化。

另外,特别是针对全球减排的趋势,民航业应着力推动飞机节油改造,推进生物燃油研究和应用,制定应对全球气候变化对航空影响的对策措施。制订实施绿色机场建设标准,推动节能环保材料和新能源的应用,实施合同能

源管理。建立大型机场噪声监测系统,加强航空垃圾无害化处理设施建设。

2. 组合效率——多式联运

《联合国国际货物多式联运公约》对国际多式联运所下的定义为:按照国际多式联运合同,以至少两种不同的运输方式,由多式联运经营人把货物从一国境内接管地点运至另一国境内指定交付地点的货物运输。

由于“一带一路”经济带地形复杂、气候多变,需要各种不同交通工具的组合运用。一般来说,水路运输具有运量大,成本低的优点;公路运输则具有机动灵活,便于实现货物门到门运输的特点,铁路运输的主要优点是不受气候影响,可深入内陆和横贯内陆实现货物长距离的准时运输;而航空运输的主要优点是可实现货物的快速运输。

因此,结合特定地区的特点,民航与其他交通运输方式形成组合优势,达成共赢。以海空联运为例,目前远东至欧洲航线有以温哥华、西雅图、洛杉矶为中转地,也有以我国香港特别行政区、曼谷、海参崴为中转地,此外还有以旧金山、新加坡为中转地。而通过“一带一路”经济带的中转形成了以我国香港特别行政区、曼谷为中转地至中近东、非洲的运输服务。在特殊情况下,还有经马赛至非洲、经曼谷至印度、经我国香港特别行政区至澳洲等联运线,但这些线路货运量较小。因此,这就为民航未来借助“一带一路”战略进一步开拓中近东市场留有诸多机遇。

(二)从单一运输业拓展到多种经济产业

我国实施“一带一路”建设的背景因素之一,在于中国传统的出口国较为单一和狭窄,美欧日占据出口的核心位置,但这些传统的出口市场已经开拓得较为充分,增量空间已经不大。因此,出现过剩产能对经济的运行的持续影响。

民航固然在承担“一带一路”交通运输任务中占有重要一环,但是其更加重要的任务是发掘东亚经济圈与欧洲欧经济圈之间广袤区域的经济潜力。因此,在民航业面前的并非仅仅是交通运输这块“小蛋糕”,而是多种经济产业的“大蛋糕”。《推动共建丝绸之路经济带和21世纪海上丝绸之路的愿景与行动》中将贸易发展表述为“投资贸易合作是‘一带一路’建设的重点内容。宜着力研究解决投资贸易便利化问题,消除投资和贸易壁垒,构建区域内和各国良好的营商环境,积极同沿线国家和地区共同商建自由贸易区,激发释放合作潜力,做大做好合作‘蛋糕’”。

因此,采取以民航业传统交通运输产业为基础,积极拓展多种经济产业竞争力的强化,是我国民航运输产业在激烈的市场竞争中求得生存和发展亟须解决的问题,也是我国实现民航强国宏伟目标实现,达成“一带一路”战略任务的必然之路。

交通运输是经济的“动脉血管”,但仅有“动脉血管”本身还不够,对于“动脉血管”周围的经济掌控才是重中之重,这就要求民航业依托“动脉血管”大力推动航空经济发展。通过民航业科学发展促进产业结构调整升级,带动区域经济发展。鼓励各航空公司结合自身条件和特点,研究发展航空客货运输、通用航空、航空制造与维修、航空金融、航空旅游、航空物流和依托航空运输的高附加值产品制造业,打造航空经济产业链,从而真正带动建设国际经济、金融、贸易、航运中心。

四、中国民航安全运行的法律经验

(一)拥有行政许可的航空公司之间监护制度

2015年1月28日中国民用航空局下发《关于控股航空公司实施统一运行有关问题的通知》,就统一运行问题作出简要说明。根据《立法法》的规定,《关于控股航空公司实施统一运行有关问题的通知》属于规范性文件,其效力低于法律、行政法规和部门规章。其结构如下。

1. 目的

根据《关于控股航空公司实施统一运行有关问题的通知》,统一运行的目的在于“提高企业效率和整体安全水平”。因此,从上述3个文件分析来看,统一运行所要达到的目的在于“效率”和“安全”。

2. 统一运行的主体

根据《关于控股航空公司实施统一运行有关问题的通知》,统一运行的主体是“母公司控股达到51%或以上的母子公司”。这就意味着统一运行是在具有绝对控股关系独立公司法人之间进行的。这实际上与中国民航业的现实是相符合的。目前,全国53家航空运输企业中仅有14家没有相互参股或控股;四大航空集团其27家子公司或者是100%全额控股,或者是51%以上控股或部分持股。

3. 统一运行的结构

根据《关于控股航空公司实施统一运行有关问题的通知》,统一运行是对于子公司绝对控股的母公司,将其运行管理和安全管理覆盖到子公司。由于母公司具有相当的运行管理经验和安全管理经验,因此通过此举可以将使子公司运行管理能力和安全管理能力在短时间获得极大提升。

另外,为了贯彻这种“覆盖”,母子公司之间将会进行四种具体行为:母子公司本着自愿的原则,通过企业法定代表人签订安全管理协议的方式,明确各自应当承担的安全责任;统一运行按照补充运行合格审定的程序,逐步过渡的原则进行;实施统一运行的被控股航空公司在所持有的运行合格证没有注销之前,规章要求的证书和文件必须持续持有并保证有效,相应的管理机构和人员必须保持在位;实施统一运行的航空公司共用母公司IATA二三字代码的,按照相关要求执行。

根据上述分析,我们可以发现统一运行的目的在于通过母公司将具有相对优势的管理经验“覆盖”子公司,从而达成对于子公司“行为能力”的监护。

传统的监护理论认为只有自然人可以被监护,根据我国《民法通则》的规定,监护制度在于保护无民事行为能力与限制民事行为能力的人身、财产以及其他合法权益,所以目前我国将监护制度的对象限于自然人。

法人作为民事主体的一种,是指法律上具有人格的组织,具有民事权利能力和民事行为能力,依法独立享有民事权利和承担民事义务。对比自然人,如果公司法人的民事行为能力出现瑕疵,其是否可以适用监护制度,从而对于公司行为能力作出补强呢？特别是对于取得某项行政许可的公司法人,其若不能完整地履行相关行为,且尚未达到撤销行政许可的要求,如果能够使其被其他公司法人监护,将是对于公司治理结构的优化以及社会资源的合理配置。

(二)对于超售行为的解决方案

1.可存放资源与不可存放资源

但是,例如,10月15日北京到上海8:30航班上的某个座位的运输服务(注意不是座位,而是运输服务)可能就难以存放了。这就成为超售的原因,如果旅客改签,将使航班的客运资源被消耗,这就促使航空公司多卖几张票,最大化保证企业成本。

2.超售作为行业惯例的法律窘境

超售,就宏观而言,降低了航空企业的亏损风险,并且一定程度上使票价低廉。但是超售的法律性质一直是个饱受争议的问题。

如果航空公司明知机上只有100个座位的运输服务,而卖出了120张票,似乎存在欺诈的故意。并且航空公司总是以“超售是国际惯例”为由进行抗辩。在我国《民法总则》第10条中规定:

“处理民事纠纷,应当依照法律;法律没有规定的,可以适用习惯,但是不得违背公序良俗。”

但是,超售可以被作为管理而被法律所保护吗?《美国联邦法规汇编》(Code of Federal Regulations,CFR)对于超售进行了规定,首先采取了有偿征询,其次采取座次优先选择机制(seating priority policy)进行旅客筛选。当然也通过对于年度拒绝登机的赔付数额进行审查的方式对航空企业进行监督。

显然对于中国来说,超售尚未规定于法律之中,并且旅客在购买机票的时候,并不知道超售的概率是多少,旅客对于航空运输的期望值使超售难以被接受。特别是航空公司以“行业惯例”来进行抗辩的时候,往往会被司法机关认为是严重侵害消费者权益。

3. 超售的性质是附条件运输合同

笔者认为超售的法律性质是附条件运输合同,我国《合同法》第45条规定:

“当事人对合同的效力可以约定附条件。附生效条件的合同,自条件成就时生效。附解除条件的合同,自条件成就时失效。

当事人为自己的利益不正当地阻止条件成就的,视为条件已成就;不正当地促成条件成就的,视为条件不成就。”

这是由于超售实际上有可能使已经订座的旅客无法获得运输服务,因此运输合同实际上附了一个条件,并且这个条件是难以预测的。例如,有可能由于某些旅客临时改签,而使剩下的旅客都获得了运输服务。

这就要求航空企业在签订合同时需要履行告知义务,旅客在获得告知后,就已经确知其所签订合同的风险,并且基于对风险的承受而自愿签订合同,从而不能再以欺诈为由提出主张。

当然最高人民法院《关于贯彻〈中华人民共和国民法通则〉若干问题的意见(试行)》第75条规定:“附条件的民事行为,如果所附的条件是违背法律规定或者不可能发生的,应当认定该民事行为无效。”

4. 公共运输与超售

航空运输作为一项公共运输服务,受到我国《合同法》不得拒绝旅客、托运人合理的运输要求的约束。笔者认为,航空企业是否可以在附条件运输合同中规定超售后的预案以及补偿条款,从而肩负起公共运输的责任。另外,可考虑对潜在超售的航班的票价上需要进行相应的优惠(当然,这是商业考虑)。

(三)航空器与航空器权利融资多功能平台

当前退租后的航空器处置成为一个令人困扰的问题,这是在租赁市场蓬勃发展的早期就需要重点考虑的问题。在实务操作中,出租方会在合同中埋伏各种“陷阱”(特别是退租检修的部分),使航空器尽量存留于承租方手中,从而避免昂贵的航空器保管费用与维护费用。

笔者认为,租期实际上是有限的时间点,那么在可预期的租赁期内,对于租赁物的远期权利实际上是可以进行交易的。例如,某架737－800客机租赁期满后的租赁权实际上是可以进行期货交易的,甚至融资租赁中的承租方亦可以对其未来的所有权进行远期交易。

1. 资产标准化的门槛——评估制度

但是,作为资产标准化的重要一环——评估,在我国是缺乏的。简而言之,评估就是我们如何对未来航空器的状况进行预测。境外存在航空器状况及时报告制度,但是笔者并不看好此种制度。如果将航空器状况的评估交付使用者或者所有者,必然会引发道德风险,对期货市场具有毁灭性的打击。

因此,需要引入第三方评估机构,对航空器价值进行评估。是否需要联合保险公司进行联合监督,需要进一步考量。

2. 航空器实际使用者的因素评估

航空器作为标准化的机械设备,具有天然的标准性。但是,就评估航空器远期价值而言,其实际使用者因素无疑具有重要的参考意义。例如,某航空公司经营状况以及安全飞行情况必然会对于航空器状况产生一定影响。此外,其运行所在的区域以及此区域的风险性(如国际民航组织高度关注的冲突区)也会成为重要的参考。

3. 航空器权利融资多功能平台

建立一个类似淘宝或者阿里巴巴的航空器资产交易平台应该更符合航空业的需求。

此平台至少应当包括以下功能:航空器的买卖、航空器的融资租赁、航空器权利登记、航空器与航空器权利资产评估、航空器与航空器期货或期权交易、担保参与体系、航空器权利动态变化发布系统。

(四)远期航空运力有效利用制度

提单是海上货物运输中最重要的单据,其发展前景是当今航运界乃至整个国际贸易界关注的焦点之一。而提单的发展很大程度上取决于对其物权性的认识。提单物权性,即提单能代表货物本身的性质居于提单各种特性的中心,是提单价值的基础。

航空货物运输凭证不同于海运提单,其本质是债权凭证。由于航空运输速度快,因此并不能从货物的角度对于航空货运进行与海运一样的设计,而是需要从运力的方面着手。

1. 第一步:航空货物运输凭证证券化

我国的航空货物运输凭证主要为航空运单。目前,各航空公司所使用的航空运单则大多借鉴国际航空运输协会所推荐的标准格式,不同的航空公司会有自己独特的航空运单格式,但差别并不大。航空运单的这种标准格式,也称中性运单。

航空运单分为主运单(Master Air Way bill,MAWB)与分运单(House Air Way bill,HAWB)。主运单,或称航空公司运单:货运代理将揽收后拼装的货物交航空运输公司,由航空运输公司签发的运输单据即航空主运单。主单的收、发货人分别是起始港的货运代理和目的港的货运代理,由航空公司统一运到目的港后,然后由目的港的代理将货物分别交由不同的收货人。分运单,或称代理人运单:在(收)发货人委托其货运代理人发运货物时,或货运代理人采用集中托运形式向航空公司交付货物时,或运费到付,或货物到达目的港后由收(发)货人、发货港运输代理人指定的目的港运输代理人接收货物等情况下,一般使用分运单。

从形式上看,我们可以发现,航空运单各部分都已经初步具备了标准化的形式。虽然航空运单中写有"与海运提单不同,因为空运单不可转让,所以'凭指示'之类的字样不得出现",但是这是仅针对货物而言的。

就运力而言,并不存在像货物的诸多时效限制,其存在在一个较长的时间段内进行预订的可能性,而正是这种可能性使运力配置获得可以充分市场化的机会。

按照目前2012年修正的《期货交易管理条例》期货合约具备时间、地点、标的物、数量的规定,航空运力基本已经符合。因此,航空运力合约的标准化实际上是规定在未来谁有权与航空公司签订航空货运合同的合约。这就将货物运输与运力相分离,从而实现了将航空运力从由于运输速度制约而面临的困境中解放出来。

2. 第二步:航空货物运输凭证期货化

(1)从非远期化交易到远期化交易

但仅仅成为标准化合约,还无法深入降低航空货物运力的交易成本。目前航空运力的预定时间较短,这使航空运力无法充分响应市场变化。一方面,航空公司在短时间内无法根据市场变化即使对于运力安排作出调整,并且也无法对于价格进行相应的制定;另一方面,货主在选择航空货物运力的时候,由于可预订时间过于短暂,极易出现“供过于求”或者“供大于求”的情况。

另外,航空货运代理公司在这种情况之中,能与航空公司、货主签订较长期的航空货物运力合同。但是这种模式并不能反映市场调节价格机制,在一定程度上航空货运代理公司操纵航空货物运力价格。

因此,如果将前述标准化合约远期化,即在标准化的前提下,允许航空货物运力远期交易。这就使航空货物运力产生了远期价格和即期价格。

(2)航空货运凭证期货运行

例如,2014 年 6 月某航线标准化航空货物运力当前价格为 20 元 ×10 吨 ×1000 公里,此即期价格即为 200 000 元。并且 2014 年 6 月,该标准化航空货物运力 12 个月后的价格为 15 元 ×10 吨 ×1000 公里,此远期价格为 150 000 元。

这样的一个远期价格与即期价格之差,就会产生套期保值的功能。套期保值(Money Market Hedge),是指企业为规避外汇风险、利率风险、商品价格风险、股票价格风险、信用风险等,指定一项或一项以上套期工具,使套期工具的公允价值或现金流量变动,预期抵销被套期项目全部或部分公允价值或现金流量变动风险的一种交易活动。为在货币折算或兑换过程中保障收益锁定成本,通过外汇衍生交易规避汇率变动风险的做法叫套期保值。外汇远期合约是进行套期保值的最基本的金融衍生工具之一。其优点在于:当金融体系不完备、运行效率低下时,它是成本最低的套期保值方式。原因是其交易相对简单,不需要保证金,涉及资金流动次数少,公司决策方式简明等。

例如,2014 年 6 月某航空公司卖出 12 个月后该标准化航空货物运力 4 个单位,获得 800 000 元。而实际上到 2015 年 6 月,该标准化航空货物运力跌至 10 元 ×10 吨 ×1000 公里,不考虑通货膨胀及其他因素,航空公司成功规避了 12 个月内可能发生的价格风险。

3. 第三步:航空货物运输凭证期权的建立

一般而言,期货市场的价格会存在一定的起伏,这也是航空货物运力期货化后所形成的套期保值功能和投资功能的体现。如果要使这些功能得到更加充分的发挥,就需要给予期货市场参与者更加充分的自由度。

期权又称为选择权,是在期货的基础上产生的一种衍生性金融工具。指在未来一定时期可以买卖的权利,是买方向卖方支付一定数量的金额(指权利金)后拥有的在未来一段时间内(指美式期权)或未来某一特定日期(指欧式期权)以事先规定好的价格(指履约价格)向卖方购买或出售一定数量的特定标的物的权利,但不负有必须买进或卖出的义务。

例如,2014 年 6 月某航线标准化航空货物运力当前价格为 20 元 ×10 吨 ×1000 公里,此即期价格即为 200 000 元。并且 2014 年 6 月,该标准化航空货物运力 12 个月后的价格为 15 元 ×10 吨 ×1000 公里,此远期价格为 150 000 元。

某航空公司认为 2015 年 2 月由于春运该标准化航空货物运力将上涨为 23 元 ×10 吨 ×1000 公里,某货主认为 2015 年 2 月由于春运,该标准化航空货物运力将上涨为 25 元 ×10 吨 ×1000 公里,因此某货主与航空公司签订期权合约,在 2015 年 2 月其将有权以 24 元 ×10 吨 ×1000 公里。因此,航空公司与货主均获利且化解风险。

(五)天气期货对于航班正常化的保证

2016 年年初,中国民用航空局创造性地提出了坚持"真情服务"的理念,为民航业未来的发展指明了正确方向。“特别是航班正常问题,一直都是旅客反映最强烈、投诉最集中、媒体最关注的首要问题。”中国民用航空局局长冯正霖指出,“这个问题也是当前民航业坚持真情服务,提高服务质量的一个关键”。

1. 天气原因成为阻碍民航企业真情服务的风险点

虽然《航班正常管理规定》规定,由于天气、突发事件、空中交通管制、安检以及旅客等非承运人原因,造成航班在始发地出港延误或者取消,承运人应当协助旅客安排餐食和住宿,费用由旅客自理。2017 年中国民用航空局发布《关于国内航空公司、机场实施〈航班正常管理规定〉相关工作情况的通告》(以下简称《通告》),《通告》显示,中国国航、东方航空、南方航空等主要航空公司切实落实“真情服务”理念,主动扩大化责任承担范围。国航表示,航班在经停地点延误或取消,或者国内航班发生备降,“无论何种原因,我们将向您提供餐食或住宿服务”。南方航空、东方航空的补偿条件及标准与中国国航类似。不过,东方航空的补偿条件中多了“商务”造成的航班延误或者取消这一补充条件,对旅客进行补偿的可能是东航自身,也可能是东航的地面服务代理人。有的航空公司直言“无论何种原因导致航班延误或取消都不提供经济补偿”。

在中国民用航空局发布的《2015 年民航行业发展统计公报》中,全部航空公司航班不正常原因中“天气原因”为 29.53%,比上年度上涨 5.19 个百分点;主要航空公司航班不正常原因中“天气原因”为 30.16%,比上年上涨 5.37 个百分点。

因此,“天气原因”在延误原因中占据了重要地位,特别是对于扩大化责任承担的航空公司,这就成为具有重要意义的企业运行风险点,也成为阻碍真情服务继续推进的阻碍。

2. 天气期货运行原理

实际上,我国民航业迫切需要天气风险管理。从美国、日本等国际上发展较为成熟的天气风险管理市场来看,主要包括以下几类:第一,农业、电力、天然气、建筑、冷饮、旅游业等的现货企业,这些现货企业通过天气风险管理市场规避经营活动中的天气风险。第二,保险公司、再保险公司、银行及各类基金,这些金融机构本身并不具有在天气风险管理市场套期保值的直接需求,它们是天气风险管理市场的积极参与者,如保险公司、再保险公司,一方面为客户提供天气保险产品,另一方面积极参与天气衍生品交易,对冲其自身承担的天气风险。第三,个人投资者,天气风险管理市场为个人投资者提供了具有特色的、有别于一般金融产品的投资工具,个人投资者是天气风险管理市场的重要参与者。

笔者认为,发展天气期货对于民航业保证民航安全第一,贯彻落实真情服务理念,以及企业可持续发展具有重要意义。

天气指数期货是商品期货中的新成员,在类别上它属于能源类期货交易品种。目前,全球交易天气指数期货的只有美国的芝加哥商业交易所(CME)和英国的伦敦国际金融期货交易所(Euronext. Liffe)两家交易所,所选择的天气指数仅仅是温度指数,交易量相对较小。但是对于受天气影响巨大的行业具有重要意义。

实际上天气期货和其他期货的交易原理是一样的。在每个月的开始,期货市场主管机构都会根据过去10年当月的气温情况,为降温度日数或升温度日数确定初始数值,如20摄氏度。为了使市场运转起来,指定的“做市商”将接着喊出“出价”和“要价”,前者比初始值稍低,后者稍高,这是投资者可以买进或卖出的度数。随着天气的变化和市场的反应,这些交易值在1个月内将起伏不定。到了月底,交易所根据实际温度进行结算,以1摄氏度等于100美元的价格兑现所有期货合同。而投资者所要做的,就是预测一下未来的天气变化,然后进行“天气期货”买卖赚取利润。举例来说,如果整个月都是30摄氏度,10点×30天=300个指数点。每个指数点价值100美元,300点就是3万美元(每张合约的按金为1400美元)。

3. 天气期货对于民航企业真情服务的积极作用

诚如上述,如果我们以航空公司最低运行天气标准为依据建立天气期货,并且运用于民航业,将会产生以下效应。

首先,期货市场具有一定的预期功能,通过期货市场的价格波动,航空公司可以在一定程度上预计未来天气情况,从而有效地安排未来的航班,保证民航安全第一的持续安全理念。

其次,航空公司可以通过天气期货对冲掉因为天气原因所造成的企业损失,从而使民航企业健康、可持续发展。

最后,航空公司可以通过在天气期货市场上所获得的利润,来更好地保障旅客权益。虽然依据《航班正常管理规定》,由于天气、突发事件、空中交通管制、安检以及旅客等非承运人原因,造成航班在始发地出港延误或者取消,承运人应当协助旅客安排餐食和住宿,费用由旅客自理。但是,具有“真情服务”精神的航空企业用于将自身责任范围扩大,从成本上看无疑增大了企业负担。因此,如果能通过天气期货市场来弥补这部分企业运行风险,无疑将更有利于民航企业继续深入推进“真情服务”。

(六)违法处罚的科学预测性

我国《民用航空法修订征求意见稿》终于揭开神秘面纱,在百余项变动中,多项新规欲治疗行业痼疾和助推产业发展。其中,关于在航空器内违规使用手机、抢占座位、霸机等行为,最高可罚款5万元等规定,被视为民航局有意对安全管理升级。

2015年2月26日国家统计局首次发布的全国居民人均可支配收入数据:2014年全国居民人均可支配收入为20 167元,将罚款数额列为5万元。2015年全年全国居民人均可支配收入21 966元,比上年增长8.9%,扣除价格因素,实际增长7.4%;农村居民人均可支配收入11 422元,比上年增长8.9%,扣除价格因素,实际增长7.5%。因此,中国人均可支配收入是X×(1+0.075)^n,就现行商业贷款的对折保证生活水平而言,50 000×2=20 167×(1+0.075)^n,n=22.1392。所以5万元的额度,是可以在相当长的时间(22年)内对于潜在干扰性旅客进行有效限制的,并且这个时间是符合修法周期的。

五、中国示范法的路径

(一)从本土民航发展为世界民航

1. 跨太平洋伙伴关系协议的挑战

就世界经济秩序而言,随着中国经济的发展,美国在亚太经济合作组织(Asia - Pacific Economic Cooperation,APEC)的话语权逐渐被削弱了,因此美国一直在推动跨太平洋伙伴关系协议(Trans - Pacific Partnership Agreement,TPP)。希望通过TPP的建设,在政治、经济等方面稀释中国的地区影响力。

从目前的现实情况来看,短期内不加入TPP,对中国经济的总体影响是有限的,特别是实际上加入TPP的综合收益不及"10 + 3",但TPP对中国参与推进东亚区域合作已构成现实的制约,不利于中国提升在东亚事务中的地位和影响力。从中长期来看,TPP的持续推进,可能会使全球经济规则出现较大改变,从而使中国与周边国家关系趋向复杂,甚至会增加中国地缘政治与防卫安全压力,不利于中国继续运用重要战略机遇期,对中国实现持续科学和平发展实现"中国梦"带来较大挑战。

2. 中国民航的历史任务

拉杰斯卡教授(J. Rajasekar)通过对美国、欧洲、亚洲以及南美洲等国家和地区59家民航公司的收入、旅客承载率以及各自占有的市场份额等指标进行分析,认为国内民航公司如果与国际航空公司实行代码共享,对于国际市场开拓和自身竞争力的提高具有重要的作用。①

中国民航业借由"一路一带"建设的历史机遇,通过协同模式,真正带动建设国际经济、金融、贸易、航运中心。掌控国际贸易主导权,定价权和资源配置权。中国主动加速主导区域经济整合,提升自己的区域经济影响能力。

---

① See James Rajasekar, "The Impact of Air lines Alliances: The Effect of Codesharing on the Performance of Domestic Airlines", Dissertation of PH. D., School of Business, Golden Gate University, 2000.

这就要求中国民航在一过程中迅速成长为世界意义的民航。不仅在交通运输意义上开拓更多的市场,而且需要以交通运输为基础,以点带面,促进相关经济的发展,并且更加主动融入当地文化,增加认同感,使中国民航业更加适应多元市场。不仅能对冲掉美国主导的试图绕开孤立中国而推进 TPP,还能有机会在“一带一路”经贸中抢占全球贸易新规则制定权。

(二)中国示范法的基本构架

20 世纪,美国曾经推出针对于第三世界国家的民用航空法示范文本,促使美国航空运输安全经验在世界范围内的推广。在当时的历史条件下有力地促进了全球民航安全。

当前,中国进入新时代,中国民航作为实际上最安全的交通运输体系之一,与政策法规体系密不可分,因此有必要将中国先进民航安全经验贡献“一带一路”建设。

(1)民航政策方面。在数十年的发展过程当中,中国民航安全政策用事实证明了其有效性。中国民航局的行政管理创造出了如“一二三三四”等理念,特别是按照建设民航强国战略“两步走”的推进方案,至 2020 年我国将初步建成民航强国。有必要撰写《“一带一路”国家民航安全政策指导白皮书》,供沿线各国参考,将中国民航多年来积累的安全经验造福“一带一路”。

(2)民航法律方面。民航是“一带一路”发展的大动脉,《民用航空法》经历了 20 余年的实践检验,目前根据时代进步与发展要求进行了修改,充分体现了中国民航的制度发展特点。因此,借鉴美国向第三世界国家所发布的民航法示范文本,有必要撰写《“一带一路”国家民用航空法示范文本》,供沿线各国参考,将中国民航先进法治经验贡献“一带一路”交通运输建设。

(3)民航规章方面。中国作为民航大国,民航规章体系一方面充分对接了国际先进经验,另一方面凝结本土安全发展理念,成为连接具有应对性的政策与具有稳固性的法律之间的桥梁,也成为中国民航安全制度体系中最重要的部分之一。因此,有必要撰写《"一带一路"国家民用航空规章示范结构》,供沿线各国参考,助力"一带一路"建设。

航空器融资租赁

飞机融资租赁的法律适用

——以《开普敦公约》为视角

陈　胜*

飞机航运业是资金密集型产业,无论是建造新飞机还是购置二手飞机,抑或是运营航运企业,均需要大量资金的支持。飞机融资租赁作为飞机融资方式的一种,凭借其贷款额度高、融资期限长、抵押品较少,并且具有节税作用等而越来越受到人们的关注。但是在飞机融资租赁过程中,往往存在相对复杂的交易结构,易产生法律风险。我国于2008年10月审议批准了《开普敦公约》,虽然其是调整航空器设备融资和租赁的国际法律制度,但该公约能否适用于飞机依旧存在可探讨的空间。本文正是基于这样的思考,探讨新时期《开普敦公约》对飞机适用的可行性。

---

* 复旦大学经济学院博士后,金杜律师事务所合伙人。

一、我国飞机融资租赁的现状

(一)航空工业的特点及现状

航空行业是典型的资金密集型企业,具有资金需求量大、投资回报率低、还款周期长的特点。当前的飞机租赁情况最显著的特征就是寡头市场,飞机制造商被波音公司和空中客车公司所垄断,机型也比较有限,产品标准化的程度相对其他行业而言非常高。这也导致资产价值的透明。新飞机和二手飞机的估值几乎是完全市场化和透明的。因此,飞机资产具有高度的安全性。

(二)飞机融资的主要方法

飞机融资,是指以飞机资产(含在建飞机)抵押或以飞机资产使用产生的现金流质押作为第二还款来源,满足借款人建造、购置、租赁、维修、使用飞机资产需求的贷款、保函等信贷业务,用途限于借款人主营业务相关支出。飞机融资业务主要适用于资产规模大、市场竞争力强、财务效益好、管理水平高、净现金流充裕的客户。[①]

飞机融资的主要方式包括银行贷款、出口信贷、股票市场融资、债券市场融资及融资租赁等。

1. 银行贷款

银行贷款是航空行业较为常见并且体系稳定成熟的一种融资方式。银行会对借款人进行贷前审查,审查的内容包括借款人能力、资金流量、对于航空公司管理及运营的能力,甚至需考察其在行业内的声誉及地位。同时,基于进一步风险的管控,银行往往还会对飞机自身情况作详细考察,包括飞机的大小、机龄、注册国,以及由此而适用的法律。

---

① 参见吕香茹主编:《商业银行信贷文化》,中国金融出版社2010年版,第12页。

相对于其他融资方式,银行贷款结构简单、直接,并且由于有较长的实践经验,也构建起了较为成熟的制度,便于借款方及银行的操作。同时,由于制度较为标准化,可以大大减轻文件制作的负担,申请审核流程简单,也节省了贷款人的时间和成本。但银行贷款的融资成本较高,并且实践中银行普遍不接受完全出资,须由借款人动用自己的权益,承担部分资金,这也给借款人带来了一些压力。

2. 出口信贷

出口信贷是有关国家为支持和扩大本国大型设备等资本货物的出口,加强国际竞争能力,由该国的出口信贷机构通过直接向本国出口商或外国进口商(或其银行)提供利率较低的贷款,或通过担保、保险或给予利率贴补等鼓励本国商业银行向本国出口商或国外进口商(或其银行)提供中长期的贷款,以解决本国出口商资金周转的困难,或满足国外进口商对本国出口商支付货款需要的一种融资方式,是国家干预外贸经济争夺国外销售市场的一种手段。①

实践中,如果飞机所有人和制造商属于不同的两个国家,出口信贷便可以成为一个很好的融资方式。相较直接性的飞机贷款,出口信贷机构是整个交易结构中不可获取的一部分,其须提供对贷款额度的保险,这在很大程度上加强了贷款的安全性。

由于出借方有保险保障其出借资金,因此借款方将能够借到更多的资金。并且通过出口信贷进行融资的利息率也往往比银行贷款低,这对贷款人也是一个很重要的吸引。但是,出口信贷也有其弊端。首先,在融资过程中,出口信贷机构往往对融资比率设定上限,一般约为合同价格或项目成本的80%。其次,虽然信贷利率较低,但是作为额外成本的保险费也会增大融资总体成本。再次,贷款人若想通过出口借贷的方式进行融资往往需要具备出口背景,如果从本国飞机制造商处购买飞机,则无法适用出口借贷的条件。

---

① 参见郭金刚、师国敏:《我国出口信贷的现状分析及发展对策》,载《经济师》2008 年第 3 期。

最后,该融资方式多用于新机买卖或建造,较难适用于二手飞机交易市场。

3. 股票市场融资

这种融资方式是指通过公司上市的途径来获得资金。通过股票融资,融资人免于提供担保及支付利息的负担,可在很大程度上减轻其融资压力。但是股票投资在这往往倾向于将低风险高收益的企业作为投资对象,而航空市场分析资料的缺乏也是阻碍融资人通过 IPO 募集资金的因素之一。

除了免于担保及支付利息,股票市场募集的资金也没有期限及利率的限制;同时,为了实现 IPO,企业为了达到证监会及交易所的规定,其企业信息、资金状况及内部结构将更为透明,因此对投资人及资金出借方也更具吸引了;股票融资也更为灵活,融资人可基于其企业需求调整融资方案。

但股票融资也存在上市程序复杂,时间成本高的弊端。同时,由于其作为上市公司负有信息披露义务,竞争对手能够轻松获取公司的关键信息,增大了竞争压力。并且,公司若经营不善也时刻面临着被竞争对手收购的风险。

4. 债券市场融资

债券市场融资,是指融资人通过债券市场,选择公司债券、高收益债券、飞机证券化产品等进行融资。通过债券市场,飞机所有人可以募集到大量长期限资金,如果公司有良好的业绩,在行业中有较高的知名度,投资人认可度高,也会很大程度上降低融资成本。但是此种融资方式过程较为复杂,需经过评级机构测评、路演等环节,需花费较长时间来筹备。同时,此过程中需专业法律人士的参与,法律服务费用也是融资成本中不可忽略的一部分。

5. 融资租赁

飞机融资租赁是出租人根据承租人对飞机的特定要求和对生产商的选择,出资向飞机制造商购买新建飞机或够买二手飞机,并租给承租人使用,承租人则分期支付租金。在租赁期内飞机所有权属于出租人所有,但承租人占有并使用飞机,租期届满、租金支付完毕并且承租人根据融资租赁合同规定履行完全部义务后，飞机所有权即转归承租人所有。飞机融资租赁将融资与融物相结合，通过租约的形式同时实现了融资和融物的目的。

融资人通过此方式能够获得更高的融资额度，且具有融资期限长、质押品少、税收负担轻等优势，同时融资租赁也相对不受营运资金及信用额度的束缚。但是融资租赁通常包含复杂的交易结构，导致较高的法律服务费用；并且出租方在挑选飞机及承租人时需要有严格的挑选标准，并非所有承租人和所有种类的飞机都能运用此种融资产品。

（三）国内飞机融资租赁的法律法规

目前我国与飞机融资租赁相关的法律法规主要有《民法通则》，《合同法》第四章“融资租赁合同”《物权法》，《民用航空法》，《航空器权利登记条例》，《外商投资租赁业管理办法》（2015 年修订，商务部令 2015 年第 2 号），《金融租赁公司专业子公司管理暂行办法》（银监办发〔2014〕198 号），《关于审理融资租赁公司纠纷案件适用法律问题的解释》（法释〔2014〕3 号），财政部、国家税务总局《关于全面推开营业税改征增值税试点的通知》（财税〔2016〕36 号），财政部、海关总署、国家税务总局《关于在全国融资租赁货物出口退税政策试点的通知》（财税〔2014〕62 号）。

我国还参加了有关飞机融资租赁的国际公约，如《日内瓦公约》。公约对飞机的登记、抵押权设立、优先权等有较为系统的规范；《开普敦公约》对飞机租赁融资交易中债权人、债务人的权利和义务进行了约定，还设立国际权益登记机构进行监督。通过加入这些国际公约，为我国飞机融资租赁公司参与国际融资租赁交易活动提供了直接适用的法律基础。此外，可供参考的国际公约还有《国际统一私法协会国际融资租赁公约》（1988 年 5 月在加拿大渥太华召开的国际统一私法协会上通过），《国际统一私法协会租赁示范法》（国际统一私法协会全体代表大会及政府专家委员会联席会议于 2008 年 11 月 13 日正式审议通过）。

因此，我国国内涉及飞机融资租赁的法律法规众多，同时也参与了关于飞机融资租赁的国际公约,形成了法律适用的较为完整的体系。

二、《开普敦公约》的简要分析

2001年10月29日至11月16日,由国际民航组织和国际统一私法协会共同倡导,在南非开普敦举行外交会议,通过了《开普敦公约》,包括《移动设备国家利益公约》及其《航空设备议定书》。《开普敦公约》的实施,是对《国际承认航空器权利的公约》的延伸,两者相辅相成。该公约也已于2006年正式生效,中国也于2008年签署并批准了《开普敦公约》。

(一)公约的主要目标

公约及议定书的主要目标是"在三类高价值且具有特殊性质的移动设备上创设、实施、完善优先担保利益以及附条件的卖方或出租人的利益"。[①] 具体而言,主要为了实现以下目标。

1. 创设为所有缔约国所承认的国际利益。[②]

2. 为债权人提供一系列基本的违约和破产救济方式,在有违约证据的情况下,为债权人提供临时快速救济办法。[③]

3. 设立电子化的国际登记处,登记国际利益,使第三方能够知悉国际利益的存在,使债权人获得其已经登记利益以及未经登记利益的优先权,并对抗债务人的破产管理人。[④]

4. 通过具体议定书的制定,满足相关行业的特殊需求。

5. 通过这些措施使债权人增加作出融资决定的信息,提高设备获得者的

---

① 杨国华、成进:《〈开普敦公约〉及其〈有关航空器设备特定问题议定书〉简介》,载《法学评论》2002年第4期。

② 《开普敦公约》第2章。

③ 《开普敦公约》第3章。

④ 《开普敦公约》第4章。

信用登记,降低各利益相关方的交易成本。[1]

其中关于国际利益的创设及其规则的设定,以及国际登记系统的创设是公约内容中最大的亮点。

(二)公约的主要原则

《开普敦公约》的起草者通过"政策为导向"的方法来统一构建一个有利于不同国家的法律框架。为了达成上述目标,确认了以下基本原则。

1. 意思自治原则。公约虽然力求使有关高价值移动设备登记为国际利益的担保权益的保护规范在全球范围内保持高度一致,但同时也给予了当事方高度的意思自治空间,尊重当事方之间达成的协议,认可合同中对公约规定的可以协议修改的规则自由约定的有效性。

2. 可预见性原则。公约在条文的拟定,规则的明晰方面要求尽可能的简洁、明确、便捷,电子登记系统的设置正是这一原则的体现。

3. 透明度原则。通过登记规则,可以使第三方清楚便捷地查询有关登记情况。公约不仅使当事方了解有关登记情况,更可以清楚地知晓有关已登记国际利益和已登记购买人的权利优先权的位次。

4. 灵活性原则。由于不同国家存在现实法律背景的差异,公约允许成员国基于自身特殊经济利益考虑,坚持在某些问题上适用本国重要的法律原则。对缔约国对其认为不合适的条款允许其加以保留或者排除适用。

(三)公约的要点和实际意义

《开普敦公约》主要涉及航空器及航空器标的物的买卖和租赁问题。依照该公约登记后的担保权益将优先于没有进行登记的在航空器上的其他权利。一旦融资债务人或者航空器的承租人不履行合同义务,融资人和出租人就可以主张其优先受偿的登记权益。在融资债务人或承租人不履行债务时,

---

① 参见[英]罗伊·古德:《移动设备国际利益公约和有关航空器设备特定问题议定书正式注释》,孙士柱译,中国民航出版社 2004 年版,第 7 页。

融资人或者出租人可以对航空器进行占有、控制、出售、出租,并可以收取因管理和使用该航空器而产生的收益。

公约和议定书还规定了债务不履行时的临时救济措施,主要有提存、监管、冻结、管理航空器并取得其收益。在融资债务人或承租人破产的情况下,如果航空器权益登记时间在破产程序开始之前,航空器的登记利益也受到特别的保护。破产管理机构或者债务人应当将航空器交由融资人或者出租人占有。航空器的登记利益不受破产程序中债权人受偿顺序的影响。

《开普敦公约》为债权人从破产航空公司取得飞机的控制权提供了便利,降低了购买或租赁飞时的融资风险,并大大降低了融资成本。航空公司可节省大量成本,并有望提高业内对新飞机的需求。

《开普敦公约》生效后,美国进出口银行已经把针对一些国家的预付风险费削减了1/3。据分析,在《开普敦公约》生效后的未来20年中,低收入国家可以节省资金约50亿美元。

三、飞机融资租赁法律实践基本分析

如前文所述,我国目前并没有飞机融资租赁方面的专门法律,飞机租赁和融资租赁的相关立法条文散见于各个不同的法律法规中。虽然,我国的立法者也注意到了融资租赁不同于一般的租赁,并在制定合同法时,单设一章对其加以规定,在其他法律法规中也规定了融资租赁交易的许多“特色”。但整体而言,我国的相关立法仍然把融资租赁当成了一种“租赁”。我国法律没有明确承租人没有合同解除权,也没有明确出租人不负有租赁物的瑕疵担保义务。而这些制度的建立对于融资租赁具有重要意义,倘若缺失,会导致融资租赁制度的不完整。

(一)《合同法》的基本规定

就我国《合同法》而言,根据有关融资租赁合同的规定和航空器融资租赁交易的实践,飞机融资租赁交易有如下基本特点。

1. 交易标的物由承租人决定,即作为承租人的航空公司向出租人提出或直接从航空器制造厂处,选择和决定飞机的型号、规格和数量。

2. 承租人和出租人遵循租赁合同的基本规范。具体而言,双方签订租赁飞机的合同,出租人是飞机的所有权人,承租人则占有飞机并进行使用、收益,并按照约定支付租金。

3. 租赁期间,承租人需要遵循收益和风险一致的原则,即飞机运营收益归承租人,据此产生的风险也归于承租人。

4. 租赁期满后,当事人可选择多种交易模式,如根据合同约定,承租人既可续租,也可直接购买飞机,或者把飞机返还出租人。

(二)飞机融资租赁合同解除的特点

飞机融资租赁合同在解除方面主要有以下特点:

1. 融资租赁合同不适用任意解除等制度。由于在航空器融资租赁交易中,出租人的实际地位是融资方,选择并使用租赁物的权利在承租人,即航空公司。航空公司对租赁物的型号、规格、制造厂商等有选择权与决定权。不难发现,承租人实际上是借款方,出租人是贷款方,承租人有权决定所借款项的使用。与之相对,在单纯的飞机租赁关系中,飞机作为租赁物,归出租人所有,并不受承租人的意愿支配。而在飞机融资租赁关系中,出租人虽然提供资金购买航空器,但通过向承租人收取租金,实质上补足了其出资金额。可以说,通过融资租赁合同,实现了对出租人资金的合理利用,满足了承租人使用飞机的需求,也缓解了承租人现实的资金压力。融资租赁合同的稳定性,关系各方当事人的根本利益。而站在出租人的角度,其关心的仅是航空器购置资金的筹措和回收,以及适当的利润,对航空器本身的使用则完全无须关心。如果允许承租人在履约途中任意解除,则对于缺乏实际使用经验的出租人而言,相当于接收了一个无用之物。而且由于飞机的定制往往体现各航空公司个性化的使用要求,如需转手出售,势必带来修正飞机的巨大成本支出,造成出租人的重大损失,极不合理。站在承租人的角度,进行融资租赁的目的在于融资购买所需使用之物,由于飞机价格昂贵,且使用价值单一,如果允许出租人中途解约,则将导致承租人丧失生产经营工具,而蒙受巨大经济损失。进一步,站在制造商的角度,制造商从出租人处接到订单开始根据承租人的要求定制飞机,如果飞机交付之前,出租人与承租人的融资租赁合同终止,那么制造商很可能因无法寻觅到合适买家而遭受重大损失。因此,考虑到各方的实质利益,以及避免资源浪费,航空器融资租赁合同不可任意解除或者终止。

事实上,我国合同法在一般情况下否认承租人的解除权。从航空器融资交易的市场情况看,这种模式一方面保障了承租人合理的救济权,另一方面又提高了出租人融资的积极性,具有合理性。

2. 融资租赁合同中出租人不应承担租赁物瑕疵担保义务。这是由融资租赁交易的特殊性决定的。(1)融资租赁的出租人提供的主要是资金,而并非产品。当租赁物存在瑕疵时,如果允许承租人擅自解除合同,则出租人的利益就难以保护。(2)在融资租赁交易中,承租人决定了航空器的规格、质量以及供应商等,出租人只是依照承租人的指示签订买卖合同。因此,承租人应当对航空器的性能、质量、供应商的信誉、资质等更为了解,要求出租人承担瑕疵担保义务不具备合理性。

四、《开普敦公约》在我国的适用

《开普敦公约》作为国际航空行业的统一标准,对促进缔约国航空行业发展具有重要意义。公约作为我国航空法律领域的重要补充,对进一步完善我国航空法律体系具有重要作用。我国在加入该公约时结合了我国国情,作了保留声明,其中就包括公约不适用于我国国内交易。所谓国内交易,根据《开普敦公约》第1条第n项的表述,指的是“在缔结合同时,所涉各方的主要利益中心和(依据议定书确定的)相关标的物的所在地都位于同一个缔约国内”,同时,第 1 条第 n 项还要求“该交易所产生的利益已经在该缔约国的国家登记处登记,且该缔约国已根据该公约第 50 条第 1 款作出声明”。笔者理解,此处的主要利益中心应当限于承租人与出租人。当承租人与出租人为境内公司,即使融资方为境外银行,该笔交易仍被认为是国内交易而不适用开普敦公约。

就目前中国的实践而言,租赁行为也是被看作独立于融资行为的。尽管有境外融资机构的介入,但由于飞机的租赁人和承租人都是中国企业,该交易仍旧适用国内规定。

然而,即使我国对公约作出了部分保留声明,但由于国内已有的法律体系,不可避免地存在一些与《开普敦公约》不一致的规定。例如,在违约救济方式方面,国内法律和公约的规定就存在一些差别。《开普敦公约》第 10 条规定,遭遇违约一方可采用解除合同的方式进行自我救济,并占有航空器。而依据我国法律,合同的解除除了经双方同意的约定解除外,只有发生了法律规定的情形,方可进行法定解除。而法律规定的情形均需达到根本违约、无法实现合同目的的程度。如果仅以履约瑕疵而主张违约进而要求解除合同的,并不构成法定解除。对此,公约在违约程度上并没有进行充分说明。此种与国内法不一致的情形,也需要由合同双方协商,约定操作的细节,以避免后续争议。

优先于担保物权的法定优先权未经在国际登记处登记,优先于在国际登记处登记的担保物权,包括破产费用及共同债务请求,破产企业职工工资,航空器抵押、质押、流质税,航空器救助请求,航空器扣押维护费用等。提供公共服务的中国政府或政府机构,政府间国际组织,或其他组织提供服务产生费用,扣押航空器的权利,不受《开普敦公约》影响。法院判决允许扣押航空器以履行判决的,判决债权人的权益为可在国际登记处登记的法定权益。

《开普敦公约》不适用于中国国内交易。担保权人不得在中国境内出租航空器。

《开普敦公约》规定的国际利益受到中国国内法的一些限制。

五、结　语

近年来,我国政府对扶持国产飞机租赁十分重视,并给予了资金来源、财政贴息等方面的政策支持。各路业内人士也纷纷呼吁大力开展飞机租赁业务。目前,我国行业主管部门也积极致力于配套政策的制定。同时,我国自主开发的飞机工业也在稳步推进。我们有理由相信,随着政府层面的重视,我国飞机租赁领域将逐步完善,飞机工业也将有巨大的发展。作为法律工作者,笔者也盼望更多地参与到飞机融资租赁法律服务中来。

“一带一路”视野下中国航空器融资租赁登记制度的完善

李毅阳[*]　丁达人[**]

“一带一路”经济合作模式的构建思路最先由中国政府提出，旨在加强全球经济一体化建设及打造跨区域间各国经济合作的新构架。本文从“一带一路”的视角分析中国航空器融资租赁登记制度的不足，提出了我国《民用航空法》第33条中“占有权”概念界定不明、有关中国航空器融资租赁登记客体之规定缺乏灵活性、有关航空器的登记机关冗余等几个问题，并通过价值层面分析探讨中国航空器融资租赁登记制度完善之必要，进而提出几点建议，旨在为中国航空器融资租赁登记制度的完善尽一点绵薄之力。

一、问题的提出

“一带一路”指“丝绸之路经济带”和“21世纪海

* 福建远大联盟律师事务所副主任、高级合伙人。

** 福建远大联盟律师事务所律师助理。

上丝绸之路",是中国政府最先提出的,旨在加强全球经济一体化建设及打造跨区域间各经济体合作的新构架。"一带一路"并未局限于字面表征的空间范围内,其具有更深层,更广义的含义。即借助"陆上丝绸之路"和"海上丝绸之路"的历史典故,深刻表明本经济合作模式所提倡的"和平合作、开放包容、互学互鉴、互利共赢"的构建主旨及文化内涵。① 而通过"一带一路"视野下研究中国航空器融资租赁登记制度,即以更多的维度和更深的广度去探索分析中国航空器融资租赁登记制度,旨在发现更多的问题,并针对上述问题提出相对较为有效的解决办法。②

航空器融资租赁登记制度,指通过行政登记,将航空器融资租赁之承租人承租航空器的基本承租情况、承租主体信息等基本信息或其他予以审查确认,进而对外公示的行政确认制度。该制度的构建旨在明确融资租赁合同中出租人和承租人构建融资租赁关系的法律事实存在,并起到公示公信的作用,保护出租人和承租人及第三人的基本权益,保障融资租赁交易活动高效、便利、安全的开展。笔者基于"一带一路"合作、开放、公平、公正的理念及视角,对比《开普敦公约》和其他国家关于融资租赁登记制度的相关规定,结合现行的中国法规及实务操作中出现的矛盾和分歧,归纳出以下几个亟待解决的问题。

首先,中国有关航空器融资租赁登记制度的规范在我国《民用航空法》第33条中有所体现。③ 而该法律规范中"占有权"一词该如何理解,中国现行的法律规范及司法解释并没有给予明确的界定。

其次,中国航空器融资租赁登记客体之规定缺乏灵活性。我国《民用航空法》第33条规定,航空器的融资租赁登记所公示确认的客体为承租者"占有航空器的权利"。那么对于航空器没有整体上融资租赁,仅针对机身或航

① 参见刘卫东:《"一带一路"战略的科学内涵与科学问题》,载《地理科学进步》2015年第5期。

② 参见季卫东:《法治秩序的建构》,商务印书馆2014年版,第146页。

③ 我国《民用航空法》第33条:"民用航空器的融资租赁和租赁期限为六个月以上的其他租赁,承租人应当就其对民用航空器的占有权向国务院民用航空主管部门办理登记;未经登记的,不得对抗第三人。"

空器发动机或其他航空器零部件的融资租赁该如何登记？对于上述问题，我国《民用航空法》及其他相关规范性文件并没有明示。但航空器的部分关键零件及发动机财产价值较高，尤其在航空器维修环节，单独对航空器关键零件和发动机的融资租赁在实务中极为常见。例如，在机场维修时，安装新的融资租赁的发动机在航空器上，后该航空器所属的公司破产，在破产清算时，该融资租赁的发动机在没有融资租赁登记的情况下该如何保护发动机出租人的产权利益的问题，值得研究和探讨。

最后，中国有关航空器各项权项的登记机关冗余且并不统一。中国现今航空器的抵押权、融资租赁权、所有权的登记皆为民用航空主管部门。现行航空器相关零件及发动机的抵押登记机构为国家工商行政管理局。此外，中国现行法律规范性文件对动产融资租赁的登记机构有明确规定，即由中国人民银行征信管理中心统一管理。综上所述，中国有关规范航空器登记部门职能的规定存在职能重叠，行政资源浪费的问题，最终有碍于登记工作的开展。

二、我国《民用航空法》第 33 条中“占有权”概念之解读

我国《民用航空法》第 33 条对融资租赁登记的客体仅用了“占有权”一词来限定表述。但现今主流的民法基本理论对“占有”的认定已经由“法律权属形态”转变为“事实形态”。“占有权”不再被认定为法律规定的物权权属状态，而是需要“本权”依托的“事实状态”，即需以物权或债权为本权。[①] 那么我国《民用航空法》第 33 条中的“占有权”一词该如何理解和界定？占有作为一个“事实状态”依法受法律保护，但并非归属于权利的范畴，“占有权”应认定为法益。那么我国《民用航空法》第 33 条中的“占有权”一词就必须进一步解释或修改，否则有失偏颇。

---

① 参见隋彭生：《论占有之本权》，载《商法研究》2011 年第 2 期。

参照民法基本理论可知,学界常以登记的法定效果为区分标准,把航空器融资租赁登记的立法例分为登记生效主义和登记对抗主义。对于航空器融资租赁登记制度来讲,登记生效主义,指航空器融资租赁的承租权以融资租赁登记的设立为起点开始生效,如尚未经过登记,融资租赁关系便难以成立,也就无从谈起对抗任意善意第三人之说。登记生效主义,通常以严格谨慎的实质审查为主,有较强的行政干预性。登记对抗主义指航空器融资租赁的承租权不以登记为生效条件,双方达成合意后交付航空器即成立融资租赁关系,但不能对抗善意的第三人,仅通过融资租赁登记,才能构建良好的权利外观,在占有状态加登记信息吻合的情况下,可以对抗善意第三人。且该模式常常配套规定较为宽松的形式审查规定。①

根据我国《民用航空法》第 33 条中明确的"未经登记的,不得对抗第三人"的规定可知,已经经过合法登记的,便可以对抗善意第三人。没有经过登记的,虽然不能对抗善意第三人,但并不影响融资租赁合同的效力。根据上述相关规定及对本法其他相关规定进行体系化解释,便可推断出中国航空器融资租赁登记制度适用的立法例为登记对抗主义立法例。既存在融资租赁权益登记的登记事实,又持续对同一融资租赁物保持占有状态,方可对抗善意第三人的融资租赁制度。

通过分析生效对抗主义立法例的基本特征可知,此处的"占有权"登记旨在保证确认承租人占有租赁物的状态得以公示于众,进而达到使善意第三人明确租赁物的租赁状态的效果。那么该"占有权"即指"融资租赁权"。但追溯到《民用航空法》的生效时间即 1995 年 10 月,在尚没有融资租赁合同的立法规范,且我国《合同法》尚未颁布生效的情况下,立法者难以直接使用"融资租赁权"一词于法律规范中。若直接使用"融资租赁权"一词,就应在我国《民用航空法》中对该词作出明确的界定和释义,而"融资租赁权"的相关词源在民法及合同法基本理论中。显然,在民用航空法内不适合规范合同

① 参见郝秀辉:《航空器权利变动公示的研究——兼论特殊动产的权利公示问题》,载《烟台大学学报》(哲学社会科学版)2007 年第 4 期。

法基础理论用词。此外,从融资租赁的民事行为本身来讲,需要合同双方达成一致意愿并签订合同时债权方才生效,但交付融资租赁的标的物方可最终形成融资租赁权。这也就意味着,在占有转让交付完成后,融资租赁权才能相应地产生,即承租人处于占有状态的事实情况下,才可以完成申请融资租赁登记。由此,立法者引用“占有权”一词,旨在确保承租人已经实际控制融资租赁物的基本状况。此外,从融资租赁制度本身的基本特征来讲,承租人在融资租赁合同期限结束后,若在合同中约定或双方达成新的合意,便可取得该融资租赁物的所有权,即具有对该租赁物所有权的期权。融资租赁合同虽然本质上应归为债权的范畴,但立法赋予其登记对抗善意第三人的效力,即其已经突破了债权相对性的基本原则。合同双方通过对抗登记来对抗善意第三人,这便具有一定的物权属性,立法者直接以“占有权”来描述,显然是源于本文中以上几个原因所致。①

三、中国航空器融资租赁登记客体规定之不足——以《开普敦公约》的实然分析为参照

《开普敦公约》即《移动设备国际利益公约》及《移动设备国际利益公约关于航空器设备特定问题的议定书》,主要规范航空器、铁路等移动设备的保护和登记等问题。对于航空器的登记制度,该公约有着明确详细的规定,《开普敦公约》在参照《日内瓦公约》的基础上,着眼于解决更高层次、更广范围的国际实务问题,制定了更具完善性的规定,旨在更好地保护航空器的所有人、出租人、抵押权人等相关各项权益。相较于《开普敦公约》,中国现行的《民用航空法》对航空器的登记制度规定便显得较为落后、片面。且很多细小、翔实的旨在解决实务中普遍出现之琐碎问题的规范制度在中国现行《民用航空法》中并没有体现。可生活是充斥着细小和琐碎之矛盾的,是亟

① 参见谷丰:《我国航空器融资租赁承租人“占有权”登记制度探析——以民用航空法第三十三条为剖析视角》,载《理论探讨》2014年第6期。

待立法者更新规范进而解决弥补问题的。不从细节着手,解决不了新的社会矛盾,法规的操作性和指引性便会大打折扣。

有关于航空器登记之客体规定,《开普敦公约》便有独到、严谨的规范内容:航空器登记的客体范围不仅仅为“国际利益”,还包括预期国际利益、国际利益的转让及预期转让。① 此外,登记客体甚至拓展到了可根据准据法,法定或约定取得的国际利益。可见,《开普敦公约》规定的航空器融资租赁登记的客体范畴从航空器整体已推展至可单独登记航空器的发动机、机身甚至拓展到单独登记航空器的各个细小零件。《开普敦公约》不但明确了已存在的众多权益可以登记,亦明确了预期权益也可以登记。这便与大多数国家对于动产仅能登记已经稳定确认的权利的规定不同。② 除此之外,《开普敦公约》第29条第5款规定了权利义务的双方,仅通过自愿平等的协议就可改变登记的相关权益内容。③

中国有关于航空器融资之客体的法律规定仅于我国《民用航空法》第33条有明确体现,即航空器融资租赁登记的客体为承租人“占有航空器的权利”,即以整个航空器为登记客体。④ 而对于航空器的发动机或航空器的重要零件是否可以单独作为融资租赁登记的客体,并没有明确规定。而融资租赁登记制度,旨在于设立明确承租人融资租赁权的基础上,保障出租人对融资租赁物的所有权,进而对善意第三人起到风险警示的作用。在实务中,经常出现仅对飞机发动机融资租赁或对某重要零件融资租赁。缺失对该部分

① 参见于丹:《开普敦公约体制下的国际利益研究》,载《当代法学》2011年第2期。

② 参见莫世健:《WTO、开普敦公约和中国飞机租赁市场法律的完善》,载《北京理工大学学报》(社会科学版)2011年第1期。

③ 《开普敦公约》第29条第5款:“本条规定的对抗利益或权利间的优先次序,可以通过此种利益持有人之间的协议加以变更。但是,从属权利益的受让人不受将该利益置于从属地位的协议约束,除非在转让时与该项协议有相关的该从属利益已被登记。”

④ 《民用航空法》第33条:“民用航空器的融资租赁和租赁期限为六个月以上的其他租赁,承租人应当就其对民用航空器的占有权向国务院民用航空主管部门办理登记;未经登记的,不得对抗第三人。”

单独融资租赁登记制度的规定，显然不利于对该类融资租赁行为的保护。[①]正如本文开头所论述的案例，在航空器整体被承租人占有，仅该航空器内部的发动机或部分关键性零件为融资租赁客体的情况。承租人基于占有该航空器整体的明显权利外观转让航空器给善意的第三人，有碍于对附有融资租赁权利负担的发动机或关键性零件的相关出租人所享有的合法权益的保护，亦难以提前警示、明确提醒善意第三人旨在订立买卖合同的标的物存在其他权利负担的客观事实，即租赁物的占有人和所有人不同，极易出现法规保护不协调之缺陷。对比分析中国有关航空器融资租赁登记制度与《开普敦公约》之关于航空器融资租赁登记的规定可知，我国关于航空器融资租赁客体范围的规定较为僵化和狭隘，缺乏一定的灵活性。

四、有关航空器的登记机关冗余之现状分析

中国现行有效的有关调整航空器登记制度的规范性文件，设置了多个行政登记机关。根据不同的登记客体，主要分为以下几个登记机构：

1. 中国人民银行征信管理中心。《中国人民银行征信中心中征动产融资统一登记平台操作规则》明确规定：中国人民银行征信管理中心和中国人民银行征信分中心以及中征动产融资统一登记平台为动产融资租赁的登记机构。此外，中国人民银行征信管理中心以完善的互联网信息技术为媒介，建立了融资租赁登记公示系统，并通过该系统为全国范围内的各动产融资租赁公司或权利人构建了一个集办理融资登记业务、查询融资租赁登记公示公信信息为一体的互联网平台。但我国现行《物权法》《合同法》等法律效力层次的法律规范中并没有明确约定一般动产融资租赁的登记机构，仅以《中国人民银行征信中心中征动产融资统一登记平台操作规则》这一行政规章来确立一般动产的融资租赁登记机构，显然缺乏法律效力。

---

① 参见高圣平：《中国融资租赁法制：权利再造与制度重塑——以〈开普敦公约〉及相关议定书为参照》，载《中国人民大学学报》2004 年第 2 期。

2. 国家工商行政管理局。该部门机构主要针对动产抵押权的登记。根据我国《物权法》[①]《动产抵押登记办法》[②]的规定,一般动产的抵押登记机关为县一级的工商行政管理部门,对于航空器发动机、各部门零件的抵押登记,均需在国家工商行政管理局登记备案。

3. 民用航空主管部门。根据我国《民用航空法》第14条、[③]第16条、[④]第33条[⑤]的规定,民用航空器的所有权、抵押权、融资租赁权的登记部门均为国务院民用航空主管部门。

上述三个登记机构的登记对象具有极大的关联性,并在某些登记客体上存在登记范围重叠的问题。虽然精密化的登记分工,有利于登记工作的切实开展,使行政职能分散开来,行政职责之负担得以均衡分配。但这有碍于公众对登记信息的查询和融资租赁活动的持续开展。

融资租赁物除了融资租赁权登记情况外,其所有权属状态、抵押状态对于第三人和融资租赁合同当事人都极为关键。分开登记也就意味着当事人需要分开查询以上权属状况。这便使行政程序烦琐化,不利于当事人方便、快捷地了解信息进而合理、安全有效地作出民事行为。此外,我国《民法总则》《物权法》《民用航空法》等基本法律均没有明确确立一个统一的有关航

---

① 《物权法》第189条第1款规定:"企业、个体工商户、农业生产经营者以本法第一百八十一条规定的动产抵押的,应当向抵押人住所地的工商行政管理部门办理登记。抵押权自抵押合同生效时设立;未经登记,不得对抗善意第三人。"

② 《动产抵押登记办法》第2条规定:"企业、个体工商户、农业生产经营者以《中华人民共和国物权法》第一百八十条第一款第四项、第一百八十一条规定的动产抵押的,应当向抵押人住所地的县级工商行政管理部门(以下简称登记机关)办理登记。抵押权自抵押合同生效时设立;未经登记,不得对抗善意第三人。本办法所称工商行政管理部门,包括履行工商行政管理职责的市场监督管理部门。"

③ 《民用航空法》第14条规定:"民用航空器所有权的取得、转让和消灭,应当向国务院民用航空主管部门登记;未经登记的,不得对抗第三人。民用航空器所有权的转让,应当签订书面合同。"

④ 《民用航空法》第16条规定:"设定民用航空器抵押权,由抵押权人和抵押人共同向国务院民用航空主管部门办理抵押权登记;未经登记的,不得对抗第三人。"

⑤ 《民用航空法》第33条规定:"民用航空器的融资租赁和租赁期限为六个月以上的其他租赁,承租人应当就其对民用航空器的占有权向国务院民用航空主管部门办理登记;未经登记的,不得对抗第三人。"

空器各个权属登记机关(《民用航空法》仅明确民用航空器的所有权、抵押权、融资租赁权的登记均属于国务院民用航空主管部门,但对于民用航空器的发动机或是单个零件的融资租赁登记、抵押权登记的机构并没有明确规定)。从法律效力层面上考量,仅仅靠行政规章、各部门工作规章的规定来分配行政机构的登记职能其效力还远远不足。若各规范性文件规定的内容适用出现矛盾,显然难以区分效力熟大熟小的问题。这便给行政人员增加了行政工作的开展难度和不可确定性。①

五、"一带一路"视角下融资租赁登记机关登记制度完善之价值分析

"一带一路"倡议构架的提出,显示了中国经济体计划进一步更广泛、更多样、更深层、更规范地和世界经济接轨。"一带一路"倡议也掀起了中国既加入WTO后的新一轮区域经济一体化建设热潮,亦顺应了全球经济一体化的国际大趋势。在坚持"开放、包容、均衡、普惠"的基本原则下,积极构建区域经济互通合作的经济蓝图,这正和"一带一路"倡议构架的精髓相契合。②中国政府在"一带一路"的深层次文化内涵引导下,不断完善自身经济、行政规范制度,才能更好地贯彻习近平主席反复提出的"走出去"政策,才能更好地构建"一带一路"区域经济合作的战略蓝图,才能更快地引导中国走上真正的法治之路。

构建公平、安全的交易环境是维护良好的经济秩序的前提条件,也是维护地区经济稳定发展的重要因素,也是"一带一路"经济带设立的基础。只有保证经济合作区域内部交易秩序的稳定、公平,才能吸引大量的外来资金、技术、人才、文化投入经济合作区,进而衍生出一个良性合理的经济循环体。

---

① 参见孟强:《论不动产登记机构登记错误的赔偿责任——兼评〈不动产登记暂行条例(征求意见稿)〉相关规定》,载《政治与法律》2014年第12期。

② 参见刘卫东:《"一带一路"战略的科学内涵与科学问题》,载《地理科学进步》2015年第5期。

这就意味着,构建“一带一路”倡议构架的前提条件,就是要尽快解决扰乱本国交易安全、经济秩序的矛盾问题。

融资租赁制度便是为稳固经济秩序解决经济矛盾的“强心剂”,在国际经贸高速发展的今天,融资租赁合同关系无处不在。通过成立融资租赁合同关系,巧妙地把金融投资和生产经营两个社会活动连接在一起,从而保障融资租赁行为安全、有效之开展。而融资租赁登记制度作为规范公示融资租赁物权属情况及出租情况的基本制度,为上述灵活的融资租赁关系之安全性、公开性提供了保障。而在航空产业中,航空器的购买和租赁事宜,大部分以融资租赁的形式完成。尤其是中国各大航空公司在设立初期,均是以融资租赁方式起步,通过融资租用航空器的方式开展航空客运或货运的商业服务,不断发展壮大。尽管现今各大航空公司营业模式有部分改变,但大部分航空器仍为融资租赁所得。根据本文第二部分的详细论述可知,中国现行的航空器的融资租赁登记的相关立法规范,严格贯彻登记对抗主义的立法例精神。而融资租赁合同为诺成合同,即仅依当事人的意思表示一致即可成立的合同。[①] 以融资租赁合同签订之日起,融资租赁之债权生效产生。以交付即转移占有为履行融资租赁义务的前提条件,以登记为对抗善意第三人的充要条件。在既确定了占有事实又确定了登记事实的情况下,可明确对抗善意第三人。不但保证了承租人融资租赁权的稳固,而且确保了出租人对融资租赁物所享有的所有权不被承租人侵犯,此外还明示于任意的第三人,方便第三人作出合理明智的交易安排。该登记制度本身便极为符合“一带一路”“开放、包容、均衡、普惠”的基本思想。

从制度价值的角度分析,航空器的融资租赁登记制度本身的制度价值便是在于保障商事主体在开展航空器融资租赁活动中能够公平、安全、均衡地完成交易。

首先,航空器融资租赁登记制度明确公示了融资租赁物的租赁权属状

---

① 参见韩世远:《合同法总论》,法律出版社2011年版,第58页。

况,即融资租赁物为承租人承租,出租人所有的特殊状态。使第三人可以明确方便地知悉该航空器是否附加租赁权负担,进而作出正确、安全的商事行为,从而保证整个交易秩序的稳定、平衡。

其次,登记使出租人避免承担出租物被承租人无权处分的风险,保证了融资租赁合同履行之安全性。承租人基于融资租赁关系,享有长期占有融资租赁物的权益。基于动产的"占有"推定原则,承租人具有易于使第三人混淆的权利外观。除此之外,融资租赁关系具有长期存续性。出租人一般不承担维修义务,这便给予承租人宽松、自由的使用权。在没有融资租赁登记制度的保障下,承租人可以较为容易地出售承租物,进而导致矛盾纠纷产生。而融资租赁登记制度的确立避免了上述风险。

最后,明确权属登记的次序,保障了买卖不破租赁制度的适用。融资租赁登记制度本身便是租赁登记制度的一种,在登记确定的情况下,明确了产生对抗善意第三人效力的时间。根据买卖不破租赁制度的规定,出租人转让其所有的出租物,并不影响承租人占有使用承租物的权利,即所有权主体的变更并不影响承租人既存的承租权。但买卖不破租赁制度适用是有明确的前提条件的,即租赁关系的成立早于所有权变动的发生,这也意味着租赁关系早于房屋买卖关系产生。融资租赁行为作为特殊的租赁行为,同样适用买卖不破租赁制度。而融资租赁登记不但可以明确融资租赁物的产权状况和租赁状况,亦可以明确融资租赁物于何时转移交付给融资租赁的承租人。且基于公权力的行政确认行为,融资租赁登记之公信力要远远高于融资租赁合同上记载的签订时间,更有利于保障买卖不破租赁制度的适用。此外,我国《合同法》第5条明确规定了合同公平之原则。[①]该原则不但指双务合同中合同双方当事人之间的对待给付义务应具等值性,亦指合同双方当事人之间合同履行风险的合理分配。[②] 中国现行法律、法规对融资租赁合同的规范内容为《合同法》分则部分的规范内容。该部分内容应遵循该法总则部分的原则

---

① 《合同法》第5条规定:"当事人应当遵循公平原则确定各方的权利和义务。"

② 参见韩世远:《合同法总论》,法律出版社2011年版,第39~40页。

性规定。而上述原则正与中国提出“一带一路”战略构架的基本原则之均衡原则相契合。这也从侧面反映出“一带一路”之视野和融资租赁登记制度的内在一致性。

综上所述,以“一带一路”之视野,去分析中国航空器融资租赁登记制度的问题,进而弥补制度之不足,显然有利于中国航空器融资租赁登记活动的开展。以更加开放、包容、均衡、普惠的视野去改善中国融资租赁登记制度,显然更具有建设性和实践意义。

六、完善我国民用航空器融资租赁登记制度的几点建议

对比国际法律规范之状况,中国融资租赁登记制度的发展还处于初期阶段,理论研究和实务探索之路均任重而道远。对于我国民用航空器融资租赁登记制度的几点不足,笔者在本文已经作出了详尽的分析。根据上述分析,笔者提出以下几点建议,希望能为我国民用航空器融资租赁登记制度的完善尽一些绵薄之力。

首先,笔者认为我国《民用航空法》第33条中“占有权”应通过修订《民用航空法》或颁布相关司法解释明确统一界定为“融资租赁权”,在我国《物权法》《合同法》已经相继出台的法律体系支撑下,明确融资租赁登记的对象为“融资租赁权”并无不当。和《民用航空法》的制定背景、时间不同,现今,中国融资租赁制度有《物权法》《合同法》《民法总则》等系列完备的基础法规为前提,直接引用《合同法》中“融资租赁权”一词并无不可。如此,便绕开了中国学界“占有权”为“事实状态”还是“法律权属状态”之分歧,又准确无误地规范了登记内容。

其次,在“一带一路”的视野下,我国可以借鉴国际大环境下其他发达国家的优良立法经验,对比《开普敦公约》,以修订我国《民用航空法》的形式,扩大我国航空器融资租赁登记的客体之范围。根据本文有关登记客体的论述可知,现有的规定明确融资租赁登记的客体为航空器的概括性整体,包括

发动机,各个航空器零件。但如果仅是航空器的发动机、单个航空器零件为融资租赁的租赁物,而在并不涉及航空器其他部分的情况下该如何登记处理的问题,是由民用航空主管部门登记登记,还是由其他工商行政机关登记,还是由中国人民银行征信管理中心登记等问题,仅依据现行规定,仍难以解决。由此,明确把航空器发动机、单个航空器零件列入至融资租赁登记的客体范围内,明确可单独融资租赁登记上述零件或重要部分,有益于增强该登记制度的灵活性。

最后,通过修正我国《民用航空法》,明确统一由民用航空主管机关专项管理所有的与航空器相关的权属登记事项(如抵押权、所有权、融资租赁权等),并明确界定其他行政登记机关不得干涉或从事航空器的权属登记工作。此外,应确保配套设施的完善:第一,应构建全国范围内的登记状况查询平台,且任何一个明确提供身份证明和联系方式的自然人或法人均可以在该平台上查询权属登记状况;第二,在该查询平台官方网站上明确操作指引,开通查询操作指导的咨询热线;第三,明确申请登记的程序和申请递交的文件要求,并明确申请受理时间和受理部门;第四,在网站上明确开通投诉热线和复议程序,贯彻服务型政府的理念。这便解决了中国航空器融资租赁登记机关冗余的问题。

Legal Market for Aircraft Financing in China

Luping Zhang *

The paper assesses the legal market for aircraft financing① in China. It offers an overview of the economic market and legal market of the development of aircraft financing in China. The introduction covers domestic laws, international conventions and the conflict in the application of the international conventions. Further, the analysis embraces two types of cases as well as proposals for future changes in aircraft financing in China. Changes include normative adaption, institutional support and professional training for the legal market.

---

* Ph. D. Candidate, King's College London.

① For the purpose of this introductory paper, aircraft financing adopts a broad definition, with a focus on aircraft financial leasing while with no distinction between operating leasing and financial leasing, unless otherwise specified.

Introduction

Aircraft financing is a promising practice field in the 21st century. As a major air power with a growing legal market, China is a prominent player in the legal market for aircraft financing. This paper aims at offering an overview of the current legal market in China and proposals for future development in aircraft financing by the following four chapters. Section 1 will introduce the economic and legal market of aircraft financing in China using statistics reported by major airlines and International Financial Law Report 1000 (IFLR1000); Section 2 will focus on the governing laws including domestic law, international law and the application of international law in China's domestic setting. For Chinese domestic law, there are Contract Law, Property Law, Guaranty Law, Civil Aviation Law, Tax Law, as well as relevant regulations and judicial opinion. For international law, there are two relevant conventions and protocol: Geneva Convention, Cape Town Convention, and Aircraft Protocol. [①] Section 3 will focus on case studies of aircraft financing as illustrations of potential legal risks and recent development in China. The first set of cases is a recent development in China—Export Credit Agency supported deals. The second case is a famous bankruptcy case of East Star Airline. Section 4 will make proposals for future development including normative adaption, institutional support, and professional training.

---

① Cape Town Convention and Aircraft Protocol are regarded as a single document for interpretation. For the purpose of this paper, the reference to the Cape Town Convention will include the Aircraft Protocol unless noted otherwise.

1. Current Market of Aircraft Financing

1.1 Economic Market

The economic market in aircraft financing has the following two features: first, it is a huge and growing market for the leasing market based on the industrial estimation; second, foreign capitals predominantly control the current market. Statistically speaking, China will be the second largest civil aviation market following the United States in 2024, based on a prediction of Boeing.① According to the Boeing report, China will operate around 200 aircrafts in total by the time of 2024.② The CEO of the Airbus also estimated that China needs 1600 new aircrafts before 2020.③ Based on the calculation, 1200 aircrafts will be through the leasing channel. Aircraft manufacturers are not alone in having confidence in the Chinese market. The mid-to-long term development plan of the China Civil Aviation Authority is to transform from a major country into a great power in civil aviation.④

Besides the size of the market, foreign capitals have a strong presence in China, covering 95% of the current market, of which GE Capital Aviation Services (GECAS), International Lease Finance Corporation (ILFC) and Boeing Capital Corporation (BCC) consisting of over 80%.⑤ Chinese leasing companies still have a long way to go. However, due to non-discrimination obligation under the WTO, China will face a serious competition vis-à-vis foreign competition in

① See F. He, "Legal Research on Aircraft Financial Leasing", *Jiang Su Aviation* 4, 2006, p. 6.

② Ibid.

③ See L. Zhao, "Legal Research on Finance Leasing of Domestically Manufactured Aircrafts", Master's thesis, Northwest University, 2010, p. 15.

④ Ibid.

⑤ See S. Mo, "WTO, Cape Town Convention and Improvement of Chinese Law on Aircraft Leasing", *Journal of Beijing Institute of Technology* 13(6), 2011, p. 80.

the aircraft financing market. Meanwhile, domestic aircraft manufacturers will join the competition as well. In 2004, Shenzhen Financial Leasing Co. , Ltd. signed a finance leasing agreement of Modern Ark 60 aircraft with Xian Aircraft Industry(Group)Co. ,Ltd. and Wuhan Airline in 2004, marking the beginning of the domestic aircraft financing in China. ①

1.2 Legal Market

Multiple parameters may apply when measuring the maturity of a legal market: the number of law firms, the sectoral groups within a law firm and specialized lawyers. Currently, there is no specialized aviation law firm in China. The banking and finance group of a major law firm often handle the legal business of aircraft financing in China. Three top Chinese law firms have established practice in this field: Han Kun Law Firm, Junhe LLP, and King & Wood Mallesons. ② Ms. Ling Wang, the managing partner of King & Wood Mallesons, is a key figure in the Chinese aircraft financing market. She is one of the few Chinese lawyers who have rich experience in aircraft financing. ③ Besides representing deals, she has also shared her observations by aircraft financing by writing commentaries, for example, on the application of Cape Town Convention

---

① See L. Zhao, "Legal Research on Finance Leasing of Domestically Manufactured Aircrafts", Master's thesis, Northwest University, 2012, p. 33. Also, due to the declaration of China made for the ratification of the Cape Town Convention, the Cape Town Convention does not apply to the internal transaction, which means domestic aircraft financing leasing agreements will be governed by Chinese domestic laws to a great extent, even though not excluding the application of the Cape Town Convention completely.

② See "Top law firms ranking of banking and finance group by IFLR 1000", Accessed https://www.zhihedongfang.com/2017/12/47138, December 19, 2017.

③ See profile of Wang Ling, Accessed http://www.kwm.com/zh/cn/people/wang-ling, December 20, 2017.

in China.[①] Another leading lawyer in aircraft financing in China is Ms. Shu Wang from Han Kun Law Firm. She has represented various stakeholders in aircraft financing, including leasing companies, airlines, and banks.[②] Also, Mr. Zhenfeng Yan, who was the director of legal affairs in Commercial Aircraft Corporation of China (COMAC) is now a partner in Junhe LLP, who has boosted the firm's aviation practice.[③]

2. Governing Laws

The governing laws of aircraft financing in China are multiple layers. The basic characters of laws in this field are as follows. First, there is no specialized law regarding aircraft financing in China. Second, the governing laws in this area cover a broad scope. According to the Chinese categorization of legal departments, there are seven major legal departments in the current legal system.[④] They are criminal law, civil law, procedure law, international law, economic law, environmental law and military law. For aircraft financing, it includes the application of civil law, administrative law, international law and economic law departments. Third, there are two ways to apply an international convention, such as the Cape Town Convention in China: transformation and

---

① See L. Wang and J. Canning, "Aircraft financing in China: are Cape Town protections available for PRC internal transactions?", Accessed http://www.kwm.com/en/au/knowledge/insights/aircraft-financing-china-are-cape-town-protections-available-internal-transactions-20150519, December 20, 2017.

② See profile of Wang Shu, Accessed https://www.hankunlaw.com/professionals/professionalDetail.html? id = 5f4aa842550b97b00156692040330202, December 20, 2017.

③ See profile of Yan Zhenfeng, Accessed http://www.junhe.com/professionals/210, December 19, 2017.

④ See "White Paper of the Construction of Rule of Law in China", Accessed http://www.china.com.cn/policy/fzjs/node_7041734.htm, December 20, 2017.

adoption.① Once applied, the international convention supersedes Chinese domestic law.② Based on the current legal practice in China, the distinction between transformation and adoption depends on the content of the international convention. Generally speaking, if the international convention is governing private legal rights, it is often directly applicable. If the international convention is governing human rights, it has to be transformed into domestic law to be applicable in China.③

2.1 Domestic laws

2.1.1 Civil Laws

China does not have a civil law code at present. The primary law in the civil law system is General Principles of Civil Law. It governs the most fundamental rules in civil legal matters in China. Inevitably, it does not go specifically into a particular area of law, such as aircraft financing. However, for each aircraft financing transaction, there shall be no violation of the General Principles of Civil Law. The second category of law is the Contract Law. Under the current structure of Contract Law, Chapter XIV is Contracts for Finance Lease. It contains thirteen articles governing finance lease relationships. The third category of law is the Property Law. The most related part is Part Four Security Interest in Property. It governs general stipulations of the security interest in the property, interest obtained from the mortgage and interests acquired through the pledge.

The fourth category of law is the Guaranty Law. There are special articles directly related to the aircraft financing, for instance, Art. 42 of the Guaranty Law stipulates that the department responsible for the registration of a mortgaged

---

① See H. Li, *Introduction to Treaty Law*, Beijing, the Law Press, 1988, p. 380.

② See *General Principles of Civil Law* 1987, Art. 142.

③ See J. Zhao, "The Status of International Convention in the Chinese Legal System", *Chinese Journal of Law* 6, 2010, pp. 196 – 197.

aircraft is the registration department for means of transport. ①

2.1.2 Civil Aviation Laws

China has a Civil Aviation Law safeguarding the national sovereignty of territorial airspace and the rights of civil aviation. In the Chapter III Rights of Civil Aircraft, there is a Section Four Lease of Civil Aircraft. There are seven articles under this section governing aircraft leasing. Meanwhile, based on the Civil Aviation Law, China has also enacted the Regulations of the People's Republic of China on Civil Aircraft Rights Registration. Regulation in China belongs to the category of general administrative law. Twenty articles in this regulation are governing the formalities of the aircraft registration.

2.1.3 Other Laws and Regulations

Tax law in China consists of by layers of laws and regulations. State Administration of Tax has issued a Letter on Collecting Stamp Duties Regarding the Aircraft Leasing Contracts 1992. State Administration of Tax and the Ministry of Commerce issued a Circular on Issue Concerning Taxation on the Turnover of the Business Tax of the Financing Leasing in 1999.

Besides general laws, there is a second tier of regulations enacted among cooperation of different departments governing the aircraft financing issues. Provisions on Foreign Investment in Civil Aviation were issued by China Civil Aviation Administration (dissolved), Ministry of Foreign Trade & Economic Cooperation (incl. former Ministry of Foreign Economy & Trade), State Development & Reform Commission (incl. former State Development Planning Commission) in 2002.

① The official English translation can be referred to at the official website of National People's Congress. However, some lower-ranking regulations do not have an official English translation. The Lawinfo website provided by Peking University Law School has offered great help. *See Guaranty Law* 1995, Art. 42.

2.1.4 Judicial Opinion

The Supreme People's Court in China has also contributed by issuing judicial opinions on this matter. Judicial opinions issued by the Supreme People's Court has a huge influence on guiding courts in adjudication in China. In 2014, the Supreme People's Court issued a judicial opinion on the issue of applicable laws of adjudicating cases involving finance leasing contracts.

2.2 International Conventions

2.2.1 Geneva Convention

The first Convention that specifically targeted at the aircraft financing issues is the Geneva Convention① in 1948. It aims at international recognition of the rights in aircraft mostly based on national laws. After the conclusion of the Chicago Convention, the International Civil Aviation Organization (ICAO) is actively strengthening international mandates by acknowledging state interests in the protection of rights in aircrafts. ②

In the summary of the Geneva Convention, it clearly states the purpose of this Convention: "to facilitate the financing for the purchase of aircraft employed in international air services." ③ The Geneva Convention has a limited application in the current aircraft financing transactions due to the restraint of historical background. In 1948, the air industry was dominated by the United States, who was a strong advocate for this Convention. The international legal protection regime on aircraft financing focused on the international recognition of rights

---

① See Geneva Convention on the International Recognition of Rights in Aircraft (Geneva, 19 June 1948) 310 U. N. T. S. 151, *entered into force* 17 *September* 1953.

② See Q. Chen, "Legal Aspects of Aircraft Financing and New Challenges for China", Master's thesis, McGill University, 2008, p. 52.

③ See Administrative Package for Ratification of or Adherence to the Geneva Convention (1948).

created under the domestic law, rather than the creation of any new supranational rights. ①

In addition, in 1948, the People's Republic of China was not even established. The People's Republic of China ratified the Geneva Convention in 2000 with two statements on the non-recognition of the signing of this Convention by the old government and non ex-tempore application in Hong Kong unless otherwise notified. ②

2.2.2 Cape Town Convention and Aircraft Protocol

Cape Town Convention③ is an international convention on international interests in mobile equipment effective in 2006. The Aircraft Protocol④ also became effective in 2006. China ratified both Cape Town Convention and Aircraft Protocol in 2009. ⑤ The relationship between the Convention and the Protocol is illustrated in Art. 6 of the Convention: (a) The Convention and the Protocol shall be interpreted together as a single instrument; (b) If there is any inconsistency between the Convention and the Protocol, the Protocol shall prevail. ⑥

The Cape Town Convention is by far the most important international legal instrument in the aircraft financing industry. The following features determine the ground-breaking status of the Capet Town Convention: first, it creates the concept of "international interest". Under Art. 7 of the Convention, ⑦ an international

---

① See Q. Chen, "Legal Aspects of Aircraft Financing and New Challenges for China", Master's thesis, McGill University, 2008, p. 53.

② Ibid., p. 55.

③ See Cape Town Convention on International Interests in Mobile Equipment (Cape Town, 19 November 2001), 2307 U. N. T. S. 285, entered into force 1 March 2006.

④ See Protocol to the Convention on International Interests in Mobile Equipment (Cape Town, 19 November 2001), 2307 U. N. T. S. 285, entered into force 1 March 2006.

⑤ On 28 October 2008, the Fifth Session of the Eleventh Standing Committee of National People's Congress has approved the Cape Town Convention and the Aircraft Protocol. They became effective on 1 June 2009.

⑥ Cape Town Convention, Art. 6.

⑦ Cape Town Convention, Art. 2(2).

interest can be created through one or more the following channels: a. granted by the chargor under a security agreement; b. vested in a person who is the conditional seller under a title reservation agreement; or c. vested in a person who is the lessor under a leasing agreement. The creation of the international interest is, in essence, a shift of jurisprudence in the protection of interests from a domestic level to an international level. This fundamental change also limits the application of the Geneva Convention in the current and future transactions to a great extent.

Second, the priority rule of the legal interests is straight-forward: a registered interest has priority over any other interest subsequently registered and over an unregistered interested under the Art. 29 of the Cape Town Convention.① To better protect international interests, it also creates a registry for international interests in Ireland called the "Aviareto".②

Third, since the Cape Town Convention is a creditor-oriented convention, it grants many self-remedies when there is adefault. Under the Art. 15 of the Cape Town Convention, there is a restraint for the creditors to conduct in a commercially reasonable manner.③

Forth, another critical aspect of the Cape Town Convention is the insolvency provisions. Art. 11 of the Protocol offers two options for the member states: "hard" or rule-based option and "soft" or discretion-based option.④

The Cape Town Convention is effective in China since June 1st, 2009. However, China has made both opt-in and opt-out declarations when ratifying the

---

① Cape Town Convention, Art. 29.
② See www. aviareto. aero, December 20, 2017.
③ Cape Town Convention, Art. 15.
④ Aircraft Protocol, Art. 11.

Convention. The declarations are made under Art. 39,40,43,50,53 and 54. [①]In particular, the declaration under Art. 50(1) of the Convention stipulates that the Convention shall not apply to a transaction which is an internal transaction in relation to the PRC. [②] This article may limit the application of the Cape Town Convention under the background of the development of domestic aircraft manufacturers. However, this will not exclude the application of the Convention in total, as it is stipulated in Art. 50(2) that the priority provisions will still apply to such transaction. [③]

2.2.3 Application of the Cape Town Convention and the Conflicts

For an international convention to be applicable in a domestic setting, it needs to be accepted by the state either by transformation or adoption. Transformation means to transform the international convention into domestic laws. Adoption means a direct application without any transformation. China does not have a uniformed legislation governing the application of international conventions in a domestic setting. In practice, it has applied both transformation and adoption methods. [④]

Concerning the application of the Cape Town Convention, which is governing civil law rights, the General Principles of Civil Law and Civil Procedural Law have both acknowledged the prioritized application of the international convention. Meanwhile, the most practical way is to modify the

---

① See http://www. unidroit. org/meetings/142-instruments/security-interests/cape-town-convention-mobile-equipment-2001/depositary/declarations-by-contracting-state/463-declarations-lodged-by-the-people-s-republic-of-china-prc-under-the-cape-town-convention-at-the-time-of-the-deposit-of-its-instrument-of-ratification, December 20, 2017.

② Ibid.

③ See See L. Wang and J. Canning, "Aircraft financing in China: are Cape Town protections available for PRC internal transactions?", Accessed http://www. kwm. com/en/au/knowledge/insights/aircraft-financing-china-are-cape-town-protections-available-internal-transactions-20150519, December 20, 2017.

④ See H. Li, *Introduction to Treaty Law*, Beijing, the Law Press, 1988, p. 380.

following conflicting provisions in the domestic laws. Since China has made declarations with regards to the insolvency provisions and self-remedies, there is no direct conflict in these two parts. ① However, the Cape Town Convention has a direct conflict with Chinese domestic laws on enforcement of the right of mortgage. The current Property Law and Guaranty Law follow the same principle of the forbidden of a fluidity contract. Art. 186 of the Property Law stipulates that "before maturity of the debts, the mortgagee may not enter into an agreement with the mortgagor that the mortgaged property shall come under the ownership of the creditor when the debtor defaults." ② Art. 40 of the Guaranty Law has a similar provision. ③ Under the Art. 9(1) of the Cape Town Convention, "at any time after default as provided in Art. 11, the chargee and all the interested persons may agree that ownership of (or any other interest of the chargor in) any object covered by the security interest shall vest in the chargee in or towards satisfaction of the secured obligations". This is a direct conflict with China's domestic legal jurisprudence. Based on the Cape Town Convention, China has to take steps to modify the strict forbidden on the fluidity contract.

Besides the fluidity clause, some scholars also argue that the Property Law and Guaranty Law also have a conflict with the Cape Town Convention on the independence of the security interests in a guaranty contract. ④ Art. 172 of the Property Law stipulates that "... A guarantee contract is an ancillary contract of the principal claim-debt contract. When the principal claim-debt contract is null and void, the guarantee contract shall be null and void accordingly, unless

---

① See S. Peng, "Legal Issues on the Application of Cape Town Convention in China", Master thesis, East China University of Political Science and Law, 2010, p. 27.

② Property Law, Art. 186.

③ Guaranty Law, Art. 40.

④ See S. Mo, "WTO, Cape Town Convention and Improvement of Chinese Law on Aircraft Leasing", 6 *Journal of Beijing Institute of Technology* 13, 2011, p. 84.

otherwise provided for by law. After it is confirmed that a guarantee contract is nullified, the debtor, the guarantor and the creditor who are in fault shall, on the merits of each case, bear civil liability respectively."① However, the Cape Town Convention emphasizes the independence of a registered international interest.

In conclusion, the Property Law and Guaranty Law are two domestic legislation that need substantial modifications to comply with the Cape Town Convention.

3. Case Studies of Aircraft Financing in China

3.1 Export Credit Agency Supported Deals

The consideration in an aircraft financing deal is comparatively heavy. Therefore, the financial condition can be too risky for commercial banks. Some countries have provided export credit finance to airlines so that their orders do not necessarily have to go through commercial markets.② Export credit finance is "either direct financing provided by an export credit agency (ECA) or a guarantee pursuant whereto an ECA assumes the default risk of the airline under loan agreements provided by banks to the airline for the funding of the acquisition of the aircraft."③ In an ECA-supported transaction, it is the sovereign credit of the exporting country that commercial banks are counting on.

In the United States, Export-Import Bank of the United States (Ex-Im) cooperates closely with Boeing-related deals. In Europe, banks deal with their respective ECAs: Compagnie Française d'Assurance pour le Commerce Extérieur

① Property Law, Art. 172.

② See B. Crans, "Chapter 9 Rights in Aircraft", in I. H. Ph. Diederiks-Verschoor and Pablo Mendes de Leon, eds., *An Introduction to Air Law*, Netherlands, Kluwer Law International, 2012, p. 380.

③ Ibid.

(Coface) in France, (now) Euler Hermes Kreditversicherungs-AG (Euler Hermes) in Germany and the Export Credits Guarantee Department (ECGD) in the UK. ①

The first ECA-supported deal in Chinese aviation finance history is a 2011 – 2012 deal between Air China and a Delaware trust entity guaranteed by Export-Import Bank of the United States (US Ex-Im Bank). ② In a series of transactions, Air China leases the Boeing 777 – 300ER aircraft from the Delaware trust entity financed through credit facilities and issuance of bonds guaranteed by the US Ex-Im Bank. This deal has been a milestone for Chinese aircraft financing from two perspectives: first, this deal is the first deal that US Ex-Im Bank has financed Chinese airlines after the ratification of the Cape Town Convention, which sends a signal to the Chinese market that the Cape Town Convention has facilitated aircraft financing transactions especially from a credit security perspective; second, this deal has become formed a model for this kind of Chinese airlines in acquiring wide-bodied Boeing aircraft.

Even though the ECA-supported transaction is a newly developed model in China, it has gone through rapid growth. Recent developments include the China Aircraft Leasing Group Holdings Limited completed its debut aircraft financing backed by a guarantee by UK Export Finance for an Airbus A320 aircraft leased to Air India. ③ The ECA-supported structure is said to enhance the

---

① See J. Wool and A. Jonovic, "Chapter on Export Credit Financing", in Rob Murphy and Nasreen Desai, eds., *Aircraft Financing*, 4th Edition, UK, Euromoney, 2011, p. 93.

② See L. Wang and J. Zhou, "China Aviation Finance Market on the Rise-A Look Back at 2012", Accessed http://www.chinalawinsight.com/2013/01/articles/corporate/china-aviation-finance-market-on-the-rise-a-look-back-at-2012/, December 20, 2017.

③ See D. Gebrial, "China Aircraft Leasing Lands First ECA-backed Financing", Accessed http://www.txfnews.com/News/Article/3831/China-Aircraft-Leasing-lands-its-first-ECA-backed-financing, December 20, 2017.

competitiveness and geographical coverage of the transaction. ①

3.2 East Star Airline Bankruptcy Case

Nevertheless, not all aircraft financing transactions have a happy ending. The East Star Airline case in 2005 tolls a bell as a reminder of potential risks in leasing aircrafts in China. In November 2005, East Star Airline and GECAS signed leasing agreements, which stated the lessor would buy ten new A321/319 as requested by the East Star Airline. ②GECAS ran the risk of signing such a contract with big consideration without any guarantee for the rent provided by banks. However, due to the economic crisis in 2008, the East Star experienced great difficulty in economy turnovers during around 2006 - 2008. Since July 2008, East Star Airline has dragged off in paying rents to GECAS. The Chinese government injected billions of yuan into Air China, China Southern Airlines and China Eastern Airlines, the three major state-owned carriers, to help them ride out the downturn. ③ However, private airlines were less lucky. The bankruptcy proceedings were launched on March 30, 2009, at the request of six creditors, according to the Communications Commission of Wuhan City. GE Commercial Aviation Services, one of the creditors, has recalled all nine aircraft it had leased to the airline. The acknowledgment of the recall rights by the Wuhan court is said to be influenced by the Cape Town Convention since there is no corresponding

---

① See "China Aircraft Leasing Group Completed First ECA Financing for A320 Aircraft Operated by Air India", Accessed http://calc.com.hk/en/Newsinfo.aspx?languageType=3&id=393, December 20, 2017.

② See D. Yu, "A Legal Analysis on Finance Leasing Aircraft—A Case Study of East Star Airline", 2 *Journal of Beijing Univeristy of Aeronautics and Astronautics* 23, 2010, p. 37.

③ See "Chinese Airline Goes Bankrupt with Huge Debts", Accessed http://www.chinadaily.com.cn/china/2009-08/27/content_8625656.htm, December 20, 2017.

rule in the domestic Bankruptcy Law. ①

The tragedy of the East Star Airlinebankruptcy has offered at least three lessons: first, the credit security is crucial in the aircraft financing transactions particularly in China. It is too risky to close a deal purely based on the market confidence at that time rather than solid guarantees from the banks; second, the very nature of an aircraft finance leasing contract is irrevocability, which burdens heavily on the airlines if the business goes beyond the weather as happened on the East Star Airline; third, the application of the Cape Town Convention has provided protection for international lessors, as shown in the recall rights in this case. It is foreseeable that the Cape Town Convention will promote the industry of aircraft finance leasing in China to a greater extent.

4. Proposals for Future Changes

4.1 Normative Adaption

There are two kinds of legislation models in aircraft financing. One is separate legislation such as in the United States. Instead, there are a series of commercial laws governing this area of legal relationships. One is uniform legislation such as in France. There are specified legislations such as leasing law and civil aviation law. ②China does not have a uniform leasing law but does have a civil aviation law. Because of the complexity of the aircraft financing, it is inevitable that multiple layers of laws will be applied in order to close a transaction.

In 2003, the Standing Committee of the People's Congress listed the finance

---

① See S. Mo, "WTO, Cape Town Convention and Improvement of Chinese Law on Aircraft Leasing", 6 *Journal of Beijing Institute of Technology* 13, 2011, p. 83.

② See S. Dong, "Research on Applicable Laws in Aircraft Financing in China", *Legal System and Society* 1, 2015, p. 87.

leasing law in the legislation plan in the People's Congress. In 2005, the draft was finished. However, it was never enacted. ①Ten years have passed, and a lot of new laws have been made, especially the conclusion of the Cape Town Convention. If China is going to make a uniform finance leasing law, the relevant provisions of the Cape Town Convention need to be taken into consideration. However, the most urgent modifications are the conflicting clauses in the Property Law and Guaranty Law.

However, China is setting up its own standard in the aircraft financing industry by making model aircraft financing agreement, which is currently publically seeking advice. ② In this proposed model agreement, there are 22 articles with 8 annexes. ③What has been highlighted is its dispute resolution and applicable law clauses, which specify that "any issue referred to this agreement and this agreement per se will apply the Chinese law and will be interpreted according to the Chinese law." ④ "Any dispute raised by or related to this agreement, both parties shall negotiate amicably; If there is no agreement reached, any party can submit the dispute to the Shanghai International Economy and Trade Arbitration Commission (Shanghai International Aviation Court of Arbitration), and the arbitration will be conducted based on the court's arbitral rules and Chinese law." ⑤Referring cases to the Shanghai International Aviation Court of Arbitration and applying Chinese law will set the tune of China's status in the aircraft financing industry.

---

① See J. Zhao, "The Status of International Convention in the Chinese Legal System", *Chinese Journal of Law* 6, 2010, pp. 196 - 197.

② See "Aircraft Financing Agreement will Have a Chinese Standard", Accessed http://www.legaldaily.com.cn/index/content/2017 - 10/24/content_7366540.htm? node = 20908, December 19, 2017.

③ Ibid.

④ Ibid.

⑤ Ibid.

4.2 Institutional Support

One of the important factors of securing aircraft financing is credit investigation. The State Council issued a Regulation on the Administration of Credit Investigation Industry in 2013. In fact, the People's Bank of China has established a Credit Reference Center for credit investigation for both individuals and enterprises. This can be an effective platform for aircraft financing. Meanwhile, international conventions have also offered an accountable platform to secure transactions, such as the Aviareto.

Moreover, there are growing numbers of Chinese leasing companies in China. They have not occupied the majority of the market, however are worth noting in the future development. Since 2011, the main players are: Bank of China (BOC) Aviation, registered in Singapore; ICBC Financial Leasing Co., Ltd., registered in Tianjin Binhai New District; Changjiang Leasing, Co., Ltd., registered in Tianjin Free Trade District; China Development Bank Leasing Co., Ltd., registered in Shenzhen; China Construction Bank Financial Leasing Co., Ltd., registered in Beijing; China Transportation Bank Financing Leasing Co., Ltd., registered in Shanghai; Minsheng Financial Leasing Co., Ltd., registered in Tianjin Binhai New District; China Merchant Bank Financial Leasing Co., Ltd., registered in Shanghai; Bank of China International Leasing co., Ltd., registered in Shanghai. ①

Since most lessors are state-controlled banks, the supervisory agencies are China Banking Regulatory Commission and the Ministry of Commerce. The Measures for the Administration of Finance Leasing Companies were issued by China Banking Regulatory Commission in 2007. The Measures for the

---

① See S. Mo, "WTO, Cape Town Convention and Improvement of Chinese Law on Aircraft Leasing", 6 *Journal of Beijing Institute of Technology* 13, 2011, p. 80.

Administration of Foreign Capital Lease Industry were issued by the Ministry of Commerce in 2000. Both are effective for governing aircraft financing.

Also, especially with the future development of the domestic aircraft manufacturing, it is worth considering by the Chinese government to establish its own Export Credit Agency. As the facilitative role played by the Ex-Im Bank to the Boeing and the Coface to the Airbus, having a supportive ECA will be important for competition worldwide.

4.3 Professional Training

Currently, there is no specialized aviation law firm in China. Top law firms, such as Han Kun Law Firm, Junhe LLP, and King & Wood Mallesons, have some lawyers from the banking or financing group in charge of aircraft financing transactions. There are also some small firms, such as Long An Law Firm[①] and Zhong Wen Law Firm[②] that declare a practice in this field. Based on the growing business need, it is foreseeable in future there will be growing numbers of aviation lawyers in China. It is possible to foresee that there will be specialized aviation firms in future. To this end, Chinese law schools should also add aircraft financing as their optional course in the curriculum, especially on a master level to equip future lawyers with the professional knowledge.

Conclusion

The legalmarket for aircraft financing is a newly developed field in China. With the ratification of the Cape Town Convention and the growth in aircraft manufacture industry, China will be a huge market for aircraft financing. Legal

---

① See Accessed http://english.longanlaw.com, 20 December, 2017.

② See Accessed http://www.zwlawyer.com/detail/business-57.html, 20 December, 2017.

risks are comparatively high given the consideration of the aircraft financing deal. As shown in the East Star Airline case, it could be lead to a large-scale bankruptcy. However, recent developments in ECA-backed deals have proved China is catching up with the global trend. This paper concludes with the proposed changes in domestic legislation, institutional support as well as professional training. All these will contribute to enhancing the competitiveness of China in the aircraft financing market.

航空法前沿

上海国际航空仲裁院仲裁程序之完善

张婉露[*]

一、引　　言

2014年6月上海国际经济贸易仲裁委员会（上海国际仲裁中心）设立上海国际航空仲裁院，该院是上海国际仲裁中心下设提供国际航空仲裁服务的工作平台。[①] 现今，该院是国际上唯一专注于航空相关仲裁的仲裁机构。该院涉及航空产业领域多种纠纷，包括但不限于航空运输、飞机制造、飞机销售、飞机金融租赁、航空保险、普通航空信托、地面服务和机票代理等。[②] 中国航空运输协会、国际航空运输协会和上海国际仲裁中心联合成立上海航空仲裁院。上海航空仲裁院致力于为解决航空争端提供法律手段。但是，上海航空仲裁院在及时、公正和专业履行

---

* 荷兰莱顿大学航空航天法研究所博士研究生。

① 参见《上海国际航空仲裁院简介》，载上海国际仲裁院网：http://www.shiac.org/Aviation/aboutus_E.aspx?page=2，最后访问日期：2017年4月19日。

② 同上。

其职能方面仍存在一些机构上和实体上亟待解决的问题。

本文将通过以下三方面内容加以介绍:一是争端的管辖权及性质;二是争端适用的准据法;三是第三技术专家的引入。上述问题并非航空仲裁所独有,亦见诸国家之间的仲裁、海洋法仲裁等其他形式的仲裁。本文将根据最近国际仲裁程序中相应内容阐释以上三个问题。进而论及航空纠纷中的一些特殊问题。综上所述,上海航空仲裁院可以考虑通过提升其规格和机制,为高效解决航空争端提供良好环境。

二、航空仲裁程序相关法律问题

国际仲裁是与司法程序并行的一种争端解决机制。① 仲裁参与方在仲裁程序中需要获得绝对的公平和公正,并且要求及时、保密和高效地解决纠纷。② 本文讨论增强仲裁程序的有效性以激活上海国际航空仲裁院,这将使上海国际航空仲裁院成为具有吸引力的解决航空纠纷的平台。

(一)判断航空法律争端存在的意义和方法

仲裁庭的管辖权依据双方协议产生。③ 仲裁庭的设立和正当性直接源于双方授权。争端是否存在,以及是否是法律争端,是研究仲裁庭管辖权范

---

① See C. H. Brower, "The Functions and Limits of Arbitration and Judicial Settlement Under Private and Public International Law", *Duke Journal of Comparative & International Law* 18, 2009, pp. 259 – 309.

② See P. Sands, "The Permanent Court of Arbitration: Remarks on the Celebration of the Centenary of the PCA", Accessed https://pca-cpa. org/wp-content/uploads/sites/175/2016/01/Reflections-on-the-CurrentRelevance-of-the-PCA-Presentation-by-Professor-Philippe-Sands-QC. pdf, July 15, 2017.

③ See L. Ervo, "Party Autonomy and Access to Justice", in A. Jokela, L. Ervo and M. Gräns, eds., *Europeanization of Procedural Law and the New Challenges to Fair Trial*, Groningen, Groningen Europa Law Publishing, 2009, p. 21. R. Stürner and M. Kawano eds., *International Contract Litigation, Arbitration and Judicial Responsibility in Transnational Disputes*, Tübingen, Mohr Siebeck, 2011, p. 147.

围首先要解决的问题。

1. 公共和/或私人争端

上海国际航空仲裁院解决双方为个人或公司的纠纷。该种形式的仲裁为私人纠纷,以区别于国家间的纠纷。①

上海国际航空仲裁院仲裁规则(以下简称《上海仲裁规则》)②明确其涉及的纠纷限于下述两种:一是合同纠纷;二是中国(上海)自贸区财物权利和利益相关的纠纷。③ 上述范围实际上比较局限,尤其是将财物权利和利益限于"与中国(上海)自贸区相关"。该种设计排除了处理其他国家间争端的可能。这会限制上海国际航空仲裁院作为航空纠纷解决平台先驱者的定位。

更为重要的是除了私人争端,航空领域存在其他形式的航空仲裁,例如,一是国家间仲裁;二是混合仲裁,即国家和个人间的仲裁。④ 上述两种仲裁的区别比较模糊,因为在多数情况下航空的纠纷包含公共和私人因素,或者诉讼程序在公共和私人间转换。航权和时刻便是著例,因为它们涉及公共机构和商业航空公司。上海国际航空仲裁院可以考虑一并办理上述案件。

---

① See G. van Harten, "The Public-Private Distinction in the International Arbitration of Individual Claims Against the State", *International and Comparative Corporate Law Quarterly* 56, 2007, pp. 371 – 394. J. G. Merrills, *International Dispute Settlement*, 4th ed., Cambridge, Cambridge University Press, 2005, pp. 107 – 108.

② 《中国(上海)自由贸易试验区仲裁规则》,2015年1月1日起施行,载上海国际仲裁院官方网:http://www.shiac.org/Aviation/arbitrate_rules_detail_E.aspx? id = 14,最后访问日期:2017年4月22日。

③ 《中国(上海)自由贸易试验区仲裁规则》第1条规定:"上海国际经济贸易仲裁委员会为公正、专业、高效地解决涉及中国(上海)自由贸易试验区的合同和其他财产权益纠纷,根据《中华人民共和国仲裁法》和有关法律的规定制定本规则。"

④ See J. G. Merrills, *International Dispute Settlement*, 4th ed., Cambridge, Cambridge University Press, 2005, pp. 108 – 110.

机场时刻的可用性、时刻的分配和时刻的分布是航空法中重要的部分。[①] 规则制定者面临的困境是航权由双边条约调整,机场时刻则由国家或区域(欧盟)机构和国际航空运输协会调整。但是航权是由经由国家间航空服务协议交易或协商确定,该权利仅在指定航空公司进入许可国境内机场时才可实现。因此航权和机场时刻分配存在实际关联,航权许可进入一国领空而时刻分配许可进入机场。对于机场时刻的限制将有可能损害航空权的行使。

如果两国间基于自由贸易,实现了不受限制的国际航空运营服务协议,即"开放领空协议"。[②] 那么对于机场时刻的限制,如严重的航班延误和取消,将损害两国间达成的国际航空服务的自由贸易。因为暂停空域的使用将损害承运人从事国际航空服务的公正机会以及不正当地影响每家航空公司的运营。[③] 因此,航空公司或其所在国应该可以通过双边航空协议中公平竞争权条款寻求救济。

从程序上讲,提前告知航空公司可能的时刻问题是正当程序的一部分。[④] 从实体上讲,如果不能使用预定的时刻,私人公司应当可以向有关机

---

① See P. Mendes de Leon, "A Multifunctional Approach Towards Slot Allocation", *Zeitschrift für Luft-und Weltraumrecht* 62, 2013, pp. 553 – 578. C. Naumann, "New Proposal to Amend the System of Airport Slot Allocation in the European Union", *Air and Space Law* 37, 2012, pp. 185 – 211. K. Brecke, "Airport Slot Allocation: Quo Vadis, EU?", *Air and Space Law* 36, 2011, pp. 183 – 200. See also, ICAO, "Slot Allocation", ATConf/6 – WP/11, 10/12/12. Council Regulation (EEC) No. 95/93 of 18 January 1993 on common rules for the allocation of slots at community airports.

② On "Open Skies", see P. Mendes de Leon, "Before and After the Tenth Anniversary of the Open Skies Agreement Netherlands-US of 1992", *Air and Space Law* 27, No. 4/5, 2002, pp. 280 – 314. B. F. Havel, "A Substantive and Procedural Critique of the US Open Skies Policy", in Pablo Mendes de Leon ed., *From Lowlands to High Skies: A Multilevel Jurisdictional Approach Towards Air Law: Essays in Honour of John Balfour*, Leiden, Martinus Nijhoff Publishers, 2013, pp. 1 – 18.

③ See R. Abeyratne, *Competition and Investment in Air Transport*, The Hague, Springer International Publishing, 2016, pp. 83 – 85. P. Fitzgerald, *A Level Playing Field for Open Skies: The Need for Consistent Aviation Regulation*, The Hague, Eleven International Publishing, 2016, pp. 89 – 136. See also ICAO Secretariat, "Existing ICAO Policy and Guidance Material on Fair Competition", ATRP/13 – IP/1, 30/6/15. ICAO Doc 9587, *Policy and Guidance Material on the Economic Regulation of International Air Transport*, 4th edition provisional version, 15 August 2016.

④ See G. della Cananea, *Due Process of Law beyond the State: Requirements of Administrative Procedure*, Oxford, Oxford University Press, 2016, chapter 8. R. McCarl, "ICSID Jurisdiction over International Mass Investment Arbitrations: Due Process and Default Rules", *Stanford Journal of International Law* 51, 2015, pp. 173 – 194.

构寻求补偿,其法律基础是期待利益的落空。[①] 那么这种公共和私人混合的纠纷能否被提交至上海国际航空仲裁院?

这一问题会给中国国内交通管理带来特殊的影响。[②] 繁复的、不合理的延误已经证实时刻的可用性和有效性并不能让人满意。[③] 鉴于此,航空公司和乘客间长期存在对于航班延误的不满。[④] 中国的立法者一直以来积极致力于颁布管理时刻的法规,如《航班正常管理规定》和《航班延误取消原因确认工作程序》。[⑤] 这些法规 2017 年 1 月正式生效。在法规生效的同时,却没有一个合适的平台解决将来可能的公共私人混合型纠纷。

应该允许将这些争端提交至上海国际航空仲裁院解决,尤其是外国航空公司和中国监管机构间涉及运输权和机场时刻的纠纷。也就是说,上海国际航空仲裁院需要将其管辖权从仲裁规则第 1 条的范围扩展至混合仲裁。通过这种方式,航空争端不必诉诸外交渠道。这将带来两项优势:一是争端解决的时间将大大缩短,这是因为可以通过更加高效的仲裁解决;二是相比于外交渠道的解决,仲裁程序中将最大限度地排除政治因素的影响。这将使航空运输争端解决进入良性发展快车道。

---

① See A. Brown, "Justifying Compensation for Frustrated Legitimate Expectations", *Law and Philosophy* 30, 2011, pp. 699 – 728. C. R. Campbell, "House of Cards: the Relevance of Legitimate Expectations Under Fair and Equitable Treatment Provisions in Investment Treaty Law", *Journal of International Arbitration* 30, 2013, pp. 361 – 379. F. Dupuy and P-M. Dupuy, "What to Expect from Legitimate Expectations? A Critical Appraisal and Look into the Future of the 'Legitimate Expectations' Doctrine in International Investment Law", in M. A. Raouf et al., *Festschrift Ahmed Sadek El-Kosheri: from the Arab World to the Globalization of International Law and Arbitration*, Alphen aan den Rijn, Wolters Kluwer, 2015, pp. 273 – 298.

② 2016 年 12 月,中国与澳大利亚签署"开放天空"协定("Open Sky" agreement),载 http://australianaviation. com. au/2016/12/australia-signs-open-a-skies-agreement-with-china/, April 29, 2016。

③ See Justin Bergman, "This is why China's airports are a nightmare", Accessed http://www. bbc. com/capital/story/20160420-this-is-why-chinas-airports-are-a-nightmare, April 19, 2017.

④ See Justin Bergman, "This is why China's airports are a nightmare", Accessed http://www. bbc. com/capital/story/20160420-this-is-why-chinas-airports-are-a-nightmare, April 19, 2017.

⑤ 中国民用航空局:《航班正常管理规定》,2017 年 7 月 23 日发布,2017 年 1 月 1 日正式实施。中国民用航空局运输司:《民航局关于印发航班延误取消原因确认工作程序的通知》,2016 年 12 月 6 日发布。

2. 政治/法律争端

虽然上海国际航空仲裁院可以解决公共和私人这种混合型争端,但是其中涉及的政治和法律因素则较难解决。仲裁裁决基于法律作出,法律争端的前提是确有管辖权。这主要取决于《上海仲裁规则》的语言表述。①

争端中的政治因素可能会因争端中并不存在法律争端从而阻碍仲裁庭的管辖权。② 在航空领域,多数纠纷通过协商解决,并且由航空领域交易双方的实力或一方强制力决定。③ 不得不承认的是航空纠纷多数是通过非法律途径解决的。

因此,航空纠纷的特殊性就在于:首先,争端是否会因为含有政治因素而导致无法仲裁?其次,如何确定是否存在法律问题?毕竟上述两个问题归结

---

① 例如,该规则示范仲裁条款一:"凡因本合同引起的或与本合同有关的任何争议,均应提交上海国际经济贸易仲裁委员会仲裁"。参见上海国际仲裁院网:http://www. shiac. org/Aviation/aboutus_E. aspx? page =2,最后访问日期:2017 年 4 月 19 日。

② See generally S. Gent and M. Shannon, "The Effectiveness of International Arbitration and Adjudication: Getting into a Bind", *Journal of Politics* 72, 2010, p. 366; S. M. Mitchell and P. R. Hensel, "International Institutions, and Compliance with Agreements", *American Journal of Political Science* 51, 2007, p. 721; T. L. Allee, and P. K. Huth, "Legitimizing Dispute Settlement: International Legal Rulings as Domestic Political Cover", 2 *American Political Science Review* 100, 2006, pp. 219 – 234; B. Simmons, "Capacity, Commitment, and Compliance: International Institutions and Territorial Disputes", *Journal of Conflict Resolution* 46, 2002, p. 829; F. Cede, "The Settlement of International Disputes by Legal Means—Arbitration and Judicial Settlement", in J. Bercovitch et al., *The Sage Handbook of Conflict Resolution*, London, SAGE Publications Ltd., 2009, pp. 358 – 359.

③ P. Dempsey, "P. Flights of Fancy and Fights of Fury: Arbitration and Adjudication of Commercial and Political Disputes in International Aviation", *Georgia Journal of International and Comparative Law* 32, 2004, pp. 231 – 306. See also P. Manzini and A. Masutti, "The Application of the EU ETS System to the Aviation Sector: From Legal Disputes to International Retaliations?", *Air and Space Law* 37, 2012, pp. 307 – 324. R. Abeyratne, "The settlement of commercial aviation disputes under the General Agreement on Trade in Services and the ICAO Council: a comparative analysis", in Ernst-Ulrich Petersmann ed., *International trade law and the GATT/WTO dispute settlement system*, The Hague, Kluwer Law International, 1997, pp. 375 – 411. I. Diederiks-Verschoor, "The Settlement of Aviation Disputes", *Annuals of Air and Space Law* 20, 1995, 335 – 341. T. C. Atherton and Trudie-Ann Atherton, "The Resolution of International Civil Aviation Disputes", *Journal of International Arbitration* 9, 1992, pp. 105 – 122. J. P. Griffin, "A Proposal for Mid-Atlantic Tribunal to Resolve UK-US Aviation Disputes", *Journal of International Arbitration* 4, 1987, pp. 167 – 173.

为管辖权问题和行使管辖权问题的区别。这一问题在学界引发广泛讨论,"管辖权之管辖权"或"决定管辖权的管辖权"。①

国际纠纷解决机制使用了"可裁决性"(justiciability)这一概念。② 国际法院认为法律问题本身如果包含政治因素并不能剥夺其作为法律问题的性质,进而使国际法院丧失管辖权。国际法院不能拒绝承认某一需要其履行司法职能解决问题本身所存在的法律性。③ 一般来说,国家间航空争端会涉及政治因素或影响,因为它可能涉及一国的重大利益或荣誉。当有纠纷出现时,国家之间一般也会通过国际民航组织理事会(ICAO Council)④进行协商解决。⑤

值得注意的是,《芝加哥公约》第 84 条规定,如果缔约方不接受理事会的

---

① See generally for instance, M. Boucaron-Nardetto, *Le principe competence-competence en droit de l' arbitrage*, Presses universitaires d' Aix – Marseille, 2013. Galina Zukova, "Lettonie: le principe 'competence – competence' n' exclut pas le recours aux tribunaux etatiques pour statuer sur la validite de la clause compromissoire", *dans Les cahiers de l' arbitrage* 3, 2015, pp. 493 – 503.

② According to Lauterpacht, "it is the refusal of the State to submit the dispute to judicial settlement, and not the intrinsic nature of the controversy, which makes it political". H. Lauterpacht, *The Function of Law in the International Community*, London, Clarendon Press, 1933, pp. 147 – 148. See also, E. McWhinney, "Judicial settlement of disputes: jurisdiction and justiciability", in *Recueil des Cours de L' académie de Droit International de la Haye*, 1990, pp. 157 – 191. D. French et al., eds., *International Law and Dispute Settlement: New Problems and Techniques*, Oxford, Hart Publishing Ltd., 2010, pp. 345 – 388.

③ 国际法院"威胁使用或使用核武器的合法性"咨询意见(*Legality of the Threat or Use of Nuclear Weapons, Advisory Opinion*), Accessed http://www. icj-cij. org/files/case-related/95/095-19960708-ADV-01-00-EN. pdf., p. 234, para. 13. M. Koskenniemi, "The Function of Law in the International Community: 75 Years After", *British Yearbook of International Law* 79, 2008, p. 1. 参见优素福法官(Judge Yusuf)在"关于停止核军备竞赛的协商义务"一案中的反对意见(*Obligations Concerning Negotiations Relating to Cessation of the Nuclear Arms Race and to Nuclear Disarmament, Marshall Islands v. United Kingdom*), Accessed http://www. icj-cij. org/docket/files/160/19202. pdf。

④ 国际民用航空组织是一个联合国专门机构,于 1944 年创建,旨在对《国际民用航空公约》(《芝加哥公约》)的行政和治理方面进行管理。载 http://www. icao. int/about-icao/Pages/default. aspx,最后访问日期:2017 年 4 月 22 日。

⑤ ICAO Doc 9587, *Policy and Guidance Material on the Economic Regulation of International Air Transport*, 4th edition provisional version, 15 August, 2016.

决定,可以向仲裁庭提出上诉。[①]上海航空仲裁院或许可以作为听取这类纠纷的"上诉机构"。因此,有必要探讨如何识别争端中的法律问题,并对这些问题予以管辖。

早在1927年年初,关于如何界定"争端",常设国际法院(Permanent Court of International Justice,PCIJ)在"马弗若麦蒂斯巴勒斯坦特许案"中提出,争端是"对法律或事实的分歧,或者是两个国家/国际组织之间有关法律观点或者利益的冲突"。[②]

然而,在2016年的马绍尔群岛案件中(Marshall Islands),国际法院脱离了以前关于管辖权的裁决,认为"争端的存在在于,根据证据证明被告知道,或不可能不知道,其意见被原告'积极反对'(positively opposed)"。[③] 托姆卡(Tomka)法官和克劳福德(Crawford)法官持不同意见,并且批评该论述。这个新标准可能会削弱国际法院在管辖权问题上的话语权,因为根据其逻辑,存在一个客观的门槛来确定当事双方之间是否有争端。这与传统上由国际法院在个案中决定是否已经有争端的做法相矛盾。

例如,就航空争端而言,如果一国拒绝允许某些航班飞越,可能违反《芝加哥公约》第6条。被飞越的国家可以主张,被飞越国保留要求飞机获得特别许可或其他授权的权利。这种许可是由国家自行决定的,国家不能意识到这样的决定将受到飞机的"积极反对"。因此,如果采用马绍尔群岛判决的

---

① 原文为,"If any disagreement between two or more contracting States relating to the interpretation or application of this Convention and its Annexes cannot be settled by negotiation, it shall, on the application of any State concerned in the disagreement, be decided by the Council... Any contracting State may, subject to Article 85, appeal from the decision of the Council to an ad hoc arbitral tribunal agreed upon with the other parties to the dispute or to the Permanent Court of International Justice. Any such appeal shall be notified to the Council within sixty days of receipt of notification of the decision of the Council"。

② 常设国际法院,"马弗若麦蒂斯巴勒斯坦特许案"(*Mavrommatis Palestine Concessions, Greece v. Great Britain*), Jurisdiction, PCIJ Rep Series A No. 2。

③ 国际法院,"关于停止核军备竞赛的协商义务"案(*Obligations Concerning Negotiations Relating to Cessation of the Nuclear Arms Race and to Nuclear Disarmament, Marshall Islands v. United Kingdom*),载 http://www.icj-cij.org/files/case-related/158/158-20161005-JUD-01-00-EN.pdf, p. 270, para. 34, 最后访问日期:2017年4月2日。

标准,则几乎没有适格的航空争端。

航空争端的法律解决途径如此之少,有多种原因。[①] 这里要指出的是,与航空争端法律解决途径有关的任何发展,本质上都是航空界真正希望更多的航空纠纷通过法律途径来解决。也就是说,如果航空界真的希望争端交由仲裁等法律途径解决,办法和手段总是有的。例如,国家间双边协议可以约定通过仲裁解决争端。

(二)国际航空仲裁中准据法的选择与适用

仲裁规则,如《上海仲裁规则》和《国际航空运输协会仲裁规则》,[②]是"程序法"(*lex arbitri*)。它适用于仲裁及其外部程序问题。缔约方有绝对的自由来界定程序法和修改这些仲裁规则。只要尊重公平的基本原则(*audi alterem partem*),就可以按照双方的约定便利行事。

与程序法不同,法律适用是另一个重要问题。在"法律适用条款"中,双方当事人共同选择适用于其协议的法,可以是国际法也可以是国内法。它涉及仲裁庭"解释和适用"法律的能力范围。

如果双方在合同/双边协议中没有具体规定适用法律的争端解决条款,仲裁庭适用什么法律? 按照《上海仲裁规则》,"仲裁庭应当根据事实,依'法'公正合理地作出裁决"。

相比之下,《国际航空运输协会仲裁规则》第 18 条规定:"仲裁庭应确定适用于案情的法律,除非双方达成一致。"这种做法可以很好地避免了法律适用方面的争端,并将自由裁量权都提交给仲裁庭。这也意味着仲裁员可能更多地承担友好调解人的角色(*amiable compositeur*),不用严格地适用某些具

---

① P. Dempsey, "P. Flights of Fancy and Fights of Fury: Arbitration and Adjudication of Commercial and Political Disputes in International Aviation", *Georgia Journal of International and Comparative Law* 32, 2004, pp. 231 – 306.

② 参见《国际航空运输协会仲裁规则》(IATA Arbitration Rules. 1999 International Air Transport Association), 载 https://www.iata.org/whatwedo/workgroups/Documents/legal/iata-arbitration-rules.pdf,最后访问日期:2017 年 4 月 22 日。

体的法律,只要找到当事人双方同意的解决办法即可。①

如果适用《上海仲裁规则》,其第 55 条中的"法"包括哪些,如何确定呢?② 该"法"是指国际法,一般法律原则还是仅仅是国内法? 在这个问题上,爱尔兰和英国有关海洋环境保护的仲裁案(OSPAR Arbitration)的裁决颇有启发性。③ 法律适用问题,取决于当事双方如何制定合同/双边协议的法律适用条款。

载有仲裁协议或仲裁条款(compromissory clause)的合同/双边协议本身适用于争端解决。实质性的权利义务首先可以在合同/双边协议本身中找到。其次,如果合同的法律适用条款提到了"国际法",则仲裁庭可以适用其他相关公约,习惯国际法甚至一般法律原则。也就是说,有关国际条约所规定的权利义务将适用,除非双方之间有特别安排。④

由此而来的一个问题是,仲裁庭对如何"解释"可能有不同的理解。例如,在飞机融资纠纷中,由于疏忽,双方可能不会对某些条款作出具体定义。如果他们不是《开普敦公约》⑤缔约国,但是某些有疑义的概念在《开普敦公约》中有所定义,仲裁法庭可否参照《开普敦公约》第 1 条定义解释双方的合同/双边协议?

这个问题涉及相关的协议和实践是否可以用来解释当事人双方的协议,

---

① J-F Poudret and S. Besson, *Comparative Law of International Arbitration*, London, Sweet & Maxwell, 2007, p. 623. J. Lew ed., *Contemporary Problems in International Arbitration*, The Hague, Springer Netherlands, 1987, p. 70.

② 《国际航空运输协会仲裁规则》第 18 条;《上海仲裁规则》第 55 条。

③ *Ireland v. United Kingdom*(*OSPAR Arbitration*), 资料来源:https://pcacases.com/web/view/34,最后访问日期:2017 年 4 月 10 日。

④ *Ireland v. United Kingdom*(*OSPAR Arbitration*), final award,资料来源:https://pcacases.com/web/view/34,最后访问日期:2017 年 4 月 10 日。

⑤ 《移动设备国际利益公约》, Convention on International Interests in Mobile Equipment, 2307 U. N. T. S. 285; UN Doc. No. A/AC. 105/C. 2/2002/CRP. 3(2001)。

在理论界已经争论很久。① 很明显,如果允许的话,法庭将根据其他协议或惯例向现在增加实质性义务。通过参考后续协议或惯例对一个协议中的条款进行解释,可能对双方造成额外的义务负担并超出当事人预期,因为各方在缔结合同时可能没有设想到这些实质性的义务。这就是所谓的"额外义务"。②

此外,如果当事方在仲裁协议中提到"争端应当按照国际法决定",可以极大地扩大仲裁庭的管辖权,这意味着仲裁庭可以就是否违反其他国际条约作出裁决。③ 原因在于,如果当事人如此宽泛地设定法律适用条款,则有理由推断他们可以接受仲裁庭的管辖权可以扩张到合同/条约以外。

因此,如果当事方打算把法庭的管辖权限制到合同/双边协议本身,必须谨慎起草适用的法律条款。仲裁协议/条款必须与实体法条款相联系,例如,法律适用条款写明"仲裁庭应按照本合同/双边协议的规定……做出裁决"。④

回到《上海仲裁规则》第55条,该条规定适用法律为"依法"。这个"法"的外延可能是非常全面的,法庭可以引用超出合同或双边协议书写的其他有关规范。因此,制定妥协条款的关键不仅在于限制法庭的管辖权,而且还限

① Report of the International Law Commission, Sixth-seventh session, A/70/10, 2015, chap. VIII, § § 118 – 128, pp. 84 – 103; Report of the International Law Commission, Sixty-sixth session, A/69/10, 2014, chap. VII, § 76 (excerpt), pp. 205 – 217 (Commentary on Draft Conclusion 10, 'Decisions adopted within the framework of a Conference of State Parties'); Report of the International Law Commission, Sixty-fifth session, A/68/10, 2013, chap. IV, § 39 (excerpt), pp. 42 – 48. (Commentary on Draft conclusion 5, 'Attribution of subsequent practice'). See also WTO, *United States-Measures Affecting the Production and Sale of Clove Cigarettes*, Appellate Body Report, WT/DS406/AB/R, 4 April 2012, pp. 83 – 101, paras. 237 – 297. A. Bianchi, D. Peat and M. Windsor eds., *Interpretation in International Law*, Oxford, Oxford University Press, 2015. Georg Nolte ed., *Treaties and Subsequent Practice*, Oxford, Oxford University Press, 2013.

② C. Adam, *The Politics of Judicial Review: Supranational Administrative Acts and Judicialized Compliance Conflict in the EU*, London, Palgrave Macmillan UK, 2016, p. 35.

③ *Ireland v. United Kingdom* (*OSPAR Arbitration*), final award, 载 https://pcacases.com/web/view/34, 最后访问日期:2017年4月10日。

④ 《东北大西洋海洋环境保护公约》, The Convention for the Protection of the Marine Environment of the North-East Atlantic (the "OSPAR Convention"), 第2条和第9条。

制适用法律的范围。如果各方有宽泛的妥协条款,仲裁庭可以裁决争端的许多方面。

总之,按照《上海仲裁规则》,除了当事人之间的合同/双边条约,上海航空仲裁院可以适用的一般原则和习惯国际法,除非双方之间约定排除。

(三)国际航空仲裁中专家报告的法律效力

航空争端解决中,专家对技术问题的评估是不可或缺的。这种情况可能需要进行法律和技术的双重考量。航空专门知识只能来自经过适当培训的技术专家,帮助仲裁庭澄清面前事实的复杂性。仅仅经过法律训练的仲裁员可能无法对复杂的技术证据进行充分评估和权衡。

仲裁员被设定,应该知道相关的适用规则和事实,如果不知道,就应该尽量去发现事实(*jura novit curia* doctrine)。[①] 因此,仲裁实践中,专家参与是非常频繁的。例如,在"莱茵铁路案"中,各方设立了一个技术专家委员会;[②]在"圭亚那苏里南争端"中,法庭任命了一名独立的水文专家。[③]

关于在法律程序中如何认定科学技术事实,有三个理论:(1)内部认定;

---

① J. Verhoeven, "Jura novit curia et le juge international", in P-M Dupuy et al., eds., *Common Values in International Law, Essays in Honour of Christian Tomuschat*, Kehl, N P Engel Verlag, 2006, pp. 635 - 653. See for some qualification of this idea, see ICJ, *Asylum (Colombia/Peru)*, 20 November 1950, ICJ Report, pp. 226 - 277; ICJ, *Rights of Nationals of the United States of America in Morocco (France v United States of America)* 27 August 1952, ICJ Report, 1952, p. 200. See also ICJ, *Fisheries Jurisdiction (Federal Republic of Germany v. Iceland)*, 25 July, 1974, ICJ Report, 1974, p. 181, para. 18.

② Award in the Arbitration regarding the Iron Rhine ("Ijzeren Rijn") Railway between the Kingdom of Belgium and the Kingdom of the Netherlands, decision of 24 May, 2005. Accessed http://legal.un.org/riaa/cases/vol_XXVII/35 - 125.pdf, April 20, 2017.

③ Award in the arbitration regarding the delimitation of the maritime boundary between Guyana and Suriname, Award of 17 September 2007—Sentence arbitrale relative à la délimitation de la frontière maritime entre le Guyana et le Surinam, Sentence du 17 septembre 2007. Accessed http://legal.un.org/riaa/cases/vol_XXX/1 - 144.pdf, April 20, 2017.

(2)私人认定;(3)外包认定。[①]考虑到航空仲裁员可能无法在内部确定所有事实,他们通常需要回答各方和/或专家证明的事实。事实的认定通常需要外部专家的协助。

1.《国际航空运输协会仲裁规则》

根据《国际航空运输协会仲裁规则》,任命专家有以下规则:(1)在仲裁员任命阶段,国际航协的总干事可以任命他认为合适的任何专家,该决定是终局的;[②](2)庭审期间,仲裁庭可以任命1名或多名专家,界定其职权范围。仲裁庭可以收取他们的书面报告进行书面审查,也可以在当事双方出席或不出席的情况下传唤专家听取意见。[③]

《国际航空运输协会仲裁规则》非常灵活,它没有具体规定如何在程序中利用专家的意见/报告。尤为关键的是,各方是否可以对专家报告发表评论?此外,如果一方不认可专家小组,他是否可以质疑该专家,甚至任命自己的专家,这些问题仍然是有争议的。

值得注意的是,如果仲裁庭在没有当事人出席的情况下接受专家报告和/或听取专家意见,这将引起"幽灵专家"(*expert fantômes*)的问题,[④]可能剥夺了当事人的知情权而且有程序不够公正透明的问题。如果争端只涉及

---

① For details, see J. D' Aspremont and M. M. Mbengue, "Strategies of Engagement with Scientific Fact-Finding in International Adjudication", *Journal of International Dispute Settlement* 5, 2014, pp. 240 – 272. M. Kamto, "Les moyens de preuve devant la Cour internationale de Justice à la lumière de quelques affaires récentes portées devant elle", *German Yearbook of International Law* 49, 2007, pp. 259 – 292; K. Del Mar, "Weight of Evidence Generated through Intra-Institutional Fact-Finding before the International Court of Justice", *Journal of International Dispute Settlement* 2, 2011, pp. 393 – 415; A. Mawdsley, "Evidence before the International Court of Justice", in R. St John MacDonald ed., *Essays in honour of Wang Tieya*, Dordrecht, Martinus Nijhoff Publishers, 1994, pp. 533 – 550; M. W. Mouton, *The Impact of Science on International Law*, The Hague, Kluwer Law International, 1999, pp. 210 – 227.

② 《国际航空运输协会仲裁规则》第12条。

③ 《国际航空运输协会仲裁规则》第17条。

④ M. M. Mbengue, "Scientific Fact-finding at the International Court of Justice: An Appraisal in the Aftermath of the Whaling Case", *Leiden Journal of International Law* 29, 2016, pp. 529 – 550. J. D' Aspremont and M. M. Mbengue, "Strategies of Engagement with Scientific Fact-Finding in International Adjudication", *Journal of International Dispute Settlement* 5, 2014, pp. 240 – 272.

零星技术问题,这种方法没有问题。[①] 然而,航空争端通常与复杂的技术问题相互交织在一起,因此专家报告可能成为事实调查的重点,从而对案情审议产生重大影响。剥夺各方对专家报告的评论能力可能是一种省时的做法,但有违反程序正义之虞。[②]

2.《上海仲裁规则》

相比之下,《上海仲裁规则》规定了更多细节。总之,专家可以通过几种方式参与仲裁:(1)法庭可以咨询或任命专家,就其认为必要的案件的具体问题进行澄清;(2)缔约方可以共同任命一名专家;如果失败,仲裁庭应当作出委任;(3)专家意见转交各方,当事人可以对报告发表意见;(4)应任何一方的要求,经仲裁庭批准后,专家或评估人可在听证会上听取并作证。[③]

各方有两个阶段对专家报告发表评论。随着书面报告的传递,第二个口头阶段值得关注。因为它为小组和各方提供了解释科学论证基础的概念、方法和原则的机会,从而提高了他们对案件技术问题的了解。

一个潜在的问题是,这种书面和口头交流程序可能不适当地拖延诉讼程序,从而违反了仲裁作为迅速的争端解决方法的性质。但是,上述程序仅仅在当事人没有意思自治的情况下启动,如果当事人将为了快速解决争端明确排除该种程序,则当事人意思自治优先。

关于当事人任命专家,《上海仲裁规则》的中英文之间有些不一致。英文版本指出,"这样的'一名'专家或评估人员可能由双方共同任命",[④]而中文版没有规定各方可以任命的专家人数。因此,目前还不清楚有多少专家在一个案件中可以被任命,以及各方是否有可能任命自己的专家,并向法庭提交各自的报告。到目前为止,没有任何判例来帮助我们了解程序是如何实践的。

---

① 乌拉圭河纸浆厂案,*Pulp Mills on the River Uruguay* (*Argentina v. Uruguay*), Joint Dissenting Opinion of Judge Al Khasawneh and Judge Bruno Simma, Accessed http://www. icjcij. org/docket/files/135/15879. pdf, pp. 109 - 117, 20 April, 2010。

② 同上。

③ 《上海仲裁规则》第 46 条。

④ 《上海仲裁规则》第 46.2 条。

如果双方的专家得出了显著不同的结论，法庭是否可以任命另一位专家进行终局认定。该做法在“圭亚那苏里南争端”中得到实践，各方不同意彼此的专家，后来的法庭必须任命第三专家。① 最后法庭任命的专家报告赢得了各方的认可，之后被法庭通过。类似的程序可考虑引入上海航空仲裁。

值得注意的是，专家报告应该只有一份，不应该把专家当作律师，对于事实问题进行辩论。原因是专家根据科学技术知识及其个人经验处理事实问题，而不是法律事实认定。②

随着航空技术的逐步提高，上海航空仲裁院会处理与复杂的航空技术相关的争端。在这方面，国际仲裁实践积累了很多法律技术实践，值得借鉴。

三、结　　论

设立上海航空仲裁院作为航空争端解决的专门机构，这在中国和国际航空历史上是一件具有里程碑意义的重要事件。机场时刻的可用性、时刻的分配和时刻的分布争端中的法律争端，应被纳入上海国际航空仲裁院的管辖范围。在准据法方面，除了当事人之间的合同/双边条约，上海航空仲裁院可以适用的一般原则和习惯国际法。关于专家报告，报告是专家根据科学技术知识及其个人经验对于事实问题的阐释，如果双方的专家得出了显著不同的结论，仲裁庭应该可以任命另一位专家进行终局认定。考虑到航空争端的特殊性，仲裁院可考虑进一步完善其规则，以提高效率。这种开放和创新的姿态一定会帮助这个年轻的机构迎接即将到来的挑战。

---

① Award in the arbitration regarding the delimitation of the maritime boundary between Guyana and Suriname, Award of 17 September 2007 – Sentence arbitrale relative à la délimitation de la frontière maritime entre le Guyana et le Surinam, Sentence du 17 septembre 2007. Accessed http://legal. un. org/riaa/cases/vol_XXX/1 – 144. pdf, p. 20, April 20, 2017.

② 乌拉圭河纸浆厂案, Joint Dissenting Opinion of Judge Al Khasawneh and Judge Bruno Simma, *Pulp Mills on the River Uruguay* (*Argentina v. Uruguay*), April 20, 2010, Accessed http://www. icjcij. org/docket/files/135/15879. pdf, para. 168。

亚太民航委员会的构建问题：国际组织法的视角

赵劲松*

60多年前的亚非万隆会议是亚非两大洲历史上的一个重要里程碑，具有伟大的国际意义和深远影响。亚非会议高举独立、和平、友好与合作的旗帜，形成了举世闻名的万隆精神。这个精神贯穿于会议所通过的各项决议之中，并产生了深远的影响。1955年4月周恩来总理率领中国代表团出席了亚非万隆会议，他在万隆会议上所展示的大智大勇、顾全大局的气度、非凡的领袖魅力，以及为会议成功作出的巨大贡献赢得了与会的各国代表和国际舆论的高度评价。万隆会议后，我国的对外关系打开了一个新局面，出现了一个外国同我国建交的高潮，在中国外交史上写下了辉煌篇章，同时也为开辟国际关系新时代做出了宝贵贡献。2015年4月24日国家主席习近平与来自亚洲、非洲和其他地区的国家领导人一

* 中国民航科学技术研究院法规标准研究所副研究员，主要从事国际法和国际航空法研究。

起前往印度尼西亚万隆,纪念万隆会议召开60周年。在纪念大会上,习近平同印度尼西亚总统佐科和斯威士兰国王姆斯瓦蒂三世共同签署《2015万隆公报》,将进一步推动亚非发展中国家合作,合作的内容以尊重国家主权、独立、平等、不附加任何政治条件、不干涉别国内政、互惠互利等为指导原则,这些原则能有效地促进和维护国际社会的和平与安全。此外,经济、社会和文化等领域的合作也有助于亚非国家共同繁荣。60多年来,中国一直都是万隆精神的践行者。今天,中国提出"一带一路"倡议以及设立受到诸多国家和地区支持的亚洲基础设施投资银行,这都表明中国与世界其他国家共同发展的决心。

民用航空运输是世界不同文明沟通交流的重要桥梁,正如英国著名华裔航空法专家郑斌教授所言,"希望天空成为各国人民交往的纽带"。各国与我国发展双边关系过程中,民航事务始终是一些国家非常关注并不断提及的议题。在推进区域合作方面,航空运输也是其中重要的合作内容。近年来,亚太地区经济持续增长。其中,中国和印度加快了亚太地区乃至全球经济发展和航空运输业的繁荣,必会成为世界第二和第三大经济体。预计这一地区的人口到2030年将增加到50亿,约占全球人口的60%,经济快速发展、地区间双边航空运输协定签订等将刺激本地区航空运输业的发展。中国已成为该地区航空运输业发展的中坚力量,预计到2021年,亚太地区旅游人次将达到约18亿人,该地区航空市场需求量大。正因如此,2014年11月23日至27日,中国民航代表团出席了在我国香港特别行政区举行的第51届亚太地区民航局长会议。在会议上,周来振先生代表中国民航局倡议成立亚太地区民航委员会,得到与会各方和国际民航组织的积极广泛回应。

一、亚太民航委员会:区域一体化的推动

近几年,亚太地区经贸一体化以多元化、多轨道态势不断演进,陆续达成数十项多边和双边自贸协定,跨太平洋伙伴关系协定(Trans-Pacific

Partnership Agreement, TPP)和区域全面经济伙伴关系协定(Regional Comprehensive Economic Partnership,RCEP)也在加紧谈判之中。尽管如此,亚太地区的经贸一体化发展水平与欧洲和北美等地区相比,尚处于发展的初中期阶段。例如,欧盟已经制定了一个单一市场,通过一个标准化的法律制度,其中适用于所有会员国,保证人、货物、服务和资本的迁徙自由。它保持了一个共同的贸易政策,包括农业和渔业政策和区域发展政策。在对外民航关系上,代表其成员以单独缔约方的名义与其他国家签订双边航空运输协定。亚太经合组织(Asia-Pacific Economic Cooperation,APEC)是一个区域性的官方经济论坛,在此合作模式下,不存在超越成员体主权的组织机构,成员体自然也无须向有关机构进行主权让渡。坚持亚太经合组织官方论坛的性质,是符合亚太地区经济体社会政治经济体制多样性、文化传统多元性、利益关系复杂性的现实情况。由此可见,就法律属性而言,欧盟是国际法中自成一类的国际组织,而亚太经合组织只是一个论坛而已。显而易见,亚太地区的经贸一体化路途漫漫。

就亚太地区的民航合作而言,其情况大体类似。欧盟内部的民航合作已经走向高度的一体化,欧洲民航会议成立于1955年,由44个欧洲国家和地区民航部门组成。主要负责协调成员国民用航空重大问题上的政策立场,推动成员国航空运输的协作与发展。在欧洲民航会议(European Civil Aviation Conference,ECAC)第139届局长会议上,欧盟委员会同44个欧洲民航会议会员国的民用航空局局长们确定,将尽可能在一切国际论坛上恪守承诺,通力合作,一起支持和促进欧洲航空运输业的进一步发展,以利于欧洲人民和地区经济。世界其他地区在推动区域民航合作方面也不甘落后。

(一)拉丁美洲民用航空委员会

2012年出席中国民航发展论坛的拉美民航委员会主席路易斯·阿历兹在《拉美民航委员会为地区和全球航空运输业所作的贡献》中指出:拉丁美洲民航委员会是个国际的组织,由22个国家组成,都是来自北美、中美和南美、加勒比地区的,主要目标是提供民航当局各个成员国一个很好的框架,在这个框架下讨论、安排、实施所有的民航合作、协调方面的工作。我们是按照民主的方式进行工作,我们会通过讨论形成决议、结论,经基准之后都收录到各国家自己的民航条例中去。在上次国际民航区域会议上,包括拉丁美洲民航委员会和其他各大洲民航委员会都签订了一些相互合作的协议,和民航组织推动我们建立一个共同的合作平台,这些拉美民航委员会和国际民航机构签订的协议能够很好地推行,涉及几个不同的机构。

(二)非洲民用航空委员会

非洲民用航空委员会(African Civil Aviation Commission,AFCAC)是非洲统一组织(Organization of African Unity,OAU,现称非洲联盟)的一个专门机构,于1969年1月在埃塞俄比亚首都亚的斯亚贝巴成立。它向所有具有非统组织成员身份的非洲国家,以及经非统组织批准的联合国非洲经济委员会(Economic Commission for Africa,ECA)的其他成员国开放。2014年我国开启了对非区域航空合作,李克强总理在访问期间倡议实施“中非区域航空合作计划”,双方未来合作的内容包括建立合资航空公司、提供民用支线客机、转让成熟技术、培训专业航空人才和建设配套保障设施等。

(三)阿拉伯民用航空委员会

阿拉伯民用航空委员会在阿拉伯国家联盟的支持下于1995年成立,接替了阿拉伯民用航空理事会。该委员会总部设在摩洛哥拉巴特,其成员面向身为阿拉伯国家联盟成员的所有国家。阿拉伯民用航空委员会的目标为:制订一项发展阿拉伯民用航空和确保其安全的计划,促进成员国之间在民用航空领域的合作与协调并制定取得一致性所必需的规章条例,以及确保民航的成长与发展,以满足阿拉伯国家对安全、高效和正常的航空运输的需求。

亚太地区民航局长会议创建于1960年,每年一届,轮流在亚太地区各国举行,是由国际民航组织主持的、亚太地区唯一定期举行的民航领域的高级别论坛。我国曾于1991年在北京承办了第27届亚太地区民航局长会议。由此可见,欧洲民航会议、拉美民航委员会、非洲民航委员会和阿拉伯民用航空委员会都是政府间国际组织,而亚太地区民航局长会议只是一个高级别论坛。

综上所述,亚太民航委员会呼之欲出,实乃“世界大势,浩浩荡荡”!

二、亚太民航委员会:法律机制之构建

如上文所述,呼之欲出的亚太民航委员会,其法律属性是政府间国际组织。那么,从国际法的角度来看,其治理机制为何?

国际组织是具有国际性行为特征的组织,可以解决国与国之间的各项事务,国际组织可分为两种主要类型:政府间国际组织——成员都是主权国家或其他成员不必为主权国家的国际组织(如欧盟和世界贸易组织)。非政府间国际组织(Non-Governmental Organizations,NGOs):任何国际组织,凡未经政府间协议而建立,均被视为是为这种安排而成立的非政府国际组织。包括独立组织、民间组织、第三部门、志愿协会。从法律角度来讲,政府间的国际组织必须有一部公约作为基础,并且具备法律人格。

一般性政府间国际组织设立了三级结构,那就是最高权力机关、执行机关和行政机关。最高权力机关由全体会员国组成,一般称为大会、代表大会或全体会议,在某些国际经济组织中则称为管理董事会。最高机关的职能是讨论、审议其职权范围内的任何问题与相关事项,以及组织内其他机构的职权,并就重大问题作出决议,制定本组织的方针、政策,接纳新成员国,选举有关机构的成员,审议有关机构的年度报告,审议本组织的预算和决算,以及修改基本文件等。执行机关由一定数目的成员国组成,其职能是负责具体执行组织所承担的专门性任务,执行机关就其职权范围内的事项作出的决议和决定,有的对所有会员国有拘束力。行政机关由行政首长和若干工作人员组成,通常称为秘书处。秘书处的职能是负责处理国际组织的行政管理事务,如提供会议场所,发放、复制、翻译文件,对内负责行政管理,对外代表该组织

参与国际活动,等等。

1971 年联合国大会通过了第 2758 号决议,恢复中华人民共和国的合法权利。1971 年 11 月 19 日国际民航组织秘书长通知我国政府,国际民航组织第 74 届理事会通过决议,承认中华人民共和国政府的代表为中国驻国际民航组织的唯一合法代表。1974 年 2 月 15 日我国政府致函国际民航组织,承认《芝加哥公约》并从即日起恢复参加国际民航组织的活动,同时声明,1949 年 10 月 1 日以后,台湾地区当局盗用中国政府名义在《芝加哥公约》的其他议定书上的签字和批准都是非法的和无效的。同时,对不定期飞行,我国声明需事先向我国政府申请,在得到答复接受后方能进入;对公约第十八章"争端和违约"的执行,以不损害我国主权为原则。1974 年 9 月 24 日至 10 月 15 日,中国代表团出席了国际民航组织第 21 届会议并当选为理事国。同年 12 月,在蒙特利尔设立中国驻国际民航组织理事会代表处,派出了驻国际民航组织理事会的代表。

应当说,40 多年来,我国民航局积极参与了国际民航组织的一系列活动,取得了令人瞩目的成就。尤其是近年来,中国民航的国际化步伐加快,影响力与日俱增,话语权逐步扩大,建设了一支高素质的民航外事工作队伍,也积累了丰富的对外交涉经验。因此,笔者认为,可以借鉴国际民航组织的经验,建立"亚太版民航组织"——亚太民航委员会,其内部治理结构是"大会—执行委员会—秘书处"。

(一)议事与决策机构——亚太民航委员会大会

这类机构是国际组织根据各自的基本文件设立的最高权力机关,由全体成员国组成,负责该组织的全面工作。无论是普遍性的国际组织还是区域性或专业性的国际组织,这一机构向全体成员国提供了讨论其业务领域所有相关事项的论坛,并就重大问题作出决策。

由全体成员国组成的议事与决策机构作为本组织最高机关,除了向成员国提供论坛,用于各国交流外交立场和主张这一职能外,仍然承担着一系列对本组织活动极为重要的任务,如接纳新成员国、选举下属的执行与主管机构成员并审议其年度报告、选举最高行政管理官员、修正基本文件并审批本组织的财政报告。目前,各国际组织的议事与决策机构多每年或数年定期举行一次全体会议。例如,国际民航组织每三年举行一次大会。在决策时,国际组织的各成员国享有平等的投票权,除另有规定外,会议以各成员国的多数票作出决定。

(二)执行与主管机构——亚太民航委员会执行委员会

这类机构一般是由本组织中部分成员国组成,在一定任期内轮换。机构的成员由本组织高一级的议事与决策机构选举产生。执行与主管机构负责具体处理本组织承担的专业性问题。

目前,执行与主管机构在国际组织中发挥了最为重要的作用。在实践中,执行与主管机构根据授权不仅处理主管事务,而且积极参与最高机构的决策过程。因此,执行与主管机构常常是决策过程中整个链条的实质环节。

从执行与主管机构的活动方式上看,在工作中根据需要定期或不定期地召开会议,有权作出本机构职权范围内的决议和决定。执行与主管机构的成员往往依据公平分配的原则确定数额,经全体会议选举产生,当选后在一定期间内参与机构的活动,并享有平等的投票权。由于此类机构的活动比议事与决策机构灵活和便利,更易于深入讨论和处理专业问题,因此更受到各国政府的重视,在国际组织活动的实践中,此类机构继续呈不断加强的趋势。

(三)行政与管理机构——亚太民航委员会秘书处

行政与管理机构被称为秘书处,其最高首长被称为秘书长、总干事或执行秘书等。

行政与管理机构负责国际组织正常活动运转的所有后勤事务,向本组织提供各项活动的管理服务,并执行各机构制订的方针与政策、落实各业务机构制订的各项活动计划与方案。该机构的最高首长一般为本组织的对外代表,由最高权力机关选举产生,获选后在一定期限内为本组织服务。行政与管理机构的成员由最高行政首长聘任的各国公民组成,他们以个人身份担任国际公务员,为本组织服务,不寻求或接受任何政府或本组织以外的任何当局的指示,以保持其公正和独立性。

(四)辅助与工作机构——亚太民航委员会专家委员会

在各国际组织运转中,除了以上议事与决策、执行与主管以及行政与管理机构外,在不同级别建立一定数量的辅助与工作机构也是必不可少的。辅助与工作机构,是指各国际组织及其主要机关根据其基本文件的规定而设立,在实现本组织目标,完成各机构职能时必需的工作性机构。

在实践中,由于各组织、各机构所承担的职能和管辖的业务范围、特点各不相同,它们所设立的辅助与工作机关更是多种多样、千差万别。如果从不同角度分析,它们可能是由所有成员或部分成员组成;可能由政府代表组成也可能由政府选派的专家组成,还可能是个人专家组成;可能是常设的也可能是临时的;可能是对某一专业领域问题进行审议,提出建议,也可能专门负责处理某一专业技术问题。由于这类机构的组成和形式很灵活,在国际组织活动时在工作层承担了具体实务,为各组织正常运转所必需,因此,它们在当前国际组织中广泛存在。例如,国际民航组织理事会下设的行政委员会、财务委员会、技术委员会、运输委员会、法律委员会、航行委员会、非法干扰委员会、联营委员会,等等。因此,从这个角度来看,亚太民航委员会设立专家委员会是必要的。

(五)司法机构——亚太民航委员会行政法庭

在一些国际组织中存在的行政法庭虽然与联合国国际法院具有不同的管辖范围,但从性质和工作特点上均属于国际组织的司法机构类型。既然作为国际公务员的国际组织雇员不受其本国或者所在国家有关雇佣条件的法律保护,因此,为使各国际组织的工作人员在与雇主发生劳务或人事纠纷时可以得到必要的法律救助,一些国际组织设立了自己的投诉体系——行政法庭。在这方面最具有代表性的是联合国大会在1949年设立的联合国行政法庭。根据有关规定,联合国的工作人员在其内部投诉程序已经全部使用后,便可向行政法庭起诉。行政法庭在接受案件并进行审理后作出的判决具有约束力。国际民航组织也建立了类似的行政法庭,以处理本组织与职员之间的争端。

三、建议:亚太民航委员会的筹建问题

诚然,我国的"和平崛起"的思想是2003年提出来的,但是,自20世纪70年代以来,随着国际社会多极化的趋势日益凸显,我国的国际地位不断提高,逐步成为多极化世界中不可忽视的重要一极。在这样的国际背景下,我国揭开了融入国际社会的帷幕,其中以1971年中国恢复在联合国的合法席位为主要标志。20世纪80年代以后,我国开始全面融入国际社会,参加了为数不少的国际体制。随着我国国际地位逐步提高,需要进一步扩大我国在全球治理中的影响力和话语权,主动参与到国际经济治理改革的活动中。在民航局领导工作报告中,也多次提出,参与国际民航公约、惯例和标准的制定工作,让中国民航的理念、经验和标准走向国际舞台,这是建设民航强国不可或缺的重要一环。那么,如何实现这一良好的愿景呢?笔者认为,借"亚太民航委员会"出海,不失为一条良好的途径。我国顺应了好评如潮的"亚洲基础设施投资银行"的"东风",更顺应了我国民航的国际化战略。因此,我们完全可以借助"亚太民航委员会"这艘"大船"扬帆出海。

笔者认为,为了让呼之欲出的这艘"大船"顺利下海,我国政府应未雨绸缪,做好各项准备工作。

第一,迅速组织行业内外的有关专家和实务人士,进一步做好亚太民航委员会的可行性研究,形成有分量的研究报告,在适当时机提交国务院民用航空主管部门,以决定是否启动亚太民航委员会的筹建工作。

第二,如果决定筹建亚太民航委员会,则应争取其落户中国。当今世界各国,正在积极打造“总部经济”,其原因在于国际组织落户本国,既可以扩大本国的国际影响力,又可以拉动本国经济的发展。例如,素有世界民航之都的加拿大蒙特利尔,正因为国际民航组织落户于此,不仅仅提升了蒙特利尔的国际声誉,更为当地带来了可观的收入。2012 年卡塔尔政府多方活动试图将国际民航组织迁往本国,加拿大政府经过多次外交活动,成功阻止了卡塔尔政府的搬迁建议。又如,瑞士政府全力打造总部经济,众多国际组织总部落户日内瓦,如联合国欧洲总部(国际联盟的前身)、国际电信联盟、国际红十字会、世界贸易组织和世界卫生组织;著名的国际清算银行落户瑞士巴塞尔。目前,落户中国的国际组织不多,如上海合作组织、国际竹藤联盟等,因此,希望我国在民航领域有重大突破。

第三,如果决定筹建亚太民航委员会,应组织政治外交、法律、经济和技术专家起草《亚太民航委员会章程》,完善其内部治理结构。

第四,如果决定筹建亚太民航委员会,应争取中国公民出任亚太民航委员会行政首长——秘书长或者总干事。同时,迅速建立国际化人才的培养机制,打造通晓外语,熟悉政治外交、法律、经济和技术等领域的专业人才队伍,将其选派到亚太民航委员会工作,以提升中国在该组织的影响力。

民用无人机国际立法的新近发展与反思

张雪莹*

一、民用无人机的实践发展引发法律挑战

对航空器的现代理解显示,①无人航空器(Unmanned Aircraft,UA,以下简称无人机)最早出现于第一次世界大战前后,但其真正大规模的投入使用是在第二次世界大战时期。以1944年6月德国攻击英国时首次使用的"*Vergeltungswaffe* 1"(V1)为例,这种无人机当时是一种依赖事先的程序设定,在设置好的一段飞行期间后下落的巡航导弹。② 现代

* 华东政法大学国际法学院硕士研究生。

① 《国际民用航空公约》(以下简称《芝加哥公约》)框架下,"航空器"被定义为"可以在大气中从空气的反作用,而不是从空气对地面的反作用获得支撑的任何机器"。参见ICAO Annex 7 to the Convention on International Civil Aviation-Aircraft Nationality and Registration Marks,6th Edition,2012,p.1。

② See Matthew T. DeGarmo,"Issues Concerning Integration of Unmanned Aerial Vehicles in Civil Airspace", *The MITRE Corporation*,2004,pp.1-3.

军事应用,如美国空军的无人机"捕食者"(Predator),曾出现在美国与伊拉克、阿富汗、波斯尼亚、科索沃和朝鲜等国的武装冲突中。它能够完成的军事任务包括实时录像以捕捉敌方行动并传送给军方、释放装载的武器来摧毁目标等。[①] 尽管无人机的发展历史一度以军用为主导,随着现代科技进步,生产力的高速提升和无人机相关产品的逐渐平价化,无人机的民商事应用在实践中变得越发普遍。其商业用途,如航拍、航空测绘、实地测量、运输等,均显示出在民用服务领域的巨大潜力,甚至在部分领域有替代有人驾驶航空器的可能性。[②]

为适应行业发展和实践需求,许多国家已经建立了针对无人机的授权运行制度,以保障其安全飞行。[③] 以美国为例,其当前法律框架主要针对起飞重量小于55磅(约25千克)的民用小型无人机,并以2016年6月颁布的《联邦法规》第107部分为主,对遥控驾驶员证照及其他人员管理进行了规定,同时对无人机飞行作业作出限制。[④] 而澳大利亚则在无人机实践早期就出台了相应的可操作性规定,目前以1998年《民用航空安全规章》下的第101部分为主,规定了无人机的事前授权和飞行规则等。[⑤] 2016年颁布的《民用航空立法修订规章》对第101部分进行了大幅修订,主要是针对风险较小遥控驾驶航空器降低了规制力度,并要求澳大利亚民用航空安全局针对第101部分制定具体的运作指南,以更为灵活和易于应对的方式适应这一迅速发展的

---

① See Aleš Završnik ed., *Drones and Unmanned Aerial Systems: Legal and Social Implications for Security and Surveillance*, Switzerland, Springer, 2016, p. 185.

② See Kristian Bernauw, "Drones: The Emerging Era of Unmanned Civil Aviation", in Nikoleta Radopmpv, et al., Collected Papers of Zagreb Law Faculty-Zbornik Pravnog Fakulteta U Zagrebu, Zagreb, Zagreb Law Faculty, 2016, pp. 223 - 248.

③ 如澳大利亚、加拿大、芬兰、意大利、马来西亚、瑞典、南非、英国和美国针对无人机运行开始实行特别授权制度。参见 ICAO Working Paper of the Exploratory Meeting on Unmanned Aerial Vehicles(UAVs), The Sixteenth Meeting of the Apanpirg, 2006(ATM/AIS/SAR/SG/16)。

④ 参见郑派:《美国新近民用小型无人机管控立法析评》,载《北京航空航天大学学报》(社会科学版)2017年第5期。

⑤ See Federal Register of Legislation, "Civil Aviation Legislation Amendment (Part 101) Regulation 2016", Accessed https://www.legislation.gov.au/Details/F2016L00400, May 9, 2018.

领域。[①] 各国在开展立法的同时,也已经预见了无人机的未来市场。根据业界研究,预计到2035年欧洲无人机市场的市值每年将超过100亿欧元,而到2050年每年将超过150亿欧元。[②]

考虑到无人机产业日新月异的发展与其越发广泛的应用,把它融入现存的有人驾驶航空器管理系统予以监管成为各国主要的发展趋势。同时,考虑到无人机未来在部分区域——特别在欧洲大陆和东亚地区——从事国际空中飞行与运输的可能,开展作业活动主要面临的挑战有两类,分别来自当前和未来从事国际空中航行和主要在国内运行的无人机。后者虽不参与国际飞行,但对于从事国际飞行的同一空域中的其他民用航空器,仍可能存在安全风险和隐患。同时,在不同国家与地区,无人机的融入程度及对其监管的政策方面均可能存在巨大差异。基于此,明确现有规则,并制定一套针对无人机的统一规范成为目前国际社会密切关注的议题。在这一方面,各国已经达成共识:国际民用航空组织(International Civil Aviation Organization, ICAO,以下简称国际民航组织)应充分利用其在促进全球民航系统互通与和谐方面的影响力,在技术专家建议的基础上,通过制定与无人机相关的"国际标准和建议措施"(Standards and Recommended Practices, SARPs,以下简称"标准和建议措施"),发展出全球协调一致的规则,促进实现无人机被安全纳入非隔离空域和机场来开展运行。[③]

---

① See Federal Register of Legislation, "Civil Aviation Legislation Amendment (Part 101) Regulation 2016-Explanatory Statement", Accessed https://www.legislation.gov.au/Details/F2016L00400/Explanatory%20Statement/Text, May 9, 2018.

② ICAO Working Paper of the Thirteenth Air Navigation Conference, Committee A, Remotely Piloted Aircraft System (RPAS), 2018 (AN-Conf/13-WP/6).

③ ICAO Global Aviation Safety Plan, 2nd Edition 2016 (Doc 10004), pp. 3 - 5.

二、国际民航组织针对民用无人机的最新“立法”进展

（一）制定和通过“标准和建议措施”是国际民航组织的“立法”模式

1.“标准和建议措施”的含义与功能

现代民航业建立在一套极为复杂且高度精确的管理系统之上，通过为各国所接受的全球性规则，能够保障该管理系统的有序运作。实现这种规则的统一化，依赖于各国在程序和实体规定上最大限度地实现协调一致，这也是《国际民用航空公约》（以下简称《芝加哥公约》）下“标准和建议措施”的发展目标。[①] 1944 年于美国芝加哥制定的《芝加哥公约》是国际航空法领域的“大宪章”，目前已有 192 个缔约国，[②]国际民航组织依据该公约建立。根据公约第 44 条，国际民航组织的宗旨和目的在于“发展国际航行的原则和技术，并促进国际航空运输的规划和发展”。在规则制定方面，国际民航组织主要是通过其理事会制定相关标准和建议措施，履行其“准立法”职能。[③]

《芝加哥公约》第六章对标准和建议措施进行了规定。公约第 37 条要求国际民航组织随时制定并修改关于包括“空中规则和空中交通管制办法”等 11 个方面的标准和建议措施。为保证各国对“标准”的遵守，公约第 38 条为缔约国设定了“通知义务”：任何国家在无法遵照标准时，或在标准被修订后其国内法与该标准不符时，或有必要采取不同于标准的国内实践时，应当立即将本国的措施和标准所规定的措施之间的差别，通知国际民航组织理事会。[④] 此外，公约本身并未对“标准和建议措施”下定义。在 1947 年国际民航组织第一届大会上，各国统一了理解——认为“标准”（standards）是指凡有

---

① Convention on International Civil Aviation (the Chicago Convention 1944), signed at Chicago, 7 December 1944. 15 UNTS 295.

② 《芝加哥公约》现已经有包括我国在内的 192 个缔约国，资料来源：https://www.icao.int/secretariat/legal/List%20of%20Parties/Chicago_EN.pdf，最后访问日期：2018 年 5 月 9 日。

③ Bin Cheng, *The Law of International Air Transport*, London, Stevens & Sons, 1962, p. 63.

④ 《芝加哥公约》第 38 条。

关物理特征、结构、材料、性能、人员或程序的规格,其统一应用被认为对国际航行的安全或正常是“必需的”(necessary),对此,缔约各国将按照公约予以遵守;如不可能遵照执行时,按照公约第38条,“必须”通知理事会。而“建议措施”(recommended practices)是与“标准”同类别的规格,但其统一应用被认为是“可取的”(desirable),所以各国仅“力求”根据公约予以遵守。①

《芝加哥公约》第54条进一步明确标准和建议措施的通过和修订由国际民航组织理事会完成,且为便利起见,将此种标准和建议措施称作为公约的“附件”(annex)。国际民航组织的“立法”职能主要涉及国际民航业的诸多技术方面的问题,包括航路与通讯控制、航空器的适航性、航空器的登记与识别等。在这些方面,已经通过了19个附件,除《附件九——简化手续》(Annex 9 - Facilitation)和《附件十七——安保》(Annex 17 - Security)外,其他附件均属于技术性规定。

2. “标准和建议措施”作为公约“附件”的法律地位问题

显然,国际民航组织制定的标准和建议措施的实施需要缔约国的配合。但从《芝加哥公约》的用语及实践来看,除特定情形外,各国并没有必须执行或遵照生效附件及其修正案的法定义务,除非他们认为“遵照”适合其国内实践。② 如此一来,标准和建议措施与公约文本间的法律地位似乎并不相同。

从形式上看,标准和建议措施构成了《芝加哥公约》的各项附件,而条约附件的国际法效力需要在具体的语境下分析。首先,对于存在附件的条约,通常应当有明确规定表明该附件文本构成公约整体文本的一部分,否则应作

---

① ICAO Assembly Resolution A1 - 31 “Definition of ‘International Standards’ and ‘Recommended Practices’”,1947[Doc. 4411(A1 - P/45)].

② 《芝加哥公约》第22条、第23条、第37条和第38条;See Thomas Buergenthal, *Law-Making in the International Civil Aviation Organization*, New York, Syracuse University Press, 1969, p. 76。

出相反的解释。[①]《芝加哥公约》显然没有这类表述。其次,公约第38条把是否遵照国际标准的权利留给了缔约各国,但设定了提交"背离通知"的义务以敦促各国保障实施,实际效果是允许缔约国背离标准,表明缔约国并没有遵照标准(以及建议措施)的义务。若附件确属公约规则的一部分,则与"条约必须遵守"(*pacta sunt servanda*)原则相悖。最后,从修订程序上来看,《芝加哥公约》第90条规定附件的修订与通过均由理事会会议2/3多数通过,而根据第94条,对公约的修正必须经大会2/3多数通过。理事会作为国际民航组织的常设机构,仅由大会选出的36个缔约国组成。[②] 这些均表明《芝加哥公约》下的19个附件与公约规则地位并不相同,因此不能认为其具有等同公约规则的法律拘束力。

尽管不具有等同于公约的拘束力,但通过其特有的机制,公约仍然要求缔约各国以制定国内规则的方式,与公约附件所列的标准和建议措施实现最高程度的一致,其主要基础是《芝加哥公约》第1条所承认的领空主权原则,同时也是习惯法规则,即各国对其领土之上的空气空间享有完全排他的主权。[③] 各国在行使主权制定相关规章制度时,应不分国籍地适用于所有在其辖域内的航空器。[④] 根据公约第12条,缔约国负有保证载有其国籍标志的航空器在飞越他国领空时遵守当地"空中规则"的义务,且在设置"空中规则"方面,公约要求各国最大限度地与公约《附件二——空中规则》(Annex 2 - Rules of the Air,以下简称《附件二》)规定的"标准"相一致。而在其他方面,公约第37条和第38条规定,各国承诺将通力合作,尽量保证其关于航空器、人员、航路及各种辅助服务方面的国内规则,与"标准和建议措施"一致,当

---

① 如1993年《关于禁止发展、生产、储存和使用化学武器及销毁此种武器的公约》第17条规定:"各附件为本公约的组成部分。凡提到本公约也就包括提到其附件。" See Anthony Aust, *Modern Treaty Law and Practice*, London, Cambridge University Press, 2013, p. 377; Duncan B. Hollis et al., *The Oxford Guide to Treaties*, Oxford, Oxford University Press, 2012, p. 698.

② 《芝加哥公约》第50条a项。

③ See Bin Cheng, *The Law of International Air Transport*, London, Stevens & Sons, 1962, p. 120.

④ 《芝加哥公约》第11条。

无法使其本国实践在一切方面遵照国际民航组织制定的“标准”时,该国负有向国际民航组织理事会报告背离的义务。

另外,考虑到在公海上空,虽不属国家主权覆盖区域,但因安全因素仍需要相关“空中规则”对其中运行的航空器进行管理,故《芝加哥公约》第12条规定:“在公海上空,有效的规则应为根据本公约制定的规则”。国际民航组织理事会在1948年4月通过《附件二》时,以及在1951年11月第一次修订该附件时,明确了公约第12条下的“有效的规则”就是《附件二》。① 换言之,在公海上空,《附件二》的法律效力等同于公约文本,这意味着实践中各国不能对这方面的“标准”依据第38条提交背离。②

3. “标准”和“建议措施”具有不同的法律效力

通过前文讨论可知,国际民航组织所制定的“标准”和“建议措施”具有不同的法律拘束力:对于“标准”,如非递交“背离”的情形,各缔约国将按照公约予以遵守;而对于“建议措施”,各缔约国仅力求按照公约予以遵守。从公约约文上看,虽然《芝加哥公约》第37条规定了对标准及程序的采用,并明确由国际民航组织制定并随时修改在此方面的“国际标准及建议措施和程序”,但并未对其中的“标准”和“建议措施”作出区分。同时,尽管公约通过第38条为缔约各国设定了在背离“国际标准和程序”时通知国际民航组织的义务——也是唯一的义务——该义务却并不涵盖背离“建议措施”的情形,这表明没有“提交背离”这样的措施来敦促各缔约国遵守“建议措施”。

实际上,在公约起草阶段,当时的技术性标准与程序委员会(The Committee on Technical Standards and Procedures)在提交给会议的报告中就明确了“建议措施”的地位。③ 委员会认为,仅在某些特定项目上的技术性规

---

① ICAO Annex 2 to the Convention on International Civil Aviation-Rules of the Air, 10th Edition 2005, 2.1.1 Note.

② See Michael Milde, *International Air Law and ICAO*, The Hague, Eleven International Pub., 2012, p.46.

③ Proceedings of the International Civil Aviation Conference: Chicago, Illinois, November 1 – December 7, 1944, Vol. I, U.S. Government Printing Office, 1948, p.708.

范是需要被完全统一化的,除此之外,包含"建议措施"的国际性协议文件只能作为"不带义务性质的建议",但其同时表达出希望各国在其"可行的程度上尽力遵照"。即便在未来这类建议可能会变成国际性标准,在没有得到充分一致的承认前,也仅仅作为建议而已。① 由此可见,"标准"在一定情况下是具有强制效力的,而"建议措施"比"标准"效力低,不具有强制效力。

基于上述讨论,能够得出下述结论:尽管遵照国际民航组织制定的"标准和建议措施"并非强制性的公约义务,但在各国没有依据《芝加哥公约》第38条向理事会提交"背离通知"时,应根据公约遵守"标准";对于"建议措施",则由各国尽力予以遵照。至于在公海上空,《附件二》规定的"标准"应当毫无例外地得到适用。

(二)国际民航组织通过"标准和建议措施"对无人机术语进行统一

一直以来,民用航空活动主要建立在这样的观念之上——有驾驶员(和空勤人员)在航空器上(航空器机舱内部)进行驾驶且机上往往搭载有乘客。对于机上没有驾驶员的航空器作业,势必会产生一系列技术和运行相关的问题。而早在2007年国际民航组织关于无人飞行器的非正式会议上就曾提及,在无人机问题上,对于相关概念、术语进行统一是非常必要的。② 实际上,无人机自其发端起就存在各种各样的称谓,如广为政府、媒体所用,公众熟知的"无人机"(Drone),或是形象的称为"自动飞机"(Automatic Airplane)等。③

---

① 报告原表述为"A particular problem of status is that of recommended practice. The committee believes that in certain branches of regulatory action some subjects should be fully standardized, while upon others the internationally agreed documents should present only recommendations implying no obligation, but expressive of a hope that the several nations will follow the recommendation as closely as may be practicable under their particular circumstances"。

② ICAO Unmanned Aircraft Systems(UAS), 2011(Cir 328 AN/190), p. 1.

③ See Benjamyn Scott ed., *The Law of Unmanned Aircraft Systems: An Introduction to the Current and Future Regulation Under National, Regional and International Law*, the Netherlands, Kluwer Law International, 2016, p. 9.

纷繁的名称并不利于对无人机进行统一规制,需要有能够反映其本质属性且相对准确的术语。针对这一需求,《芝加哥公约》第 8 条特别提到了"无人驾驶的航空器"(Pilotless Aircraft),但没有给出清晰的定义。或许是考虑到早期的"无人驾驶的航空器"大多为军事用途,国际民航组织并没有采用该术语,反而尽量避免使用它。同样,国际民航组织也没有采用"无人飞行载具"(Unmanned Aerial Vehicle,UAV)的说法,而是最终着眼于作为整体的"无人航空器系统"(Unmanned Aircraft Systems,UAS)。这与美国联邦航空局、①欧盟,②包括欧洲航空安全局③所采纳的方案是一致的。

2011 年国际民航组织针对无人航空器系统出台了一份《无人航空器系统咨询通告》,④为之后制定的标准和建议措施提供指导。其中,该咨询通告建议将"无人航空器系统"定义为"没有驾驶员在机上操作的航空器及其相关部件",而"无人航空器"(Unmanned Aircraft,UA)这一概念仅用于指称作为此系统组成部分之一的"航空器"。值得注意的是,文件描述了国际民航组织当前的研究重心,是无人航空器概念下的"遥控驾驶航空器"(Remotely Piloted Aircraft,RPA)。⑤

2012 年 3 月 7 日理事会第 195 届 5 次会议上通过了对公约《附件七——航空器国籍和登记标志》(Annex 7 – Aircraft Nationality and Registration Marks,以下简称《附件七》)的第 6 次修订,其中特别加入了关于"遥控驾驶航空器"的内容,尤其是明确了其在航空器中的分类。⑥ 根据《附件七》,凡是

---

① US FAA,"Unmanned Aircraft Systems (UAS): Frequently Asked Questions", Accessed https://www.faa.gov/uas/faqs/, May 9, 2018.

② European Commission, "Unmanned Aircraft Systems (UAS)", Accessed https://ec.europa.eu/transport/modes/air/uas_en, May 9, 2018.

③ EASA, "Opinion 01/2018 Unmanned Aircraft System (UAS) Operations in the 'Open' and 'Specific' Categories", Accessed https://www.easa.europa.eu/document-library/opinions/opinion-012018#group-easa-downloads, May 9, 2018.

④ ICAO Unmanned Aircraft Systems (UAS), 2011 (Cir 328 AN/190).

⑤ ICAO Unmanned Aircraft Systems (UAS), 2011 (Cir 328 AN/190), p. (x).

⑥ ICAO, "Adoption of Amendment 6 to Annex", Accessed https://www.icao.int/Meetings/UAS/Documents/Adoption%20of%20Amendment%206%20to%20Annex%207.pdf, May 9, 2018.

机上没有驾驶员飞行的航空器统称为"无人航空器",而无人航空器(下文仍简称其为无人机)既包括"无人自由气球"(Unmanned Free Balloon),如气象气球,也包括持照航空专业人员操作的"遥控驾驶航空器"。① 后者在《附件七》中被明确定义为"(驾驶员)通过遥控站驾驶的无人机"。因此,《附件七》通过对航空器的定义和分类,明确规定了无人机是《芝加哥公约》项下的航空器,且遥控驾驶航空器属于无人机的一种,是其下位概念,也是航空器。

另外,对《附件二》的第43次修订也在这次会议中通过,其中新纳入了与遥控驾驶航空器相关的一系列概念,包括"遥控驾驶航空器系统"(Remotely Piloted Aircraft Systems,RPAS)和作为其组成部分的"指令与控制链路"(C2 link)、"遥控站"(Remote Pilot Station)等,并特别增设了"附录四"(Appendix 4)——具体规定了与遥控驾驶航空器系统相关的规则。② 同时,由于《附件二》与《附件七》中都只包含"标准",而没有"建议措施",各国在不通知"背离"的情况下必须遵守,如通过纳入其国内法规的形式予以实施,由此保障了对术语统一理解的执行效力,有利于实现无人在国际和国内层面规则的协调与衔接。

尽管国际民航组织通过制定并通过标准和建议措施,出台一系列文件,确认并统一了当前涉及无人机的主要术语,但仍需解决从《芝加哥公约》层面对无人机进行特别调整的问题。而这就涉及对公约第8条规定的"无人驾驶的航空器"的条约解释问题。从字面上看,公约第8条似乎是针对航空器"没有驾驶员操作"的情况,据此则只能用于调整不需要驾驶员控制的"自主航空器"(Autonomous Aircraft)。③ 鉴于无人机系统体系庞杂,且不排除未来会有更多分类出现的可能,自主航空器目前只是无人机的一类很小的分支,

① ICAO Annex 7 to the Convention on International Civil Aviation-Aircraft Nationality and Registration Marks,6th Edition 2012,p. 2.

② ICAO,"Adoption of Amendment 43 to Annex 2", Accessed https://www. icao. int/Meetings/UAS/Documents/019e. pdf,May 9,2018.

③ "自主航空器"被定义为:"在管理飞行过程中不需要驾驶员介入操作的无人航空器。" ICAO Unmanned Aircraft Systems (UAS), 2011 (Cir 328 AN/190), p. (ix); ICAO Manual on Remotely Piloted Aircraft Systems,2015(Doc 10019 – AN/507),p. (xiv).

也不是当前国际民航组织关注的重心。[①] 与之相对,作为目前规则制定所重点关注的"遥控驾驶航空器"才最应当被第 8 条所涵摄。国际民航组织在多份文件中屡次表明:第 8 条应当被理解为是在规范没有驾驶员在航空器上(航空器机舱内部)驾驶的航空器,这与《芝加哥公约》起草者之意图相符,也与当前采取的术语概念一致。因此,所有无人机,无论是否遥控、完全自主或二者兼而有之,都需要遵守《芝加哥公约》第 8 条的规定。[②] 于此背景下,国际民航组织依据公约先制定了专门调整"遥控驾驶航空器系统"的标准,并将其纳入《附件二》,同时也在着手完善其他类型的标准。

(三)"遥控驾驶航空器系统"规则是国际民航组织的最新"立法"成果

按照前述附件的规定,遥控驾驶航空器属于无人机的一种。由于它的运行处于实时可控的状态,被视作是最有可能被纳入有人驾驶航空器作业环境中的一类无人机。有人驾驶航空器的作业活动,经过国际社会的不懈努力,已经处于谨慎监管且完善建立的一套管理体系之中,而无人机的运行环境则欠缺此种法律环境。考虑到遥控驾驶航空器系统功能广泛、种类多元,同时又具有巨大的经济发展潜力,国际民航组织明确表示要针对其优先制定标准和建议措施。[③] 在这一方面,已经完成了在《附件七》、《附件十三——航空器事故和事故征候调查》(Annex 13 – Aircraft Accident and Incident Investigation)中制定各项相关规定,以及于 2012 年在《附件二》中增加了"附录四",规定从事国际作业的遥控驾驶航空器必须满足《芝加哥公约》的各项要求。另外,2014 年国际民航组织还出版了《遥控驾驶航空器系统手册》,[④] 对将遥控驾驶航空器纳入非隔离空域和机场开展作业提供了技术及运行指导。

---

① ICAO Unmanned Aircraft Systems(UAS),2011(Cir 328 AN/190),p. 1.

② ICAO Unmanned Aircraft Systems(UAS),2011(Cir 328 AN/190),p. (x).

③ ICAO Working Paper of the Thirteenth Air Navigation Conference, Committee A, Remotely Piloted Aircraft System(RPAS),2018(AN-Conf/13 – WP/6).

④ ICAO Manual on Remotely Piloted Aircraft Systems,2015(Doc 10019 – AN/507).

《附件二》下的附录四——“遥控驾驶航空器系统”,是当前国际民航组织针对民用无人机规则制定所取得的最新立法成果。其中不仅涉及遥控驾驶航空器的一般运行规则,还涵盖了航空器证书、人员执照以及运行特许的内容。鉴于在其他附件中特别针对遥控驾驶航空器系统的相关规则还没有制定完全,附录四采取了要求缔约国依据国内法进行管控的方式,来应对当前可能存在的监管空缺状况。

为了弥补对驾驶员证照要求的空白,2018 年 3 月 7 日国际民航组织理事会还审议通过了对《附件一——人员执照的颁发》(Annex 1 – Personnel Licensing,以下简称《附件一》)的第 175 次修订,涉及遥控驾驶员及遥控驾驶航空器系统执照颁发的监管框架,支持在仪表飞行规则下运行的国际飞行。① 同时,会议还通过了对《附件二》的第 46 次修订,针对《附件一》所引入的新规定对《附件二》附录四的第 2 节“合格审定和执照办法”进行修订。② 两项附件的修订内容中有关遥控驾驶航空器系统的部分都将至 2022 年 11 月 3 日才开始适用。当前,《附件二》的附录四仍然发挥着规范遥控驾驶航空器的主导作用。

三、“遥控驾驶航空器系统”规则的主要法律问题

《芝加哥公约》的《附件二》第 43 次修订时,在其第三章“一般规则”下新增了第 3.1.9 节——“遥控驾驶航空器系统”规则,概括性地规定了遥控驾驶航空器的运行方式应当使其对人员、财产或其他航空器可能造成的危险最小化,并明确遥控驾驶航空器应具体依照《附件二》附录四所列之规则进行运行。鉴于“附录”本身属于“标准和建议措施”的组成部分,且《附件二》中的所有规则均为“标准”,因此《附件二》项下的附录四具有等同于标准的法律

① See Adoption of Amendment 175 to Annex 1, Accessed http://www.atcguild.com/IWEN/IWEN1318/ICAO/011e.pdf, May 9, 2018.

② See Adoption of Amendment 46 to Annex 2, Accessed http://www.atcguild.com/IWEN/IWEN1318/ICAO/020e.pdf, May 9, 2018.

效力。[1] 附录四由三个部分组成,分别针对遥控驾驶航空器的一般运行规则、证书与执照规则及其运行特别许可的申请进行了详细规定。

(一)遥控驾驶航空器的一般运行要求

附录四的"一般运行规则"概括性规定了从事国际空中飞行的遥控驾驶航空器的运行要求,包括事前应获取哪些国家颁发的飞行"许可",运行过程中应当遵守哪国法规,以及需要符合哪些国家对于遥控驾驶航空器系统的性能、所载设备的要求。

附录四下对遥控驾驶航空器系统运行所必需的"许可",可以根据其表述不同分为"一般许可"和"特别许可"(以下简称"特许")。从事国际空中航行的遥控驾驶航空器系统需获取由起飞地所在国授予的一般许可才可以开展相关作业,并且应在遥控驾驶航空器起飞前取得。与此同时,当存在跨越他国空域的飞行阶段时,遥控驾驶航空器还应取得其将要飞经的国家授予的"特许"(special authorization)。通常在计划作业时,就可以预先确定遥控驾驶航空器将要飞经哪些国家的领空;计划飞经多国时,则必须事前获得每一将飞经国颁发的"特许"。这样的协调工作能够使遥控驾驶航空器的飞行作业活动符合各飞经国的具体情况。另外,在不能合理预见的突发的紧急情况下,可以不需要事前计划或事前许可。[2]

按照国际民航组织的说明,遥控驾驶航空器属于《芝加哥公约》第 8 条规制的"无人驾驶的航空器"范围内,附录四中所要求的飞经国"特许"正是依据第 8 条。该条规定:"任何无人驾驶而能飞行的航空器,未经一缔约国特许并遵照此项特许的条件,不得无人驾驶地在该国领土上空飞行。各缔约国承允对此项无人驾驶的航空器在向民用航空器开放的地区内的飞行一定加以

---

① See ICAO Annex 2 to the Convention on International Civil Aviation-Rules of the Air, 10th Edition, 2005, p. vi.

② See ICAO Manual on Remotely Piloted Aircraft Systems, 2015 (Doc 10019 - AN/507), p. 3 - 1.

管制,以免危及民用航空器。”

实际上,《芝加哥公约》框架下除第 8 条,也有其他相似的“特许”要求存在,如《芝加哥公约》第 6 条对“定期航班”要求的“特准或其他许可”。① 虽然遥控驾驶航空器是公约调整的航空器,属于该条调整的范围,但公约第 6 条规定的特许并不意在考虑其运行问题,而是主要着眼于航空器的经济利用和航线经营权,且一般以双边航空运输(或航空服务)协定方式互相授予特许,是国家间交换航权的形式。而公约第 8 条要求的是“无人驾驶的航空器”在他国领空飞行时的“特许”,主要着眼于航空器的飞行安全,反倒与公约第 3 条规定的“国家航空器”在他国领土上空飞行或在其领土上着陆时需获得的“特别协定或其他方式的许可”更为类似,②也与公约第 8 条在此前一直针对的是军用无人机的实践是相符的。③ 在许可形式上,附录四第 1.2 节明确了飞经国的“特许”可能以所涉国家间的协议形式存在。④

除“特许”外,附录四第一部分还要求在遥控驾驶航空器作业时,应当满足航空器注册国、运营人国籍国(如与注册国不同)及飞经国的在运行方面所指定的条件。表现为对航空器设备(如配置二次雷达应答机)、航空器的运行和性能标准的要求等。飞行计划的提交原则上依照《附件二》第三章进行,但航空器的飞经国如对此另有规定,应按照其规定实施。而在运输性能和设备方面,则应完全符合飞经国的要求。

---

① 《芝加哥公约》第 6 条规定:“除非经一缔约国特准或其他许可并遵照此项特准或许可的条件,任何定期国际航班不得在该国领土上空飞行或进入该国领土。”

② 《芝加哥公约》第 3 条 b 项规定:“用于军事、海关和警察部门的航空器,应认为是国家航空器。”其 c 项还规定:“一缔约国的国家航空器,未经特别协定或其他方式的许可并遵照其中的规定,不得在另一缔约国领土上空飞行或在此领土上降落。”ICAO Working Paper of the Legal Committee – 36th Session, Study of Legal Issues Relating to Remotely Piloted Aircraft, 2015(LC/36 – WP/2 – 4), p. A – 2.

③ See Michael Milde, *International Air Law and ICAO*, The Hague, Eleven International Pub., 2012, p. 66.

④ See ICAO Annex 2 to the Convention on International Civil Aviation-Rules of the Air, 10th Edition 2005, Appendix 4 Remotely Piloted Aircraft Systems, 1.2.

(二)遥控驾驶航空器与遥控驾驶员的证照要求

《附件二》附录四第二部分关于遥控驾驶航空器系统的证书和其相关人员执照的规定,涉及《附件一》、《附件六——航空器的运行》(Annex 6 - Operation of Aircraft)和《附件八——航空器的适航性》(Annex 8 - Airworthiness of Aircraft)中的相关标准和建议措施。由于在这些方面,涉及遥控驾驶航空器的标准和建议措施尚未制定完成,现有的附件规则并不能直接适用于遥控驾驶航空器。① 鉴于此,附录四要求考虑到遥控驾驶航空器系统中各个部分的独立性,在遥控驾驶航空器的适航证明、型别设计中所列明的遥控驾驶航空器系统各部分之认证与维护、运营人执照以及遥控驾驶员执照等方面,应当依照航空器登记国或其他会受影响的国家的国内规定来操作,同时应与相关附件规则保持一致。②

另外,根据《芝加哥公约》第33条,缔约国在承认证书与执照时必须要参考相关的标准,而考虑到当前相关标准和建议措施的缺失,③附录四特别以"注"(Note)的形式纳入了国际民航组织大会"第A38-12号决议"的内容,以对这部分标准进行说明。该决议决定:在相关标准和建议措施出台前,对于一些特别类型的航空器,其依据航空器登记国所颁发或核准有效的证书,为了这些航空器在缔约国的飞行(包括起飞和降落)目的,该飞经国应承认其有效。④ 这意味着,在当前相关标准和建议措施空缺的情形下,各缔约国对他国对遥控驾驶航空器的管理要予以承认。尽管如此,《芝加哥公约》第8

---

① ICAO Annex 2 to the Convention on International Civil Aviation-Rules of the Air, 10th Edition 2005, Appendix 4 Remotely Piloted Aircraft Systems, Note 2.

② ICAO Annex 2 to the Convention on International Civil Aviation-Rules of the Air, 10th Edition 2005, Appendix 4 Remotely Piloted Aircraft Systems, 2.1, 2.2, 2.3.

③ 《芝加哥公约》第33条规定:"登记航空器的缔约国发给或核准的适航证和合格证书及执照,其他缔约国应承认其有效。但发给或核准此项证书或执照的要求,须等于或高于根据本公约随时制定的最低标准。"

④ ICAO Annex 2 to the Convention on International Civil Aviation-Rules of the Air, 10th Edition 2005, Appendix 4 Remotely Piloted Aircraft Systems, Note 2.

条还是以“特许”的形式保障了各缔约国对其领空的绝对主权。

值得注意的是,附录四第2.3节明确要求各国应依照《附件一》对“遥控驾驶员”(Remote Pilot)颁发执照,且前述“第A38-12号决议”要求各国对遥控驾驶航空器的相关证照予以承认。那么决议中要求的“承认”,是否也包括对遥控驾驶员执照的承认?可以确认的是,《芝加哥公约》第32条下的“驾驶员”(Pilot)指的是“在航空器上操作航空器飞行的驾驶员”,因而“遥控驾驶员”并不在此概念范围内。[①] 公约第33条在“驾驶员”的理解上与第32条相同,故其对执照的认可也不包括“遥控驾驶员”执照,仅应对遥控驾驶航空器的适航性合格证书适用。[②] 由此,应当认为,根据公约第33条出台的“第A38-12号决议”也没有将“遥控驾驶员”的证书和执照包括在内。

在《附件一》的第175次修订中,加入了有关遥控驾驶员执照颁发的相关标准和建议措施。相应地,《附件二》的第46次修订对其附录四中关于人员执照的内容作了更新。[③]《附件一》修订中的一个重要变化是引入了“遥控空勤组成员”(Remote Flight Crew Member)及“遥控驾驶员”在训练、运行和执照方面的标准。在此之前,《附件一》及《芝加哥公约》针对的都是“在航空器上的”空勤组成员和其他机组成员。

鉴于遥控驾驶员的特殊性,在纳入新规定的同时,仍有一些问题需要解决。例如,此前出台的《无人驾驶航空器系统咨询通告》就提及,遥控驾驶航空器的运作给人员的执照监管带来了一个新的视角——遥控驾驶员究竟是应该从属于遥控驾驶航空器,还是遥控站?这一问题的答案将进一步决定是由遥控驾驶航空器的登记国还是遥控站所在国(如不是同一国家的情形下)给遥控驾驶员颁发执照。[④] 不过从《附件一》的修订情况来看,应该由遥控驾

---

① 《芝加哥公约》第32条a项规定:“从事国际航行的每一航空器驾驶员及飞行组其他成员,应备有该航空器登记国发给或核准的合格证书和执照。”

② ICAO Manual on Remotely Piloted Aircraft Systems(Doc 10019-AN/507)(2015),p.8-2;ICAO Unmanned Aircraft Systems(UAS),2011(Cir 328 AN/190),p.1-7.

③ 《附件一》的第175次修订及《附件二》的第46次修订中有关遥控驾驶航空器系统的部分将于2022年11月3日适用。

④ ICAO Unmanned Aircraft Systems(UAS),2011(Cir 328 AN/190),p.33.

驶航空器系统的运营人的主要营业地所在国颁发执照,或由该国相关的机关予以核准。[①] 此外,由于遥控驾驶员执照不在《芝加哥公约》第 33 条互相认可的范围内,需要制定相应的标准来解决这个问题。与之相似,公约第 29 条要求"机上"携带证书、执照和记录簿等文件。[②] 针对遥控驾驶航空器系统,可能需要新的办法来解决这些问题,而《附件一》的第 175 次修订里尚未给出这些问题的答案。

(三)遥控驾驶航空器运行的特许"申请"问题

《附件二》附录四的最后部分对"一般运行规则"中提及的遥控驾驶航空器运行所必需的特许申请作出了规定,主要列举了国家在颁发特许时应当参考的信息(除非该国另有规定),包括遥控驾驶航空器系统的运营人基本信息、遥控驾驶航空器的性能及运行特征和相关证书等。考虑到遥控驾驶航空器可能存在不同于有人驾驶航空器的运行风险,比如,没有一个驾驶员在机上应对突发情况。申请特许时就包括一项"紧急程序"(emergency procedures),要求提交能有效应对航空器与空中交通管制单位无法对接交流,或出现指令与控制链路(C2 link)失效,或遥控驾驶员与遥控驾驶航空器观察员失联这些情况的紧急预案。[③] 在符合附录四"一般运行规则"的情形下,此特许应至少在遥控驾驶航空器计划飞行的 7 日前,由拟飞经国的有权机关颁发,除非该国对此另有规定。[④] 这表明,在该部分中所规定的特许就是前述《芝加哥公约》第 8 条中对"无人驾驶的航空器"规定的特许要求。同时,附录四还规定了获取特许后应履行的"通知义务",如应当通知相关空中

---

① See Adoption of Amendment 175 to Annex 1, Accessed http://www.atcguild.com/IWEN/IWEN1318/ICAO/011e.pdf, May 9, 2018.

② 根据《芝加哥公约》第 29 条,缔约国的每一航空器在从事国际航行时,应按照公约规定的条件携带如航空器登记证、航空器适航证、每一机组成员的适当的执照等文件。

③ ICAO Annex 2 to the Convention on International Civil Aviation-Rules of the Air, 10th Edition 2005, Appendix 4 Remotely Piloted Aircraft Systems, 3.2 n.

④ ICAO Annex 2 to the Convention on International Civil Aviation-Rules of the Air, 10th Edition 2005, Appendix 4 Remotely Piloted Aircraft Systems, 3.1.

交通管制单位，并配合其协调工作等，但没有具体表明由哪一方来履行该义务。由于此项义务是依据颁发特许的国家之要求来实施的，义务主体的具体确定可能会留给当事国自行协商。

附录四关于特许申请的规定还存在其他一些模糊不清的地方。例如，关于申请特许的主体，以及应以何种形式获得特许，附录四并未明确阐述。这些问题在2014年出版的《遥控驾驶航空器系统手册》中得到了部分回应。从该文件的描述来看，提交特许申请的主体应该是遥控驾驶航空器系统的运营人。而获取特许的形式，尽管附录四第1.2节中表明特许可以是以国家间的协议形式存在，实践中，为了便于特许的授予，这一程序可能会被简化。国家间可能会通过双边、多边协议或对具体的遥控驾驶航空器运行作出特别安排。同时，这一目标还可以在区域范围内通过采取规范性措施来实现。[①] 不过，应当明确，特许的授予单位是国家民航局或其他同等级机关，体现的是国家对其领空绝对的主权。在此意义上，尽管申请特许所提交的信息与向空中交通管制单位递交飞行计划或有相似之处，但性质则完全不同。

此外，前述对附录四的理解出自《遥控驾驶航空器系统手册》，它作为对技术和运行提供"指导"的文件，效力十分有限，不一定能实现相关实践的统一化。当前如果尚未形成"由运营人申请特许"的惯例，可能会出现申请人混乱的局面。如果遥控驾驶航空器的登记国与其运营人国籍国为不同国家，应由哪一国与航空器拟飞经国签订双边协议来获取特许？而如果同时采取其他形式获取特许，出现冲突规定的情况又应如何解决？这些问题的解决有赖于之后出台的标准和建议措施提供有效方案。

四、民用无人机国际立法对我国的启示

我国自1974年恢复参加国际民航组织活动以来，已多届连任国际民航

---

① See ICAO Manual on Remotely Piloted Aircraft Systems, 2015 (Doc 10019 - AN/507), p. 3 - 1.

组织的一类理事国。[①] 作为民航大国,近年来我国的航空运输业和航空制造业都以惊人的速度在持续发展。在世界各国纷纷迎来民航新生力量——无人机带来的无限机遇时,我国的无人机产业也展现出了巨大实力。无人机研究公司"Skylogic Research"的数据显示,成立于2006年的中国企业大疆公司目前在全球市场上所占的份额已超过70%。[②] 此外,我国目前的无人机应用环境也比较乐观,不仅在商业上备受关注,在公用事业上也被用于检查电缆、调查火情和灾区、喷洒农药及监测空气质量等。面对无人机运行活动不断增多与其应用领域不断扩展之现实,并考虑到其将来应用于国际民用航空——如跨境作业——的广阔前景,如何在对接国际标准的同时形成规则导向,在规范无人机安全作业的同时从法律层面助推产业发展,极大程度上决定了我国无人机事业未来的发展。这也是其他国家和国际社会正在密切关注的问题。

从世界范围来看,各国在努力开展对无人机认识、定义和最终使之统一完善之工作的同时,亦在对国际规则的制定产生持续的动态影响,而这也是我国当前已经参与并应当继续积极参与的工作。国际民航组织当前的规则发展状况能够基本反映各国的需求。遥控驾驶航空器产业的蓬勃发展和遥控驾驶技术复杂的运行机制,促成了当前国际层面和国内层面对其优先进行立法调整的局面。应当指出,许多国家业已形成了针对无人机——特别是遥控驾驶航空器——运行的监管框架,在此基础上进一步开始采取按照无人机风险进行分类监管的举措,并积极建议国际民航组织在规则制定上充分考虑遥控驾驶航空器系统的技术创新驱动特点,给予其恰如其分的灵活性。例如,美国[③]和法国、德国[④]等欧盟成员国就积极倡导应以绩效为导向并基于风

---

① 参见《我国连任国际民航组织一类理事国》,载中国民用航空局网:http://www.caac.gov.cn/XWZX/MHYW/201610/t20161001_40006.html,最后访问日期:2018年5月9日。

② See The New York Times, "At an Air Show in China, Drones, Not Jets, Are the Stars", Accessed https://cn.nytimes.com/china/20171228/china-drones/, May 9, 2018.

③ See ICAO Working Paper of the Assembly – 39th Session, Technical Commission, Prioritize Unmanned Aircraft Systems Integration, 2016(A39 – WP/103), p. 2 – 3.

④ See ICAO Working Paper of the Assembly – 39th Session, Technical Commission, Remotely Piloted Aircraft Systems(RPAS), 2016(A39 – WP/95), p. 2.

险进行监管干预，以便实现维持和加强航空安全、安保、运行效率、经济有效性和环境效率等目标。

我国在积极从事国内无人机规则的制定和完善，但立法进程较为缓慢。自2013年11月发布了《民用无人驾驶航空器系统驾驶员管理暂行规定》后，陆续出台了对无人机空中交通管理、实名制登记管理等相关规定。2018年1月底发布了《无人驾驶航空器飞行管理暂行条例》的征求意见稿，[①]目前还没有正式文件公布。在这份意见稿中，出现了无人机及其系统的基本构成与定义，也按照运行风险对无人机进行了分类，同时对无人机驾驶员、飞行空域、无人机运行等与无人机安全作业最密切相关的事项进行了规定，体现了与当前《芝加哥公约》相关附件标准较高程度的一致性。此外，该文件规定了四种可以不划设隔离空域的无人机飞行情况，[②]对于如执行特殊任务的国家无人机或者经充分安全认证的中型、大型无人机，可与有人驾驶航空器混合飞行。[③] 这充分显示出我国在积极促进无人机纳入非隔离空域作业方面的工作进展。但是对于当前调整有人驾驶航空器的法律法规对无人机的适用与衔接等方面，文件中并没有进行说明。

与此同时，在参与国际规则制定方面，我国也在积极推进全球监管建设，如建议引入全球范围融合空域内民用无人机运行关键数据的分享机制，以及采纳通过无人机云系统对轻小型无人机进行监管的模式等。[④] 但这些提案的重点针对无人机运行的技术性航空安全保障，而非政策导向性建议。在当前规范国内无人机监管的同时，也应重视在国际规则制定上的政策性规则导向能力，适当考虑我国民用无人机的产业利益，充分发挥民航大国的关键

① 参见《关于征求〈无人驾驶航空器飞行管理暂行条例（征求意见稿）〉意见的通知》，载中国民用航空局网：http://www.caac.gov.cn/XWZX/MHYW/201610/t20161001_40006.html，最后访问日期：2018年5月9日。

② 《无人驾驶航空器飞行管理暂行条例（征求意见稿）》第30条。

③ 《无人驾驶航空器飞行管理暂行条例（征求意见稿）》第43条。

④ 国际民用航空组织工作文件：大会——第39届会议技术委员会，轻小型无人机运行和监管（A39－WP/335），载国际民用航空组织网：https://www.icao.int/Meetings/a39/Documents/WP/wp_335_zh.pdf，最后访问日期：2018年5月9日。

优势。

五、结　语

近年来,民用无人机的迅猛发展为全球带来了巨大的应用机遇与商业前景,同时也使其面临来自监管缺失、法律适用不明确等各方面的新生问题与挑战。各国达成的共识表明,需依托国际民航组织,在国际法层面制定一套使民用无人机安全运行且成功融入现行有人驾驶航空器空域管理体系的统一规则,并优先促进最具发展潜力的"遥控驾驶航空器系统"实现这一目标。在《芝加哥公约》框架下,近来国际民航组织以"标准和建议措施"的"立法"模式,制定出"遥控驾驶航空器系统"规则,代表了其针对民用无人机所取得的最新国际立法进展。该规则涉及遥控驾驶航空器系统的一般运行要求,还涵盖了遥控驾驶航空器证书、人员执照以及运行特许等内容。考虑到民用无人机未来在国际民用航空中广阔的应用前景,持续跟进研究相关标准和建议措施,对我国积极参与国际规则的制定,有效促进民用无人机融入非隔离空域开展作业活动意义重大。

论航空运送人之责任限制

吴光平[*]

一、前　　言

航空运送人民事责任体制采行责任限制之制度，系沿袭船舶所有人责任限制之制度。按船舶所有人责任限制制度之起源并不明确，且目前已难考，可确认的是国际法之父格劳秀斯（Hugo Grotius，1583～1645年）于1625年即主张船舶所有人责任限制制度合于正义要求，而1681年《法国海商条例》则于“第二编　海员及船舶”将船舶所有人责任限制制度纳入，于第八章中规定船舶所有人应对船长之行为负责，但仅以其船货抵充之，此即“委弃主义”（我国台湾地区文献称“委付主义”），该规定经略加修正后成为1807年法国《商法典》之内容，其他各国亦多遵循，采行船舶所有人责任限制制度直至今日（但历经海产主义、委付主义、船价主义、金额主义、选择主义、并用主义

* 台湾开南大学法律学系暨研究所专任副教授、法律硕士在职专班执行长。

之演变递擅);而在国际公约法方面,则有 1924 年《关于海船所有人责任限制某些法律规则之统一国际公约》(International Convention for the Unification of Certain Rules of Law relating to the Limitation of the Liability of Owners of Seagoing Vessels)、1957 年《关于海船所有人责任限制国际公约》(International Convention relating to the Limitation of the Liability of Owners of Seagoing Ships)、1976 年《海事求偿责任限制公约》(Convention on Limitation of Liability for Maritime Claims)三个主要之国际公约。而由于船舶所有人责任限制制度系针对因利用船舶所生非契约之债之损害赔偿,故针对因利用船舶所生契约之债之损害赔偿则另于运送契约加以规范,而惯称为海上运送人单位责任限制,如 1924 年《统一关于载货证券某些法律规则之国际公约》(International Convention for the Unification of Certain Rules of Law relating to Bills of Lading,以下简称《海牙规则》)第 4 条第 5 项第 1 段、1968 年《修正统一关于载货证券某些法律规则之国际公约议定书》(Protocol to Amend the International Convention for the Unification of Certain Rules of Law relating to Bills of Lading,以下简称《威士比规则》)第 2 条、1978 年《海上货物运送联合国公约》(United Nations Convention on the Carriage of Goods by Sea,以下简称《汉堡规则》)第 8 条、1979 年《修正经 1968 年 2 月 23 日议定书(威士比规则)所修正 1924 年 8 月 25 日之统一关于载货证券某些法律规则之国际公约(海牙规则)之议定书(特别提款权议定书)》[Protocol (SDR Protocol) amending the International Convention for the Unification of Certain Rules of Law relating to Bills of Lading of 25 August 1924 (The Hague Rules), as amended by the Protocol of 23 February 1968 (Visby Rules),以下简称《布鲁塞尔议定书》]第 2 条、2009 年《全程或部分海上货物运送契约之联合国公约》(United Nations Convention on Contracts for the International Carriage of Goods Wholly or Partly by Sea,以下简称《鹿特丹规则》)第 59 条等货物运送国际公约法、1961 年《统一关于海上旅客运送某些规则之国际公约》(International Convention for the Unification of Certain Rules Relating to the Carriage of

Passengers by Sea)第 6 条、1967 年《统一关于海上旅客行李运送某些规则之国际公约》(International Convention for the Unification of Certain Rules relating to Carriage of Passenger Luggage at Sea)第 6 条、1974 年《关于海上载运旅客及其行李之雅典公约》(Athens Convention relating to the Carriage of Passengers and their Luggage by Sea)第7 ~ 8 条、1976 年《修正 1974 年关于海上载运旅客及其行李之雅典公约之 1976 年议定书》(Protocol of 1976 to amend the Athens Convention relating to the Carriage of Passengers and their Luggage by Sea)第 2 条、1990 年《修正 1974 年关于海上载运旅客及其行李之雅典公约之 1990 年议定书》第 2 条、2002 年《1974 年关于海上载运旅客及其行李之雅典公约之 2002 年议定书》(Protocol of 2002 to the Athens Convention relating to the Carriage of Passengers and their Luggage by Sea)第 6 ~ 7 条等旅客运送国际公约法。就我国台湾地区"海商法"而言,船舶所有人责任限制系规定于"第二章　船舶"第 21 ~ 23 条,而海上运送人单位责任限制则规定于"第三章　运送"第 70 条。

由于海上运送之历史相当悠久,在发展演进之过程中海商法已建立起如船舶国籍制度、船舶登记制度、船舶所有人责任限制制度、海事优先权制度、船舶抵押权制度、海上运送人单位责任限制制度等完整而独立之法律体系,①而到 20 世纪才起步之航空运送,依循着海上运送之足迹,仍属自然,故航空法乃仿海商法建立航空器国籍制度、航空器登记制度、航空器营运人责任限制制度、航空器优先权制度、航空器抵押权制度、航空运送人单位责任限制制度等法律体系。② 因此,本文乃就航空运送人单位责任限制制度与航空

① 关于此等有别于民法之海商法上制度之由来与功能,以及以此等制度为元素所形成之海商法固有性(或独自性),参见吴光平:《海商法与海事国际私法研究》,台北,台湾财产法暨经济法研究协会 2007 年版,第 20 ~ 43 页。

② 就国际公约法而言,1919 年《关于飞航管理之公约》(Convention Relating to the Regulation of Aerial Navigation,以下简称《巴黎公约》)与 1944 年《国际民用航空公约》(Convention on International Civil Aviation,以下简称《芝加哥公约》)涉及航空器国籍制度与航空器登记制度,1948 年《国际承认航空器权利公约》(Convention on the International Recognition of Rights in Aircraft,以下简称《日内瓦公约》)涉及航空器优先权制度与航空器抵押权制度。

器营运人责任限制制度加以介绍、分析。

自1783年6月5日,法国孟戈菲兄弟[约瑟夫－米歇尔·孟戈菲(Joseph-Michel Montgolfier)与雅克－艾蒂安·孟戈菲(Jacques-Étienne Montgolfier)]首次将可用于运送之热气球升空,人类开启了航空活动。由于航空活动既不受海洋分隔,也无高山阻挡,此为船舶、火车、汽车等交通工具所不能者,故以航空器从事运送遂逐渐发展,尤其时至今日,航空旅客运送更是几乎取代了海上旅客运送。而航空运送所生之民事责任有二者极为重要,一是旅客或托运人因飞航意外事故,致造成旅客死亡、伤害或托运货物、行李之毁损、灭失时,航空运送人之民事责任;二是地面第三人因航空器在航行中对地面造成损害时,航空器使用人之民事责任,①此二者航空法借镜海商法之责任体制,前者师法海商法之海上运送人单位责任限制制度而于航空法形成航空运送人单位责任限制制度,后者师法海商法之船舶所有人责任限制制度而于航空法形成航空器营运人责任限制制度,二者共同构筑了航空法上民事责任为有限责任之基本原则,使无论是利用航空器所生契约之债之损害赔偿抑或利用航空器所生非契约之债之损害赔偿,航空运送人之赔偿责任皆有最高额度,此与民法上债务人以其财产为担保对债权人负无限清偿责任,有明显差异,此堪称航空法之一大特色,故就航空运送人责任限制(航空运送人单位责任限制＋航空器营运人责任限制)加以介绍、分析,实饶富意义。

二、航空运送人责任限制之国际公约法

(一)航空运送人单位责任限制

1. 华沙体系

(1)华沙体系之形成

1918年第一次世界大战结束后,因国际航空运送迅速发展,有关航空运

① 参见刘铁铮:《外国飞机对地面第三人造成损害有关国际立法之研究——从一九三三年罗马公约到一九七八年蒙特利尔议定书》,载《政大法学评论》1982年第26期。

送契约当事人所生权利义务规则之统一，成为当时迫切之需求，在法国努力下，于 1925 年 10 月 27 日至 11 月 6 日在巴黎召开了第一次国际航空私法会议。法国于会中曾提出一份公约草案，但因各国意见不一致而未能通过，唯与会各国同意指派专家成立一常设机关国际航空法律专家委员会（Comité International Technique d'Experts Juridiques Aériens，CITEJA）①，就法国提出之公约草案加以研议，并于 1928 年 5 月于西班牙马德里召开之第三次会议通过了最后版本之草案。第二次国际航空私法会议由波兰召集，自 1929 年 10 月 4 日至 12 日于华沙集会，会中就 CITEJA 所通过最后版本之草案加以审议后，通过了以法文为官方版本之《统一关于国际航空运送某些规则之公约》（Convention for the Unification of Certain Rules relating to International Carriage by Air，以下简称《华沙公约》）供各国签署，于 1933 年 2 月 13 日生效，至今已有 152 个缔约国。

《华沙公约》共五章 41 条，整部公约建立在航空运送人推定过失责任、航空运送人单位责任限制之原则、航空运送人单位责任限制之排除三基柱上，由此三基柱所建构之航空运送人责任制度对于国际航空运送人责任制度之统一具有相当贡献。随着航空技术之日新月异以及经济情势之变迁，《华沙公约》制定当时之时空背景，早已不符不断进步之现代航空运送之需求，故于各方不断要求修正之呼吁下，《华沙公约》历经数次修正、补充，然由于《华沙公约》之缔约国未必批准历次修正、补充《华沙公约》之国际公约与协定，故《华沙公约》本身、历次修正、补充《华沙公约》之国际公约与协定，以及于《华沙公约》之基础上航空运送人之私人协议，交杂成一极为庞大且错综复杂之"华沙体系"（Warsaw System or Warsaw Regime）。详言之，"华沙体系"除作为其中心之《华沙公约》外，尚包括 1955 年《修正 1929 年 10 月 12 日于华沙所签署统一关于国际航空运送某些规则之公约之议定书》（Protocol to Amend the Convention for the Unification of Certain Rules Relating to

① CITEJA 已于 1947 年解散，其业务则移交由国际民用航空组织（International Civil Aviation Organization，ICAO）下之法律委员会（Legal Committee）继续执行。

International Carriage by Air signed at Warsaw on 12 October 1929,以下简称《海牙议定书》)、1961年《为补充华沙公约之统一关于由契约运送人以外之人履行国际航空运送某些规则之公约》(Convention, Supplementary to the Warsaw Convention, for the Unification of Certain Rules Relating to International Carriage by Air Performed by a Person Other than the Contracting Carrier,以下简称《瓜达拉哈拉公约》)、1971年《修正由1955年9月28日海牙议定书所修正之1929年10月12日于华沙所签署统一关于国际航空运送某些规则之公约之议定书》(Protocol to Amend the Convention for the Unification of Certain Rules Relating to International Carriage by Air signed at Warsaw on 12 October 1929 as Amended by the Protocol done at The Hague on 28 September 1955,以下简称《瓜地马拉议定书》)、1975年《修正1929年10月12日于华沙所签署统一关于国际航空运送某些规则之公约之第1号追加议定书》(Additional Protocol No. 1 to Amend the Convention for the Unification of Certain Rules Relating to International Carriage by Air signed at Warsaw on 12 October 1929,以下简称《蒙特利尔第1号追加议定书》)、1975年《修正由1955年9月28日海牙议定书所修正之1929年10月12日于华沙所签署统一关于国际航空运送某些规则之公约之第2号追加议定书》(Additional Protocol No. 2 to Amend the Convention for the Unification of Certain Rules Relating to International Carriage by Air signed at Warsaw on 12 October 1929 as Amended by the Protocol done at The Hague on 28 September 1955,以下简称《蒙特利尔第2号追加议定书》)、1975年《修正由1971年3月8日所修正经1955年9月28日海牙议定书所修正之1929年10月12日于华沙所签署统一关于国际航空运送某些规则之公约之议定书之第3号追加议定书》(Additional Protocol No. 3 to Amend the Convention for the Unification of Certain Rules Relating to International Carriage by Air signed at Warsaw on 12 October 1929 as Amended by the Protocols done at The Hague on 28 September 1955 and at Guatemala City on 8 March 1971,以下简称《蒙特利

尔第3号追加议定书》)、1975年《修正由1955年9月28日海牙议定书所修正之1929年10月12日于华沙所签署统一关于国际航空运送某些规则之公约之蒙特利尔第4号议定书》(Montreal Protocol No. 4 to Amend the Convention for the Unification of Certain Rules Relating to International Carriage by Air signed at Warsaw on 12 October 1929 as Amended by the Protocol done at The Hague on 28 September 1955,以下简称《蒙特利尔第4号议定书》)等国际公约与协定,以及1966年航空公司就进出美国之国际航空运送与美国签订之《有关华沙公约与海牙议定书与责任限制有关之协议》(Agreement Relating to Liability Limitation of the Warsaw Convention and the Hague Protocol,以下简称《蒙特利尔协议》)、1992年日本航空运送人修订国际航空运送契约条款之《日本倡议》(Japanese Initiative of 1992)、1995年《国际航空运送协会》(International Air Transport Association,IATA)所通过《旅客责任之运送人间协议》(Intercarrier Agreement on Passenger Liability,IIA)、1996年国际航空运送协会所通过《实施国际航空运送协会运送人间协议之措施之协议》(Agreement on Measures to Implement the IATA InterCarrier Agreement,MIA)等航空运送人之私人协议。

(2)华沙公约之航空运送人单位责任限制

《华沙公约》系建立在航空运送人推定过失责任、航空运送人单位责任限制之原则、航空运送人单位责任限制之排除三基柱上。以航空运送人推定过失责任言,《华沙公约》第17条、第18条规定,旅客于飞机上或登机、离机作业过程中发生意外事故致旅客发生伤亡,或其他任何身体上之伤害,①以及已登记行李或货物交予运送人保管期间发生毁损、灭失,运送人皆应负赔

① Article 17:The carrier is liable for damage sustained in the event of the death or wounding of a passenger or any other bodily injury suffered by a passenger, if the accident which caused the damage so sustained took place on board the aircraft or in the course of any of the operations of embarking or disembarking.

偿责任,[①]且第 19 条亦规定,运送人就旅客、行李、货物因航空运送迟延所生之损害应负赔偿责任。[②] 然第 20 条规定,运送人如能证明其已采取一切必要措施防止意外事故发生,或采取该措施为不可能者,不负赔偿责任。[③] 由此可知,若有第 17 ~ 19 条所规定损害之发生,除非运送人能依第 20 条所规定之抗辩负举证,否则即需负赔偿责任,此显示出《华沙公约》系采取推定过失责任(presumed liability)。

由于运送人负推定过失责任,故《华沙公约》就运送人之赔偿责任以航空运送人单位责任限制之原则使之负有限责任,于公约第 22 条规定,航空运送人就旅客运送所负之责任以每一旅客赔偿 125 000 金法郎为限,交托之行李及货物以每公斤 250 金法郎为限,旅客随身物品以每件 5000 金法郎为限,而金法郎系指含有 90‰成色的 65.5 毫克黄金之法国法郎,此金额可以折合

① Article 18:1. The carrier is liable for damage sustained in the event of the destruction or loss of, or of damage to, any registered luggage or any goods, if the occurrence which caused the damage so sustained took place during the carriage by air. 2. The carriage by air within the meaning of the preceding paragraph comprises the period during which the luggage or goods are in charge of the carrier, whether in an aerodrome or on board an aircraft, or, in the case of a landing outside an aerodrome, in any place whatsoever. 3. The period of the carriage by air does not extend to any carriage by land, by sea or by river performed outside an aerodrome. If, however, such a carriage takes place in the performance of a contract for carriage by air, for the purpose of loading, delivery or transshipment, any damage is presumed, subject to proof to the contrary, to have been the result of an event which took place during the carriage by air.

② Article 19:The carrier is liable for damage occasioned by delay in the carriage by air of passengers, luggage or goods.

③ Article 20:1. The carrier is not liable if he proves that he and his agents have taken all necessary measures to avoid the damage or that it was impossible for him or them to take such measures. 2. In the carriage of goods and luggage the carrier is not liable if he proves that the damage was occasioned by negligent pilotage or negligence in the handling of the aircraft or in navigation and that, in all other respects, he and his agents have taken all necessary measures to avoid the damage.

成任何国家之货币取其整数。①

运送人之赔偿责任《华沙公约》虽采取航空运送人单位责任限制之原则，但又规定排除航空运送人单位责任限制之事由，使航空运送人于以下四情形即不得主张单位责任限制而仍应负无限清偿责任：①损害之发生系因运送人、运送人之受雇人或代理人之故意不法行为所致（第25条）；②②当事人间有特别协议（第23条反面解释）；③③托运人声明登记货物或行李依目的地价值计算，并加付运费者（第22条第2项但书）；④④运送文件有瑕疵（第3

① Article 22:1. In the carriage of passengers the liability of the carrier for each passenger is limited to the sum of 125 000 francs. Where, in accordance with the law of the Court seised of the case, damages may be awarded in the form of periodical payments, the equivalent capital value of the said payments shall not exceed 125 000 francs. Nevertheless, by special contract, the carrier and the passenger may agree to a higher limit of liability. 2. In the carriage of registered luggage and of goods, the liability of the carrier is limited to a sum of 250 francs per kilogram, unless the consignor has made, at the time when the package was handed over to the carrier, a special declaration of the value at delivery and has paid a supplementary sum if the case so requires. In that case the carrier will be liable to pay a sum not exceeding the declared sum, unless he proves that that sum is greater than the actual value to the consignor at delivery. 3. As regards objects of which the passenger takes charge himself the liability of the carrier is limited to 5 000 francs per passenger. 4. The sums mentioned above shall be deemed to refer to the French franc consisting of 65 milligrams gold of millesimal fineness 900. These sums may be converted into any national currency in round figures.

② Article 25:1. The carrier shall not be entitled to avail himself of the provisions of this Convention which exclude or limit his liability, if the damage is caused by his wilful misconduct or by such default on his part as, in accordance with the law of the Court seised of the case, is considered to be equivalent to wilful misconduct. 2. Similarly the carrier shall not be entitled to avail himself of the said provisions, if the damage is caused as aforesaid by any agent of the carrier acting within the scope of his employment.

③ Article 23: Any provision tending to relieve the carrier of liability or to fix a lower limit than that which is laid down in this Convention shall be null and void, but the nullity of any such provision does not involve the nullity of the whole contract, which shall remain subject to the provisions of this Convention.

④ Article 22:2. In the carriage of registered luggage and of goods, the liability of the carrier is limited to a sum of 250 francs per kilogram, unless the consignor has made, at the time when the package was handed over to the carrier, a special declaration of the value at delivery and has paid a supplementary sum if the case so requires. In that case the carrier will be liable to pay a sum not exceeding the declared sum, unless he proves that that sum is greater than the actual value to the consignor at delivery.

条第 2 项、第 4 条第 4 项、第 9 条)。[①]

(3)修正、补充华沙公约航空运送人单位责任限制之国际公约与协定

①1955 年《海牙议定书》

1955 年《海牙议定书》仍然维持《华沙公约》航空运送人推定过失责任、航空运送人单位责任限制原则之基柱,但适度且合理地增加运送人单位责任限制之额度,将《华沙公约》第 17 条旅客赔偿限度额从 125 000 金法郎提高至 250 000 金法郎(《海牙议定书》第 11 条第 1 项),[②]并将《华沙公约》第 25 条之故意不法行为不得主张单位责任限制修正为损害之发生系因运送人、其受雇人或代理人之故意或重大过失,或有所认识之过失行为所致者不得主张单位责任限制(《海牙议定书》第 13 条),且明定限于运送人之受雇人或代理人如证明损害之发生系因其执行职务范围内之行为所致者,方得主张单位责

① Article 3:2. The absence, irregularity or loss of the passenger ticket does not affect the existence or the validity of the contract of carriage, which shall none the less be subject to the rules of this Convention. Nevertheless, if the carrier accepts a passenger without a passenger ticket having been delivered he shall not be entitled to avail himself of those provisions of this Convention which exclude or limit his liability. Article 4:4. The absence, irregularity or loss of the luggage ticket does not affect the existence or the validity of the contract of carriage, which shall none the less be subject to the rules of this Convention. Nevertheless, if the carrier accepts luggage without a luggage ticket having been delivered, or if the luggage ticket does not contain the particulars set out at(d),(f) and(h) above, the carrier shall not be entitled to avail himself of those provisions of the Convention which exclude or limit his liability. Article 9: If the carrier accepts goods without an air consignment note having been made out, or if the air consignment note does not contain all the particulars set out in Article 8(a) to (i) inclusive and(q), the carrier shall not be entitled to avail himself of the provisions of this Convention which exclude or limit his liability.

② Article XI: Article 22 of the Convention shall be deleted and replaced by the following: "Article 22:1. In the carriage of persons the liability of the carrier for each passenger is limited to the sum of two hundred and fifty thousand francs. Where, in accordance with the law of the court seised of the case, damages may be awarded in the form of periodical payments, the equivalent capital value of the said payments shall not exceed two hundred and fifty thousand francs. Nevertheless, by special contract, the carrier and the passenger may agree to a higher limit of liability."

任限制(《海牙议定书》第13条)。[1]

②1961年《瓜达拉哈拉公约》

1961年《瓜达拉哈拉公约》主要系针对《华沙公约》以及经1955年《海牙议定书》修正后之《华沙公约》关于运送人所为之补充规范(第1条第1项),而将运送人区分为契约运送人及实际运送人,前者系指与旅客、托运人或其代理人缔结应受《华沙公约》所规范之运送契约之本人(《瓜达拉哈拉公约》第1条第2项),后者系指缔约运送人以外之基于缔约运送人之授权从事全部或一部运送之人(《瓜达拉哈拉公约》第1条第3项)。[2] 然无论是契约运送人抑或实际运送人,均得主张《华沙公约》之单位责任限制(第2条),[3]且其各自或其代理人及受雇人所为之行为,视为自己之行为(《瓜达拉哈拉公

① Article XIII: In Article 25 of the Convention, paragraphs 1 and 2 shall be deleted and replaced by the following: "The limits of liability specified in Article 22 shall not apply if it is proved that the damage resulted from an act or omission of the carrier, his servants or agents, done with intent to cause damage or recklessly and with knowledge that damage would probably result; provided that, in the case of such act or omission of a servant or agent, it is also proved that he was acting within the scope of his employment."

② Article I: In this Convention: (a) "Warsaw Convention" means the Convention for the Unification of Certain Rules Relating to International Carriage by Air signed at Warsaw on 12 October 1929, or the Warsaw Convention as amended at The Hague, 1955, according to whether the carriage under the agreement referred to in paragraph (b) is governed by the one or by the other; (b) "contracting carrier" means a person who as a principal makes an agreement for carriage governed by the Warsaw Convention with a passenger or consignor or with a person acting on behalf of the passenger or consignor; (c) "actual carrier" means a person other than the contracting carrier, who, by virtue of authority from the contracting carrier, performs the whole or part of the carriage contemplated in paragraph (b) but who is not with respect to such part a successive carrier within the meaning of the Warsaw Convention. Such authority is presumed in the absence of proof to the contrary.

③ Article II: If an actual carrier performs the whole or part of carriage which, according to the agreement referred to in Article I, paragraph (b), is governed by the Warsaw Convention, both the contracting carrier and the actual carrier shall, except as otherwise provided in this Convention, be subject to the rules of the Warsaw Convention, the former for the whole of the carriage contemplated in the agreement, the latter solely for the carriage which he performs.

约》第3条)。①

③1971年《瓜地马拉议定书》

国际民用航空组织为因应美国于1965年退出《华沙公约》,故着手进行修正《华沙公约》之相关作业,并于1971年2月在瓜地马拉市(Guatemala City)召开外交会议,同年3月8日通过《瓜地马拉议定书》。《瓜地马拉议定书》系修正《海牙议定书》,要者有三:第一,将过失推定主义改采严格责任主义,规定旅客于飞机上、登机或离机过程中之发生人身伤亡或其他身体上之伤害除系因旅客自身之健康状态所致者外,运送人应负损害赔偿责任(《瓜地马拉议定书》第4条第1项),②又旅客发生损害而运送人能证明旅客具与有过失之情形者,运送人就该旅客与有过失之限度内得为全部或一部免责(《瓜地马拉议定书》第7条),③但于迟到之情形,无论是旅客运送抑或货物

---

① Article III: 1. The acts and omissions of the actual carrier and of his servants and agents acting within the scope of their employment shall, in relation to the carriage performed by the actual carrier, be deemed to be also those of the contracting carrier. 2. The acts and omissions of the contracting carrier and of his servants and agents acting within the scope of their employment shall, in relation to the carriage performed by the actual carrier, be deemed to be also those of the actual carrier. Nevertheless, no such act or omission shall subject the actual carrier to liability exceeding the limits specified in Article 22 of the Warsaw Convention. Any special agreement under which the contracting carrier assumes obligations not imposed by the Warsaw Convention or any waiver of rights conferred by that Convention or any special declaration of interest in delivery at destination contemplated in Article 22 of the said Convention, shall not affect the actual carrier unless agreed to by him.

② Article IV: Article 17 of the Convention shall be deleted and replaced by the following: "Article 17: 1. The carrier is liable for damage sustained in case of death or personal injury of a passenger upon condition only that the event which caused the death or injury took place on board the aircraft or in the course of any of the operations of embarking or disembarking. However, the carrier is not liable if the death or injury resulted solely from the state of health of the passenger."

③ Article VII: Article 21 of the Convention shall be deleted and replaced by the following: "Article 21: If the carrier proves that the damage was caused or contributed to by the negligence or other wrongful act or omission of the person claiming compensation, the carrier shall be wholly or partly exonerated from his liability to such person to the extent that such negligence or wrongful act or omission caused or contributed to the damage. When by reason of the death or injury of a passenger compensation is claimed by a person other than the passenger, the carrier shall likewise be wholly or partly exonerated from his liability to the extent that he proves that the damage was caused or contributed to by the negligence or other wrongful act or omission of that passenger."

运送,仍维持过失推定主义(《瓜地马拉议定书》第 6 条);[①]第二,增加运送人单位责任限制之额度,规定运送人就旅客伤亡之责任限额为每人 1 500 000 金法郎,运送人就旅客迟延之责任限额为每人 62 500 金法郎,运送人就行李运送之责任限额为 15 000 金法郎,而货物运送则维持每公斤 250 金法郎(《瓜地马拉议定书》第 8 条第 1 项、第 2 项);[②]第三,赋予运送人单位责任限制不可突破性,规定运送人对旅客运送不会因其故意或相当于故意之行为而不能主张责任限制,但货物运送则排除运送人之责任限制(《瓜地马拉议定书》第 10 条)。[③]

---

① Article VI: Article 20 of the Convention shall be deleted and replaced by the following: "Article 20: 1. In the carriage of passengers and baggage the carrier shall not be liable for damage occasioned by delay if he proves that he and his servants and agents have taken all necessary measures to avoid the damage or that it was impossible for them to take such measures. 2. In the carriage of cargo the carrier shall not be liable for damage resulting from destruction, loss, damage or delay if he proves that he and his servants and agents have taken all necessary measures to avoid the damage or that it was impossible for them to take such measures."

② Article VIII: Article 22 of the Convention shall be deleted and replaced by the following: "Article 22: 1. (a) In the carriage of persons the liability of the carrier is limited to the sum of one million five hundred thousand francs for the aggregate of the claims, however founded, in respect of damage suffered as a result of the death or personal injury of each passenger. Where, in accordance with the law of the court seised of the case, damages may be awarded in the form of periodic payments, the equivalent capital value of the said payments shall not exceed one million five hundred thousand francs. (b) In the case of delay in the carriage of persons the liability of the carrier for each passenger is limited to sixty-two thousand five hundred francs. (c) In the carriage of baggage the liability of the carrier in the case of destruction, loss, damage or delay is limited to fifteen thousand francs for each passenger. 2. (a) In the carriage of cargo, the liability of the carrier is limited to a sum of two hundred and fifty francs per kilogramme, unless the consignor has made, at the time when the package was handed over to the carrier, a special declaration of interest in delivery at destination and has paid a supplementary sum if the case so requires. In that case the carrier will be liable to pay a sum not exceeding the declared sum, unless he proves that that sum is greater than the consignor's actual interest in delivery at destination. (b) In the case of loss, damage or delay of part of the cargo, or of any object contained therein, the weight to be taken into consideration in determining the amount to which the carrier's liability is limited shall be only the total weight of the package or packages concerned. Nevertheless, when the loss, damage or delay of a part of the cargo, or of an object contained therein, affects the value of other packages covered by the same air waybill, the total weight of such package or packages shall also be taken into consideration in determining the limit of liability."

③ Article X: Article 25 of the Convention shall be deleted and replaced by the following: "Article 25: The limit of liability specified in paragraph 2 of Article 22 shall not apply if it is proved that the damage resulted from an act or omission of the carrier, his servants or agents, done with intent to cause damage or recklessly and with knowledge that damage would probably result; provided that, in the case of such act or omission of a servant or agent, it is also proved that he was acting within the scope of his employment."

④1975年《蒙特利尔议定书》

国际民用航空组织于1975年在加拿大蒙特利尔召开第九次国际航空私法会议,会议原本之召开目的系解决《瓜地马拉议定书》制定时漏未处理《海牙议定书》有关货物及邮件运送等条项之修正,但于会议中,有人鉴于运送人责任限额以黄金为基础换算成货币带有相当之不确定性,遂有提议将责任限额改以国际货币基金会(International Monetary Fund,IMF)之特别提款权(Special Drawing Rights,SDR)计算列入议案中,经讨论后,通过了三个追加议定书及一个议定书。

《蒙特利尔第1号追加议定书》系将《华沙公约》责任限额之以金法郎计算修正为以特别提款权表示,将航空运送人就旅客运送所负之责任以每一旅客赔偿125 000金法郎为限修正为每一旅客8300 SDR为限,交托之行李及货物以每公斤250金法郎为限修正为以每公斤17 SDR为限,旅客随身物品以每件5000金法郎为限修正为以每件332 SDR为限(《蒙特利尔第1号追加议定书》第2条第1~3项)。[①]

《蒙特利尔第2号追加议定书》系将《海牙议定书》责任限额之以金法郎计算修正为以特别提款权表示,将航空运送人就旅客运送所负责任以每一旅客250 000金法郎为限修正为每一旅客16 600 SDR为限,旅客随身物品则以每件5000金法郎为限修正为以每件332 SDR为限,交托之行李及货物则规

---

① Article II: Article 22 of the Convention shall be deleted and replaced by the following: "Article 22: 1. In the carriage of passengers the liability of the carrier for each passenger is limited to the sum of 8300 Special Drawing Rights. Where, in accordance with the law of the court seised of the case, damages may be awarded in the form of periodic payments, the equivalent capital value of the said payments shall not exceed this limit. Nevertheless, by special contract, the carrier and the passenger may agree to a higher limit of liability. 2. In the carriage of registered baggage and of cargo, the liability of the carrier is limited to a sum of 17 Special Drawing Rights per kilogramme, unless the consignor has made, at the time when the package was handed over to the carrier, a special declaration of interest in delivery at destination and has paid a supplementary sum if the case so requires. In that case the carrier will be liable to pay a sum not exceeding the declared sum, unless he proves that that sum is greater than the consignor's actual interest in delivery at destination. 3. As regards objects of which the passenger takes charge himself the liability of the carrier is limited to 332 Special Drawing Rights per passenger."

定以每公斤 17 SDR 为限(《蒙特利尔第 2 号追加议定书》第 2 条第 1 ~ 3 项)。[①]

《蒙特利尔第 3 号追加议定书》系将《瓜地马拉议定书》责任限额之以金法郎计算修正为以特别提款权表示,将航空运送人就旅客运送所负责任以每一旅客 1 500 000 金法郎为限修正为每一旅客 10 000 SDR 为限,且如同《瓜地马拉议定书》,运送人对旅客运送不会因其故意或相当于故意之行为而不能主张责任限制,而旅客运送迟到责任则规定以每一旅客以 4150 SDR 为限,行李(无论交付托运或旅客随身物品)发生毁损、灭失或迟到则规定对每一旅客所负责任以 1000 SDR 为限,货物发生毁损、灭失、迟到所负责任则规定

① Article II: Article 22 of the Convention shall be deleted and replaced by the following: "Article 22:1. In the carriage of persons the liability of the carrier for each passenger is limited to the sum of 16 600 Special Drawing Rights. Where, in accordance with the law of the court seised of the case, damages may be awarded in the form of periodic payments, the equivalent capital value of the said payments shall not exceed this limit. Nevertheless, by special contract, the carrier and the passenger may agree to a higher limit of liability. 2. (a) In the carriage of registered baggage and of cargo, the liability of the carrier is limited to a sum of 17 Special Drawing Rights per kilogramme, unless the passenger or consignor has made, at the time when the package was handed over to the carrier, a special declaration of interest in delivery at destination and has paid a supplementary sum if the case so requires. In that case the carrier will be liable to pay a sum not exceeding the declared sum, unless he proves that that sum is greater than the passenger's or consignor's actual interest in delivery at destination. (b) In the case of loss, damage or delay of part of registered baggage or cargo, or of any object contained therein, the weight to be taken into consideration in determining the amount to which the carrier's liability is limited shall be only the total weight of the package or packages concerned. Nevertheless, when the loss, damage or delay of a part of the registered baggage or cargo, or of an object contained therein, affects the value of other packages covered by the same baggage check or the same air waybill, the total weight of such package or packages shall also be taken into consideration in determining the limit of liability. 3. As regards objects of which the passenger takes charge himself the liability of the carrier is limited to 332 Special Drawing Rights per passenger."

以 17 SDR 为限(《蒙特利尔第 2 号追加议定书》第 2 条第 1 ~ 2 项)。①

《蒙特利尔第 4 号议定书》系就《海牙议定书》所规定之运送规则作出修正,故称为议定书而非如同第 1 ~ 3 号因未修正运送规则故称为附加议定书。《蒙特利尔第 4 号议定书》除规定运送文件得以电磁方法为之(第 3 条),②更

---

① Article II: Article 22 of the Convention shall be deleted and replaced by the following: "Article 22: 1. (a) In the carriage of persons the liability of the carrier is limited to the sum of 100 000 Special Drawing Rights for the aggregate of the claims, however founded, in respect of damage suffered as a result of the death or personal injury of each passenger. Where, in accordance with the law of the court seised of the case, damages may be awarded in the form of periodic payments, the equivalent capital value of the said payments shall not exceed 100 000 Special Drawing Rights. (b) In the case of delay in the carriage of persons the liability of the carrier for each passenger is limited to 4150 Special Drawing Rights. (c) In the carriage of baggage the liability of the carrier in the case of destruction, loss, damage or delay is limited to 1000 Special Drawing Rights for each passenger. 2. (a) In the carriage of cargo, the liability of the carrier is limited to a sum of 17 Special Drawing Rights per kilogramme, unless the consignor has made, at the time when the package was handed over to the carrier, a special declaration of interest in delivery at destination and has paid a supplementary sum if the case so requires. In that case the carrier will be liable to pay a sum not exceeding the declared sum, unless he proves that that sum is greater than the consignor's actual interest in delivery at destination. (b) In the case of loss, damage or delay of part of the cargo, or of any object contained therein, the weight to be taken into consideration in determining the amount to which the carrier's liability is limited shall be only the total weight of the package or packages concerned. Nevertheless, when the loss, damage or delay of a part of the cargo, or of an object contained therein, affects the value of other packages covered by the same air waybill, the total weight of such package or packages shall also be taken into consideration in determining the limit of liability."

② Article III: In Chapter II of the Convention-Section III (Articles 5 to 16) shall be deleted and replaced by the following: "Section III. Documentation relating to cargo: Article 5: 1. In respect of the carriage of cargo an air waybill shall be delivered. 2. Any other means which would preserve a record of the carriage to be performed may, with the consent of the consignor, be substituted for the delivery of an air waybill. If such other means are used, the carrier shall, if so requested by the consignor, deliver to the consignor a receipt for the cargo permitting identification of the consignment and access to the information contained in the record preserved by such other means. 3. The impossibility of using, at points of transit and destination, the other means which would preserve the record of the carriage referred to in paragraph 2 of this Article does not entitle the carrier to refuse to accept the cargo for carriage."

规定航空运送人对货物之毁损、灭失原则上负严格责任(第 4 条)①且以每公斤 17 SDR 为限(第 7 条)。②

---

① Article IV: Article 18 of the Convention shall be deleted and replaced by the following: "Article 18: 1. The carrier is liable for damage sustained in the event of the destruction or loss of, or damage to, any registered baggage, if the occurrence which caused the damage so sustained took place during the carriage by air. 2. The carrier is liable for damage sustained in the event of the destruction or loss of, or damage to, cargo upon condition only that the occurrence which caused the damage so sustained took place during the carriage by air. 3. However, the carrier is not liable if he proves that the destruction, loss of, or damage to, the cargo resulted solely from one or more of the following: (a) inherent defect, quality or vice of that cargo; (b) defective packing of that cargo performed by a person other than the carrier or his servants or agents; (c) an act of war or an armed conflict; (d) an act of public authority carried out in connexion with the entry, exit or transit of the cargo. 4. The carriage by air within the meaning of the preceding paragraphs of this Article comprises the period during which the baggage or cargo is in the charge of the carrier, whether in an airport or on board an aircraft, or in the case of a landing outside an airport, in any place whatsoever. 5. The period of the carriage by air does not extend to any carriage by land, by sea or by river performed outside an airport. If, however, such carriage takes place in the performance of a contract for carriage by air, for the purpose of loading, delivery or transhipment, any damage is presumed, subject to proof to the contrary, to have been the result of an event which took place during the carriage by air."

② Article VII: In Article 22 of the Convention (a) in paragraph 2 (a) the words "and of cargo" shall be deleted. (b) after paragraph 2 (a) the following paragraph shall be inserted: "(b) In the carriage of cargo, the liability of the carrier is limited to a sum of 17 Special Drawing Rights per kilogramme, unless the consignor has made, at the time when the package was handed over to the carrier, a special declaration of interest in delivery at destination and has paid a supplementary sum if the case so requires. In that case the carrier will be liable to pay a sum not exceeding the declared sum, unless he proves that the sum is greater than the consignor's actual interest in delivery at destination." (c) paragraph 2 (b) shall be designated as paragraph 2 (c). (d) after paragraph 5 the following paragraph shall be inserted: "6. The sums mentioned in terms of the Special Drawing Right in this Article shall be deemed to refer to the Special Drawing Right as defined by the International Monetary Fund. Conversion of the sums into national currencies shall, in case of judicial proceedings, be made according to the value of such currencies in terms of the Special Drawing Right at the date of the judgment. The value of a national currency, in terms of the Special Drawing Right, of a High Contracting Party which is a Member of the International Monetary Fund, shall be calculated in accordance with the method of valuation applied by the International Monetary Fund, in effect at the date of the judgment, for its operations and transactions. The value of a national currency, in terms of the Special Drawing Right, of a High Contracting Party which is not a Member of the International Monetary Fund, shall be calculated in a manner determined by that High Contracting Party. Nevertheless, those States which are not Members of the International Monetary Fund and whose law does not permit the application of the provisions of paragraph 2 (b) of Article 22 may, at the time of ratification or accession or at any time thereafter, declare that the limit of liability

(4)修正、补充华沙公约航空运送人单位责任限制之航空运送人私人协议

①1966年《蒙特利尔协议》

虽然《海牙议定书》已将航空运送人对旅客人身伤亡之责任限额提高至250 000金法郎,但美国对此数额仍嫌过低,并于1965年11月15日宣布退出《华沙公约》,此事件史称为"华沙公约危机",而依《华沙公约》第39条第2项之规定,退出公约于通知后6个月发生效力,亦即美国之退出会于1966年5月15日生效。国际民用航空组织担心以美国如此之经济大国退出《华沙公约》,其他经济水准达已开发国家之列之会员国恐将效尤而退出,故邀请美国参加外交会议加以挽回,但宣告失败,之后由国际航空运送协会居中斡旋,于1966年在加拿大蒙特利尔召开会议,会中与美国达成《蒙特利尔协议》。由美国民用航空局(Civil Aeronautics Board,CAB)遂于1966年5月13日以行政命令批准《蒙特利尔协议》,故而通知波兰撤回其退出华沙公约之声明,"华沙公约危机"因而解除。

《蒙特利尔协议》内容之要者有:第一,若旅客所持机票系以美国为出发地、目的地或协议经停地,且合于《华沙公约》或《海牙议定书》所定之国际运送者,运送人同意将责任限额提高至75 000美元(含诉讼费用、律师费等,扣除后为58 000美元),并放弃《华沙公约》第20条有关"已采取一切必要措

of the carrier in judicial proceedings in their territories is fixed at a sum of two hundred and fifty monetary units per kilogramme. This monetary unit corresponds to sixty-five and a half milligrammes of gold of millesimal fineness nine hundred. This sum may be converted into the national currency concerned in round figures. The conversion of this sum into the national currency shall be made according to the law of the State concerned."

施”避免事故发生之抗辩;①第二,航空公司交付旅客之客票,其上应载有适用《华沙公约》或《海牙议定书》之文字。②

《蒙特利尔协议》为非政府形态之航空公司成功地完成一个具有可行性之和解方案,此意味着企业之私人协议将来可能被广泛使用,然《蒙特利尔协议》之效力仅以进出美国为限,但此种美国与特定航空公司间以私人协议之方式修正《华沙公约》之适用,使其具有一般国际条约法律之效力,其结果不但侵蚀《华沙公约》统一国际航空私法之作用,且与美国身为《华沙公约》之会员国负有遵守公约之义务抵触。唯《蒙特利尔协议》就航空运送人之责任标准采行严格责任,为“华沙体系”之突破,对日后之《瓜地马拉议定书》、《蒙特利尔第3号追加议定书》及《日本倡议》造成影响。

---

① 1. Each of the Carriers shall effective 16th May 1966, include the following in its conditions of carriage, including tariffs embodying conditions of carriage filed by it with any government: “The carrier shall avail itself of the limitation of liability provided in the Convention for the Unification of Certain Rules Relating to International Carriage by Air signed at Warsaw 12th October 1929, or provided in the said Convention as amended by the Protocol signed at The Hague 28th September 1955. However in accordance with Article 22(1) of said Convention, or said Convention as amended by said Protocol, the Carrier agrees that, as to all international transportation by the Carrier as defined in the said Convention, or said Convention as amended by said Protocol, which, according to the Contract of Carriage, includes a point in the United States of America as a point of origin, point of destination, or agreed stopping place (i) The limit for each passenger for death, wounding, or other bodily injury shall be the sum of US $75 000 inclusive of legal fees and costs, except that, in case of a claim brought in a State where provision is made for separate award of legal fees and costs, the limit shall be the sum of US $58 000 exclusive of legal fees and costs. (ii) The Carrier shall not, with respect to any claim arising out of the death, wounding, or other bodily injury of a passenger, avail itself of any defense under Article 20(1) of said Convention or said Convention as amended by said Protocol. Nothing herein shall be deemed to affect the rights and liabilities of the Carrier with regard to any claim brought by, on behalf of, or in respect of any person who has wilfully caused damage which resulted in death, wounding, or other bodily injury of a passenger.”

② 2. Each carrier shall, at the time of delivery of the ticket, furnish to each passenger whose transportation is governed by the Convention, or the Convention as amended by the Hague Protocol, and by the special contract described in paragraph 1, the following notice, which shall be printed in type at least as large as 10 point modern type and in ink contrasting with the stock in (i) each ticket; (ii) a piece of paper either placed in the ticket envelope with the ticket or attached to the ticket; or (iii) on the ticket envelope.

②1992 年《日本倡议》

1992 年 6 月,日本 10 家定期航班之航空公司联名宣布修正其运送条款,将其于国际运送对旅客所负责任限制提高至 100 000 SDR,并于 1992 年 11 月 20 日生效。此由日本之航空公司修正之运送条款,即为 1992 年《日本倡议》。

《日本倡议》内容之要者有:第一,《华沙公约》(含《海牙议定书》)第 17 条对于旅客死伤或其他身体上伤害之责任之任何诉讼,排除《华沙公约》(含《海牙议定书》)第 20 条第 1 项之任何抗辩;第二,上述诉讼放弃《华沙公约》(含《海牙议定书》)第 20 条第 1 项在 100 000 SDR 内之任何抗辩,此 100 000 SDR 不包含法院认为适当之诉讼费用与律师费用。由此可知,《日本倡议》最大之特色在于航空运送人责任采取"双阶制"(two tier system),航空运送人放弃依《华沙公约》(含《海牙议定书》)第 20 条第 1 项之抗辩者,采《蒙特利尔协议》之严格责任,超过 100 000 SDR 之请求,则恢复可依《华沙公约》(含《海牙议定书》)第 20 条第 1 项抗辩,此时采推定过失责任。

《日本倡议》系在《华沙体系》下以运送条款之契约形态所形成之国际航空运送人责任体制,只要该航空运送人系日本航空公司,即有适用。

③1995 年《旅客责任之运送人间协议》

国际航空运送协会于 1995 年 10 月 31 日在马来西亚吉隆坡举行之年会中,与会代表一致通过《旅客责任之运送人间协议》。

《旅客责任之运送人间协议》内容之要者有:第一,运送人就《华沙公约》第 17 条有关旅客人身伤亡之诉讼,放弃《华沙公约》第 22 条第 1 项可回复损害赔偿请求之责任限额者,得依旅客住所地法确定及判决损害赔偿数额;[①] 第二,保留所有得依公约所为之抗辩,但若情况允许,运送人得放弃任何抗

① 1. To take action to waive the limitation of liability on recoverable compensatory damages in Article 22 paragraph 1 of the Warsaw Convention 2 as to claims for death, wounding or other bodily injury of a passenger within the meaning of Article 17 of the Convention, so that recoverable compensatory damages may be determined and awarded by reference to the law of the domicile of the passenger.

辩,包括在一定请求可恢复损害赔偿数额内之金融上限制。①

观《旅客责任之运送人间协议》之内容,其究竟采行何种责任制度,颇有疑义,有认为系采单一之推定过失责任,有认为从其就特定金额放弃抗辩权可知系采推定过失责任与严格责任之“双阶制”,亦有认为就特定金额放弃其抗辩权系采单一之严格责任,但无疑的,此不明确使航空运送人责任制度更为复杂。

④1996 年《实施国际航空运送协会运送人间协议之措施之协议》

国际航空运送协会于 1996 年 2 月及 4 月分别于美国迈阿密及加拿大蒙特利尔召开会议,作成两个实施《旅客责任之运送人间协议》之草案,最后采用在于美国迈阿密所拟订之草案,即为《实施国际航空运送协会运送人间协议之措施之协议》。

《实施国际航空运送协会运送人间协议之措施之协议》内容之要者有:第一,签署《旅客责任之运送人间协议》之运送人就《华沙公约》第 17 条所引起之损害而提起之损害赔偿诉讼,不应援引《华沙公约》第 22 条第 1 项之责任限制,且在该诉讼中不超过 100 000 SDR 之范围内,原则上不得援引《华沙公约》第 20 条第 1 项之任何抗辩;②第二,签署之运送人可于其运送条款中加入下列之选项:①运送人同意依应适用之法律,就有关损害赔偿之请求,依旅客住所地或其永久居所在地之该适用之法律为之。②运送人就有关损害赔偿之诉,不超过 100 000 SDR 内之部分,不得援引《华沙公约》第 20 条第 1 项

---

① 2. To reserve all available defences pursuant to the provisions of the Convention; nevertheless, any carrier may waive any defence up to a specified monetary amount of recoverable compensatory damages as circumstances may warrant.

② I. Pursuant to the IATA Intercarrier Agreement of 31 October 1995, the undersigned carriers agree to implement said Agreement by incorporating in their conditions of carriage and tariffs, where necessary, the following: 1. …………………………………… {CARRIER} shall not invoke the limitation of liability in Article 22(1) of the Convention as to any claim for recoverable compensatory damages arising under Article 17 of the Convention. 2. …………………………………… {CARRIER} shall not avail itself of any defence under Article 20(1) of the Convention with respect to that portion of such claim which does not exceed 100 000 SDRs(*)[unless option II(2) is used].

之任何抗辩,但经政府授权特定航线另定较低额度者,其抗辩权则不受影响。①

2. 蒙特利尔公约

(1)蒙特利尔公约之制定

按制定《华沙公约》之目的系期望统一国际航空运送规则,以一套国际运送国际航空运送规则以促进民用航空业之成长及茁壮,但由于《华沙公约》所规定航空运送人责任限额于制定当时与开始生效后之航空技术与经济情势之变迁所生差距逐渐因时间因素而拉大,《华沙公约》制定当时之时空背景,早已不符不断进步之现代航空运送之需求,故于各方不断要求修正之呼吁下,自1955年后,《华沙公约》历经数次修正、补充,然由于《华沙公约》之缔约国未必批准历次修正、补充《华沙公约》之国际公约与协定,故《华沙公约》本身、历次修正、补充《华沙公约》之国际公约与协定,以及于《华沙公约》之基础上航空运送人之私人协议,交杂成一极为庞大且错综复杂之"华沙体系",附加以各国内国法及法院态度之分歧,导致《华沙公约》统一国际航空运送规则之初衷岌岌可危,整个"华沙体系"不仅面临内部规范不统一之问题,甚至整体适用上亦发生龃龉,故国际上开始出现制定新公约以取代并统一"华沙体系"之呼吁。

国际民用航空组织于1975年制定了《蒙特利尔议定书》(三个追加议定书及一个议定书),沉寂近20年,于1995年再度致力于"华沙体系"之现代化,其理事会于1997年成立华沙体系现代化及统一化特别工作小组(The Special Group on Modernization and Consolidation of the Warsaw System,

---

① II. At the option of the carrier, its conditions of carriage and tariffs also may include the following provisions: 1. …………………………………… {CARRIER} agrees that subject to applicable law, recoverable compensatory damages for such claims may be determined by reference to the law of the domicile or permanent residence of the passenger. 2. …………………………………… {CARRIER} shall not avail itself of any defence under Article 20(1) of the Convention with respect to that portion of such claims which does not exceed 100 000 SDRs, except that such waiver is limited to the amounts shown below for the routes indicated, as may be authorised by governments concerned with the transportation involved.

SGMW),将"华沙体系"相关规定加以整合,研议成新公约草案。国际民用航空组织遂于1999年5月10日于加拿大蒙特利尔召开外交会议,针对该新公约草案讨论,于同年5月28日通过了《统一关于国际航空运送某些规则之公约》(Convention for the Unification of Certain Rules Relating to International Carriage by Air,以下简称《蒙特利尔公约》)。《蒙特利尔公约》已于2003年11月4日生效,包括美国、英国与中国在内共有104个国家签署。

《蒙特利尔公约》共七章57条。《蒙特利尔公约》内容之要者有:第一,将"华沙体系"之各法律文件加以整合,因此于体系上乃将《瓜达拉哈拉公约》纳入使之成一独立章节;第二,于运送文件之格式方面,《蒙特利尔公约》较"华沙体系"更为简化、现代性;第三,于运送人旅客运送责任方面,《蒙特利尔公约》一反"华沙体系"所采行之单一责任体制而改采"双阶制",航空运送人对于旅客运送责任明确排除任何惩罚性(punitive)、惩戒性(exemplary)或其他非填补性损害赔偿(other non-compensatory damages),且责任限额亦定期视通货膨胀情形而调整;第四,新增预付金制度(advance payments);第五,强制航空运送人就其责任限额保险。

(2)旅客运送责任

航空运送人对于旅客发生人身伤亡应负之责任,《蒙特利尔公约》采取《日本倡议》所定之"双阶制",以100 000 SDR作为区分两种责任制度之分水岭。依公约第21条之规定:于100 000 SDR范围内之损害运送人适用严格责任,除非旅客与有过失,否则运送人不得主张任何抗辩,此为第一阶;于100 000 SDR范围以上之损害运送人适用推定过失责任,倘运送人不能证明损害非由其本身或其受雇人或代理人之过失所致,或损害系由第三人之过失所致者外,运送人即应负责,此为第二阶。于第二阶之范围内,实际运用之结果等于没有任何责任限制,盖责任基础从难以证明之《华沙公约》(包括《海牙议定书》)所规定之"故意不法行为"变更为"推定过失或重大过失行为",使举证责任从原告变动到运送人,其结果使第二阶已接近绝对责任,故为了因应此一变动可能动辄使运送人容易就制造人制造航空器有缺陷或恐怖攻击而负责,复规定运送人如能证明“损害完全地由于第三人之不当行为所致”者,即不负责任之免责规定。[①]

(3)行李与货物之运送责任

航空运送人对于行李运送发生毁损、灭失应负之责任,《蒙特利尔公约》维持交托及未交托行李之区分而异其责任:交托行李如系由运送人所照管者,除了行李内在缺陷以及旅客与有过失者外,运送人就交托行李因毁损、灭失所负之责任适用严格责任(第 17 条第 2 项);[②]就未交托行李包括个人物品,适用过失责任,仅在赔偿请求人证明运送人对非托运行李之损害有过失时,运送人始须负责(第 20 条)。[③] 此外,对于运送人就交托行李所负责任范围,《蒙特利尔公约》非以重量为据,且不采以往《华沙公约》(包括《海牙议定书》)仅就交托行李为规范,而系规定无论交托行李或未交托行李所负之责任以每一旅客 1000 SDR 为限,且无论此等行李是否发生毁损、灭失或迟到,

---

① Article 21:1. For damages arising under paragraph 1 of Article 17 not exceeding 100 000 Special Drawing Rights for each passenger, the carrier shall not be able to exclude or limit its liability. 2. The carrier shall not be liable for damages arising under paragraph 1 of Article 17 to the extent that they exceed for each passenger 100 000 Special Drawing Rights if the carrier proves that: (a) such damage was not due to the negligence or other wrongful act or omission of the carrier or its servants or agents; or (b) such damage was solely due to the negligence or other wrongful act or omission of a third party.

② Article 17:2. The carrier liable for damage sustained in case of destruction or loss of, or of damage to, checked baggage upon condition only that the event which caused the destruction, loss or damage took place on board the aircraft or during any period within which the checked baggage was in the charge of the carrier. However, the carrier is not liable if and to the extent that the damage resulted from the inherent defect, quality or vice of the baggage. In the case of unchecked baggage, including personal items, the carrier is liable if the damage resulted from its fault or that of its servants or agents.

③ Article 20: If the carrier proves that the damage was caused or contributed to by the negligence or other wrongful act or omission of the person claiming compensation, or the person from whom he or she derives his or her rights, the carrier shall be wholly or partly exonerated from its liability to the claimant to the extent that such negligence or wrongful act or omission caused or contributed to the damage. When by reason of death or injury of a passenger compensation is claimed by a person other than the passenger, the carrier shall likewise be wholly or partly exonerated from its liability to the extent that it proves that the damage was caused or contributed to by the negligence or other wrongful act or omission of that passenger. This Article applies to all the liability provisions in this Convention, including paragraph 1 of Article 21.

除非损害系因运送人故意不法行为所致(第 22 条第 5 项),且旅客于必要时得预先支付额外费用以获得较高之责任限额(第 22 条第 5 项)。①

航空运送人对于货物运送发生毁损、灭失应负之责任,《蒙特利尔公约》不采以往《华沙公约》(包括《海牙议定书》)之推定过失责任,而改采严格责

① Article 22:1. In the case of damage caused by delay as specified in Article 19 in the carriage of persons, the liability of the carrier for each passenger is limited to 4150 Special Drawing Rights. 2. In the carriage of baggage, the liability of the carrier in the case of destruction, loss, damage or delay is limited to 1000 Special Drawing Rights for each passenger unless the passenger has made, at the time when the checked baggage was handed over to the carrier, a special declaration of interest in delivery at destination and has paid a supplementary sum if the case so requires. In that case the carrier will be liable to pay a sum not exceeding the declared sum, unless it proves that the sum is greater than the passenger's actual interest in delivery at destination. 3. In the carriage of cargo, the liability of the carrier in the case of destruction, loss, damage or delay is limited to a sum of 17 Special Drawing Rights per kilogram, unless the consignor has made, at the time when the package was handed over to the carrier, a special declaration of interest in delivery at destination and has paid a supplementary sum if the case so requires. In that case the carrier will be liable to pay a sum not exceeding the declared sum, unless it proves that the sum is greater than the consignor's actual interest in delivery at destination. 4. In the case of destruction, loss, damage or delay of part of the cargo, or of any object contained therein, the weight to be taken into consideration in determining the amount to which the carrier's liability is limited shall be only the total weight of the package or packages concerned. Nevertheless, when the destruction, loss, damage or delay of a part of the cargo, or of an object contained therein, affects the value of other packages covered by the same air waybill, or the same receipt or, if they were not issued, by the same record preserved by the other means referred to in paragraph 2 of Article 4, the total weight of such package or packages shall also be taken into consideration in determining the limit of liability. 5. The foregoing provisions of paragraphs 1 and 2 of this Article shall not apply if it is proved that the damage resulted from an act or omission of the carrier, its servants or agents, done with intent to cause damage or recklessly and with knowledge that damage would probably result; provided that, in the case of such act or omission of a servant or agent, it is also proved that such servant or agent was acting within the scope of its employment. 6. The limits prescribed in Article 21 and in this Article shall not prevent the court from awarding, in accordance with its own law, in addition, the whole or part of the court costs and of the other expenses of the litigation incurred by the plaintiff, including interest. The foregoing provision shall not apply if the amount of the damages awarded, excluding court costs and other expenses of the litigation, does not exceed the sum which the carrier has offered in writing to the plaintiff within a period of six months from the date of the occurrence causing the damage, or before the commencement of the action, if that is later.

任(第18条第1项),[①]除了第18条第2项所定内在缺陷、战争以及公约第20条所规定与有过失抗辩等情形外,运送人始得主张免责。又鉴于实务上经托运之货物通常投保财产保险,故运送人对于货物所负责任限额,仍然维持与《华沙公约》相同数额,即由每公斤250金法郎换算成每公斤17 SDR(第22条第3项),且托运人于必要时如预先支付额外费用以获得较高之责任限额(第22条第2项)。

(4)迟到责任

航空运送人对于旅客、行李或货物因迟到所生损害之责任,《蒙特利尔公约与《华沙公约》相同,采取推定过失责任(第19条)。[②] 运送人对于货物迟到所负责任限额,为每公斤17 SDR(第22条第3项);行李之迟到则新增规定,无论该行李是否为交托行李,运送人就行李迟到所负责任限额以每一旅客1000 SDR为限(第22条第2项);运送人对于旅客运送迟到所负责任限额,以每一旅客4150 SDR为限(第22条第1项)。唯迟到系因运送人故意不法行为所致者,虽然运送人对货物所负责任限制仍维持其不可突破性,但不适用于旅客及行李运送(第22条第5项)。

(二)航空器营运人责任限制

1. 罗马公约之制定

基于《华沙公约》之经验,国际航空法律专家委员会就航空器对于地面第三人造成损害之赔偿责任规则,亦积极研议公约草案,于1933年5月在罗马召开的第三次国际航空私法会议,通过了以法文为官方版本之《统一关于航空器对地面第三人造成损害某些规则之公约》(Convention for the

---

① Article 18:1. The carrier is liable for damage sustained in the event of the destruction or loss of or damage to, cargo upon condition only that the event which caused the damage so sustained took place during the carriage by air.

② Article 19:The carrier is liable for damage occasioned by delay in the carriage by air of passengers, baggage or cargo. Nevertheless, the carrier shall not be liable for damage occasioned by delay if it proves that it and its servants and agents took all measures that could reasonably be required to avoid the damage or that it was impossible for it or them to take such measures.

Unification of Certain Rules relating to Damage Caused by Aircraft to Third Parties on the Surface)供各国签署,然仅有5个国家签署,故宣告失败。后国际民用航空组织于1947年5月的第一届大会中,决议责令其下之法律委员会研究修正1933年《统一关于航空器对地面第三人造成损害某些规则之公约》。历经数年,终于1952年10月17日在罗马召开的会议中通过了《外国航空器对地面第三人造成损害之公约》(Convention on Damage Caused by Foreign Aircraft to Third Parties on the Surface,以下简称《罗马公约》)并由15国代表签署,亦供其他国家签署,于1958年12月4日生效,至今已有49个缔约国。

2. 罗马公约之航空营运人责任限制

《罗马公约》系建立在航空营运人严格责任、航空营运人责任限制之原则、航空营运人责任限制之排除三基柱上。

就航空器对地面第三人造成损害之赔偿责任,《罗马公约》于第1条第1项规定,任何人受到地面上损害时,只须证明损害发生之原因为航行中之航空器,或由该航空器坠落之人或物所造成,即有权请求赔偿。① 质言之,除非有第4~6条所规定抗辩事由之存在(公约第4条:未经航空器航行负责人之同意擅自使用航空器,致引起地面损害时,该航行负责人若能证明其已尽应有之注意以防止航空器之非法使用,则可不负赔偿责任,否则须与非法使用人负连带责任。② 第5条:依本公约应负责之人,若能证明地面之损害系武装

---

① Article 1:1. Any person who suffers damage on the surface shall, upon proof only that the damage was caused by an aircraft in flight or by any person or thing falling therefrom, be entitled to compensation as provided by this Convention. Nevertheless there shall be no right to compensation if the damage is not a direct consequence of the incident giving rise thereto, or if the damage results from the mere fact of passage of the aircraft through the airspace in conformity with existing air traffic regulations.

② Article 4:If a person makes use of an aircraft without the consent of the person entitled to its navigational control, the latter, unless he proves that he has exercised due care to prevent such use, shall be jointly and severally liable with the unlawful user for damage giving a right to compensation under Article 1, each of them being bound under the provisions and within the limits of liability of this Convention.

冲突或内乱之直接结果,或依本公约本应负责赔偿之人,因为政府之措施致不能运用其航空器者,不负赔偿责任。[①] 第6条第1项:依本公约应负责之人,若能证明地面之损害完全由被害人或其受雇人或其代理人之过失或其他不当作为或不作为所引起,不负赔偿责任;若能证明地面之损害系由被害人或其受雇人或代理人之过失或其他不当作为所引发,其赔偿额应比例减少之;但地面之损失虽因被害人之受雇或代理人之过失或不当作为或不作为所致,但被害人若能证明其受雇人或代理人的行为非属于该人职务范围内,则本公约所定之赔偿责任,不得减免。公约第6条第2项:被害人死亡或受伤,由另一人诉请赔偿时,关于被害人或其受雇人或代理人之过失或不当作为或不作为,适用前项之规定),[②]否则只要有损害之发生,航空器营运人(第2条第2项第1款:地面损害发生之时,正在运用航空器之人,但航空器之运用权如果直接或间接来自对航空器保留航行指挥权之人,则该人仍视为航空器之营运人;公约第2条第2项第2款:为自己运用航空器或由其受雇人或代理人在雇用期间内运用航空器者,也不论后者之运用航空器是否在其职权范围

---

① Article 5:Any person who would otherwise be liable under the provisions of this Convention shall not be liable if the damage is the direct consequence of armed conflict or civil disturbance, or if such person has been deprived of the use of the aircraft by act of public authority.

② Article 6:1. Any person who would otherwise be liable under the provisions of this Convention shall not be liable for damage if he proves that the damage was caused solely through the negligence or other wrongful act or omission of the person who suffers the damage or of the latter's servants or agents. If the person liable proves that the damage was contributed to by the negligence or other wrongful act or omission of the person who suffers the damage, or of his servants or agents, the compensation shall be reduced to the extent to which such negligence or wrongful act or omission contributed to the damage. Nevertheless there shall be no such exoneration or reduction if, in the case of the negligence or other wrongful act or omission of a servant or agent, the person who suffers the damage proves that his servant or agent was acting outside the scope of his authority. 2. When an action is brought by one person to recover damages arising from the death or injury of another person, the negligence or other wrongful act or omission of such other person, or of his servants or agents, shall also have the effect provided in the preceding paragraph.

以内,该人即规为航空器营运人)①即需负损害赔偿责任,此显示出《罗马公约》系采取严格责任。

就航空器对地面第三人造成损害之赔偿数额,《罗马公约》采行责任限制之原则,且以航空器之重量(公约第11条第3项:本公约所谓航空器重量,系指该航空器适航证书中所记载该机能够起飞之最大总重量)②为决定最高赔偿额之标准,于第11条第1项规定:航空器重量在1000公斤以下者,500 000金法郎;航空器重量在1000公斤以上,不满6000公斤者,除起初之1000公斤按500 000金法郎计算外,每逾1公斤增加400金法郎;航空器重量在6000公斤以上,不满20 000公斤者,除起初之6000千公斤按2 500 000金法郎计算外,每逾1公斤增加250金法郎;航空器重量在20 000公斤以上,不满50 000公斤者,除起初之20 000公斤按6 000 000金法郎计算外,每逾1公斤增加150金法郎;航空器重量逾50 000公斤者,除起初之50 000公斤按10 500 000万金法郎计算外,每逾1公斤增加100金法郎③。此外,公约第11条第2项更规定,地面被害人因人身伤亡所应得之损害赔偿,每人不得超过

---

① Article 2:2. (a) For the purposes of this Convention the term "operator" shall mean the person who was making use of the aircraft at the time the damage was caused, provided that if control of the navigation of the aircraft was retained by the person from whom the right to make use of the aircraft was derived, whether directly or indirectly, that person shall be considered the operator. (b) A person shall be considered to be making use of an aircraft when he is using it personally or when his servants or agents are using the aircraft in the course of their employment, whether or not within the scope of their authority.

② Article 11:3. "Weight" means the maximum weight of the aircraft authorized by the certificate of airworthiness for take-off, excluding the effect of lifting gas when used.

③ Article 11:1. Subject to the provisions of Article 12, the liability for damage giving a right to compensation under Article 1, for each aircraft and incident, in respect of all persons liable under this Convention, shall not exceed: (a) 500 000 francs for aircraft weighing 1000 kilogrammes or less; (b) 500 000 francs plus 400 francs per kilogramme over 1000 kilogrammes for aircraft weighing more than 1000 but not exceeding 6000 kilogrammes; (c) 2 500 000 francs plus 250 francs per kilogramme over 6000 kilogrammes for aircraft weighing more than 6000 but not exceeding 20 000 kilogrammes; (d) 6 000 000 francs plus 150 francs per kilogramme over 20 000 kilogrammes for aircraft weighing more than 20 000 but not exceeding 50 000 kilogrammes; (e) 10 500 000 francs plus 100 francs per kilogramme over 50 000 kilogrammes for aircraft weighing more than 50 000 kilogrammes.

500 000 金法郎。①

航空器营运人之赔偿责任《罗马公约》虽采取航空器营运人责任限制之原则,但又规定排除航空器营运人责任限制之事由,使航空器营运人于以下二情形不得主张责任限制而仍应负无限清偿责任:(1)被害人若证明地面损害系由航空器营运人或其受雇人或代理人之故意作为或不作为所造成,且有造成损害之意图时,航空器营运人应负无限责任,但该损害如非航空器营运人本身之故意,而系其受雇人或代理人之故意所造成时,被害人尚须证明该受雇人或代理人之行为,系其从事职务时且在其权限范围内之行为;(2)未经合法航空器运用人之同意而非法取得并运用航空器,造成地面损害者,应负无限责任②。

3.《蒙特利尔议定书》之修正、补充

《罗马公约》自 1958 年生效以来,虽陆续有其他国家之批准或签署,但美国、英国、法国、日本、瑞典、苏联、荷兰等世界主要空运国家均未批准或签署,而作为最初批准国之一的加拿大,又于 1976 年 6 月 29 日通知退出,并已于同年 12 月 29 日生效,致使《罗马公约》成效不彰,故国际民用航空组织法律委员会自 1965 年起,即开始就《罗马公约》之修正进行研究。于国际民用航空组织于 1978 年 9 月 6 日至 23 日在在加拿大蒙特利尔举行国际航空法会议,讨论由国际民用航空组织法律委员会所提出之赔偿限额之修正,终于通过了《修正 1952 年 10 月 7 日于罗马所签署外国航空器对地面第三人造成损害之公约之议定书》(Protocol to Amend the Convention on Damage Caused by Foreign Aircraft to Third Parties on the Surface signed at Rome on 7 October

---

① Article 11:2. The liability in respect of loss of life or personal injury shall not exceed 500 000 francs per person killed or injured.

② Article 12:1. If the person who suffers damage proves that it was caused by a deliberate act or omission of the operator, his servants or agents, done with intent to cause damage, the liability of the operator shall be unlimited; provided that in the case of such act or omission of such servant or agent, it is also proved that he was acting in the course of his employment and within the scope of his authority. 2. If a person wrongfully takes and makes use of an aircraft without the consent of the person entitled to use it, his liability shall be unlimited.

1952，以下简称《蒙特利尔议定书》）。

1978年《蒙特利尔议定书》仍然维持《罗马公约》航空营运人严格责任、航空营运人责任限制之原则之基柱，但将《罗马公约》责任限额之以金法郎计算修正为以特别提款权表示，且适度且合理地增加航空营运人责任限制之额度，将《罗马公约》赔偿限度额修正为：第一，（1）航空器重量在2000公斤以下者，300 000 SDR；（2）航空器重量在2000公斤以上，不满6000公斤，除起初之2000公斤按300 000 SDR计算外，每逾1公斤增加175 SDR；（3）航空器重量在6000公斤以上，不满30 000公斤者，除起初之6000公斤按1 000 000 SDR计算外，每逾1公斤增加65 SDR；（4）航空器重量在30 000公斤以上者，除起初之30 000公斤按2 500 000 SDR计算外，每逾1公斤增加65 SDR。第二，关于人身伤亡应负的损害赔偿责任，对每一被害人不得超过125 000 SDR。①

三、我国台湾地区“民用航空法”上航空运送人之责任限制

（一）航空运送人单位责任限制

1. 责任标准

（1）航空运送人对旅客人身伤亡或迟到之损害赔偿责任

我国台湾地区“民用航空法”第91条规定：“（第1项）乘客于航空器中

---

① Article III: Article 11 of the Convention shall be deleted and replaced by the following: “Article 11: 1. Subject to the provisions of Article 12, the liability for damage giving a right to compensation under Article 1, for each aircraft and incident in respect of all persons liable under this Convention shall not exceed: (a) 300 000 Special Drawing Rights for aircraft weighing 2000 kilograms or less; (b) 300 000 Special Drawing Rights plus 175 Special Drawing Rights per kilogramme over 2000 kilogrammes for aircraft weighing more than 2000 but not exceeding 6000 kilogrammes; (c) 1 000 000 Special Drawing Rights plus 62.5 Special Drawing Rights per kilogramme over 6000 kilogrammes for aircraft weighing more than 6000 but not exceeding 30 000 kilogrammes; (d) 2 500 000 Special Drawing Rights plus 65 Special Drawing Rights per kilogramme over 30 000 kilogrammes for aircraft weighing more than 30 000 kilogrammes. 2. The liability in respect of loss of life or personal injury shall not exceed 125 000 Special Drawing Rights per person killed or injured.

或于上下航空器时,因意外事故致死亡或伤害者,航空器使用人或运送人应负赔偿之责。但因可归责于乘客之事由,或因乘客有过失而发生者,得免除或减轻赔偿。(第 2 项)乘客因航空器运送人之运送迟到而致损害者,航空器运送人应负赔偿之责。但航空器运送人能证明其迟到系因不可抗力之事由所致者,除另有交易习惯者外,以乘客因迟到而增加支出之必要费用为限。”系规范航空运送人对旅客人身伤亡或迟到损害赔偿责任之规定。本条规定就责任标准而言:第 1 项就航空运送人对于旅客人身伤亡之赔偿责任方面,本条虽然系仿《华沙公约》第 17 条之规定而设,但系使航空运送人负通常事变责任,与“华沙体系”采取过失推定主义不同,而与《蒙特利尔公约》第 21 条于 100 000 SDR 范围内之损害运送人适用严格责任之第一阶较接近,故只要旅客于航空器中或于上下航空器时,因意外事故致死亡或伤害者,航空运送人即应负责,而运送人仅于意外事故之发生系可归责旅客或旅客与有过失之情形始得免责;本条第 2 项就航空运送人对于旅客迟到之赔偿责任,与我国台湾地区“民法”第 654 条第 2 项“运送之迟到系因不可抗力所致者,旅客运送人之责任,除另有交易习惯者外,以旅客因迟到而增加支出之必要费用为限”相同,皆为不可抗力责任,故旅客仅须证明其因航空器运送人之运送迟到而受有损害者,航空运送人即应负责。

(2)航空运送人对货物及行李毁损、灭失或迟到之损害赔偿责任

航空运送人对货物毁损、灭失或迟到之损害赔偿责任方面,以及航空运送人对交托行李及未交托随身行李之毁损、灭失或迟到之损害赔偿责任方面,由于我国台湾地区“民用航空法”并无明文规定,故应回归我国台湾地区“民法”之规定,就航空运送人对货物毁损、灭失或迟到之损害赔偿责任,依我国台湾地区“民法”第 634 条“运送人对于运送物之丧失、毁损或迟到,应负责任。但运送人能证明其丧失、毁损或迟到,系因不可抗力或因运送物之性质或因托运人或受货人之过失而致者,不在此限”之规定使航空运送人负

通常事变责任。[1] 就航空运送人对交托行李毁损、灭失或迟到之损害赔偿责任,依我国台湾地区"民法"第657条"运送人对于旅客所交托之行李,纵不另收运费,其权利义务,除本款另有规定外,适用关于物品运送之规定"之规定应适用我国台湾地区"民法"第634条之规定,使航空运送人负通常事变责任。就航空运送人对未交托随身行李之毁损、灭失之损害赔偿责任,依我国台湾地区"民法"第658条"运送人对于旅客所未交托之行李,如因自己或其受雇人之过失,致有丧失或毁损者,仍负责任"之规定使航空运送人负过失责任。[2] 就航空运送人对未交托随身行李迟到之损害赔偿责任,我国台湾地区"民用航空法"与我国台湾地区"民法"第658条均未规范,有认为应随身行李系由旅客直接占有,故迟到责任成立与否应与乘客迟到作同一判断,亦即应依"民法"第634条之通常事变责任。[3] 但倘依此见,较债务不履行态样较严重之毁损、灭失仅负过失责任(我国台湾地区"民法"第658条),但债务不履行态样较轻微之迟到责任卻负较重之通常事变责任(我国台湾地区"民法"第634条),未免轻重失衡,故解释上应类推适用我国台湾地区"民法"第658条未交托随身行李之毁损、灭失之损害赔偿责任,负过失责任。[4]

2. 责任范围

(1)航空运送人对旅客人身伤亡或迟到之损害赔偿责任

航空运送人对旅客人身伤亡损害赔偿责任之责任范围,依我国台湾地区"民用航空法"第93条第1项,乘客或航空器上工作人员之损害赔偿额,有特别契约者,依其契约;特别契约中有不利于我国台湾地区居民之差别待遇者,

---

① 参见林诚二:《债法各论新解—体系化解说(中)》,台北,瑞兴图书公司2015年版,第443页;刘春堂:《民法债编各论(中)》,台北,作者自版2014年版,第441页;邱聪智著,姚志明校订:《新订债法各论(中)》,台北,元照出版有限公司2002年版,第514页。

② 参见林诚二:《债法各论新解—体系化解说(中)》(第3版),台北,瑞兴图书公司2015年版,第471页;刘春堂:《民法债编各论(中)》,台北,作者自版2014年版,第484页;邱聪智著,姚志明校订:《新订债法各论(中)》,台北,元照出版有限公司2002年版,第557页。

③ 参见洪希诚:《国际航空运送人责任:我国法之增修建议》,高雄大学法律学系2010年硕士学位论文,第111页。

④ 参见林诚二:《债法各论新解—体系化解说(中)》,台北,瑞兴图书公司2015年版,第471页。

依特别契约中最有利之规定。无特别契约者,由我国台湾地区交通主管部门依照本法有关规定并参照国际间赔偿额之标准订定办法,报请我国台湾地区行政管理机构核定之,若无特别契约者,应适用我国台湾地区"航空客货损害赔偿办法"之规定,特别契约依我国台湾地区"航空客货损害赔偿办法"第2条第2项之规定,应以书面为之,且约定之损害赔偿额不得低于我国台湾地区"航空客货损害赔偿办法"所定之标准。旅客人身伤亡之损害赔偿额,依我国台湾地区"航空客货损害赔偿办法"第3条"(第1项)……但被害人能证明其受有更大损害者,得就其损害请求赔偿:一、死亡者:新台币三百万元。二、重伤者:新台币一百五十万元。(第2项)前项情形之非死亡或重伤者,其赔偿额标准按实际损害计算。但最高不得超过新台币一百五十万元。(第3项)第一项第二款所称重伤,依刑法第十条第四项之规定"之规定,以单位责任限制为原则,而为限额赔偿,但倘被害人能证明其受有更大损害者,则例外不依单位责任限制之限额赔偿,而为完全赔偿,复依同办法第6条第1项"航空器使用人或运送人因故意或重大过失致生客货之损害者,其赔偿责任不受本办法赔偿额标准之限制"之规定,航空运送人因故意或重大过失致生旅客人身伤亡者,亦例外不依单位责任限制之限额赔偿,而为完全赔偿,但依举证责任之原理,航空器运送人之故意或重大过失应由旅客证明。

航空运送人对旅客迟到损害赔偿责任之责任范围,由于我国台湾地区"民用航空法"及"航空客货损害赔偿办法"未有规范,故应回归我国台湾地区"民法"第216条:"(第1项)损害赔偿,除法律另有规定或契约另有订定外,应以填补债权人所受损害及所失利益为限。(第2项)依通常情形,或依已定之计划、设备或其他特别情事,可得预期之利益,视为所失利益。"完全赔偿原则之规定,计算赔偿数额,亦即并无责任限制。

(2)航空运送人对货物及行李毁损、灭失或迟到之损害赔偿责任

航空运送人对货物与交托行李毁损、灭失损害赔偿责任之责任范围,我国台湾地区"民用航空法"与"航空客货损害赔偿办法"皆有规定,我国台湾地区"民用航空法"第93条之1第1项规定:"航空器使用人或运送人,就其

托运货物或登记行李之毁损或灭失所负之赔偿责任,每公斤最高不得超过新台币一千元。”与《航空客货损害赔偿办法》第4条第1款“航空器使用人或运送人对于载运货物或行李之损害赔偿,其赔偿额依下列标准:一、货物及登记行李:按实际损害计算。但每公斤最高不得超过新台币一千元”之规定相同,皆以单位责任限制为原则,而为限额赔偿,实则2003年5月28日我国台湾地区“民用航空法”增订第93条之1前,我国台湾地区“民用航空法”就航空运送人对货物与行李之毁损、灭失损害赔偿责任之责任范围并未有规定,故此部分乃由我国台湾地区“航空客货损害赔偿办法”于第4条加以规范以补我国台湾地区“民用航空法”之阙如,其后,2003年5月28日我国台湾地区“民用航空法”修订时,乃将我国台湾地区“航空客货损害赔偿办法”第4条之规定内容纳入我国台湾地区“民用航空法”而增订为第93条之1,故于我国台湾地区“民用航空法”增订第93条之1后,航空运送人对货物与行李毁损、灭失损害赔偿责任之责任范围,即应依我国台湾地区“民用航空法”第93条之1而不再依我国台湾地区“航空客货损害赔偿办法”第4条。依我国台湾地区“民用航空法”第93条之1第1项,航空运送人对货物与交托行李毁损、灭失损害赔偿责任之责任范围虽采取单位责任限制,而为限额赔偿,但依同条项但书“但托运人托运货物或行李之性质、价值,于托运前已向运送人声明并载明于货物运送单或客票者,不在此限”之规定,则例外不依单位责任限制之限额赔偿,而为完全赔偿,复依同条第3项“航空器使用人或运送人因故意或重大过失致生前二项所定之损害者,不得主张赔偿额之限制责任”之规定,航空运送人因故意或重大过失致生货物与交托行李毁损、灭失者,亦例外不依单位责任限制之限额赔偿,而为完全赔偿,但依举证责任之原理,航空器运送人之故意或重大过失应由托运人或旅客证明。

航空运送人对未交托随身行李毁损、灭失损害赔偿责任之责任范围,我国台湾地区“民用航空法”与“航空客货损害赔偿办法”皆有规定,我国台湾地区“民用航空法”第93条之1第2项:“乘客随身行李之赔偿责任,按实际损害计算。但每一乘客最高不得超过新台币二万元。”与我国台湾地区“航空客货损害赔偿办法"第4条第2款"航空器使用人或运送人对于载运货物或行李之损害赔偿,其赔偿额依下列标准:……二、随身行李:按实际损害计算。但每一乘客最高不得超过新台币二万元"之规定相同,皆以单位责任限制为原则,而为限额赔偿,但于我国台湾地区"民用航空法"增订第93条之1后,航空运送人对未交托随身行李毁损、灭失损害赔偿责任之责任范围,即应依我国台湾地区"民用航空法"第93条之1而不再依我国台湾地区"航空客货损害赔偿办法"第4条。依我国台湾地区"民用航空法"第93条之1第2项,航空运送人对未交托随身行李毁损、灭失损害赔偿责任之责任范围虽采取单位责任限制,而为限额赔偿,但依同条第3项之规定,航空运送人因故意或重大过失致生货物与交托行李毁损、灭失者,亦例外不依单位责任限制之限额赔偿,而为完全赔偿,但依举证责任之原理,航空运送人之故意或重大过失应由托运人或旅客证明。

航空运送人对货物与交托行李迟到损害赔偿责任之责任范围,由于我国台湾地区"民用航空法"及我国台湾地区"航空客货损害赔偿办法"皆未有规范,故若无特别契约者,应回归我国台湾地区"民法"之规定。依我国台湾地区"民法"第638条第1项"运送物有丧失、毁损或迟到者,其损害赔偿额应依其应交付时目的地之价值计算之"之规定(交托行李依我国台湾地区"民法"第657条之规定亦适用第638条),仅以货物与交托行李之价值为赔偿范围,亦即仅就所受损害加以赔偿而不及于所失利益,故为限额赔偿,[①]但依同条第3项"运送物之丧失、毁损或迟到,系因运送人之故意或重大过失所致者,如有其他损害,托运人并得请求赔偿"之规定,航空运送人因故意或重大过失致生货物与交托行李迟到者,则例外为完全赔偿,[②]责任范围除同条第1项之所受损害外,尚及于所失利益,但依举证责任之原理,航空器运送人之故意或

① 参见刘春堂:《民法债编各论(中)》,台北,作者自版2014年版,第448~449页;邱聪智著,姚志明校订:《新订债法各论(中)》,台北,元照出版有限公司2002年版,第522~524页。

② 参见林诚二:《债法各论新解—体系化解说(中)》,台北,瑞兴图书公司2015年版,第446~449页;刘春堂:《民法债编各论(中)》,台北,作者自版2014年版,第444页;邱聪智著,姚志明校订:《新订债法各论(中)》,台北,元照出版有限公司2002年版,第519~521页。

重大过失应由托运人或旅客证明。至于航空运送人对未交托随身行李迟到损害赔偿责任之责任范围,因其责任标准系类推适用我国台湾地区“民法”第658条未交托随身行李之毁损、灭失之损害赔偿责任,负过失责任,故责任范围亦应类推适用未交托随身行李之毁损、灭失损害赔偿责任之责任范围,依第638条定之,但因迟到之损害赔偿额,不得超过因灭失可得请求之赔偿额(我国台湾地区“民法”第640条)。

(二)航空器营运人责任限制

1.责任标准

我国台湾地区“民用航空法”第89条规定:“航空器失事致人死伤,或毁损他人财物时,不论故意或过失,航空器所有人应负损害赔偿责任;其因不可抗力所生之损害,亦应负责。自航空器上落下或投下物品,致生损害时,亦同。”第90条规定:“航空器依租赁、附条件买卖或借贷而使用者,关于前条所生之损害,由所有人与承租人、附条件买卖买受人或借用人负连带赔偿责任。但附条件买卖、租赁已登记,除所有人有过失外,由承租人、附条件买卖买受人单独负责。”系航空器营运人对地面第三人损害赔偿责任之规定。本条规定就责任标准言,与《罗马公约》相同,皆为严格责任,盖只要航空器失事致人死伤或毁损他人财物,或自航空器上落下或投下物品致生损害,无论故意或过失,亦无论是否为不可抗力,航空器营运人即需负损害赔偿责任。第89条规定之赔偿义务人为航空器所有人,与《罗马公约》规定航空器营运人有所不同,此应系我国台湾地区“海商法”就船舶所有人责任限制之主体规定为船舶所有人有关,故本条之航空器所有人,不妨参酌我国台湾地区“海商法”第21条第2项“前项所称船舶所有人,包括船舶所有权人、船舶承租人、经理人及营运人”之规定,将航空器所有人解释为包括航空器所有权人、经理人及营运人,至于航空器承租人与航空器借用人,因已于第90条明定,故不包括于此之航空器所有人之范畴。

2. 责任范围

我国台湾地区"民用航空法"第89条及第90条损害赔偿责任之范围,由于我国台湾地区"民用航空法"第93条之1系针对与航空运送人间订有航空运送契约始有适用,而我国台湾地区"民用航空法"对第89条及第90条损害赔偿责任之范围并无明文规定,故应回归我国台湾地区"民法"之规定,而令航空器所有人负无限责任,此与《罗马公约》采取航空器营运人责任限制之原则,有非常大之不同。亦即,于我国台湾地区法制上,航空器营运人并无责任限制之适用。

四、航空运送人责任限制之存废辩证

(一)肯否之对立

航空运送人民事责任体制采行责任限制之制度,系沿袭自船舶所有人责任限制之制度,20世纪方起步之航空运送,依循海上运送之足迹,就运送人责任亦采行单位责任限制制度。航空运送人责任限制与船舶所有人责任限制之制度基础极为相近,亦即因活动之高风险性,故以责任限制之方式鼓励活动,以利活动之发展。著名航空法学者德理翁(Huibert Drion,1917～2004年)即分析航空运送人责任限制之基础有八:①(1)海商法也采用了类似船舶所有人责任限制;(2)保护航空业于资金上之脆弱;(3)不应使航空运送人单独承担人类尚无能力防止之风险;(4)有利于航空运送人对此风险取得保险;(5)为潜在的赔偿请求权人自行保险创造机会;(6)责任限制是《华沙公约》加重运送人责任(推定过失责任)之补偿或交换;(7)责任限制下能快速解决纷争;(8)有利于赔偿金额之统一。

第二次世界大战前,对于航空运送人责任限制几未质疑,但第二次世界大战后,质疑声开始涌现。美国首先提出反对,之后也得到其他已开发国家

① See Huibert Drion, *Limitation of Liabilities in International Air Law*, Hague, Nijhoff, 1954, pp. 12－13.

的支持，其反对理由有五：(1)航空运送于设备、技术上已大幅提升，资金、运量、营收亦大幅增长，航空运送人之经济实力今非昔比，较《华沙公约》制定时已不可同日而语，航空运送人已足承担更高甚至无限责任；(2)航空运送人可通过责任保险转嫁责任，而保险业之发达使保险人具有足够之实力承担巨额之保险金给付；(3)随着科技之进步，航空事故发生之概率减少，从而保险费于航空运送业之总成本中已不构成庞大之负担，赔偿责任数额之提高未必使保险费增加，赔偿责任数额于今已非航空业之投资者、提供贷款之金融业所考量之因素；(4)旅客人身伤亡之损害系依受害人之医疗费用、预期收入、对受抚养权利人责任等数额计算所得，已开发国家之生活水准高于开发中国家，故已开发国家受害人之损害数额自高于开发中国家之受害人，且于已开发国家，非财产上(精神)损害赔偿之请求极为普遍，且其数额往往庞大，采取责任限制显不利于受害人之求偿；(5)采取责任限制，则于已开发国家，于国际航空运送中旅客所获之赔偿远低于国内航空运送之旅客，显失公平，且责任限制道致损害赔偿数额过低之现象，更会因通货膨胀而加剧。

针对以美国为首的已开发国家对于航空运送人责任限制的质疑与反对，开发中国家反而肯定与支持航空运送人责任限制，盖：(1)开发中国家仍需借由航空运送任责任限制以保护其航空业之发展；(2)开发中国家保险业之风险承担能力，无法与已开发国家相提并论，其并无充分之财力给付航空事故发生时之巨额理赔；(3)在保险费率上，开发中国家航空技术水准相对较低，其事故发生率高于已开发国家，致使开发中国家航空责任保险之保险费率对赔偿责任数额极为敏感，倘不采取航空运送任责任限制，则保险费率将大幅提高，此无疑将成为开发中国家航空业之庞大负担；(4)开发中国家航空业之经济实力显不及已开发国家之航空业，倘不采取航空运送任责任限制，无异于在经济实力差距极大之航空业间订立相同之责任标准，迫使开发中国家势力弱小之航空业面对已开发国家航空运送旅客庞大之赔偿请求，此不公平之现象，较已开发国家国际航空运送旅客与国内航空运送旅客间赔偿额之失衡更难被接受。

由上述可知,对于航空运送人责任限制之反对与支持,实即已开发国家与开发中国家之对立。

(二)评析

就航空运送人责任限制之肯否主张,各有所据。按一国之法律于事业经营者之利益与消费者之保护间如何抉择,端视该国经济发展之程度,若处于经济发展中阶段,法律往往偏重于保护事业经营者,等到了经济发达成熟阶段,法律则转而偏向保护消费者,故已开发国家反对航空运送人责任限制而开发中国家支持,乃属必然。虽说航空科技已进入成熟阶段,航空事故风险概率已得较精密估算,且国际航空运送业也已进入稳定期而无强制要求旅客与航空运送人分担运送风险之正当性与必要性,而航空运送责任保险于技术上亦能精确地估算无赔偿责任上限之情形,使航空运送人责任限制之正当性令人质疑,[①]但对开发中国家而言,已开发国家也是从航空运送人责任限制中逐步走来,且已从中获得利益,如今却要求开发中国家接受其提高责任限额甚至废除责任限制之主张,牺牲开发中国家航空业之利益,以满足已开发国家消费者之漫天要价,另开发中国家无法接受。[②] 虽说航空运送人责任限制系在特定历史时空下国家资本间妥协之产物,创设当时所拟制之利益平衡的有效性于今有必要加以检讨,但航空运送人责任限制确实也具有减轻航空运送人责任以鼓励航空业、航空业攸关国力之强弱故于国家政策上实有特加保护之必要、有利保险之取得、维持国际竞争力等优点,更何况航空运送人责

---

① 参见黄居正:《国际航空法的理论与实践》,台北,新学林出版股份有限公司2006年版,第286~287页。

② 在国际民用航空组织理事会成立华沙体系现代化及统一化特别工作小组会议中,开发中国家便对已开发国家倾向无责任限制之主张提出反对。首先,印度反对无金额限制之赔偿责任,其认为"双阶制"中第二阶之举证责任倒置之推定过失(《蒙特利尔公约》采行),无异于严格责任(strict liability),此不利于航空运送人,尤其是中小型之航空业,甚至危及其生存,而当航空运送人面对更高之保险费率时,无限制责任下主要之受益者,将会是已开发国家之旅客。此观点获得53个非洲会员国之热烈回响,甚至进而提议"三阶制",此提议受到阿拉伯民航委员会16个会员国之支持,而越南甚至提议请求超过100 000 SDR之情形,应要求损害赔偿请求人证明航空运送人之过失。

任限制制度模型之船舶所有人责任限制虽亦受质疑,但仍继续维持,且其制度精神更由“船舶所有人责任限制”演进至“海事求偿责任限制”,亦即由船舶所有人得享何种程度之责任限制演变为以法律扩大广义下之债权人如何得就海上企业所造成之损害主张求偿范围,①使航空运送人责任限制恐难完全弃之不顾,故而面对争议,较稳当且平衡之做法,应是逐步提高责任限额之额度,而非贸然废除责任限制。但无论如何,航空运送人责任限制之肯否,已非单纯之法律议题,而是国际政治议题,此甚明显。

五、结　　论

航空运送人单位责任限制及航空器营运人责任限制共同构筑了航空法上民事责任为有限责任之基本原则,使无论是利用航空器所生契约之债之损害赔偿抑或利用航空器所生非契约之债之损害赔偿,航空运送人之赔偿责任皆有最高额度,此航空运送人责任限制制度,与民法上债务人以其财产为担保对债权人负无限清偿责任,有明显差异,为航空法之一大特色。但随着航空科技的进步与航空运送业之稳定发展,对航空运送人责任限制已有诸多质疑与反对。就航空运送人责任限制之质疑与反对,乃为应然层次之问题,就实然层次而言,航空运送人责任限制乃为当前之国际公约法与较多国家立法例所继续接受,故而如何正确地解释、适用航空运送人责任限制,应为当前较应受重视者。就我国台湾地区航空法制而言,亦采行航空运送人责任限制,就航空运送人对旅客人身伤亡之损害赔偿责任(我国台湾地区“民用航空法”第93条第1项、我国台湾地区“航空客货损害赔偿办法”第3条)、航空运送人对货物及行李毁损或灭失之损害赔偿责任(我国台湾地区“民用航空法”第93条之1、我国台湾地区“航空客货损害赔偿办法”第4条)、航空运送人对货物及行李迟到之损害赔偿责任(我国台湾地区“民法”第638条)为限

---

① 参见吴光平:《海商法与海事国际私法研究》,台北,台湾财产法暨经济法研究协会2007年版,第28~29页。

额赔偿,但对于航空运送人对旅客迟到之损害赔偿责任及航空器营运人对地面第三人损害赔偿责任,则仍依我国台湾地区“民法”损害赔偿之基本原则,为完全赔偿,此应注意及之。

美国对国际航空运输法律自由化的影响论析*

周亚光**

自1978年完成国内航空运输自由化改革后,美国先后采用多种模式将美式航空自由论从双边向诸边推行。首先,1979年《国际航空运输竞争法》成为美国航空自由化法律输出的战略支点,该法规定了美国对外航空运输协定自由化的战略目标及实现保障机制。其次,美国利用"比荷卢模式",采用各个击破策略瓦解航空秩序论同盟。再次,美国利用双边"开放天空模式"加速国际航空运输自由化协定网络的形成。最后,美国与分别与大西洋与太平洋国家达成诸边航空自由化协定,"两洋模式"不仅建立了准组织化的国际体系,而且几乎囊括所有关键议题,明确表达了为世界立法的雄心以及重塑国际航空运输法律秩序的远景目标。美国在推动国际航空自由化过程中采取的相关策

---

* 本文的核心内容与主要内容最先以《美国航空运输协定的模式演进及我国的借鉴》为题发表于《法商研究》2017年第4期。

** 西北政法大学郑斌航空与空间法研究所讲师,法学博士。

略对我国参与国际航空运输秩序的全球法律治理具有重要的借鉴意义。

一、前　　言

在制度设计上,一方面,由于1919年《巴黎公约》第5条禁止缔约国与非缔约国交换航权,另一方面,《巴黎公约》赋予了附件与公约相同的法律地位,同时将对其修正的权利交由委员会行使,因此批准公约意味着签署了一张空白支票——缔约国需对未来的任何修正无条件接受。① 在美国当时持有孤立主义外交立场的背景下,美国没有批准《巴黎公约》,这在客观上使《巴黎公约》不具有普遍性。②

---

① See Michael Milde, *International Air Law and ICAO*, Hague, Eleven International Publishing Press, 2008, p. 12.

② 米尔德(Miled)认为《巴黎公约》的主要缔约国是欧洲国家,因此缺乏普遍性,see Michael Milde, *International Air Law and ICAO*, Hague, Eleven International Publishing Press, 2008, pp. 10 – 11。但是,肯尼思·克莱格夫(Kenneth Colegrove)认为,《巴黎公约》缔约国中有日本、非洲国家及其他国家,其仍然是具有普遍性的。从宏观上看,美国参加《巴黎公约》的谈判与条约约文的起草但最终并未批准该公约的原因是受到美国的孤立主义外交政策的影响。美国在1928年第六次泛美会议上与拉美国家共同签署了《泛美商业航空公约》,该公约是美国航空门罗主义外交政策的体现,并不代表普遍性航空合作模式,也并非《巴黎公约》的补充。《泛美商业航空公约》既没有要求国内管制统一性,也没有在所有权登记、海关程序、标识标记、航空器适航认证与飞行员许可等方面确立高标准,《泛美商业航空公约》是在美国国务院的推动下形成的互惠安排,其目的在于拓展美国航空公司在拉美地区的运营网络。See Kenneth Colegrove, "The International Aviation Policy of the United States", *The Journal of Air Law* 2, 1931, pp. 450 – 456. 从微观上看,《巴黎公约》第5条在事实上对美国的参与造成了制度障碍。1929年4月25日,美国时任国务卿亨利·刘易斯·史汀生向胡佛总统汇报时指出了美国不批准《巴黎公约》的5个原因:(1)美国私人飞机应被允许飞越他国领空,而《巴黎公约》第3条则要求外国航空器飞越他国领空应得到东道国许可。(2)美国通过与巴拿马在1926年签订的双边协定,已经控制了巴拿马运河上空的空域。《泛美商业航空公约》认可了该美国—巴拿马双边协定的合法地位,而《巴黎公约》第5条则禁止缔约国与非缔约国签订航空运输协定。因此在巴拿马没有加入《巴黎公约》的情况下,美国加入《巴黎公约》将会造成美国丧失巴拿马运河上空空域的控制权。(3)美国不打算修改其当时的海关条例。(4)美国更倾向于将公约项下的争端提交常设国际法院解决而非空中航行国际委员会(international commission for air navigation, CINA)项下的仲裁。(5)《巴黎公约》第34条规定公约项下的空中航行国际委员会应在国际联盟的指导下运作,美国不愿意因加入《巴黎公约》而与国际联盟产生任何关系。See Alan P. Dobson, *Peaceful Air Warfare*, Oxford, Clarendon Press, 1991, pp. 27 – 29.

第二次世界大战后,持有航空自由论的美国与持有航空管制论英国就双边航空协定的谈判进行了多次激烈的双边磋商而未能达成共识。经英国的强烈请求,美国在多重因素的考虑下最终同意在 1944 年 9 月召开芝加哥会议。[①] 美国在此次会议上的航空自由论受到多数国家的反对,最终各国以英国航空秩序论为基础达成了《芝加哥公约》。[②] 由于多数国家在当时均持"航空秩序论"立场,[③]《芝加哥公约》本身并没有解决航权交换问题,而是将航权交换问题留给了成员国根据"航空绝对主权原则"在双边模式下进行航权交换。

此后,美国并未放弃航空自由论的主张,其一方面在国际层面与英国于 1946 年达成了实现部分市场要素放松国家管制的《美英双边航空运输协定》(《百慕大协定 I》),[④]另一方面在国内联邦法层面进行航空运输自由化改革。在 1978 年完成国内航空运输自由化改革后,美国于次年开始了对国际航空运输法律秩序的美式再造进程。

---

① 我国学界认为芝加哥会议是美国应英国请求而召开的,但对《芝加哥公约》召开的背景以及美国为何同意多语焉不详。事实上,美国同意召开国际会议主要是基于以下三点考虑:(1)"二战"后,进行多边自由化条约的观点在美国国内对外政策争论中逐渐占据上风;(2)在英国坚持通过国际会议解决国际航空运输法律秩序的立场坚定的情况下,如果美国与英国在此问题上产生激烈冲突,那么美国将会面临欧洲、中东、非洲以及除加拿大外其他英联邦国家的压力;(3)将国际会议作为美国进军全球商业航空的入口,先渐进地达成双边模式,而后通过多边国际协定将其替代。See Alan P. Dobson, *Peaceful Air Warfare*, Oxford, Clarendon Press, 1991, pp. 160 - 161.

② 值得注意的是,百慕大协定尽管在运价、航线、受指定承运人方面受到国家的强烈管制,但在运力方面却较为宽松,为该国正式指定的航空企业有公平的机会去向旅行公众展示它可提供的服务,而航空公司营运额的分配比例则是消费者选择的结果。参见赵维田:《国际航空法》,社会科学文献出版社 2000 年版,第 111 页。

③ 54 个参会国有 45 个国家反对航权的多边交换体制,因为这将会减损他们在双边体制可以享有的议价能力。See Thomas Burke, "Influences Affecting International Aviation Policy", *Law and Contemporary Problems* 11, 1946, p. 608.

④ "百慕大协定 I"是航空自由论与航空秩序论的妥协性产物,是美国以接受航线由国家管制、运价受国际航协(IATA)协调为代价,换取英国开放第 5 航权和受指定承运人数量的多数化。该协定签订后为其他各国所效仿,此类双边航空运输协定被称为"百慕大模式"。尽管美国与英国在 1977 年达成修正《百慕大协定 I》的《百慕大协定 II》,但前者在出台后即为各国所效仿,而后者因其强烈的管制色彩甫一出台即饱受非议,不代表国际主流实践,因此"百慕大模式"仅指以《百慕大协定 I》为代表的协定类型。

二、《国际航空运输竞争法》:战略支点

在1978年颁布《航空公司放松管制法》①后,美国的航空法理论与实务界掀起了批判美国与英国在1977年签订的《百慕大协定II》的浪潮。② 卡特政府在1978年《美国国际航空运输谈判行动政策声明》中明确提出美国应将国内航空运输业的自由化改革成果向国际层面输出,特别是推动增加国际航

① Airline Deregulation Act 中的"deregulation"一词的翻译有两种译法。一方面,我国学者刘伟民教授认为应当翻译为"不管制"或"解除管制"或"去管制",理由是,如果翻译为"放松管制",仍然是行政力量管制航空市场的范畴,只不过是管制程度减弱而已。参见[英]郑斌:《国际航空运输法》,徐克继译,刘伟民校,中国民航出版社1996年版,校译说明第2页。持类似观点的欧洲学者也认为,美国的航空去管制化是一夜之间(overnight),see Eugenie Kalshoven-van Tije, "The EEC Commission as the European Version of the CAB?",*Air Law* 15,1990,pp. 257 - 271。而欧洲学者布通(Button)尽管采用了"大爆炸"(big bang)这一措辞,但是其强调,根据当时的立法背景,布通所指的大爆炸是在"国内航空市场管理方式的变化,不是突然间放开市场,而是制定了逐步放松价格与市场准入的时间表"的意义上讲的。See Kenneth Button, "Institutions, Regulations and Markets in Transportation", Accessed http://www.transport-research.info/Upload/Documents/201003/20100325_144733_55633_Stella%20Final%20Publishable%20Report.pdf , June 4, 2004. 另一方面,我国学者唐明毅主张"放松管制"的译法,赵维田先生也持有"放松管理"的译法。参见唐明毅主编:《现代国际航空运输法》,法律出版社1999年版,第22页;赵维田:《国际航空法》,社会科学文献出版社2000年版,第127页。笔者认同第二种观点。同时,对于当代航空法学界兴起的 regulation-deregulation-re-regulation 的提法,笔者窃以为应翻译为"管制—去管制—再监管",第一个管制是行政管制,第二个管制指的是在从美国1978年放松管制开始至各国不同程度国内自由化与全球航空自由化趋势的宏观语境下而言的,是一个逐渐放松的进程,是以市场代替行政、竞争代替垄断为落脚点的,不仅仅是指如美国等国家某一时间点的立法现象,而是指航空市场竞争充分、有效的进程以及达致充分的状态。最后一个 re-regulation 则是针对去管制化导致的政府成为"守夜人"的过度、无效的竞争状态而言的,是对航空竞争放任主义(laze faire)经济学的反思,但又不是旨在回到"管制"的时代,而是在市场经济前提下旨在对必要事项进行行政监管,但政府的角色仍然不是管理者(regulator),是对过度竞争导致的不必要经济风险的监管者(monitor)角色,如果严格按照直译或者图求押韵而翻译为"管制—去管制—再管制",无法精准表达航空法发展过程中的精髓,因此笔者拙译为"管制—去管制—再监管"。

② See Richard W. Bogosian, "Aviation Negotiations and the U. S. Model Agreement", *Journal of Air Law and Commerce* 46,1981,pp. 1007 - 1013. 此外,有律师甚至认为该协定违反了美国联邦宪法,损害了美国的国家利益,并要求追究谈判代表的刑事责任。See Robert R. Gray, "The Impact of Bermuda II on Future Bilateral Agreements",*Air and Space Law* 3,1978,p. 22.

线数量、运价自由以及排除运力限制障碍等竞争要素的自由化。[①] 美国以1974年《国际航空运输公平竞争实践法》[②]为基础,在1979年出台了目标更为多元、立场更为明确的《国际航空运输竞争法》。

(一)《国际航空运输竞争法》对美国航空运输协定的影响

《国际航空运输竞争法》是美国旨在通过单边立法将美式航空自由论进行国际输出的“战略支点”,其核心是推动国际航空运输业的市场化并提高美国航空公司的国际竞争力。该法首次明确了美国对外航空运输协定谈判的指导原则与战略目标:[③](1)强化美国承运人的国际竞争力与盈利能力;(2)保证国际承运人基于市场消费需求的定价自由;(3)降低对包机运输的限制;(4)最大限度地提高美国受指定承运人的数量及其在许可航线上的权利授予,使美国承运人能根据市场需求的变化迅速作出反应;(5)排除运力、运次等经营限制;(6)整合国内与国际航空运输市场;(7)增加美国的直达门户城市的数量;(8)结合外国对美国航空公司的权利授予与撤销情况,在美国与他国的自由化互惠安排使美国承运人和消费者获得等量利益的情况下,增加外国承运人飞往美国的航线数量;(9)消除美国航空公司在国际运输中面临的歧视与不公平竞争行为(包括歧视性的落地费与用户费、不合理的地面服务要求、不正当的营运限制、禁止改换机型等类似限制);(10)促进、鼓励与发展包括运输在内的美国民用航空业。

一方面,《国际航空运输竞争法》确立的战略目标(除目标10难以在特定期间量化外),在美国1979年至1983年对外签订的22个双边航空运输协定中均获得了不同程度的实现,如表1所示。

---

① Jimmy Carter, International Air Transportation Negotiations Statement of U. S. Policy for the Conduct of the Negotiations, August 21, 1978. 对该政策声明的作出背景与分析参见 Rigas Doganis, *Flying off Course: The Economics of International Airlines*, New York, Routledge Press, 1991, p. 49。

② See International Air Transportation Competitive Practices Act of 1974, Pub. L. No. 98 - 443, 98 Stat. 1706.

③ 49 U. S. C. A. 40101(e).

表 1 《国际航空运输竞争法》对美国《双边航空运输协定》(1979～1983 年)的影响①

主体	签订日期	实现的目标(序号)	未实现的目标(序号)	备注
韩国	3/22/1979	2、3、4、5、7、9	8	
新加坡	9/14/1979	2、3、4、5、7、9	8	
泰国	12/7/1979	2、3、4、5、7、9	8	
英国	1/1/1980	7、9	2、3、4、5、8	
芬兰	5/12/1980	2、3、4、5、7、9	8	
中国	9/17/1980	2、7、9	3、4、5、8	临时协定
日本	9/20/1980	9	2、3、4、5、7、8	
比利时	10/23/1980	2、3、4、5、7、9	8	
新西兰	11/25/1980	2、3、4、5、7、9	8	
阿根廷	3/11/1981	7,8	2、3、4、5、9	
加拿大	8/28/1981	4、7、9	2、3、5、8	
欧洲民航会议	8/1/1982	2		与 12 个欧共体成员国谈判,谈判内容仅涉及目标 2
日本	6/4/1982	9	2、3、4、5、7、8	
巴西	6/23/1982	7、9	2、3、4、5、8	
中国	8/19/1982	2、7、9	3、4、5、8	
菲律宾	9/16/1982	2、7、9	3、4、5、8	
委内瑞拉	11/9/1982		5	谈判内容仅涉及目标 5
欧洲民航会议	2/1/1983	2		与 17 个欧共体成员国谈判,谈判内容仅涉及目标 2
巴西	5/2/1983	2、7、9	2、3、4、5、8	原协定延长适用 1 年

① See Rex S. Toh and Nathan S. Shubat, "The Impact and Effectiveness of the International Air Transportation Competition Act of 1979", *Transportation Journal* 25, 1985, pp. 48 – 49.

续表

主体	签订日期	实现的目标（序号）	未实现的目标（序号）	备注
阿根廷	9/9/1983	7、8	2、3、4、5、9	原协定延长适用1年
欧洲民航会议	11/1/1983	2		与15个欧共体成员国谈判，谈判内容涉及目标2
菲律宾	11/23/1983	2、7、9	3、4、5、8	

另一方面，从实现效果上看，相关目标在美国的对外航空运输条约实践中的实现程度存在一定差异，如表2所示。

表2 《国际航空运输竞争法》战略目标的实现效果①

目标序号	实现该目标的航空运输协定的数量
9	16
7	16
2	15
4	7
3	6
5	6
8	2

结合表1与表2，可以得出以下几个结论。第一，目标9（消除美国承运人面临的歧视与不公平竞争行为）、目标7（增加美国的直达门户城市数量）与目标2（价格市场化）的实现效果最为明显，这为美国航空公司的国际自由化竞争提供了"公平竞技场"（level playing field）。② 第二，由于日本等国家在当时只有一个国际航空公司，其运力提供能力有限，因此目标3（被指定承运人数量增加）与目标5（排除对运力的限制）对此类国家的实现效果较差。

① See Rex S. Toh and Nathan S. Shubat, "The Impact and Effectiveness of the International Air Transportation Competition Act of 1979", *Transportation Journal* 25, 1985, p. 49.

② See Mike Tretheway and Robert Andriulaitis, "What Do We Mean by a Level Playing Field in International Aviation?" *Transport Policy* 43, 2015, p. 96.

第三,由于新加坡、泰国、韩国等国的航空运输能力有限,在其本土与美国之间的航线市场较小的情况下,其航空公司仅通过行使往返于本国与美国的第3航权与第4航权无法盈利,更愿意通过第5航权自由化以实现本国航空公司的盈利,因此《国际航空运输竞争法》的战略目标在美国与此类国家的协定中获得较好实现。① 总之,美国首先从议价能力较弱的国家入手推进航空自由化,而英国、日本等当时的航空强国在这一阶段对美国的让步仍然较为有限。

(二)《国际航空运输竞争法》的软硬两面性

作为美国对国际航空运输法律秩序进行自由化重塑的单边涉外立法,《国际航空运输竞争法》兼具"软法"与"硬法"的混合特性。②

一方面,《国际航空运输竞争法》的软法性是就其对《芝加哥公约》这一"硬国际法"而言的。《国际航空运输竞争法》本身不是国际法渊源,其仅是对《芝加哥公约》"公平"理念③的美国化解读,即机会公平而非结果公平。④换言之,该法是美国对国际航空运输法律秩序自由化的立场表达,其国内法

---

① 航权(traffic rights, droit de trafic)按国际惯例被称为"空中自由"(freedoms of the air),我国学者也将航权翻译为运营权。芝加哥会议确定了5种航权,当前已发展至9种航权,其中第3航权是指本国航机可以在协议国境内卸下乘客、邮件或货物;第4航权是指本国航机可以在协议国境内载运乘客,邮件或货物返回;第5航权是指某国或地区的航空公司在其登记国或地区以外的两国或地区间载运客货,但其班机的起点与终点必须为其登记国或地区;第6航权是指本国航机可以用两条航线的名义,接载甲国和乙国乘客及货物往返,但途中必须经过本国,第6航权是第3与第4航权的结合;第7航权是指本国航机可以在境外接载乘客和货物,而不用返回本国。即本国航机在甲、乙两国间接载乘客和运载货物。参见[英]郑斌:《国际航空运输法》,徐克继译,刘伟民校,中国民航出版社1996年版,第3页(校译说明)、第4~14页。

② See Brain F. Havel, *Beyond Open Skies: A New Regime for International Aviation*, Hague, Kluwer Law International Press, 2009, p. 273.

③ 根据《芝加哥公约》的缔约历史资料,《芝加哥公约》所指的公平是航空秩序论国家所指的国际航空利益的公平分配。在芝加哥会议上,英国代表斯温顿(Swinton)勋爵明确认为,国际航空运输法律机制应当服务于国际航空运输的公共性以及保证各国公平分享(fair share)航运资源,see Ruwantissa Abeyratne, *Convention on International Civil Aviation—A Commentary*, Springer Press, 2013, pp. 103 - 105。

④ See Mike Tretheway and Robert Andriulaitis, "What Do We Mean by a Level Playing Field in International Aviation?" *Transport Policy* 43, 2015, pp. 97 - 98.

的性质无法对国际航空运输法律秩序产生实质性影响。①

另一方面,《国际航空运输竞争法》的硬法性是就其对外国政府及外国航空公司的实施效果而言的。当时几乎任何国家的航空公司均有涉美运输业务,美国当局可以根据该法对外国政府及其航空公司的反竞争行为实施管辖。

1. 从制裁对象看,与 1974 年《国际航空运输公平竞争实践法》仅针对机场用户费的歧视性收取相比,《国际航空运输竞争法》的制裁对象拓及任何航空承运人的不正当或不合理的歧视性、掠夺性的反竞争行为,以及对美国承运人进入外国市场强加不正当、不合理限制的外国政府行为。② 例如,美国密克罗西亚航空与大陆航空在涉日本的国际运输中遭受日本籍航空公司不公平竞争行为,而日本航空当局的相关行为也违反《美日双边航空运输协定》反竞争条款的规定,因此美国当局对日本籍航空公司以及日本政府分别提出将会采取禁飞措施、中止双边运输协定的警告。③

2. 从制裁措施看,当外国政府或外国航空公司的行为损害、限制或拒绝美国航空公司行使根据条约享有的运营权,或对于美国航空承运人前往、来自、通过、飞越该外国领空的航空运输活动实施不公平、歧视性或限制性措施并对竞争产生实质性损害时,美国当局可在不经听证(需要总统批准)的情况下中止或修正外国航空公司在美国的运营许可、对外国政府采取中止双边航空运输协定等制裁措施。④ 此外,为强化制裁效果,美国当局甚至将相关措施用于从制裁目标国起飞飞往美国的第三国航空公司,即对行使涉美第 5

① See Brain F. Havel, *Beyond Open Skies: A New Regime for International Aviation*, Hague, Kluwer Law International Press, 2009, pp. 273 – 274.

② See Gloria Schaffer and Stephen H. Lachter, "Development in United States-International Air Transportation Policy", *Lawyer of the Americans* 12, 1980, pp. 595 – 596.

③ See Diane L. Welch, "Air Micronesia v. The Japan Civil Aeronautics Bureau: A First Interpretation of the International Air. Transportation Competition Act of 1979", *Brooklyn Journal of International Law* 7, 1981, pp. 435 – 463.

④ 49 U. S. C. A. 41304(b).

航权的第三国航空公司采取次级制裁。① 1998 年美国联合航空公司向交通部控诉欧共体委员会以及部分欧共体国家的航空公司的反竞争行为侵害了其根据"双边航空运输协定"享有的利益,美国当局向欧共体发出其将根据《国际航空运输竞争法》对欧共体相关国家的航空公司实施限运或者停飞的制裁威胁后,欧共体最终迫于压力而让步。②

3. 从制裁程序看,《国际航空运输竞争法》引入了程式化的控告与调查程序,在一定程度上含有司法化的特征。③ 当然,该程序主要是为下一步的外交磋商作准备兼有安抚美国航空公司情绪的作用,当局也可以在不说明理由的情况下驳回控诉。1992 年至 1994 年,美国西北航空公司对澳大利亚政府实施的反竞争措施向美国交通部提出控诉,最终澳大利亚在双边磋商后取消了相关措施。④

三、"比荷卢模式":分而治之

在明确国际航空协定的谈判目标后,为使航空秩序论国家接受自由化立场,美国采取了分而治之、各个击破的包围战略,即通过荷兰向德国和英国施压、通过韩国向日本施压。⑤ 美国对接受航空自由论的国家开放更大的美国市场,相关国家也因此获得了更大的国际市场份额和旅游收益,这迫使英国

---

① 次级制裁的法律机理参见王淑敏:《国际投资中的次级制裁问题研究——以乌克兰危机引发的对俄制裁为切入点》,载《法商研究》2015 年第 1 期。

② See U. S. DOT, Complaint of United Air Lines, Inc., Against the European Commission and National Implementing Authorities under 49 U. S. C. 41310, Dkt. No. OST - 98 - 4030 - 2, Order, Jul. 27, 1998; Dkt. No. OST - 98 - 4030 - 2, Order Dismissing Complaint and Terminating Proceeding, Nov. 27, 2002.

③ 49 U. S. C. app. 1159(b)(1).

④ See James Baxter, "Aviation and Space Law: Australia-United States Aviation Dispute", *Australian Year Book of International Law* 15, 1994, pp. 489 - 503.

⑤ See Anthony Sampson, *Empires of the Skies: The Political Contests and Cartels of World Airlines*, New York, Random House Press, 1984, p. 24.

等航空秩序论国家重新衡量各自立场。① 时任美国民航委员会主席卡恩明确指出，"如果外国政府允许美国航空公司进入其本国航空市场并接受包机自由化、放弃运力限制以及接受定价自由，作为回报，我们将进一步对其开放富饶的美国市场"。② 荷兰与比利时首先接受美国立场，在与美国的双边航空运输协定中纷纷取消了对运价、航线、运价和受指定承运人的数量的国家管制，此类协定被称为"比荷卢(Benelux)模式"。③

(一)"比荷卢模式"的核心内容

"比荷卢模式"是美国推动国际航空运输自由化的第一个范本，主要特点为：④(1)不限制受指定航空承运人的数量；(2)对等开放第5航权，即美国航空公司可以从美国本土任何一个机场起飞，途经第三国中间点飞抵缔约国，或经缔约国飞往第三国以远点；(3)不限定受指定承运人的飞机运力、运次及机型；(4)不限制货运第6航权；(5)鼓励低票价，航空公司可以根据市场情况自行确定票价，不参考国际航协的运价协调机制；⑤(6)将政府对运价事项的干预最小化；(7)允许包机运输，适航标准采用起始国规则；(8)排除

① See Paul S. Dempsey, "The International Rate and Route Revolution in North Atlantic Passenger Transportation", *Columbia Journal of Transnational Law* 17, 1978, p. 444.

② See A Review of U. S. International Aviation Policy, Hearings Before the Subcommittee on Aviation of the House Comm. on Public Works And Transportation, 95 Cong., 1st Sess. 943, 1982.

③ Protocol Between the Government of the United States of America and the Government of Belgium Relating to Air Transport(Dec. 1978)，协定的具体内容参见 Paul S. Dempsey, *Law and Foreign Policy in International Aviation*, London, Transnational Publication Press, 1987, pp. 425 - 431, Dempsey 在该书中将将此类协定统称为"比荷卢模式"(Benelux Model)。

④ See P. P. C. Haanappel, "Bilateral Air Transport Agreements: 1913 - 1980", *International Trade Law Journal* 5, 1980, p. 261.

⑤ 具体而言，协定确定的运价机制分为两种：(1)起始国票价机制。航空承运人起始国可以否决承运人的票价，因此一国可以废止美国承运人在其本国领土起飞航班的较低票价以保护本国承运人，这种机制为美国与秘鲁、德国、波兰、荷兰的双边协定中采用；(2)双重否决制。只有当缔约双方同时否决承运人票价时，承运人票价才作废。这种模式在美国与比利时、以色列和韩国的双边协定中采用。See Klem Leister, "The Struggle for a Competitive Market Structure in International Aviation: The Benelux Protocols Take United States Policies a Step Forward", *Law and Policy in International Business* 11, 1979, pp. 573 - 574.

歧视与不公平竞争行为,缔约方均允诺禁止掠夺性定价或歧视性定价行为。

"比荷卢模式"对"百慕大模式"的自由化变革主要体现在以下四个方面。

1. 在硬权利行使方面,"百慕大模式"的运力设计主要是根据航空承运人国籍国与营运最终目的地之间(第3航权与第4航权的运营市场)的需求作为国家事先确定运力的主要标准(primary justification traffic),将进出第三国一个或几个点(第5航权的中间点或以远点)的运力作为次要标准(secondary justification traffic),并辅以事后检查制度。① 因此,在百慕大模式下,第5航权因运力分配的国家干预而难以充分行使。而在"比荷卢模式"下,彻底废除国家对运力、运次与机型的干预与限制能使航空公司不考虑协定对运力的分配,航空公司可以对第5航权的运力在第三国、缔约国之间自由分配,第5航权得以充分行使。

2. 运价自由化。与"百慕大模式"的运价双批准制相比,"比荷卢模式"采用起始国票价机制与双重否决制,这不仅降低了政府对票价市场的干预程度,而且摆脱了国际航空运输协会下的航空公司票价协商体制。②

3. 开放货运第6航权,意味着美国承运人可以将美国本土作为中间点(而不是始发点)进行全球货物运输。这在客观上将美国机场从口岸型(货物出口与进口终端)转变为国际货运物流枢纽地位(货物进出口中转中心)。

4. 强调"软权利"的获得与行使。"比荷卢模式"禁止不公平竞争行为,

---

① See Bin Cheng, *The Law of International Law Air Transport*, London, Stevens and Son Press, 1962, pp. 303 – 314.

② 国际航空运输协会(International Air Transport Association, IATA)是国际定期航班承运人间的非政府间行业组织。该组织项下设有营运会议,营运会议是承运人之间根据协商一致原则对国际运价事先确定的会议。在美国法上,对运价协商的反垄断豁免需要履行两次批准:第一次是对"运价会议"行为本身授予豁免,第二次是对"凡涉及美国航空承运人"的运价表的实施授予豁免。美国早在1946年签订《百慕大协定I》时就对IATA的运价协调机制表达了不满,因此在1956年以前一直没有给予该机制不定期反垄断豁免。美国在1956年与IATA发生第一次正面冲突,给运价协调机制冠以"卡特尔"的恶名。第二次冲突发生在1963年,美国两次拒绝对运价协调机制授予反垄断豁免,史称"钱德勒风波"。在美国打算推行比卢荷模式时,美国司法部向国际航协发布陈情令,宣称要撤销对国际航协的反托拉斯豁免。参见赵维田:《国际航空法》,社会科学文献出版社2000年版,第177~187页。

明确将竞争法作为调整国际市场秩序的基本手段。

此外,为使航空秩序论国家接受航空自由化政策,美国交通部在1990年正式推出“城市计划”(cities program),允许外国航空公司在满足特定条件下可向美国交通部申请运营其母国至美国特定城市的国际航线。① 城市计划的本质是美国对外国航空公司给予单边优惠,当局在批准申请时通常会考虑该国与美国的航空外交关系以及该国对美国自由化航空协定的接受程度,是美国推行自由化航空运输协定的战略补充。② 例如,美国交通部在1992年批准德国汉莎航空公司的城市计划申请时,就综合考虑了美国与德国之间双边航空运输协定自由化的谈判现状、对分歧议题达成一致立场的可能等因素。③

(二)“比荷卢模式”的实现效果

截至20世纪80年代中期,约70个国家接受了“比荷卢模式”,这不仅极大强化了美国国际航空运输网络的形成,而且加速了管制型国际航空运输法律体制的瓦解。④ 随着接受美式航空自由论的国家数量的迅速增加,坚持航空秩序论的欧洲国家不仅面临自由化带来的航空经济利益的丧失,而且其所采取的政府补贴行为也面临航空自由论国家的非难。一方面,尽管“比荷卢模式”对当时的国际航空运输法律秩序的影响并不明显,但其迫使英国等航空秩序论大国重新衡量自己的立场并逐步接受航空自由化政策,这为国际航空自由化奠定了观念基础。⑤ 另一方面,“比荷卢模式”为国际社会提供了明

---

① Expanding International Air Service Opportunities to More U. S. Cities, DOT Order90 – 1 – 62, 1990, as amended by Expanding International Air Serv. Opportunities to More U. S. Cities, D. O. T. Order No. 91 – 11 – 26, 1991.

② See Seth M. Warner, “Liberalize Open Skies: Foreign Investment and Cabotage Restrictions Keep Noncitizens in Second Class”, *The American University Law Review* 43, 1993, p. 291.

③ See Lufthansa German Airlines, U. S. DOT Order 92 – 2 – 35, 1992.

④ See Amir Ali Majd, “Impact of Current U. S. Policy on International Civil Aviation”, *German Journal of Air and Space Law* 32, 1983, pp. 297 – 298.

⑤ See Anthony Sampson, *Empires of the Skies: The Political Contests and Cartels of World Airlines*, New York, Random House Press, 1984, p. 444.

确的规则范本,这奠定了国际航空自由化的制度基础。① 此外,美国的"城市计划"成功地抓住了航空公司这一国际航空运输的利益相关者,德国柏林航空、德国汉莎航空、荷兰皇家航空、瑞士航空、智利拉德科航空纷纷因此受益,航空公司成为了游说本国接受航空自由化政策的影子行为体。② 可以说,"城市计划"成为了美国在随后进一步推动开放天空政策的前奏与垫脚石。③ 总之,"比荷卢模式"对欧盟成员国的国内自由化与欧盟的航空区域自由化与一体化改革起到了示范作用(role model),欧洲的航空自由化有着"美式范本"的深刻烙印。④

当然,"比荷卢模式"的推行也非一帆风顺。由于"比荷卢模式"并未对"不公平竞争"作出明确界定以及缺乏反竞争条款的实施机制,美国承运人的公平竞争利益受到极大损害。美国国际航空承运人一致认为用开放美国市场以换取他国对市场公平竞争的承诺的做法并不明智。⑤美国国会进一步指出,"我们已经让外国航空公司进入了美国的内陆市场,美国……对于歧视与垄断行为不应宽恕,应对外国航空企业的非法垄断行为采取更为强硬的制裁行动"。⑥ 美国政府由此也放慢了不惜以授予第 5 航权及稀缺航班时刻等"硬权利"换取公平竞争权等"软权利"的步伐,从急切兜售航空自由论的理想主义者变成了循序渐进的实用主义者。

---

① 美国范本参见 Richard W. Bogoslan, "Aviation Negotiations and the U. S. Model Agreement", *Journal of Air Law and Commerce* 46, 1981, pp. 1022 - 1037。

② 当时的国际航空公司多数为国有公司,也被称为该国航空运输界的"国家冠军",国际政治学者将国有公司作为国际关系中的"影子行为体",在体系层面形成由国有公司、国有公司母国与第三国共同构成的"三角外交"关系,参见孙溯源:《国际石油公司研究》,上海人民出版社 2010 年版,第11 ~ 35 页。

③ See Paul S. Dempsey and Ram S. Jakhu, *Handbook of Public Aviation Law*, New York, Routledge Press, 2016, p. 269.

④ See Sean Barrett, Deregulation and the Airline Business in Europe, New York, Routledge Press, 2009, pp. 35 - 63.

⑤ See Paul S. Dempsey, "The Evolution of Air Transport Agreements", *Annual of Air And Space Law* 33, 2008, p. 359.

⑥ Ibid., pp. 359 - 360.

四、"开放天空模式":加速推进

"比荷卢模式"使美国航空公司的盈利在步入20世纪90年代后大幅增加,这促使美国为谋求更大的国际航空市场而加速推动国际航空运输法律秩序的自由化改革。① 自1992年开始,美国通过不断修正双边航空运输自由化协定范本的方式推进国际航空运输自由化协定网络的形成。②

(一)"开放天空模式"的核心内容

为与欧洲国家展开新一轮的双边自由化航空运输协定谈判,美国在1992年发布了名为"开放天空"的政策文件,③其政策目标是排除对航线、运价、运力的所有限制,允许承运人根据市场情况自由调整竞争要素。"开放天空模式"对"比荷卢模式"的核心条款作了进一步的自由化推进:(1)开放所有航线;(2)在所有航线上不限制运力与运次;(3)无限制的第5航权;(4)第3航权与第4航权市场上运价双重否决机制,以及对缔约方承运人在第三国的第3航权与第4航权的运输市场(第三国第6航权运输市场)实施价格自由化;(5)自由化的包机安排,当政府对包机运输规定宽严不一时,适用管制最小

① 与1980年相比,美国航空公司在1990年的国际旅客运输量增长了一倍、国际市场份额增加20%、航线数量与运力情况均大幅增加。See Jeffrey N. Shane,"Air Transport Liberalization: Ideal and Ordeal", http://www.raes-montreal.org/html/en/body/events/ak/2005/AK_IILecture.pdf, July 7, 2016.

② 美国双边航空运输协定的最新范为2012范本,参见http://www.state.gov/e/eb/rls/othr/ata/114866.htm, Oct. 11。

③ 美国对开放天空采用了描述性定义,共有11条标准,主要是指运力、运价、航线、市场准入等方面的自由化,see U.S. DOT, in the Matter of Defining "Open Skies", DOT Order 92-8-13, 1992, p.8。世界贸易组织(World Trade Organization, WTO)认为新西兰与澳大利亚之间的开放天空协定比美国的开放天空协定在内容上更为丰富,前者包含了实质所有权与有效控制权的自由化、第七航权开放、特定条件下的国内载运权开放的美式开放天空范本不具有的内容。See WTO, Second Review of the Air Transport Annex: Developments in the Air Transport Sector (Part II). Quantitative Air Service Agreements Review (QUASAR) (Volumes I and II): Note by the Secretariat, Document S/C/W/270, 2006.

的国家的规则;(6)将包括多式联运在内的广义航空货物运输的市场要素全面自由化;(7)允许代码共享;(8)货币汇兑自由;(9)地面自我处理(self-handing);①(10)公平竞争,包括禁止航空公司的掠夺性定价行为以及利用国家补贴获得竞争优势地位,反对航空公司计算机订座系统(Computer Reservation System,CRS)接入的歧视性行为,禁止国家歧视性收取用户费等。

(二)"开放天空模式"的实现效果

"开放天空模式"的主要目的仍然是想敲开欧洲三巨头(德国、法国和英国)的航空大门。在战术上与"比荷卢模式"如出一辙,美国仍将荷兰作为首个谈判对象,双方于1992年9月达成新的《美荷双边航空运输协定》。与之前的协定相比,除了国内载运权与航空公司实质所有权与有效控制权未开放外,双方的任何航空公司无须指定即可从其本国任何机场飞往另一国的任何机场。② 荷兰在面积上与美国西弗吉尼亚州相当,美国以其巨大的本土市场换取了荷兰的让步,但在战略上获得了丰厚的回报:1995~2005年,美国与包括欧盟成员国在内的67个国家签订"开放天空模式"的双边协定,彻底瓦解了航空秩序论同盟。③

美国的"开放天空模式"是通过双边方式加速向他国兜售"航空自由化范本",该模式不仅通过双边条约推动了协定缔约方的国内航空运输自由化改革,而且深刻影响了缔约国国与其他国家双边航空运输协定的自由化。④

---

① 自我处理,是指任何机场使用者(airport user)自己处理一个或者多种类型的地面服务,以及包括不与任何第三方为这些服务而缔约的自由。根据此定义,机场使用者之间提供这些服务在下列情况下不应当被认为是第三方:(1)一方持有另一方的主要股份;(2)双方的主要股份共同为一个机构所持有。换言之,航空公司如果有自我提供一种或者多种地面服务的能力,任何机场当局不应强迫外国航空公司必须使用机场提供的相应服务。

② See Pablo Mendes De Leon, "Before and after the Tenth Anniversary of the Open Skies Agreement Netherlands-U. S. of 1992", *Air and Space Law* 27, 2002, pp. 280 - 289.

③ See Pat Halon, *Global Airlines-Competition in a Transnational Industry*, Oxford, Elsevier Press, 2007, pp. 335 - 336.

④ See Christopher Findlay, "Plurilateral Agreements on Trade in Air Transport Services: The US Model", *Journal of Air Transport Management* 9, 2003, pp. 211 - 220.

可以说,当前的国际航空运输是在由美国网织而成的双边航空运输自由化协定群中经营的。① 从本质上说,美国对国际航空运输法律秩序遵循着观念认同—行为认同—规则认同的进路,是“通过建构语法规则来影响国际规则的语句表达”。②

五、“两洋模式”:诸边立法

进入21世纪后,随着多数国家对美式“开放天空模式”的接受,美国先后在太平洋与大西洋两个跨区域层面(cross-regional)③采用诸边进路推动国际航空运输法律秩序的多边自由化。

(一)“两洋模式”的核心内容

1.《跨太平洋航空运输协定》。由美国在2001年发起、部分亚太国家参与的《国际航空运输自由化多边协定》(以下简称《跨太平洋航空运输协定》)是美国航空自由化政策在亚太地区的诸边化产物。④ 时任美国交通部长米

---

① 截至2016年9月,与美国签订开放天空协定的国家或地区共120个,在地理上遍布各洲,其中开放第7航权的国家共计85个(尼加拉瓜仅开放包机运输第7航权),载 http://www.state.gov/e/eb/rls/othr/ata/114805.htm,Sep. 7, 2017。

② See Brian F. Havel, “Substantive and Procedural Critique of the U.S. Open Skies Policy”, in Pablo Mendes De Leon ed., *From Lowlands to High Skies—A Multilevel Jurisdictional Approach Towards Air Law*, Hague, Martinus Nijhoff Press, 2013, p.6.

③ 随着WTO多哈僵局以及TPP、TTIP等跨区域贸易协定成为当前新的国际潮流,有学者认为其与一般的区域内贸易协定有着明显区别,认为跨区域贸易协定是大国试图重塑国际经贸秩序的新的国际场所,并最终导致当前既存体制的根本变革。笔者认为尽管当前跨区域贸易协定中航空运输并非主要议题,但其原理基本相同,美国推动下的航空诸边自由化在效果上最终可能导致以《芝加哥公约》为基础的双边机制的崩溃。参见刘中伟、沈家文:《跨太平洋伙伴关系协议(TPP):研究前沿与架构》,载《当代亚太》2012年第1期;Rafael Leal-Arcas, “Proliferation of Regional Trade Agreements: Complementing or Supplanting Multilateralism?”, *Chicago Journal of International Law* 11, 2011, pp.597-598; C. O'Neal Taylor, The U.S. Approach to Regionalism: Recent Past and Future, *ILSA Journal of International and Comparative Law* 15, 2009, p.418.

④ 协定的参与国有:美国、智利、库克群岛、蒙古、新西兰、萨摩亚、新加坡、汤加,秘鲁在2005年撤回,see Multilateral Agreement on the Liberalization of International Air Transportation, Accessed http://www.maliat.govt.nz, August 12, 2017。

内塔表示,"《跨太平洋航空运输协定》是我们超越双边体系,向21世纪的国际航空运输法律体系迈进过程中具有历史性意义的协定……它的重要意义在于该协定涵盖了日趋增长的、具有战略意义的跨太平洋市场"。① 除了秉承美国"开放天空模式"的基本要素,该协定对航空自由化又做了进一步的拓展,形成了有别于双边机制的诸边"俱乐部"。②

表3 《国际航空运输自由化多边协定》的主要内容

航空自由化的主要方面	自由化程度
航线	开放定期航班航线
货运航权开放	开放第5航权与第7航权
客运航权开放	开放第5航权
计算机订座系统	非歧视
客运国内载运权	任择议定书中开放
运价	在政府批准的最低价格之上自由化
受指定承运人数量	多数指定
运力	自由确定
代码共享	允许第三方代码共享
航空公司实质所有权与有效控制权	要求被指定的航空公司主要营业地在指定国家领土内;只对被指定的航空公司的有效控制权人有国籍要求,不再强调实质所有权的归属

① US State Department Release of May 1 2001, Accessed http://ussembassy-australia.state.gov/hyper/2001/0501/epf210.htm, August 12, 2017.

② 赵维田教授将plurilateral翻译为"复边",是指缔约国数目多于双边(bilateral)、少于多边(multilateral)者,具有未来"晋升"多边的预备阶段,参见赵维田:《最惠国与多边贸易体制》,中国社会科学出版社1996年版,第243~244页。从观念上看,"多边主义"是一种"框架式"(an architectural form)的观念或意识形态,多边主义不仅意味着形式上多数,而且意味着观念上对潜在加入方的开放,即优惠对非参与方的扩散性,这也是多边主义与区域主义(如东盟、阿拉伯国家联盟等区域自由化)的区别所在,后者具有体系封闭性。因此,下文中《国际航空运输自由化多边协定》虽然名为"多边",但事实上参与国数量仍然有限,没有达到国际社会多数(无论是国家数量还是市场占有数量)参与意义上的"多边",其性质介乎于双边与多边之间。对多边主义更为详尽的讨论参见[美]约翰·鲁杰主编:《多边主义》,苏长和等译,浙江人民出版社2003年版。

与双边机制相比,《跨太平洋航空运输协定》在规则的自由化方面有重大突破。第一,该协定为国际航空运输自由化提供了从双边到多边过渡的初步尝试。第二,全货运输第7航权的开放提高了航空运输对国际货物贸易的经济贡献,强化了航空运输在全球经济供应价值链中的作用。第三,客运无限制第5航权的开放以及附加议定书中客运第7航权和国内载运权的开放拓展了航权的交换范围。第四,对传统的"实质所有和有效控制原则"进行侧面突破,缔约方可以指定多个航空公司,受指定航空公司只需满足其为该国国民有效控制(effective control)而无须为该国国民实质所有(substantially owned),加速了国际航空运输企业之间的投融资合作与资本的全球流动。① (见表3)

但是,《跨太平洋航空运输协定》对美国利益作了过多让步,在客观上造成国际航空利益的分配失衡。美国航空公司可以在自由化的亚太区域获得利益,但其他缔约国的航空公司因其能力所限以及美国对国内运载权的限制而无法进入美国市场,这也是韩国、日本、澳大利亚等亚太航空大国迄今没有加入的原因。② 可以说,《跨太平洋航空运输协定》的现实经济效果并不理想,其在一定程度上是美国为与欧盟展开谈判进行的规则认同测试。

2.《跨大西洋航空运输协定》。美国的航空自由化极大地促使了欧盟的航空自由化浪潮并在1993年后形成了欧盟内部的开放天空,但欧盟委员会并未获得对外航空条约谈判权能,成员国仍然对外(特别是与美国)继续签订双边协定。③ 从1993年开始,委员会与成员国就对外航空条约谈判代表权

---

① 该协定的这一规定影响到了国际民航组织的立场,国际民航组织在2003年第5次世界航运大会中形成的建示范条款直接采用了有效管理控制(effective regulatory control)标准,并建议世界各国在双边和多边协定中采用。See ICAO, Consolidated Conclusions, Model Clauses, Recommendations and Declaration, Worldwide Air Transport Conference: Challenges and Opportunities of Liberalization, March 31, 2003, Agenda Item 2.1.

② 例如,货运第7航权使得美国航空公司可以在不返回美国的情况下在亚太地区的国家间从事国际货物运输,而该公约的多数缔约国的航空公司均在除其母国外的其他国家缺少足够的枢纽基地,因此没有能力充分运用第7航权。

③ See Magnus Schmauch, *EU Law on State Aid to Airlines: Law Economic and Policy*, Berlin, Lexxion Press, 2012, pp. 25 – 29.

限问题上展开旷日持久的博弈。1995年各成员国迫于“委员会向欧盟起诉”压力授予委员会在对外谈判方面的软权力(计算机订座系统、起降时刻、地面服务、航空公司实质所有权与有效所有权)。就在委员会欢欣鼓舞地认为这是一场“真正的胜利”时,美国却明确表示其拒绝与在欧盟委员会缺乏权能的情况下与之进行任何形式的谈判。① 美国的立场使英国、荷兰、意大利无视委员会的立场继续推进与美国的双边开放天空协定谈判,欧盟成员国与委员会之间就对外航空条约谈判专属权的争夺逐步升级。美国与葡萄牙2000年签订的开放天空协定不仅进一步激化了欧盟的内部矛盾,而且将欧盟航空运输协定的对外谈判权限问题推入“僵局”,迫使欧盟委员会对8个成员国在欧盟法院提起诉讼。② 欧盟法院在2002年的“开放天空判决”中明确要求各成员国必须重新与非欧盟成员方进行双边谈判,以修正之前航空运输协定中不符合欧盟法的条款。为说服成员国,欧盟委员会委托美国布拉特尔(Brattle)集团公司对“跨大西洋开放天空协定”将会带来的市场利益进行预测并得出量化结论:(1)大西洋市场年客运量从400万增到1100万,这意味着大西洋市场占全球市场的比例将从9%提升至24%;(2)欧盟市场的年客运量将会增至3570万,同比增长1360万;(3)创造的消费者利益为52亿美元,并带来竞争增加、票价降低和旅客数量增加的效果;(4)直接相关产业将会增加年经济产出36亿美元,增加的年经济总产出为81亿美元。③ 欧盟理事会迫于压力在2003年给予委员会水平授权(horizontal mandate)并代表欧盟成员国开展与美国的航空运输协定的谈判。欧盟与美国在经历多轮谈判后于2007年与2010年先后签署了第一阶段与第二阶段的开放天空协定,形

① See Paul S. Dempsey, *European Aviation Law*, Hague, Kluwer Law International Press, 2004, p. 82.

② 参见黄涧秋:《开放天空:欧盟航空运输管理体制的自由化》,载《欧洲研究》2009年第2期。

③ 事实上,根据学者对协定生效后的经济学分析,跨大西洋开放天空协定并未达到预期的经济效果, see Barry Humphreys Peter Morel, The Potential Impacts of the EU/US Open Sky Agreement: What Will Happen at Heathrow after Spring 2008, *Journal of Air Transport Management* 15, 2009, p. 77。

成了跨大西洋的共同航空市场。该协议是美国迄今为止将其航空自由化国际输出的最新成果,对以《芝加哥公约》为基础的双边体系产生了重要的影响。

在欧盟委员会获得对外航空运输协定的谈判权能后,①美国与欧盟及各成员国在经历多轮谈判,分别于2003年、2007年和2010年达成两阶段的《美国与欧盟及其成员国航空运输协定》(以下简称《跨大西洋航空运输协定》)及议定书。②《跨大西洋航空运输协定》将之前所有双边、诸边自由化协定的所有核心成果并入其中,并在以下方面作出新的突破:(1)缔约方所有的航空公司无须指定均能参与市场运营;(2)航线、运力、运价、运次等所有的竞争要素全部由市场决定;(3)以竞争法的手段代替行政管制手段,禁止政府进行损害公平与平等机会的补贴与支持;(4)环境措施协调承诺;(5)劳工标准承诺;(6)航空公司实质所有权与控制附条件的达成妥协,在互惠的基础

---

① 美国为"一揽子"解决美国与欧洲的航空自由化问题,多次利用外交手段间接促使欧盟理事会向欧盟委员会授予对外航空协定的谈判代表权。美国在1995年明确表示,其拒绝在欧盟委员会缺乏在航权等"硬权利"方面的谈判权能的情况下与之进行任何形式的谈判。美国的立场使英国、荷兰、意大利继续推进与美国的双边开放天空协定谈判,欧盟成员国与委员会之间就对外航空条约谈判权的争夺逐步升级。美国与葡萄牙2000年签订的开放天空协定不仅进一步激化了欧盟委员会与成员国的内部矛盾,而且将欧盟航空运输协定的对外谈判权限问题推入"僵局",这迫使欧盟委员会对8个成员国在欧盟法院提起诉讼。欧盟法院在2002年的"开放天空判决"中明确要求各成员国必须重新与非欧盟成员方进行双边谈判,以修正之前航空运输协定中不符合欧盟法的条款。在欧盟理事会迫于压力于2003年对委员会水平授权后,美国正式展开其与欧盟《跨大西洋航空运输协定》的谈判。See Paul Stephen Dempsey, *European Aviation Law*, Hague, Kluwer Law International Press, 2004, pp. 82 – 86;参见黄涧秋:《开放天空:欧盟航空运输管理体制的自由化》,载《欧洲研究》2009年第2期。

② 笔者所用协议为整合版本,虽然该协议在学理上存在"第一阶段"和"第二阶段"之分,但这并不是指两个协议是相互独立的,第二阶段协议是对第一阶段的补充,此外双方在2010年又达成了修正第二阶段协定的议定书。整合版文本全文请参见欧盟美国联合委员会的第8次会议,参见Eighth Meeting of the U. S. -EU Joint Committee Record of Meeting, Nov. 17, 2010。迄今为止,欧美双方最新的一联席会议是第18次会议(2016年4月19日), see Accessed http://www. state. gov/e/eb/rls/othr/ata/e/eu/227943. htm, October 2, 2017。

上实施;[①](7)美国承认"欧盟共同体承运人"的概念并对其开放"航空服务政府采购市场";(8)建立常态化联合委员会机制。

(二)"两洋模式"的实现效果

"两洋模式"是美国进入21世纪以来推动国际航空运输自由化的最新手段,其战略效果尚未充分展现,笔者仅就在其影响下可能发生的全球多边化效果进行初步分析。

1. 为国际航空运输多边自由化提供条约范本。"两洋模式"(特别是《跨大西洋航空运输协定》)不仅在内容上对之前所有自由化协定的成果进行固化并在重要方面获得突破,而且表达了旨在为国际航空运输多边自由化提供理想范本(ideal model)[②]的立法雄心与远景目标。[③] 当前,"两洋模式"对国际航空运输法律秩序的"范本化"影响正在显现。例如,新西兰等《跨太平洋航空运输协定》缔约国认为该协定为多边自由化提供了"制度范本"并鼓励其他国家加入该协定。[④] 欧盟在2007年以后与加拿大、东盟等多个国家和地区签订或正在谈判的双边与跨区域航空运输协定在内容上多以《跨大西洋航

① 美国囿于国内法的规定,允许欧盟投资者持有美国航空企业50%以上的股份,但仍存在外国投资者25%的表决权限制。由于欧盟成员国国内法允许美国投资者持有欧盟成员国航空公司49%的表决权,因此该协议第21(2)款要求根据互惠原则,欧盟及其成员国应当允许美国或其国民对欧盟航空公司享有主要所有权以及有效控制。根据协定第4条与附件4,未来欧美市场的实质所有权与控制问题有赖于美国国会修改其国内法,在互惠的基础上实施。双方在每年一度召开的联合工作组会议上持续地对该问题进行磋商与协调,致力于解决国际航空运输领域的股权并购的国际投资壁垒。

② See Russell E. Tanguay, "The Future of the U. S.-EU Agreement: A World of Open Skies?", *Issues in Aviation Law and Policy* 9, 2010, p. 345.

③ 《跨大西洋航空运输协定》第21条要求缔约方采取建议与鼓励措施使其他国家开放本国航空服务市场,提高缔约方航空公司进入全球资本市场的机会。

④ ICAO, The Multilateral Agreement on the Liberalization of International Air Transportation: A Basis for the Future Economic Regulation of Air Services, ATConf/6 – WP/34, para. 4. 4, 该协定对亚太国家国际航空运输协定自由化的影响的具体分析,参见 David Timothy Duval, *Air Transport in the Asia Pacific*, New York, Routledge Press, 2014。

空运输协定》为蓝本(除俄罗斯)。[①] 可见,一方面,美国在这一阶段已不是利用自己的力量,通过开放本国市场的方式推行航空自由化政策,而是借力于"两洋模式"的缔约方,以诸边协定为范本向全球推行自由化政策。另一方面,"两洋模式"克服了多边自由化机制建构中的制度公共产品提供不足的问题,[②]降低了国际航空运输多边自由化的条约谈判成本,使多边自由化的速度从"加数效应"向"乘数效应"变化。[③]

2. 在国际民航组织之外创设大国协调机制。根据《芝加哥公约》,国际民航组织只在安全与技术性事项有立法权,而在航空经济合作等方面只有建议权,国际民航组织也没有利用《芝加哥公约》赋予的司法裁判权通过判决"能动"地确立其在国际航空经济关系方面的权威地位,[④]导致在相关议题上长期无法形成有拘束力的多边法律机制。[⑤] 就国际事务而言,如果两个或两个以上的国家有足够的交往且对彼此决策有足够影响,从而使他们(至少在一定程度上)作为一个整体的组成部分来行为时,他们就建构了初步的国际

---

① 相关协定的主要特点参见 EU Parliament, *An Overview of the Air Services Agreements Concluded by the EU*, Brussel, European Union Press, 2013, p. 75;相关协定与"跨大西洋协定"的相似性参见 Francesco Gaspari, "Recent Developments in EU Air Transport Liberalization and Re-Regulation Policies and the New Legal Order of International Air Transport", *Issues in Aviation Law and Policy* 11, 2012, pp. 425 - 434;对欧盟与东盟的自由化协定的分析参见 Alan Khee-Jin Tan, "The Proposed E. U. -ASEAN Comprehensive Air Transport Agreement: What Might It Contain and Can It Work?", *Transport Policy* 43, 2015, pp. 76 - 84。

② 对公共产品更为详尽的分析参见徐崇利:《国际公共产品理论与国际法原理》,载刘志云主编:《国际关系与国际法学刊》(第 2 卷),厦门大学出版社 2012 年版,第 3 ~ 49 页。

③ 条约范本的形成对国际法律机制多边化谈判成本的降低与谈判效率的提高的分析参见王彦志:《新自由主义国际投资机制初探——以国际机制理论为视角》,载刘志云主编:《国际关系与国际法学刊》(第 1 卷),厦门大学出版社 2011 年版,第 154 ~ 157 页。

④ See David Marcella, "Passport to Justice: Internationalizing the Political Question Doctrine for Application in the World Court", *Harvard International Law Journal* 40, 1999, p. 120.

⑤ 对于 ICAO 安全与技术以外事项缺乏权能的现状,学界认为主要从三个方面进行变革:(1) 强化 ICAO 在经济领域的作用;(2) 完善 ICAO 的争端解决机制;(3) 修正《芝加哥公约》对 ICAO 的授权。See Ruwantissa Abeyratne, "Reinventing ICAO's Role in Economic Regulation-A Compelling Need", *Issues in Aviation Law and Policy* 13, 2013, pp. 9 - 28; Gabriel S Sanchez, "The Impotence of the Chicago Convention's Dispute Settlement Provisions", *Issues in Aviation Law and Policy* 10, 2010, pp. 27 - 39; Brian F. Havel and Gabriel S. Sanchez, "Do We Need a New Chicago Convention?", *Issues in Aviation Law and Policy* 11, 2011, pp. 8 - 22.

体系。[①]《跨大西洋航空运输协定》以条约为基础建立了常态化联合委员会机制,联合委员会每年至少召开一次,或根据一方请求,就有关竞争政策对协定适用的影响以及缔约方拒绝承担协定义务引起的协定解释问题,自请求之日起不晚于60内召开会议(除非双方另有约定)。联合委员会的职能相当广泛,包括:(1)协定的适用与解释;(2)协定的修正与现代化;(3)第三方的加入;(4)在适当时与国际组织就发展与合作问题在协商的基础上磋商;(5)对特定议题专门磋商,以确定双方在此议题上是否以及采用何种"一致的方法"(joint approach),同时允许一方参与另一方在特定议题上的立法过程。[②]因此,《跨大西洋协定》是在国际民航组织之外初步建立了以条约为基础的大国立场协调体系。[③] 联合委员会机制在实践中产生了良好的效果,例如,就美国对全球航空碳减排提出的市场机制方案、欧盟反对"共同但有区别责任原则"对航空运输碳减排领域适用的立场,[④]双方的方案与立场均在国际民航组织会议等多边场合获得对方的基本支持。

3. 建构走向全球多边主义的诸边路径。当前的国际航空运输是在极其复杂网络下运转的,试图在拥有197个成员方的国际民航组织场所下达成多边自由化协定并不现实。[⑤] 美国推动的"两洋模式"为国际航空运输的全球

---

① 参见[英]赫德利·布尔:《无政府社会:世界政治秩序研究》,张小明译,上海人民出版社2015年版,第12~13页。

② 参见《跨大西洋协定》第15条第5款a项。

③ 例如,美国在第六次世界航空大会中的立场文件就明确表明国际民航组织在国际航空市场竞争法方面不应当成为一个立法者或监管者,而是作为沟通与协调平台存在,美国此举是刻意弱化ICAO在相关事项上的影响力,参见ICAO,AT Conf/6 - WP/62,paras. 4.1 - 4.2;事实上,运输政策学学者已然提出通过大国间的诸边协定的方式解构《芝加哥公约》体系的主张。See Antigoni Lykotrafiti,"Liberalisation of International Civil Aviation-Charting the Legal Flight Path", *Transport Policy* 43,2015,pp. 85 - 95.

④ Tenth Meeting of the U. S. -EU Joint Committee Record of Meeting December 8, 2011, Accessed https://www. state. gov/e/eb/rls/othr/ata/e/eu/192096. htm,Mar. 12,2017.

⑤ 截至2016年,全球197个国家共缔结了2743个双边、多边协定及超过1000个协定修正议定书,其中2176个为非自由化的传统协定,283个是向自由化方向发展的转型协定、184个是开放天空协定。See ICAO Secretariat, Overview of Regulatory and Industry Developments in International Air Transport,September 2016,para. 3.5.1.

多边化提供了诸边进路。[①] 当前,大国诸边领导(plurilateral lead)、其他国家多边跟随(multilateral follow-up)的进路,日渐成为全球性多边法律机制形成的重要方式之一。[②] 诸边方式是在少数大国间先行达成协定,而后利用正式或者非正式的体制性(institutional power)力量对其他国家施压以使其接受该协定,当协定成员国的权重达到临界数量(critical mass)时,[③]非缔约国基于理性选择(成本—收益)对规则进行接受。[④] 一方面,《跨太平洋航空运输协定》已然在跨区域层面形成开放性"俱乐部",[⑤]《跨大西洋航空运输协定》进一步要求欧盟与美国应基于共同立场与目标追求而努力将本协定拓展第三方国家,在必要的情况下可对本协定进行必要修正以便第三方加入。[⑥] 另一方面,"两洋模式"的临界数量特征[⑦]使其有在适当时机并入、转化为多边航

---

① 诸边航空运输协定是指与地缘无关,在两个以上少数志趣相投国家间达成的但并不排除其他国家加入的协定,国际民航组织从现实效果意义上将"诸边"认为是准"多边",see ICAO Secretariat, Overview of Regulatory and Industry Developments In International Air Transport, September 2016, para. 1.5.1。

② See Armin Steinbach, "The Trend towards Non-Consensualism in Public International Law: A (Behavioural) Law and Economics Perspective", *The European Journal of International Law* 27, 2016, pp. 666 – 668.

③ 临界数量协定是当前国际贸易法研究中频繁采用的一个概念,是指当"志趣相投"的WTO部分成员方参与协定谈判并对其他缔约方开放的协定。临界数量是指缔约方的贸易量满足一定的市场权重(market weight)从而足以使其为其他国家所认同。See Peter Gallagher and Andrew Stoler, "Critical Mass as an Alternative Framework for Multilateral Trade Negotiations", *Global Governance* 15, 2009, p. 385;我国学者也认为美欧通过临界数量协定先行绕开存在明显分歧的谈判对手进行立场协定以掌握规则制定先机是其晚近经贸战略调整的重要工具,而RTAs是多边化的先导或者次优选择,参见石静霞:《国际贸易投资规则的再构建及中国的因应》,载《中国社会科学》2015年第9期。

④ 这种接受既可以是以国家同意为基础的条约加入,也可以是非参与方在实质上对相关条约所确立的标准的接受并反映在该国的条约实践中。See Armin Steinbach, "The Trend towards Non-Consensualism in Public International Law: A (Behavioural) Law and Economics Perspective", *The European Journal of International Law* 27, 2016, p. 645.

⑤ 只要是1963年《东京公约》、1971年《海牙公约》和1988年《蒙特利尔议定书》(合称三个反劫机公约)的缔约国,就可以加入该公约。

⑥ 参见《跨大西洋航空运输协定》第18条第5款。

⑦ 两洋协定的缔约国共占据全球50%以上的市场份额。值得注意的是,这一份额将会进一步增加。See Barry Humphreys Peter Morel, "The Potential Impacts of the EU/US Open Sky Agreement: What Will Happen at Heathrow After Spring 2008", *Journal of Air Transport Management* 15, 2009, p. 77.

空自由化体系或作为综合性多边贸易法律机制构成部分的可能。① 事实上,这种渐进式的多边化正在发生,美国、欧盟、智利、阿拉伯国家联盟、马来西亚、巴拿马(共占据国际航空运输市场60%的份额)在2009年已共同签署了向《跨大西洋航空运输协定》标准趋近的多边政策性声明,为未来形成多边条约的形成奠定了共识基础。② 因此,有学者认为,《跨大西洋航空运输协定》在性质上是为全球立法的造法性条约(traite-loi),与契约性(traite-contrat)的双边"开放天空模式"在国际法意义上有质的不同。③

六、我国的借鉴

自1978年至今,美国采用多种策略将美式航空自由论国际化,从国内法的双边化、双边协定的诸边化以及诸边协定的多边化,呈现出层层递进的规律。④ 尽管我国已成为全球第二大航空市场,⑤但国内市场的繁荣并没有促进

---

① 例如,在欧美跨大西洋协定第十三次和第十四次联合委员会会议上,双方就《欧美跨大西洋伙伴关系协定》与欧美跨大西洋航空运输协定之间的关系与一致性问题进行意见交换,欧盟在2016年11月28日的《欧美跨大西洋伙伴关系协定》提案中明确提出航空运输纳入《欧美跨大西洋伙伴关系协定》的讨论之中,载 http://trade. ec. europa. eu/doclib/docs/2015/march/tradoc_153263. pdf,Feb. 11,2017。《跨太平洋伙伴关系协定》尽管将航空运输业排除,但《跨太平洋伙伴关系协定》成为美国对其他《跨太平洋伙伴关系协定》国家施压的场所,see John D. Goetz and Sarah L. Thompson, "The Trans-Pacific Partnership and Its Effect on International Aviation", *Issues in Aviation Law and Policy* 15,2016,pp. 285 – 295。

② See Russell E. Tanguay, "The Future of the U. S.-EU Agreement: A World of Open Skies?", *Issues in Aviation Law and Policy* 9,2010,pp. 345 – 346.

③ See Brain F. Havel, *Beyond Open Skies: A New Regime for International Aviation*, Hague, Kluwer Law International Press,2009,p. 273.

④ 法国学者马蒂教授指出,大国通过单边立法影响国际社会,通过将自己的法律作为"商品"输出的方式影响他国,以及在区域或者发达国家集团层面推动多边条约三种法律技术推行霸权主义,参见[法]米海依尔·戴尔玛斯·马蒂:《世界法的三个挑战》,罗结珍、郑爱青、赵海峰译,赵海峰校,法律出版社2000年版,第10~18页;高鸿钧教授对美国20世纪60年代以来美国对拉丁美洲、欧洲、转型国家以及国际商法方面法律输出作了精辟的考察,参见高鸿钧:《美国法全球化:典型例证与法理反思》,载《中国法学》2011年第1期。

⑤ 根据国际航协的统计,我国在2024年前后将取代美国,成为全球最大的航空市场。IATA, "IATA Forecasts Passenger Demand to Double Over 20", Press Release No. 59,18 October 2016.

我国航空运输业国际竞争力的增强。实证研究表明，一方面，我国对国际航空运输的运力及航线等竞争要素的国家管制、国有航空公司的国际化管理水平较低、反垄断法对航空业的实施效果较差等因素是造成我国航空公司与其他航空公司间的国际竞争力差距不升反降的部分原因。① 另一方面，我国对第5、6、7航权交换的不充分导致我国国际机场的国际枢纽性不足，降低了我国机场的洲际运输中转能力及我国航空公司参与国际运输的机会。② 因此，参与国际航空运输自由化进程是提高我国航空公司国际竞争力与我国国际航空运输枢纽地位的必然选择，而美国对国际航空运输法律秩序的再造手段对我国参与国际航空运输法律秩序的全球治理具有借鉴意义。

首先，明确我国《反垄断法》对国际航空运输活动的适用。与1979年美国《国际航空运输竞争法》相比，我国缺乏保障国际航空利益的国内法根据。我国《民用航空法》(以下简称《民航法》)是调整我国国内与国际航空运输的主要国内法渊源，③由于双边航空运输协定与《民航法》对国际与国内运价、航线、运力等市场要素的管制性规定，导致我国法院认为航空公司缺乏能够控制航班价格、航班数量或者其他交易条件，或者能够阻碍、影响其他航空公

① 从定性角度看，我国东航、国航、南航三大集团公司占据全国70%的市场份额，在《反垄断法》对我国航空公司的拘束力较弱的情况下，我国大型航空公司可以利用国内市场的支配地位获得利润，缺乏与参与国际竞争的动力。从定量角度看，管理学学者使用了“总要素与部分要素生产率”“平均收益”“单位成本”“投入价格”四个测度对比了我国大型航空公司与发达国家国际航空公司国际竞争力的差距，并发现我国国际航空公司与发达国家国际航空公司的竞争力差距在晚近以来有扩大趋势，see Kun Wang et al., Benchmarking the Performance of Chinese Airlines: An Investigation of Productivity, Yield and Cost Competitiveness, Journal of Air Transport Management 38, 2014, p. 3。

② 我国国际机场与东北亚其他国家国际机场枢纽化程度的对比及其对我国航空公司国际竞争力的影响，see Xiaowen Fu et al., “Dominant Carrier Performance and International Liberalization-The Case of Northeast Asia”, *Transport Policy* 43, 2015, pp. 61–75。

③ 中国民用航空总局曾在1996年颁布《制止民用航空运输市场不正当竞争行为的规定》(1996年中国民用航空总局令第47号)，明确了“维护我国民用航空运输市场的正常秩序，鼓励和保护公平竞争”的立法目的并列举了若干不正当行为，但并未规定垄断行为。随着该规定在2007年被废止，《反垄断法》对国际民用航空运输活动的适用缺乏准用性规则。值得注意的是，《制止民用航空运输市场不正当竞争行为的规定》的废止理由是“与国家有关法律相冲突”，但废止决定并未言明是与《民用航空法》相冲突还是与《反垄断法》相冲突。参见《中国民用航空总局关于废止部分民用航空规章和规章性文件的决定》(2007年中国民用航空总局令第186号)。

司进入该相关市场能力的市场地位,我国法院据此认为航空公司无法成为《反垄断法》滥用市场支配地位规则的规制对象。① 因此,《民航法》准用性规则的缺失造成我国《反垄断法》对国际航空运输缺乏管辖基础,不利于我国国际利益的维护。在中国东方航空公司与澳大利亚航空公司的联盟案中,澳大利亚竞争与消费者委员会在2015年根据其反垄断法对申请作出初步否决决定。该案涉及中国与澳大利亚两国市场,而我国反垄断执法机构既没有对该经营者集中行为行使管辖,②也没有在澳方作出否决草案时像美国执法机构一样根据国内法采取相应措施,最终使我国航空公司被迫接受更为苛刻的豁免附加条件。因此,我国应在《民航法》的修订中:(1)明确我国推行国际航空运输自由化的基本立场,确立我国对外航空运输协定谈判的指导原则与战略目标;(2)规定我国《反垄断法》对国际航空运输活动的可适用性及执法模式。

其次,确立中国双边航空运输协定的谈判范本。与美国的"比荷卢模式""开放天空模式"相比,我国多数航空运输协定的自由化程度较低,特别体现在客货运第5航权、货运第7航权、运力限制、运价的确定方式等方面。③造成我国对外双边协定自由化程度较低的原因,一方面是我国接受航空运输自由化协定的时间较晚,更新速度较慢;另一方面是随着我国国际航空运输

① 本案仅涉及国内运输,但由于我国的多数双边航空运输协定并非自由化协定,均对市场要素存在较强的国家管制,《反垄断法》对国际航空运输适用的法理与本案相同,参见广东省高级人民法院:《顾芳诉中国南方航空股份有限公司拒绝交易纠纷案》,(2014)粤高法民三终字第1141号。

② ACCC经估算认为,在除去间接航班旅客数量和中国国际航空的直达旅客数量外,联盟申请双方共占据70%左右的市场份额。根据《反垄断法》(2007年8月30日中华人民共和国第十届全国人民代表大会常务委员会第二十九次会议通过)第21条与第22条的规定,经营者集中的当事方应向发改委申报。See Australian Competition and Consumer Commission Determination, Applications for Authorisation lodged by Qantas Airways Limited and China Eastern Airlines Corporation Limited in Respect of a Joint Coordination Agreement, Authorisation Numbers: A91470 and A91471.

③ 截至2013年,我国对外签订的双边航空运输协定共有118个,其中86个允许对承运人多数指定、26个采用开放航线表、12个不限班次的客货运第3、4航权、7个不限班次的全货运第3与第4航权、7个班次不限的第5航权,58个允许与第三国航空公司进行代码共享,ICAO, ATConf/6 - WP/97, para. 2.2.

能力的增强,部分国家不愿意向我国开放航空运输市场。因此,我国应在未来谈判过程中:(1)以2009年《中国与智利双边航空运输协定》为范本,借鉴美国"比荷卢模式",对欧洲、美洲等航空富饶市场采用分而治之的谈判策略;(2)可以借鉴美国"城市计划",将我国单边对外国空运企业开放海南的客货运第3、4、5航权的"海南模式"以及全货运第7航权的开放引入我国国内自由贸易区,允许任何满足条件的国际航空公司经申请均可进入中国自贸区。

最后,推动(跨)区域航空运输的多边自由化。随着《跨大西洋航空运输协定》的达成,亚洲航空公司国际航线网络不足的现状将进一步恶化,区域自由化将是亚太地区未来的可能选择之一。① 2010年《中国与东盟各成员国航空运输协定》是我国签署的唯一区域多边航空运输协定,该协定在航权、运价、受指定承运人数量等方面实现了一定程度的自由化。② 但同时,亚太国家的对外航空政策追求(aero-political)存在较大差异,具有巨大市场的关键国家(key states with large markets)之间缺乏集体利益认同,各方陷入了"胜利者—失败者"(winters and losers)的相对获益范式,缺乏大国驱动成为亚太航空运输多边自由化的主要障碍。③ 我国可借鉴美国的"两洋模式",一方面,将《中国与东盟各成员国航空运输协定》的成功生效定位为"规则认同测试"的通过,在"一带一路"倡议背景下推动国际航空运输自由化(特别是客运第5、6航权与货运第7航权),形成连接欧洲扇形航线网络与大洋洲扇形

① See OECD, Regional Integration in the Asia Pacific Issues and Prospects, Paris, OECD Press, 2005, p. 152.

② 该协定授予我国航空公司从东盟国家任何一点至我国任何一点的第3、4航权和有限制的第5航权,而东盟成员国的航空公司则只能经营从其本国任何一点至我国任何一点的航线。有学者认为东盟在没有完成形成"单一天空"的情况下与我国签订多边自由化协定属于"本末倒置",降低了东盟航空运输区域一体化的可能。相关分析参见 Alan Khee-Jin Tan, "The 2010 ASEAN-China Air Transport Agreement: Placing the Cart before the Horse", *Air and Space Law* 37, 2012, p. 35。

③ See Alan Khee-Jin Tan, "The Future of Multilateral Liberalisation of Air Transport in Asia", in David Timothy Duval, ed., *Air Transport in the Asia Pacific*, New York, Routledge Press, 2014, pp. 259 – 275.

航线网络的"一带一路航线"。另一方面,在"一带一路"倡议下的正式与非正式的国际机制中加入航空运输议题,建立利益协调与常态对话机制,在环境、竞争、劳工等议题上形成大国共识,奠定"空中丝绸之路"的制度基础与观念基础。

资　　讯

著名国际法学家、英国伦敦大学终身名誉教授郑斌先生向西北政法大学捐赠图书

受西北政法大学副校长、国际法研究中心主任、航空法治现代化协同创新中心首席专家王瀚教授特别委托,2017 年 5 月西北政法大学国际法学院院长刘亚军教授、丝绸之路区域合作与发展法律研究院周亚光博士,赴英国伦敦拜见年届 96 岁高龄的著名国际法学家、国际航空法学家、英国伦敦大学终身名誉教授郑斌先生,专程接受和办理图书捐赠事宜。

郑斌教授和其父郑天锡先生是我国法学史上十分鲜见的国际法研究世家,他们均在英国伦敦大学获得国际法学博士学位,都是在国际上享有盛誉的著名国际法学家。此次捐赠由西北政法大学国际法研究中心特聘教授、亚太航空法协会主席、台湾东吴大学程家瑞先生促成,西北政法大学党委书记宋觉研究员和王瀚副校长曾于 2016 年 12 月 14 日会见程家瑞教授商定接受该批图书捐赠。

此次受赠图书为国际法外文图书资料共计 3000 余种、册,创我校历史上单次接受海外赠书之最。其

中包括郑斌教授从事航空法和国际法学术研究60多年来珍藏的国际法、国际航空法及外层空间法专业图书;郑斌教授的父亲、民国时期法学家、国际联盟常设国际法院中国籍大法官郑天锡先生所收藏的国际法外文图书;其中尤为珍贵的是郑斌教授英文博士学位论文《国际法院与法庭适用的一般法律原则》打印稿及文献卡片摘录等。

此次西北政法大学受赠的图书和文献资料来源广泛、跨越百年,涉及英、德、法、韩、日和中文等语种,包括劳特派特、施瓦曾伯格等权威国际法学家的经典国际法和航空法著作,联合国国际法院的判例、联合国大会、安理会决议,部分国际条约谈判的相关历史资料,美国、德国、法国、荷兰、韩国、日本、中国等国的重要国际学术刊物,内容非常丰富,文献价值和学术价值十分珍贵。这批图书和文献资料展现了近代国际法学到现代国际法学的形成、演进和发展,其中蕴含的学术脉络和学说集成为考察、梳理和挖掘国际法学术史研究提供了珍贵的原始资料。郑斌先生撰著的《国际法院与法庭适用的一般法律原则》自1957年由英国史蒂文斯出版社出版以来已多次再版,在全球国际法学界享有盛誉,1987年曾作为对国际法和政治学界认识极具重要性的著作的格劳秀斯名著”再版,成为国际法学界公认的经典文献之一。

鉴于郑斌先生在国际法学、国际航空法学与外层空间法学研究的杰出成就与学术影响,西北政法大学荣聘郑斌先生为我校荣誉教授并对郑斌先生襄助学术之举颁发捐赠证书。为传承郑斌、郑天锡先生的学术思想,有效使用受赠图书和文献资料,西北政法大学国际法研究中心将以郑斌教授捐赠图书为基础,分别设置建设“郑斌航空法图书馆”和“郑天锡国际法图书馆”,在2017年10月西北政法大学80周年校庆期间举行图书馆揭幕仪式,向西北政法大学师生开放借阅藏书,为国际法和航空法研究者提供信息资料平台;建设郑斌、郑天锡生平图片纪念馆,编辑整理两位前辈的法学学术文集,届时将邀请中外著名学者举行第一届郑天锡、郑斌法学思想研讨会。

附一:郑天锡先生简介

郑天锡(Cheng Tien-Hsi,1884～1970),字云程,号茀庭,广东香山县人(今中山市三乡镇雍陌村),中国著名法学家、外交家,曾任大理院大法官,多所大学法学教授,司法官次长,国际联盟常设国际法院法官,民国最后一任驻英大使。

郑天锡早年肄业于香港皇仁书院,后毕业于上海圣约翰大学。1907年时年24岁的郑天锡放弃了在香港待遇优厚的工作,赴英国留学专攻法律。1912年毕业于伦敦大学法律系,翌年回国。1914年郑天锡再次赴英深造,1916年获伦敦大学法学博士学位,是第一批在伦敦大学获得博士学位的中国人之一。1917年返港任执业律师。1918年转往北京,任北洋政府司法部法律翻译监督。1919年任大理院大法官。1921年任中国出席华盛顿会议代表团专门委员。翌年返国,任中国出席关税特别会议专门委员,法权调查委员会准备处处长,国际法权委员会代表,国务院商标局法律顾问。在北京期间,曾先后兼任北京大学、朝阳大学、法政大学等校教授。1928年在上海重操律师业,并兼上海东吴大学法学院教授。1932年1月任国民政府司法行政部常任次长,7月改任司法行政部政务次长,1935年任外交部顾问。1936年10月郑天锡先生当选国际联盟常设国际法院法官。第二次世界大战结束后,国际联盟常设国际法院重新选举法官。郑天锡原是战前由中国政府推举当选的法官,由于当时中国驻美大使出缺,政府改调驻英大使顾维钧出任驻美大使,郑天锡出任驻英大使,提名人选因此改为徐谟。此外,在这次联合国大会上,荷兰政府提名郑天锡为法官候选人,这也表明郑天锡在任这一职务期间的国际影响。第二次世界大战爆发前夕,郑天锡意识到海牙将被德国法西斯侵占,因此于1940年离开海牙避居瑞士,并将常设国际法院的重要文件档案转移到中立国瑞士首都日内瓦,使这些文件在第二次世界大战期间得到妥善保存,为保存重要国际文档立下大功。1945年第二次世界大战后返回海牙,出席国际法庭全体法官会议,后被选为国际联盟清理委员会委员,同年返国并重任司法行政部次长。1946 年 8 月,任中国驻英国大使,1950 年 1 月去职留居英国。1970 年 1 月 30 日在伦敦病逝,终年 86 岁。

郑天锡先生著作甚丰,在法律与文学领域均具有卓越建树。在法律方面,先后将中国法律翻译为英文,如《民法初稿》《最高法院的判决》《捕获审判所规则与审判》等。另有中英文本《大理院判例》《大理院判例讨论》《暂行新刑律例》以及博士论文《国际私法中关于确定契约能力的法规》等。在文学方面,郑天锡先生用英文撰写了多部介绍中国文化的著作,获得国际文坛好评,如《中国文化与艺术》《孔子模型之中国人》《东方与西方》等。

附二:郑斌先生简介

郑斌(Bin Cheng,1921 ~),广东香山县人(今中山市三乡镇雍陌村),著名国际法学家、国际航空法学家和国际空间法学家,是全球国际航空法学与外层空间法学的开拓者与奠基人之一,原国际法协会英国分会荣誉秘书(1960 ~ 1967 年)、伦敦大学大学学院法学院院长(1971 ~ 1973 年)、伦敦大学法学院院长(1974 ~ 1978 年),现为伦敦大学航空与空间法终身名誉教授。其妻傅锦培女士为前国民政府驻苏联大使,司法院副院长傅秉常长女,与郑斌教授育有一子一女。郑斌教授 1944 年获得瑞士日内瓦大学法学学士,1950 年获英国伦敦大学法律系哲学博士,1966 年获伦敦大学法学博士,1980 年当选英国皇家航空学会院士。郑斌教授著述丰富,在国际法、国际航空法、国际空间法等领域均有卓越建树,享誉全球,先后发表 200 余篇学术论文与多部重要学术专著。《国际法院与法庭适用的一般法律原则》自 1957 年出版至今,在全球国际法学界享有盛誉,在 1987 年作为对国际法和政治学界认识极具重要性的著作的格劳秀斯名著再版,先后在 1997 年、2006 年被剑桥大学出版社再版,成为国际法学界的经典文献之一;1962 年出版的《国际航空法》被公认为是全球国际航空法的经典著作,1996 年由我国著名航空法学家徐克继翻译、刘伟民审校在我国出版,成为指导我国对外航空条约谈判的重要指导文献;1997年出版的《国际空间法研究》一书成为全球系统研究外层空间法的代表性与开拓性文献。多国政府及大学、研究机构为表彰郑斌教授的杰出成就,先后授予郑斌教授诸多荣誉:1978年香港中文大学授予荣誉法学博士;1998年法国政府授予学术勋章;1989年巴西政府授予"桑托斯杜蒙航空勋章";1989年当选伦敦大学学院院士;1997年韩国航空与空间法学会授予"对国际航空法与空间法多年贡献奖牌";1997年获国际航天联盟空间法国际学会"终生成就奖";1988年获国际航空运输协会"国际法航空法发展杰出贡献奖";2007年获加拿大麦吉尔大学航空与空间法研究院《航空与空间法年刊》(2007年第32卷)编委题献;2010年获欧洲航空学协会"终生成就奖",被国际航空法学界尊称"航空法之父"。郑斌教授曾讲学于全球20余国,并在中国、加拿大、英国、澳大利亚等国家的权威期刊与研究机构任咨询委员会委员、学术总监、董事。

“一带一路”民航法治实践与创新

——2017年中国法学会航空法学研究会年会综述

时杜娟*

中国法学会航空法学研究会于2017年11月17日至18日在厦门召开会议。此次会议由中国法学会航空法学研究会和中国民用航空局国际合作服务中心主办，厦门市法学会承办，厦门航空公司、厦门翔业集团、厦门远大联盟律师所协办。来自全国各地160余位航空法专家和学者参加了会议。

本次论坛暨年会主要采取了大会发言的研讨形式，代表们围绕“一带一路”航空法治、“一带一路”航空国际经营法律问题与争议解决、“一带一路”民航法制建设法律问题、“一带一路”中国航空制造与服务法律问题这四个单元的主题进行了发言与交流。现将会上代表发言及其主要观点综述如下。

---

* 西北政法大学服务西北地区稳定发展与国家安全高级法律人才培养项目2017级博士研究生。

一、"一带一路"航空法治

我国《民用航空法》颁布于 1995 年,至今已 20 年有余。1995 年《民用航空法》已经无法适应我国航空运输的发展,特别是对我国国际航空运输业务的拓展产生了诸多阻碍。在"一带一路"倡议的背景下,我国急需构建与沿线国家之间的航线网络,这一因素给《民用航空法》的修订增加了特殊的考量方面。

中国民用航空局政策法规司副司长郭仁刚指出,立法是国家治理的基础,制定一部好的法律是国家治理体系现代化的基础,落实中央要求民航局对相关政策进行立法转化是民航局践行与中央保持一致的实际做法。他认为,"一带一路"不是民航法修订的主体内容,是中国航空运输发展过程中面临的一个特殊情况。中国在"一带一路"沿线上的航空运输尚未形成市场边界和市场驱动,航线网络布局需要国家政策的引导。航空法的修订需要与中央对"一带一路"的航空运输政策保持一致。"一带一路"沿线国家的航空运输面临几个重要的问题:第一,沿线国家的政局不稳定,安全问题比较突出,在民航法的修订中可以考虑将"安保"问题单独设章。第二,保障航空运输安全是民航发展的指导思想,安全贯穿民航运输的始终,既涉及旅客运输过程中的安全保障问题,也涉及机场地面设施的安全保障问题,不能单独设章。第三,我国民航法的修订需要特别关于赔偿标准问题,与国际航空运输公约全面接轨,特别是与中国加入的 1999 年《蒙特利尔公约》的标准相接近。

南方航空公司总法律顾问陈威华指出,"一带一路"航线开放主要涉及两大风险:一是国家风险;二是法律风险。具体涉及法系差异、劳工问题、环境问题、税收问题和商业腐败等风险。针对上述风险,南方航空公司采取了一系列的防范措施:一是出具重大风险排查报告;二是制作法律风险热力地图;三是制作国别手册;四是加强海外办事处管理;五是提升合规文化培育力度;六是加强与东道国政府、金融机构的沟通。南方航空公司在平时的管理中采取航线开设法律先行,日常管理法律随行。

时任中国航空法研究会副会长聂颖指出,我国航空企业应该重视对“标准”的研究。标准是先进企业的标志,建立标准意味着话语权和市场主动权。针对中国民航企业如何创立标准的问题,聂颖副会长提出几点建议:第一,将标准工作与法律工作相结合。将国家法律细化到企业规章,再细化到行业标准。企业的标准是企业风险控制、内部控制和合规管理的基础。第二,建立法律和规章的科学体系。重视标准在企业行为决策量化和法律判断量化中的作用,完善的企业规章和标准是企业应对危机和重大事故的重要砝码。第三,要重视对标准的研究。航空产业的标准研究既要跟进国际水平,也要符合中国的实际国情。

大疆公司法律副总监黄义指出,大疆公司无人机销量占到国际市场的70%,其中80%的销量进入了海外市场。在销售的各个环节面临的法律风险呈现出多样性和复杂性。如无人机出口、运输与入境过程中的贸易术语、货损与理赔、知识产权保护、337调查等纠纷,销售环节中出现的买卖合同纠纷、价格与渠道控制和误导宣传等,售后环节中涉及的各国维保政策、产品责任认定等政策和法律上的冲突,以及在销售管理中可能因各国法律文化背景差异遇到各类纠纷。针对这些风险,黄义也提出了三点建议:一是实行“本地化”管理模式,聘请当地雇员,聘请当地律师;二是合规化经营,入乡随俗、尊重当地法律;三是经验固化,由专业人员研究当地法律,改进无人机销售流程。

二、“一带一路”航空国际经营法律问题与争议解决

上海国际仲裁中心副秘书长黄文指出航空争议解决机制的构建应该具有国际化的视野,为此,上海国际航空仲裁院进行了积极的摸索和创新。一是组建航空争议解决专家委员会,以保障航空争议解决的专业性、公平性和公正性。目前,上海国际航空仲裁院成立了专家委员会,专家委员主要来自

国际航协和中国航协的推荐。二是扩充仲裁员队伍,吸纳航空各个领域的专业人才。上海国际航空仲裁院2014年吸纳了来自61个国家和地区的仲裁员,新增仲裁员70余人。目前通用航空和无人机领域的仲裁员仍存在很大空缺。三是采用机构仲裁,有利于降低当事人的争议解决成本。国外仲裁一般是按次收费,仲裁成本较高,上海国际航空仲裁院是机构仲裁,执行标准收费。四是借助《纽约公约》较高的国际普及度,能够保障航空仲裁裁决的承认与执行。“一带一路”沿线有53个国家加入了《纽约公约》,占到沿线国家总数的83%,而签署司法互助协议的国家仅有10个,因此仲裁裁决在执行上的困难要比法院判决的承认与执行小得多。五是与国际航协临时仲裁对接,扩大中国国际航空仲裁的影响力。上海国际航空仲裁院预计发布一套航空仲裁规则,包括代理指定仲裁员、进行财务的管理、程序的协助以及硬件设施的提供。

北京盈科(深圳)律师事务所合伙人陈茜对通用航空领域争议热点和纠纷解决作了重点阐述。一是“航空中毒综合征”(Aerotoxic Syndrome)引起的纠纷及法院实践。航空中毒综合征,是指飞机通风系统将部分空气排进机舱内部引起人体不适、功能丧失等症状。在现有的案件中,当事人及其律师曾以“飞机设计缺陷”起诉制造商,以失败告终。根据世界卫生组织的认定,航空中毒综合征与排进机舱内部空气是存在关联性的。从德国法院新近审理的一起航空中毒综合征候群案来看,德国初审法院首次将航空中毒综合征对机组工作人员造成的人体伤害认定为工伤。陈茜律师认为如果德国上诉法院维持初审法院的判决,通用航空的运营商今后可能会面临大量的此类诉讼。二是通用航空目前还存严重的飞行安全问题,特别是在某些娱乐飞行领域,运营公司为了增强飞行项目的吸引力,飞行员往往在极端天气下强行执行飞行任务,多次造成机毁人亡的严重事故。陈茜认为,应该加强对通航企业飞行安全的监管,规范无证飞行、不具备航空器代管人资质等现象。

东方航空云南公司法律部总经理何英指出,中国已与“一带一路”沿线62个国家签订了双边航空运输协定,与43个国家实现了空中直航,东航

2016 年在"一带一路"沿线国家经营了 131 条航线,通航城市已达 21 国 45 城。东航在航空运输争议解决中面临法律适用的难点主要有两个方面:一是民航法规定承运人的严格责任,不以其故意和过失为前提,容易造成旅客的过度维权,如霸机、放任损失扩大等;而且受适航标准等问题的限制,客舱尚未纳入监控区,造成承运人举证困难等。二是国际公约的适用。《蒙特利尔公约》实行的是限额赔偿和无限额赔偿的双轨责任制。为了化解这一困境,何英认为,应该采用多元化的争议解决机制,并建议成立民航商事调解中心、民航业纠纷仲裁委员会等。特别建议在昆明成立与上海国际航空仲裁院类似的仲裁组织,专门用以解决南亚、东南亚、西亚等国家的航空运输争议。

台湾铭传大学法律学院副教授林盟翔以复兴航空公司的经营与监管为主线,重点阐述了与航空运输消费者紧密关联的两个问题:一是航空公司能否稳健经营、永续发展问题;二是机票的履约保证问题。林盟翔教授认为,复兴航空公司 2016 年发生毫无征兆的停飞及突然宣布解散对消费者产生了很大的困扰,应该加强对航空公司经营及退出市场的监管。在履约保证的问题上,林盟翔教授提出了四点建议:一是在现行制度的基础上,采取多元化的保险制度;二是在"一带一路"的航空运输中,建议航空公司借鉴国际上采用的履约金制度或者信托方式;三是航空公司在实施履约金等制度中产生的费用和成本可以保险的方式进行分散;四是建议台湾地区在消费者保护法中进行相关条款的设计。

众达律师事务所北京代表处资深顾问薛强指出,航空业已经成为欧盟、美国等实行反垄断监管的重点,在法律责任的追究上,逐渐将追究直接责任人员和管理层作为制止垄断的有效方式。在法律风险防范上,薛强提出了三点建议:一是避免与竞争者交换敏感信息;二是谨慎出席行业协会会议;三是加强日常的反垄断培训与合规。

民航科学技术研究院副研究员赵劲松分析了卡塔尔事件的来龙去脉,赵劲松认为在任何情况下,占据优势地位的国际民航组织理事会大多数代表是外交官或者航空专家,而不是律师,理事会不可能被视作一个真正的由法官组成的司法机构，不可能严格排他地以国际法基础来裁决，理事会的仲裁实质是一种由主权国家执行的“外交仲裁”，此种仲裁往往基于主权国家的某些政策或者某种政治考虑。

国浩（北京）律师事务所高级合伙人高峰指出，中国航空公司与“一带一路”沿线国家开展运输服务的过程中，不可避免地要与当地的机场签订诸如航线维护、机务、配餐、住游等协议，因此产生的纠纷所涉及的法系较为多样，而且此类纠纷很难在私下通过双方领导层的协调、双方律师的交流等比较平和的方式解决，更多的争议会诉诸诉讼，会给航空公司带来诸多负面影响，如诉讼成本增加、形象受损、诉讼结果不公平等。针对这一难题，高峰律师认为可以通过“航空商事调解”来化解。高峰律师所提的“商事调解”不同于调解法下的调解，或者民航局的航空调解，而是由专职律师、航空法专家甚至是仲裁员在成为调解人员的前提下，对相关争议以第三方的地位进行调解。“航空商事调解”有四大优势：一是自愿；二是保密；三是完全凭借当事人对某个调解员的信任来确定；四是调解地和程序由当事人确定。不足之处是“航空商事调解”没有强制执行力，针对这一问题，高峰律师建议将航空商事调解协议与仲裁的承认与执行制度相结合，以实现商事调解协议的跨域执行。

三、“一带一路”民航法制建设法律问题

东方航空集团政策研究室主任兼办公厅主任吴建端指出，推进“一带一路”的进程中所产生的法律问题是世界性的、普遍性的，所涉法律制度不会局限于“一带一路”沿线国家，而是涵盖了世界主要国家的法律体系。吴建端主任据此提出了 5 个可供研究的法律问题。一是双边、多边的航空运输协定的法律问题。我国与沿线 62 个国家签有双边航空运输协定，这些协定在天空开放程度上差异较大，需要深入研究这些航空运输协定的正文、备忘录等文件。二是航空联盟合作的法律问题。传统上的航空联盟已经从联程、常旅客计划、代码共享，发展到全面航班时刻、航线协调、联合经营的收入收益共

享等更高级别的股权合作,其经营风险小于单纯的航线开辟。三是政府补贴法律问题研究。“一带一路”新航线所经地区大多欠发达,经营这些航线的航空公司必然面临运营困难的问题。吴建端律师建议将“一带一路”航线纳入政府补贴范围。四是建议加强对通用航空法律问题的研究。五是建议航空法学研究应立足中国、借鉴国外、侧重研究民航“一带一路”“国际化”“全球化”等法律问题,构建中国特色航空法学研究体系。

中国民航科学技术研究院助理研究员李亚凝指出,航空器权利登记采用的是登记对抗主义,中国国籍的航空器利益相关人必须先从民航局取得授权代码后,方可在国际登记处进行利益登记。李亚凝助理研究员提出了构建航空器交易多功能平台的设想,即从航空器制造业入手,推动通用航空器制造业的网上适航认证,推动通用航空企业的设立、投资、合并与收购,吸引运输航空器的线上交易,逐步发展航空器制造业的中国标准。在航空器交易环节,继续推动航空器,特别是通用航空器的网上交易,实时为交易方办理航空器权利登记,保障交易安全,吸引航空器网上跨境交易。在航空器融资环节,鼓励和推动航空器融资方网上认证,促进航空器资产证券化。在航空器交易纠纷解决环节,从纠纷解决的便利性出发,可以推动中国规则在航空器交易过程中的适用,促进国内仲裁机构对航空器交易纠纷的管辖,并逐渐形成国内航空器交易的合同范本。

福建远大联盟律师事务所副主任李毅阳律师对航空器融资租赁登记制度的完善提出了三点建议。第一,修订《民用航空法》或颁布司法解释来完善航空器的占有权制度,统一界定为融资租赁权;第二,扩大我国航空器融资租赁登记的客体范围,明确把航空器发动机、单个航空器零件列入融资租赁登记的客体范围,增强登记制度的灵活性;第三,明确统一由民用航空主管机关专项管理所有的与航空器相关的权属登记事项,并明确界定其他行政登记机关不得干涉或从事航空器的权属登记工作。

山东航空集团规划部经理郭才森提出,空域和航班时刻是公共资源,都不归国家所有。他认为,航班时刻拍卖是政府实施行政许可职权,是一种公法上的行为，政府在此行为中不能获取利益，因此，航空时刻拍卖收入不应该归国家所有，应当归航空公司共有，同时，航空公司以抽签取得的航班时刻不应当缴纳使用费。

中国政法大学朱子勤教授介绍了航空法模拟大赛的发展历程和参赛队伍选拔规则。国际航空法模拟法庭比赛是由民航组织建议设立，由荷兰莱顿大学和印度沙林（Sarin）法律基金会主办，是国际上唯一的航空法模拟法庭比赛，在国际航空运输领域有较大的影响。中国政法大学分别于 2013 年、2014 年获得冠军和亚军，2015 年大赛由首都机场主办，中国政法大学承办。中国民航大学、中国政法大学、华东政法大学、西北政法大学、北京航空航天大学、南京航空航天大学、武汉大学分别参加过比赛。朱子勤教授建议由中国航空法研究会作为主办方，取得中国赛区授权，成立中国国内赛委员会，制定中国赛区规则，包括承办机制、法官人选的确定和赛事程序等。

中国民航大学王朝梁副教授对货物多式联运经营人的责任制度构建提出了三点建议。第一，借鉴最小网状责任制。即中国多式联运的立法应该借鉴《鹿特丹规则》的最小网状责任制。第二，引用完全过错的归责原则。王朝梁副教授认为，不完全归责原则和严格责任原则已经不适应中国运输发展的现状，在“一带一路”倡议的背景下，沿线各国的港口码头数量大大增多，海运发展渐入佳境，多式联运发展较为成熟，采用完全过错责任归责原则具有可行性。第三，规定合理的赔偿责任限额。王朝梁副教授建议参考《汉堡规则》关于赔偿责任数额的规定，完善我国多式联运经营人的相关立法。

四、“一带一路”中国航空制造与服务法律问题

中国商飞公司法律部部长唐绮霞指出，在“一带一路”国产飞机外销的过程中：一是应该坚持飞机卖到哪儿，服务跟到哪儿；二是要对销售目标国法律政治环境进行分析；三是在服务网点的建设方面，应该采用合作、合资和自建的模式；四是应该对目标国在技术合作、外商投资、场地租赁、土地买卖、工

程建设、维修中心适航管理资质等方面的相关政策进行研究。

中国商飞公司李圣别就适航认定分享了三点看法:一是适航双边协议的具体构成,一般包括了框架性协议(谅解备忘录 MOU、双边适航协定 BAA、航空安全协定 BASA)和技术性协议(技术安排 TA、工作安排 WA、监控协议 AOS)。二是关于单独 MOU(双边适航谅解备忘录)是否足以支撑型号认可审查的问题,印尼目前的做法是准许审查。三是 2017 年"中美适航实施程序(IPA 2017)"中包括诸多亮点,如实现了中美两国航空产品全面对等互认、基于安全风险的理念对认可程序进行分类和支持工业合作等。

首都机场集团资产管理有限公司总经理李纯指出,基础设施是"一带一路"互联互通的核心,机场的建设投资应进一步向社会放开,加大机场建设发展的进程。李纯认为,"一带一路"背景下机场投资建设法律风险应该从两个方面进行防范。第一,在战略层面。应该强化政府层面的规则建立;选择能够推动航线体系网络完备的城市,对投资区域进行风险评估、法律政策梳理;在探索投资基础设施建设的同时,注重机场管理的标准输出。第二,在战术层面。筹划好投资机构,做全面充分的尽调;涉及优化的投资架构;合理设计投资退出机制;对东道国风险进行评估;实行项目本地化;建立劳动者保护机制。

中航西飞民机公司法律与审计室主任于涛指出,新舟飞机在国际化拓展中主要面临四个方面的法律风险,分别是主制造商与供应商产品责任划分问题、知识产权问题、出口管制问题和争议解决机制问题。针对上述风险,于涛分别提出了防范和解决的建议。第一,供应商需对系统的性能、功能、质量等承担主要责任。无论是因系统还是机体产生的责任纠纷,应该合理划分权责,形成一套系统的处理规则,最大限度保障各方利益。第二,知识产权风险较为复杂,主制造商应该在管理过程中实行有效区分,对知识产权信息明确标识、合法使用、有效保护、防范侵权,以及在合同解除后对知识产权问题予以善后特别关注。第三,在出口管制问题上,可以通过合同条款设计,加强供应商的信息报告责任,对在销售合同中通过对可谅解的交付延迟等情形加以约定，从两端联动系统性降低风险发生的后果，并尽力将将责任传导至管制政策所在国的供应商。第四，将适用法律和争议解决机构设为招标条件，可以预防合同谈判中的被动性。

中国民航大学郝秀辉教授提出了多项防范措施，如构建跨国融资租赁平台；加强审查与信用监管；加强利率和汇率风险管理；设置保障条款；设计相应保险产品；国家政策与服务创新举措；推动更多的沿线国家加入《开普敦公约》。

中国民航大学刘胜军认为，从解释论的角度来讲，以利他合同来解释实际承运人从事的运输：一方面，契合公约和我国相关法律突破“合同相对性原则”以扩大运输责任主体，保护旅客/托运人的规范意旨；另一方面，也符合现代运输业运输的连续性、衔接性和运输商业活动中多主体相互依赖性的交易现实。刘胜军还提出，我国国际国内物流大通道建设需要以实际承运人制度为基础，完善多式联运制度，以促进我国“一带一路”战略的实施。

五、其　　他

在第一单元的点评环节，中国政法大学杜新丽教授针对民航法治提出了三点建议：第一，鉴于国际民商事条约在适用上优先于国内法，民用航空法的修订要尽可能地实现对 1999 年《蒙特利尔公约》的转化适用，防止国际国内在赔偿标准等方面出现较大的差异。第二，仲裁在航空争议解决方面具有很大的优势，特别是仲裁的专业性，上海国际航空仲裁院的成立对航空运输纠纷的解决很有必要。第三，关于航空争议的诉讼解决，杜新丽教授指出目前最为突出的两个问题，一是管辖权问题，二是承认与执行。中国已于 2017 年签署了《协议选择法院公约》，管辖权今后应当以当事人的选择为准。在判决的承认与执行方面，海牙国际私法会议正在讨论“关于判决跨国界的承认与执行”，中国一直在参加该公约的谈判，希望公约能够顺利签署，以便利国际航空争议的解决。南方航空公司法律部副总经理马选玲提出两点建议：一是“一带一路”航空法治要明确一个目标,尝试构建“一带一路”沿线国家的航空法体系,在已加入的多边公约的基础上,通过多边磋商的方式,率先对一些重点领域进行构建,如飞机的引进、飞机融资租赁、中国飞机的出售。二是要加快培养和储备国际化航空法律人才,推动“一带一路”航空法治建设。

在第二单元的点评环节,民航局国际合作服务中心主任孟庆芬指出,在断交外交关系中,两国之间虽无外交关系,但是可以有航空运输关系;希望监管机构关注中小型外国航空公司代表处关闭问题,更好地保护消费利益。孟庆芬指出目前的航空公司垄断已经不局限于代码共享、航空公司联盟合作等方式,其他的方式还有如通过单一航线或者某几条航线联营的方式,应该加强对航空公司新型市场垄断方式的研究和审查。中国航空油料集团公司法律顾问徐永建指出航空公司拖欠油款的问题在解决中目前面临依法(合同)停供与社会责任之间的困境,建议在法律法规、行业标准中细化拖欠油款的补救措施,以促进行业发展,实现互利共赢。

在第三单元的点评环节,厦门大学法学院何丽新教授提出了三点建议:一是航运中心的建设。何丽新教授认为,应该对“航运”作广义的解释。二是海运与航运的制度能否融会贯通的问题。何丽新教授认为航空器登记制度、租赁制度等与船舶制度十分接近,因此创新的航空法与古老的海商法在制度上是可以融通的。三是在多式联运的问题上,尽管国际上的多式联运规则迟迟不能生效,如果航运与海运能在归责原则、免责条款和免责条款的制度设计上能够融通,国内在多式联运问题上就可以领先国际规则,先行实践。中国民航大学王立志副教授认为,航权是“空中丝绸之路”建设的最基本的问题。航空器占有权一般是发生在干租的情况下,也不排除例外情况。航空器是合成物,包括发动机和其他零部件。航空运输已经成为多式联运的一个重要区段,人的多式联运已经超过了货物的多式联运,在航空领域目前主要在探讨人的多式联运,把之前的货物多式联运用在人的多式联运中是存在问题的,需要进一步研究。中国民航管理干部学院刁伟民副教授认为,“一带一路”倡议的实施应该贯穿法治思维,否则将成为一句空话。国际航空公约在国际范围内普及较广,但仍需要国内法的实施作为落脚点。

在第四单元的点评环节,东航集团公司法律部副部长赵进和北京大成(上海)律师事务所高级合伙人吴静静对该单元的发言进行了总结和点评。赵进指出以商飞、西飞等为代表的制造业正在成为寡头垄断行业,对目前取得的成绩表示祝贺。同时,赵进指出,全球民用航空大飞机制造主要是以空客和波音的标准和需求,逐步建立起了适航认证体系。我国目前还没有采用国际标准,生产的飞机销往任何一个国家都面临合规问题,我国制造企业在质量保障等方面的压力巨大。机场建设的融资面临着诸多不确定因素,在退出条件的设计上应该严谨周密。

西北政法大学郑斌航空与空间法研究所2017年学术活动大事记

郑斌航空与空间法研究所，是西北政法大学依托陕西省哲学社会科学重点研究基地（国际法研究中心）和陕西省哲学社会科学重点学科（国际法学科）成立的专门从事航空法与空间法学术研究、人才培养、科研服务的综合性、专业化高校智库平台。原为成立于2009年的西北政法大学航空与空间法研究所，为了弘扬全球杰出航空法专家、"航空法之父"、英国伦敦大学华裔终身教授郑斌先生的航空法治思想，培养现代航空法治人才，推进中国航空法研究现代化水平，征得郑斌先生同意，2017年8月正式更名为"郑斌航空与空间法研究所"。

1. 武汉大学国际法研究所黄解放教授就国际航空法的新发展作专题讲座

2017年1月4日在西北政法大学雁塔校区研究生综合楼三楼国际法学术报告厅举行了题为"国际航空法的新发展"的专题讲座。本次讲座由国际法学院、国际法研究中心主办，邀请了国际民用航空组织高级法律官员、武汉大学国际法研究所黄解放教授作为主讲人，并由国际法学院院长刘亚军教授作为主持人。国际法学院副院长刘萍教授、王秀梅教授、周亚光博士、张超汉博士以及2015级、2016级国际法专业研究生参加了讲座。

黄解放教授首先强调，航空安全是国际航空业永恒的主题，由于航空业具有显著的国际性，因此有必要成立相应的国际组织，推动建立航空业的统一标准以尽可能保证国际航空业的健康安全发展。接下来，黄解放教授为在场师生重点介绍了基于1944年芝加哥公约而组建的国际民航组织及其宗旨，并继而详细讲解了1963年东京公约、1970年海牙公约、1971年蒙特利尔公约、1988年蒙特利尔补充议定书以及2010年北京公约等在国际民航组织主持下的重要国际立法。此外，黄解放教授还结合马航MH17与MH370事件分析了其中的法律问题，强调了法律在外交斡旋中的重要作用。黄解放教授以其深厚的法学功底和丰富的工作经验所做的讲解不仅有专业深度，更可以从其亲身工作经历中体会到上述国际立法的理念碰撞与演变，令在场师生印象深刻。

在提问与互动环节，在场师生踊跃参与，纷纷就马航MH17事件的刑事管辖问题、航空器的环境污染问题以及机长的权利与权力问题等向黄解放教授提问，黄解放教授也对此一一作出了回应。

2. 西北政法大学王瀚教授入选陕西省第二批“三秦学者”岗位特聘教授

2017年1月17日中共陕西省委组织部发布《关于印发陕西省第二批“三秦学者”岗位特聘教授、特聘专家入选名单的通知》（陕组通字〔2017〕4号），西北政法大学国际法学科带头人、丝绸之路区域合作与发展法律研究院院长、郑斌航空与空间法研究所所长王瀚教授经竞聘申报、资格审核、匿名评审、专家答辩、会议评审和省委人才办审定获批陕西省第二批“三秦学者”岗位特聘教授，成为我省法学学科“三秦学者”岗位首位特聘教授入选者。

“三秦学者”计划是陕西省委和陕西省政府大力实施人才强省战略、更好地培养和凝聚高层次创新创业人才、全面提升陕西省人才队伍的综合实力和科技创新能力、为建设西部强省提供坚强的人才支撑和智力保障的一项重要人才计划。“三秦学者”岗位设置主要围绕陕西省经济社会发展和重大项目实施需要,重点在信息技术、新材料、航天航空、运输物流、生物技术、能源化工、现代制造业及人文社会科学等领域。全省每一学科、行业、领域原则上设置一个“三秦学者”特聘岗位。

“三秦学者”岗位包括特聘教授和特聘专家,在高等学校设置特聘教授岗位。2012 年陕西省下发《关于申报设置第二批“三秦学者”岗位的通知》(陕人才办〔2012〕44 号),按照西北政法大学人事处统一安排和部署,西北政法大学国际法学科依托陕西省哲学社会科学重点研究基地——西北政法大学国际法研究中心的学术队伍和学科优势,精心撰写三秦学者岗位设置论证报告和支撑材料,经过申报、初评答辩、专家组进校实地考察和终评,获批三秦学者岗位设置。

西北政法大学国际法学科“三秦学者”岗位特聘教授获批是我校高层次人才培养和引进工作的新突破。根据《陕西省“三秦学者”计划实施办法》,西北政法大学将在省政府的统一部署和安排下,组建高品质的三秦学者学术创新团队,紧贴一带一路发展战略和陕西省建设自由贸易实验区和深化对外开放的重大需求,聚集和培养优秀创新人才,打造优秀科研团队,强化科研协同创新,优化科研咨政和科研服务能力,不断推出高水平学术成果,持续提升学科建设和学科发展能力,为建设一流国际法学科创造条件。

3. 张超汉博士在欧洲权威航空航天法杂志发文

2017 年 3 月 1 日,欧洲权威专业性航空航天杂志《德国航空航天法季刊》(Zeitschrift für Luft-und Weltraumrecht, *German Journal of Air and Space Law*)杂志 2017 年第 1 期刊发了郑斌航空与空间法研究所张超汉博士的学术论文《航空产品责任的新发展及对中国的启示》(*Development in Aviation Product Liability and its Implication to China*)。该文以法理阐述、比较研究和实证分析等方法,全面梳理了美国和欧盟有关航空产品责任问题所涉不同法律关系、责任主体、责任性质、损害赔偿、管辖权以及法律适用等方面的立法和司法实践情况,总结了欧美航空产品责任诉讼的发展趋势及在司法实践中存在的难点和困惑问题。文章通过比较美国和欧盟的做法，结合中国C919大飞机发展战略和项目背景，对中国大飞机建造以及未来进入国内外市场与美国波音和欧洲空客飞机竞争过程中可能面临的风险和法律问题进行了预测和评估，最后从立法和司法两个层面提出了中国的应对策略。

《德国航空航天法季刊》由德国科隆大学航空与空间法研究所主办，创刊于1929年，具有近90年的历史。该刊现任主编为科隆大学航空法与空间法研究所所长斯蒂芬（Stephan Hobe）教授，郑斌（Bin Cheng），邓普西（Dempsey），帕布罗（Pablo）等教授担任编委，目前为季刊，为全球航空航天法领域唯一一家国际性刊物，由英、法、德三种语言在7国发行，主要刊发航空法、航天法以及有关航空航天立法、会议报告、司法判决、书评等方面的文章。

4. 北京理工大学法学院院长李寿平教授来我校作讲座

2017年4月25日北京理工大学法学院院长、北京理工大学空间法研究所主任、博士生导师李寿平教授在西北政法大学雁塔校区研究生综合楼国际法学术报告厅举行了题为“外空全球治理背景下国家间的博弈”的讲座。讲座由西北政法大学副校长、国际法研究中心主任、博士生导师王瀚教授主持。王秀梅教授、吕江副教授、师怡副教授、张望平博士、张超汉博士、刘学文博士以及2016级国际法专业研究生参加了讲座。

王瀚副校长首先介绍了主讲人李寿平教授的学术简历以及本次讲座的相关背景。接下来李寿平教授运用专业知识对讲座专题展开了详尽分析，他从全球治理的视角出发，分析了现有治理主体与治理模式，并指出其所关注的核心问题，由此引出了外空层面的全球治理问题。李寿平教授详细阐述了针对外空而来的联合国大会框架下国家间的博弈、裁谈会下外空安全国家间的博弈和《外空活动行为准则》下国家间的博弈等相关问题。并指出，在外空全球治理中各项规则亟待进一步完善，以实现外空“长期可持续性”这一目标。李寿平教授用生动的案例，幽默风趣的语言深入浅出地讲解了外空全球治理的一系列问题，使在场听众获益匪浅。

5. 著名国际法学家、英国伦敦大学终身名誉教授郑斌先生向我校捐赠图书

5 月 10 日受西北政法大学副校长、国际法研究中心主任、航空法治现代化协同创新中心首席专家王瀚教授特别委托,我校国际法学院院长刘亚军教授、丝绸之路区域合作与发展法律研究院周亚光博士赴英国伦敦拜见年届96岁高龄的著名国际法学家、国际航空法学家、英国伦敦大学终身名誉教授郑斌先生,专程接受和办理图书捐赠事宜。

郑斌教授和其父郑天锡先生是我国法学史上十分鲜见的国际法研究世家,他们均在英国伦敦大学获得国际法学博士学位,都是在国际上享有盛誉的著名国际法学家。此次捐赠由我校国际法研究中心特聘教授、亚太航空法协会主席、台湾东吴大学程家瑞先生促成,我校党委书记宋觉研究员和王瀚副校长曾于去年 12 月 14 日会见程家瑞教授商定接受该批图书捐赠。

此次受赠图书为国际法外文图书资料共计 3000 余种、册,创西北政法大学历史上单次接受海外赠书之最。其中包括郑斌教授从事航空法和国际法学术研究 60 多年来珍藏的国际法、国际航空法及外层空间法专业图书;郑斌教授的父亲、民国时期法学家、国际联盟常设国际法院中国籍大法官郑天锡先生所收藏的国际法外文图书;其中尤为珍贵的是郑斌教授英文博士学位论文《国际法院与法庭适用的一般法律原则》打印稿及文献卡片摘录等。

此次西北政法大学受赠的图书和文献资料来源广泛、跨越百年,涉及英、德、法、韩、日和中文等语种,包括劳特派特、施瓦曾伯格等权威国际法学家的经典国际法和航空法著作,联合国国际法院的判例、联合国大会、安理会决议,部分国际条约谈判的相关历史资料,美国、德国、法国、荷兰、韩国、日本、中国等国的重要国际学术刊物,内容非常丰富,文献价值和学术价值十分珍贵。这批图书和文献资料展现了近代国际法学到现代国际法学的形成、演进和发展,其中蕴含的学术脉络和学说集成为考察、梳理和挖掘国际法学术史研究提供了珍贵的原始资料。郑斌先生撰著的《国际法院与法庭适用的一般法律原则》自 1957 年由英国史蒂文斯出版社出版以来已多次再版,在全球国际法学界享有盛誉,1987 年曾作为对国际法和政治学界认识极具重要性的

著作的格劳秀斯名著再版,成为国际法学界公认的经典文献之一。

鉴于郑斌先生在国际法学、国际航空法学与外层空间法学研究的杰出成就与学术影响,我校荣聘郑斌先生为西北政法大学荣誉教授并对郑斌先生襄助学术之举颁发捐赠证书。为传承郑斌、郑天锡先生的学术思想,有效使用受赠图书和文献资料,我校国际法研究中心将以郑斌教授捐赠图书为基础,分别设置建设"郑斌航空法图书馆"和"郑天锡国际法图书馆",在 2017 年 10 月西北政法大学 80 周年校庆期间举行图书馆揭幕仪式,向西北政法大学师生开放借阅藏书,为国际法和航空法研究者提供信息资料平台;建设郑斌、郑天锡生平图片纪念馆,编辑整理两位前辈的法学学术文集,届时将邀请中外著名学者举行第一届郑天锡、郑斌法学思想研讨会。

6. 研究员张超汉博士荣获 2017 年度中国博士后科学基金特别资助项目

2017 年 6 月 12 日中国博士后科学基金会公布了中国博士后科学基金第十批特别资助项目获资助人员名单,我校郑斌航空与空间法研究所副所长张超汉博士获得 2017 年度中国博士后科学基金特别资助,其申报的项目"中国大飞机发展战略法律保障机制研究"获得 15 万元经费资助。

张超汉博士于 2016 年到上海交通大学凯原法学院开展博士后研究(合作导师为凯原特聘教授徐冬根博士)。张超汉博士已于 2016 年分别获得中国法学会一般项目、陕西省社科基金项目、中国博士后科学基金面上项目,2017 年再次获批中国博士后科学基金特别资助项目,是对张超汉博士在站研究工作的进一步激励和肯定,也是西北政法大学青年教师良好学术研究能力的反映。据悉,2017 年年度全国法学共 13 人获此资助,张超汉博士是上海交通大学法学唯一获得者。

中国博士后科学基金特别资助是从 2008 年开始,在中国博士后基金面上资助的基础上设立的,旨在对在站期间取得重大自主创新研究成果和在研究能力方面表现突出的一部分非常优秀的博士后研究人员给予资助,是中国博士后科学基金最高资助等级,每年评审一次。特别资助更加强调博士后的创新能力;其评审方法在单位推荐的基础上,采取专家通讯评议和会议评议两轮评审确定资助对象,评审要求更为严格。

7. 王瀚教授应邀出席“西咸新区空港新城航空物流发展扶持实施办法”专家评审会

2017年6月22日西咸新区空港新城管理委员会组织召开“空港新城航空物流发展扶持实施办法”专家评审会。陕西省发展和改革委员会、西安市发展和改革委员会、陕西省财政厅、西安市财政局、中国民航大学综合交通研究所、国家发展和改革委员会综合运输研究所、西部机场集团、北京中航建研航空设计咨询有限公司、东航西北分公司、扬子江航空货运控股公司、天驹航空、龙浩航空、顺丰航空的代表以及空港新城管委会相关部门负责人等20多人参加会议。

西北政法大学副校长王瀚教授受邀作为专家评审出席会议,并就“空港新城航空物流发展扶持实施办法(暂行)”存在的编写体例、措辞表达、实施条件等问题发表了意见。王瀚教授指出“实施办法”的补贴对象应该包括三类:一是具备货运市场开发能力的航空公司,二是开辟了新航线的航空公司,三是具有充足货源的航空公司。建议西咸新区空港新城管理委员会进一步明确各类补贴对象的补贴范围,制定切实可行的补贴方案,以引导航空运输企业开发货运市场、拓展货运航线,促进陕西省航空物流产业的发展。王瀚教授的建议受与会专家和参会代表的共鸣和肯定。会后,王瀚教授提交了对“空港新城航空物流发展扶持实施办法”修改的书面意见,以供西咸新区空港新城管理委员参考。

8. 西北政法大学国际法专业研究生李艺同学获准赴国际民航组织留学机会

为服务国家外交工作,向国际组织输送人才更好地参与国际事务,培养和储备一批国际组织人才,2017年2月至6月23日,西北政法大学、中国民航大学、中国民航飞行学院的优秀在读硕士研究生、博士研究生赴国际民航组织实习项目选拔活动结束。本次活动由西北政法大学国际法学院,国家留学基金管理委员会以及国际民航组织联合举办,根据协议条款,西北政法大学优胜学生将具备公派留学资格。经过首轮选拔，西北政法大学2人，中国民航大学4人，中国民航飞行学院2人共8人脱颖而出。

在研究所所长王瀚教授悉心指导下进行国际法专业研究的李艺，代表西北政法大学参加了后两轮面试。经过激烈角逐，李艺同学凭借缜密的分析能力，出色的应变技巧，流利诙谐的英语表达，成功通过北京淘汰赛，闯入决赛，赢得了比赛评委的好评，并最终获得录取资格。据悉，李艺同学为我校首位通过国际留学基金委获得公派资格去联合国专门机构实习的学生。

9. 中华人民共和国驻国际民航组织理事会代表处向西北政法大学发来感谢信

2017年6月22日中国驻国际民航组织理事会代表处向西北政法大学发来感谢信。该信指出，“2017年6月21日国际民航组织理事会举行第211届第9次会议，审议了巴西与美国争端的程序问题，投票决定受理巴西提交的解决与美国分歧的申请，并请理事会主席出面协调巴西和美国双方继续进行双边磋商……我处在制定处理方案过程中，得到西北政法大学郑斌航空与空间法研究所的大力支持，在此表示感谢，希今后进一步加强合作，将国际航空法研究成果更多地落实和应用到国际民航领域”。

无疑，此次中国驻国际民航组织理事会代表处的感谢来信，再次反映了西北政法大学服务于国家战略和现实需要，维护中国核心利益的积极表现；也彰显了西北政法大学郑斌航空与空间法研究所，作为我校高端特色智库，在航空法领域的影响力。

10. 研究所张望平、周亚光博士赴深圳参加无人机与法律高峰论坛

2017年6月22日我院青年教师、郑斌航空与空间法研究所研究人员张望平和周亚光博士赴深圳参加了中国航空法学研究会2017年无人机与法律高峰论坛。本次会议由中国法学会航空法学研究会、中国航空运输协会法律委员会主办，中国国际经济贸易仲裁委员会华南分会、法制日报社中国公司法务研究院协办。

论坛开幕式在深圳明华国际会议中心举行，中国民航局国际合作服务中

心主任孟庆芬、民航局法规处处长吉大鹏、中国贸仲委/中国海仲委华南分会秘书长黎晓光、中国法学会研究部副处长姚国艳等应邀出席开幕式并作主题发言。开幕式由中国法学会航空法学研究会会长、中国航空运输协会法律委员会主任、东航集团总法律顾问郭俊秀主持。来自中国民航大学、南京航空航天大学、西北政法大学、西北工业大学等各大高校的专家学者和来自工信部政策法规司、国际航协法律部、法制日报社、深圳市人民政府法制办、最高人民法院第一巡回法庭、东航、国航、南航、首都机场、云南机场、南京机场、大疆创新公司、顺丰集团以及其他无人机产业链公司法律顾问、法律部门负责人共计150余人参加了论坛。

开幕式后,与会的专家学者以及实务届人士围绕无人机产业发展的法律问题、无人机与空域管理的法律问题、无人机案件司法实务问题、无人机国内外立法问题四个议题展开了深入探讨。张望平博士就无人机的界定以及立法层级的设定参与了讨论;周亚光博士就无人机系统的武器化与《塔林手册2.0》的关系以及《芝加哥公约》修改欧盟所提出的临时适用动议两个问题与国际航空运输协会法律部高级法律顾问解兴权博士进行了探讨。

11. 研究所张超汉博士为中国商用飞机有限公司法务人员做专题培训

2017年7月6日受中国商用飞机有限责任公司法律部特别邀请,西北政法大学青年教师、郑斌航空与空间法研究所副所长张超汉博士赴上海为中国商飞公司总部及其下属公司法务人员就"中国大飞机建造中的产品责任及其法律风险防范"问题做专题培训。中国商飞公司总部法律部唐绮霞部长、闫可荣副部长,法律事务处范莉莉处长,中国商飞客服公司总会计师、总法律顾问陈林,中国商飞上海飞机设计研究院总法律顾问金靖寅,商飞公司法律部及下属公司的全体法务人员参加了培训。

中国自主研发的国产C919大飞机已于2017年5月1日成功首飞,不久将投入国内外市场运营,为了防范飞行事故发生后受害人频繁对中国航空器制造商提起产品责任诉讼,维护中国航空器制造业的利益与国家权益,张超汉博士通过欧美航空产品责任诉讼大量实践判例,系统梳理和总结了航空产品责任案件涉及的法律关系、权利义务主体、归责原则、损害赔偿、免责事由、管辖权、法律适用等实体性问题和程序性问题以及实践中存在的难点和困惑问题。通过比较欧美航空制造大国有关航空产品责任的立法与司法实践，张超汉博士指出，C919大飞机进入市场后，中国航空器制造商也有可能面临像美国波音、欧洲空客一样被受害人基于各种缘由指控和提起产品责任诉讼的情形，致使中国航空器制造商遭受不确定的损失。借此，中国应从三个方面完善航空产品责任法律体制。一是在宏观法律修订与解释上，应做好立法的解释工作，借助制定《民法典》的良机，修订和解释有关产品责任一般法中的一些模糊、原则、不周延的内容，使现有民事立法更具前瞻性、统领性。二是在微观立法上，加快民航基本法的修订和产业单行法的制定进度。可在《民用航空法》修订中进一步丰富该法序言对"国家扶持民用航空器制造业"的原则性规定，在分则中增加有关航空产品责任的实体规范或制定细化配套的部门规章。另外，为契合中国大飞机战略，切实保护刚刚起步的大飞机制造业的利益，可借鉴1994年美国《通用航空振兴法》，考虑制定中国版的单行《航空产业促进法》，为中国航空产业发展提供法律保障。三是在司法体制层面，应以开放和包容的态度加强对欧美航空产品责任诉讼经典判例的实证研究，积累和借鉴实践经验。

通过此次法律培训，实现了理论研究与实务问题的对接，也显示了我校航空法研究在全国的影响力和知名度。

12.《中国航空法评论》和中国航空法文库首批学术著作由法律出版社出版

2017年6月30日和8月1日，由陕西省哲学社会科学重点研究基地——西北政法大学国际法研究中心和西北政法大学郑斌航空与空间法研究所主办和编辑策划的《中国航空法评论》(以下简称《评论》)和《中国航空法文库》(以下简称《文库》)首批学术著作由法律出版社正式出版。西北政法大学副校长、陕西省"三秦学者"特聘教授、郑斌航空与空间法研究所所长王瀚担任《评论》和《文库》主编。

《评论》秉承弘扬学术,探究法理,注重国际国内立法与司法实践的办刊特色,力求刊发海内外与航空法律、政策相关的一切研究成果。目前开设航空法热点问题评析、航空公约述评、国际国内航空立法动态、航空案例研究、资料信息、译文摘录、学位论文等栏目。

《文库》首批学术著作为王瀚教授等撰写的《国际航空法专论》、张超汉博士撰写的《国际航空产品责任研究》、周亚光博士撰写的《国际航空运输垄断行为法律规制研究》,第二批航空法文库著作(目前已出版3本)也将于2018年7月出版。《文库》系列著作作者均为西北政法大学航空法研究团队成员。

13. 研究所所长王瀚教授应邀参加2017中国国际通用航空大会高峰论坛并作主题发言

2017年8月24日第五届中国国际通用航空大会高峰论坛在陕西西安绿地笔克国际会展中心召开。西安市副市长强晓安致欢迎词,西安市工业和信息化委员会巡视员金乾生和亚洲商务航空协会主席、德事隆中国政府事务副总裁张传勇主持论坛。国家工信部装备司副司长杨栓昌,西北政法大学副校长、郑斌航空与空间法研究所所长王瀚教授,西安航空基地管委会党工委副书记、纪工委书记张炎,中国航空规划设计研究总院有限公司副总经理白海平,中国民用航空西北地区管理局通航处处长李天宇,中捷航空协会主席虎彼得(Petr Hyl),亚洲商务航空协会主席、德事隆中国政府事务副总裁张传勇,中航通用飞机有限公司副总经理沙长安,德事隆航空中国区市场推广总监邱莉娜,德国柏林勃兰登堡州航空联盟执行董事安德烈·迪马等出席论坛并作主题发言,来自中航工业、美国航空运动协会等国内外通用航空公司、产业开发区等近百名专家参加论坛。

王瀚教授以“法治驱动与引领:中国通用航空事业的走向与未来”为题作主题发言。王瀚教授以美国通用航空发展的经验为例,详细论证了法治驱动在美国通用航空产业发展的重要作用。王瀚教授认为,通用航空法治之路是通用航空产业发展的必由之路,要在通用航空领域实行法治创新,构建中国特色通用航空法律体系。从立法上破解通用航空发展的制度性“瓶颈”，第一，要将通用航空规定从现行《民用航空法》中分离，制定单行的通用航空法，对通用航空的基本制度、原则、规范作出完整规定。第二，要推行通用航空法治教育，培养高素质的通用航空法治人才。第三，要提高现有政策性文件的法律地位，制定单行的通用航空产业发展法，为通航产业发展提供专门的法律支撑作为保障，发挥现代航空法治在通用航空中的立法驱动和引领作用。

14. 西北政法大学郑斌航空与空间法研究所召开航空法热点问题研讨会

2017年8月24日“航空法热点问题研讨会”在西北政法大学雁塔校区国际法研究中心会议室召开。西北政法大学副校长、郑斌航空与空间法研究所所长王瀚教授，中国航空集团办公厅聂颖巡视员，中国民航大学法学院杨惠教授，中国民航管理干部学院董念清教授，中国民航大学法学院王立志副教授、刘海安副教授，上海君合律师事务所合伙人闫振峰律师，山东航空集团公司统计与研究管理经理郭才森，甘肃政法学院讲师张辉，郑斌航空与空间法研究所师怡副教授、张望平博士、张超汉博士、周亚光博士、李洁博士、刘冰博士生、张丝路博士生、时杜娟博士生等人参加了本次会议。

王瀚教授向各位与会嘉宾介绍了西北政法大学郑斌航空与空间法研究所科学研究与人才培养的最新情况以及今后的方向和任务，同时就西安国际航空物流的发展前景和面临的挑战发表了自己的看法。王瀚教授表示，西安在航天航空产品制造方面具有突出优势，同时拥有全国第一个通用航空产业园区试点，但是由于相关企业对外开放意识有限，相关政府部门服务意识不足，目前还没有形成理想的国际航空物流环境。

聂颖巡视员就我国《民用航空法》修订的最新情况向参会人员作了详细介绍。聂颖表示，此次修改的初衷是弥合中国《民用航空法》与蒙特利尔公约等现行国际公约的差距，目前主要修改了第八章、第九章的内容，同时也对其他部分进行了一定程度的调整。聂颖就我国《民用航空法》修改过程中遇到的诸多实际困难与问题和各位参会代表进行了沟通。首先，相关条款的修改更多的是基于民航实践经验而作的调整,而在法理基础支撑方面相对欠缺,这导致对一些具体且关键的概念进行严格的法律界定时出现较大的不确定性。其次,实务部门在法律执行方面存在与现行法律不一致的现象,因而如何确保修改后的法律在实践中得以顺利实施也是需要进一步解决的问题。

随后,参会的各位代表围绕相关话题进行了自由发言,作为立法参与人,中国民航管理干部学院的董念清教授和中国民航大学的王立志副教授先后介绍了参与《民用航空法》修订过程中的问题与现状。郑斌航空与空间法研究所副所长张超汉博士对一些民航法的立法细节提出了自己的思考。此外,各位参会代表还就航空保险、空域管理、航空产业反补贴等问题进行了深入的交流讨论。本次会议的多位参与人参与了我国《民用航空法》修订的立法工作,相关讨论不仅归纳了未来相关立法工作的焦点、难点问题,而且提出了我国航空法研究的主要方向。

15. 西北政法大学成功主办第三届通用航空法治论坛

2017 年 8 月 25 日由西安阎良航空高技术产业基地、西北政法大学航空法治现代化协同创新中心、西北政法大学通用航空法研究所、西部机场集团以及西北通用航空协会联合主办的第三届通用航空法治论坛在西安绿地笔克会展中心举行,论坛主题为"面向'一带一路'实践创新的中国通用航空法治之路"。

论坛开幕式由西北政法大学国际法学院院长刘亚军教授主持并致欢迎辞,西北政法大学副校长、郑斌航空与空间法研究所主任、通用航空法研究所主任王瀚教授,西安阎良航空高技术产业基地副主任仝秀丽女士,中国航空集团公司巡视员聂颖,北京航空航天大学通用航空产业研究中心主任高远洋,北京航空法学研究会会长、中国民航管理干部学院董念清教授,中国民航大学法学院杨惠教授,上海国际航空仲裁院秘书长黄文,中国民用航空局空管局法规标准部副部长宋河滨,西北政法大学郑斌航空与空间法研究所,通用航空法研究所的研究人员等我国通用航空法律理论与实务界 40 余位代表参会。西安阎良航空高技术产业基地副主任仝秀丽女士和西北政法大学副校长王瀚教授作开幕式致辞。

与会专家就“中国通用航空产业发展的法治驱动与法治引领问题”“欧美发达国家通用航空产业发展的法治经验与中国通用航空的法治路径”“中国通用航空产业发展的机场建设与航空器租购、保险与产品责任法律问题”“通用航空产业发展的空域法律问题”“军民融合发展战略与中国通用航空法律实践”等问题展开热烈讨论。

论坛闭幕式由西北政法大学国际法学院副院长刘萍教授主持，中国民航大学杨惠教授致闭幕词。杨惠教授指出，本次会议聚集了我国通用航空产业法律理论与实务界的众多专家，各方观点碰撞激发，对我国通用航空产业发展的法治“瓶颈”作出深刻的分析。本次会议在我国通用航空法治史上具有重要意义。

16. 王瀚教授荣获中国社会科学院“首届十大杰出法学博士后”荣誉称号

2017 年 8 月 26 日为纪念我国哲学社会科学（法学）博士后制度实施 25 周年，第六届中国法学博士后论坛在中国社会科学院学术报告厅举行。本届论坛的主题为“回顾与展望：开创法治中国建设新局面”，由中国社会科学院、全国博士后管委会、中国博士后科学基金会共同主办，中国社会科学院博士后管委会、中国社会科学院法学研究所和最高人民法院中国应用法学研究所联合承办，腾讯研究院协办。中国社会科学院副院长、学部委员李培林研究员，最高人民法院副院长姜伟教授，中国法学会副会长、学术委员会主任张文显教授，人力资源与社会保障部专业技术人员管理司司长、全国博士后管委会办公室主任俞家栋，中国社会科学院学部委员、法学研究所所长李林教授，最高人民法院中国应用法学研究所所长蒋惠岭，中国社会科学院科研局局长马援，中国社会科学院人事教育局副局长王文成等领导，中国社会科学院荣誉学部委员、著名法学家刘海年、刘楠来教授等著名专家和来自最高人民法院、中国法学会、人力资源与社会保障部、中国社会科学院等有关部门的领导及全国法学界、法律界的专家学者和法学博士后 160 余人出席了本次论坛。中国社会科学院法学研究所所长、学部委员李林研究员主持开幕式和中国社会科学院首届十大杰出法学博士后颁奖仪式。中国社会科学院副院长李培林研究员、最高人民法院副院长姜伟大法官、中国法学会副会长张文显教授、人力资源与社会保障部专业技术人员管理司司长、全国博士后管委会办公室主任俞家栋教授分别致辞。

开幕式举行了中国社会科学院首届十大杰出法学博士后颁奖活动，我校国际法学科带头人、陕西省"三秦学者"王瀚教授荣获中国社会科学院"首届十大杰出法学博士后"称号。

颁奖仪式后由中国社会科学院法学所、国际法所联合党委书记陈甦研究员和中国社会科学院荣誉学部委员、法学研究所刘海年研究员共同主持了专家论坛，六位演讲嘉宾均为"十大杰出法学博士后"的获得者。西北政法大学副校长王瀚教授就"航空强国建设与中国特色航空法律体系的建构与完善"发表了演讲，提出要运用法治思维和法治方法破解影响和限制我国航空事业发展的制度"瓶颈"，依法确定我国空域的法律地位和使用原则，解决我国航空事业迅猛发展与空域过度军事占用之间的矛盾，为民航和通用航空事业的发展释放空域红利；制定领空和空域管理法，用立法确定通用航空的飞行高度和空间范围，设立专门的通用航空管理机构，实行全国统一的通用航空空域管理制度；将民航法中通用航空的法律规范分离出来，制定单行的通用航空法，为通用航空活动制定完备的法律规范，明确个人通用航空器所有权制度和航空器登记制度，依法确定个人飞行的权利和义务；制定通用航空产业发展法，为通用航空产业发展、市场监管提供充分的法律依据，为我国航空强国建设建构中国特色航空法律体系。

17. 张望平博士为首届无人机应用与监管国家级研修班作讲座

2017 年 9 月 14 日国际法学院青年教师、郑斌航空与空间法研究所研究人员张望平博士应邀赴成都为首届无人机应用与监管国家级研修班讲授无人机立法专题。本次国家级研修班经人力和社会资源保障部批准，由四川省人社厅主办，成都工业学院承办，四川溉亚智能科技有限公司协办。

本次讲座由成都工业学院无人机发展研究院院长余炜教授主持，来自国内高校、科研机构、无人机企业的60多名学员参加了讲座。张望平老师以“中国航空立法改革中的无人机立法调整问题”为主线,就我国航空立法的现状与改革路径、无人机立法层面所存在的问题以及解决方法为研修班的学员进行了讲授。张望平老师指出,随着无人机市场的急速扩充,无人机的研发、生产、销售、推广等环节存在大量法律规制的空白,而无人机“黑飞”的事件更是层出不穷,给现行立法出了很大的难题;无人机立法是一个迫在眉睫、亟待解决的问题,否则将导致整个行业发展乱象丛生。张望平老师以我国民事立法改革的发展为例,指出无人机最佳的立法模式是单行法,在目前条件尚不具备的情况下可以考虑专编专章的立法模式,借民用航空立法改革的东风尽快出台有关无人机的法律规定,推动整个行业健康有序的发展。

18. 张超汉博士获中国国际私法优秀学术成果二等奖

2017年9月14日中国国际私法学会网公示了2017年中国国际私法优秀学术成果奖获得名单,西北政法大学国际私法教研室教师,郑斌航空与空间法研究所研究员张超汉博士在《法律科学》2016年第6期发表的论文《国际航空运输事故承运人先行付款制度研究》获得2017年中国国际私法优秀学术成果二等奖。该文同时被中国人民大学报刊复印资料《国际法学》2017年第5期和中国社会科学网全文转载。

据悉,本年度申报成果范围从国际私法专家、学者于2012年1月1日至2016年12月31日在国内外公开出版或发表的国际私法专业学术专著、译著、教材或学术论文,以及被省部级以上党政机关采纳的与国际私法相关的研究咨询报告类成果和2016年《中国国际私法学会年会论文集》提交的学术论文中进行评选,经评审委员会专家认真评审,并进行不记名投票,最终确定一等奖作品2件,二等奖作品8件。

张超汉博士于2017年9月23~24日赴武汉参加了2017年中国国际私法学术年会和优秀成果奖颁奖仪式,并在年会第三小组就“一带一路”倡议与中国仲裁制度创新作了主题发言。

19. 王瀚教授拜访著名国际法学家、“航空法之父”、英国伦敦大学华裔终身荣誉教授郑斌先生

2017年9月15日陕西“三秦学者”、西北政法大学副校长、丝绸之路区域合作与发展法律研究院院长王瀚教授在英国伦敦专程拜访了96岁高龄的著名国际法学家、“航空法之父”、英国伦敦大学华裔终身荣誉教授郑斌先生。

在英国伦敦近郊著名国际法学家郑斌先生寓所的会客厅,郑斌先生及其夫人接待了西北政法大学副校长、丝绸之路区域合作与发展法律研究院院长王瀚教授、丝绸之路区域合作与发展法律研究院常务副院长刘亚军教授和丝绸之路区域合作与发展法律研究院研究员吕江老师三人。

王瀚教授首先代表西北政法大学向郑斌先生致以亲切的问候。感谢郑斌先生将其父郑天锡先生(常设国际法院中国籍法官)和自己的国际法和航空法藏书赠与西北政法大学。之后,王瀚教授高度评价了郑天锡法官和郑斌先生在中国国际法发展和国际航空法领域做出的卓越贡献。并向郑斌先生表示,西北政法大学将妥善保管这3000余册珍贵图书资料,西北政法大学航空与空间法研究所也将正式更名为“郑斌航空与空间法研究所”。

郑斌先生对王瀚教授代表西北政法大学,不远千里赴英专程拜访他激动不已,一再拱手表示感谢。双方落座后,郑斌先生首先回忆了其父郑天锡作为常设国际法院中国籍法官的工作以及驻英时受英国玛丽皇后接见的情景。其后,郑斌先生讲述了自己从事国际法和航空法研究的经历,并谈到了当前国际法与航空法发展的趋势,饱含深情地鼓励后辈须珍惜时光,为中国国际法与航空法事业而努力。随后,他再次感谢西北政法大学对这3000余册藏书作出的精心安排,希望这些藏书能为西北政法大学及所有中国学人在法律研究方面提供更好的便利,为中国的法学事业作出其相应贡献。

此外,王瀚教授与郑斌先生还就设置“郑斌航空法讲席教授”岗位,从全球招聘顶级航空法专家从事学术交流和研究工作,以及建设郑斌航空法图书馆交换了意见和获得支持,以服务于我国航空强国建设和陕西省临空经济发

展。会谈结束之后,郑斌先生向王瀚教授个人赠送了其父郑天锡法官签名的博士论文著作和其父的个人英文传记。

此次专程赴英拜访郑斌先生,高度反映了西北政法大学尊师重教的优良传统。无论天隔多远,西法大人都将以一颗赤诚之心,永远铭记那些为中国法学事业作出卓越贡献的前辈学者及其谆谆教诲。同时,郑斌先生能将其父及其藏书赠与西北政法大学,也充分表明西北政法大学在国际法学和航空法学研究方面所取得的成绩和影响力,并激励着西北政法大学学人在这些领域创造更多辉煌。

20. 高圣惕教授在我院作"我的国际法奇幻旅程"讲座

2017年10月13日海南大学法学院教授、国际司法与仲裁研究中心高圣惕主任受邀在西北政法大学国际法研究中心就"我的国际法奇幻旅程"作讲座。讲座由西北政法大学副校长、国际法研究中心主任、郑斌航空与空间法研究所所长王瀚教授主持,校内外部分国际法专家、教师以及2017级国际法研究生参加。

高圣惕教授从青年时代讲起,讲述了自己是如何与杰塞普国际模拟法庭大赛结缘,并传授其长期从事以及带领学生参加该项赛事的宝贵经验。高圣惕教授鼓励同学们多从对方角度去演绎思考问题;接着高圣惕教授讲起其去英国剑桥大学、英国伦敦大学国王学院、荷兰莱登大学深造等艰难苦涩而又收获颇丰的时期,谈到其在国外求学面临的语言障碍,以及如何克服种种困难最终完成学业的经验以及在我国台湾地区"飞安会"等机构的从业经历等;最后,高圣惕教授又讲到其博士毕业后至今的其他工作以及学术研究历程。讲座进入提问互动环节后,与会师生就讲座主题向高圣惕教授踊跃提问,提问涉及如何参加英文竞赛、外语对于国际法学习的重要性、两岸"三通"、MH370等问题,高圣惕教授一一回复并与提问者讨论。

在总结阶段,王瀚副校长对高圣惕教授报告的精彩内容表示感谢,希望同学们能从高圣惕教授生动的演讲中体会和学习到国际法的学习方法和研究方法,培养学习国际法的兴趣,树立起学好国际法的信心。最后,王瀚副校长宣布聘请高圣惕教授为我校“郑斌航空与空间法研究所”特约研究员。

21. 王瀚副校长等参加空港新城“自由贸易港与多式联运”研讨会

2017年10月26日应陕西省西咸新区空港新城管委会的邀请,西北政法大学副校长、“三秦学者”、郑斌航空与空间法研究所所长王瀚教授、副所长张超汉博士、丝绸之路区域合作与发展法律研究院研究员吕江副教授和周亚光博士前往空港新城管委会,参加了“自由贸易港与多式联运”研讨会。

出席此次“自由贸易港与多式联运”研讨会的空港新城管委会人员有改革发展局刘瑞菊局长、招商三局韩娜局长、副局长李晔等领导和干部10余人。研讨会由韩娜局长主持,她指出,党的十九大报告中提出,赋予自由贸易试验区更大改革自主权,探索建设自由贸易港的新理念,这在陕西自由贸易试验区建设中引起了强烈反响。为了更深入地了解自由贸易港,特别是对空港新城来说,如何将自由贸易港与多式联运相结合,亟待有一个清晰的认识。因此,此次邀请王瀚副校长及其“一带一路”研究团队和航空与空间法团队,旨在为下一步空港新城在自由贸易港与多式联运方面出谋划策和提供智识支持。

接下来,空港新城改革发展局刘瑞菊局长介绍了其收集到的有关自由贸易港与多式联运的一些相关资料,并就空港新城现在所面临的相关问题以及未来改革中不明确的地方一一列出,希望能得到王瀚及其团队在法律政策方面的解读和支持。

在听取了空港新城相关领导的介绍后,王瀚副校长对相关问题进行了详细解答。首先,王瀚教授对自由贸易港进行了介绍。他指出,党的十九大报告对自由贸易区和对外开放提出了许多新提法。而且报告中明确表达了中国对外开放的大门是不会关闭的,而且是越来越开放。其中一个重大举措就是第一次提出了中国要建设自由贸易港。自由贸易港是自由贸易区的创新和发展,许多研究中将其概括为自由贸易区的3.0版本。自由贸易港的先进之处在于大幅度地减少贸易、资金流动中政府管理的过程,它一般设立在港口,实现一线二线的管控分类。一线放开,国家让利,鼓励从事自由的商业活动。接着,王瀚教授指出,自由贸易港看似使国家在税收方面的收入减少了,但实际上却带动了国内其他生产和产品出口的扩大。这远远比单纯收税能获得更多收益,因此,应从综合经济的角度考虑。特别是打造自由贸易港与政府监管改革是密切联系的,必须在政府服务意识方面有所举动。其次,王瀚教授具体回答了空港新城在三个方面的疑问,即在空港新城引进国外的航空公司、开展航空维修业务以及外国飞行员引入此三方面的法律政策。

之后,国际法学院院长刘亚军教授、郑斌航空与空间法研究所副所长张超汉博士、丝绸之路区域合作与发展法律研究院研究员周亚光博士也就自由贸易港、航空权等方面再次进行了多视角的解读。

近年来,西北政法大学服务于"一带一路"和自贸区建设已初显成效,为国家决策和地方经济建设提供了重要的智力支持。此次空港新城"自由贸易港与多式联运"研讨会再次彰显了我校紧跟党的十九大精神,发挥法律智库作用,服务于国家和地方建设的积极影响。

22. 王瀚副校长会见国家"千人计划"学者黄解放教授和亚太航空法协会主席程家瑞教授

2017年10月29日正值我校80华诞之际,西北政法大学副校长王瀚教授在雁塔校区国际法研究中心会见前来参加我校郑斌航空法与郑天锡国际法图书馆揭牌仪式的国家"千人计划"学者、原国际民航组织高级法律官员、武汉大学国际法研究所黄解放教授和亚太航空法协会主席、东吴大学程家瑞教授。

黄解放教授和程家瑞教授对西北政法大学成立80周年和成立郑斌航空法与郑天锡国际法专业图书馆表示祝贺。在与黄解放教授的交谈中,双方同意共同策划、筹备和组建"中国航空法研究方阵",以凝聚国内航空法研究力量,形成中国航空法研究共识,助力中国航空强国建设,并与武汉大学国家高端智库(武汉大学国际法研究所)协同合作向国家出具中国航空强国建设法治驱动与法治保障咨询意见,双方同意合作培养与指导国际航空法方向博士研究生。

在与程家瑞教授的商谈中,双方就航空法人才培养与学科建设各自发表了意见,程家瑞教授表示将全力支持西北政法大学国际航空法研究与人才培养工作,力争把我校郑斌航空与空间法研究所打造建设成为亚洲一流的航空法研究所,并进一步强化我校航空法研究特色方向。另外,双方还就2018年在西北政法大学召开郑斌航空法学术思想研究暨全球航空业发展法治论坛以及首批郑斌航空法讲席教授的遴选事宜做了沟通。会见结束后,郑斌航空与空间法研究所举行了“航空强国建设与中国航空法治现代化”座谈会。

23.郑斌航空与空间法研究所召开航空强国建设与中国航空法治现代化座谈会

2017年10月29日西北政法大学郑斌航空与空间法研究所在雁塔校区研究生综合楼国际法学术报告厅召开了“航空强国建设与中国航空法治现代化”座谈会。西北政法大学副校长、郑斌航空与空间法研究所所长王瀚教授、亚太航空法协会主席、台湾东吴大学程家瑞教授,国家“千人计划”学者、原国际民航组织高级法律官员、武汉大学国际法研究所黄解放教授、西北政法大学航空法研究团队全体成员以及国际法学院部分师生参加了本次座谈会。

座谈会开始前,王瀚副校长首先为东吴大学程家瑞教授、武汉大学黄解放教授颁发了郑斌航空与空间法研究所首席专家和学术顾问聘书,赠送了首批“中国航空法文库”和《中国航空法评论》,播放了王瀚副校长、刘亚军院长专程赴英国拜访郑斌先生的访谈影录。

聘任仪式结束后,研究所进行了“航空强国建设与中国航空法治现代化”座谈会,参会人员就航空法人才培养、学术研究、中国航空强国建设的法治保障与驱动、党的十九大提出的“航空自由贸易港”等问题进行了自由发言与交流。另外,各位还谈及郑斌先生的精神和著作对自己的鼓舞和帮助。会议最后,王瀚副校长作了总结性发言,建议航空法研究团队应进一步拓宽研究领域,加大对航天法领域、外层空间法领域的研究力度,为党的十九大报告提出的建设交通强国和航天强国提供充分的智力支撑,并寄语国际法全体师生:没有平庸的时代,只有平庸的人;既然选择了国际法,只能风雨兼程加倍努力，做一个胸怀宽广，有理想、有追求的国际法学人。

24. 郑天锡国际法与郑斌航空法图书馆揭牌仪式在西北政法大学举行

2017年10月29日，正值西北政法大学80周年校庆之际，郑天锡国际法与郑斌航空法图书馆揭牌仪式在我校雁塔校区研究生综合大楼举行。西北政法大学党委书记宋觉研究员，副校长王瀚教授，台湾东吴大学程家瑞教授，武汉大学黄解放教授，澳大利亚维多利亚大学黎永强教授，中国社会科学报陕西站主任陆航先生，国际交流与合作处、研究生院、科研处、图书馆、国际法学院负责人，以及航空法团队成员参加了揭牌仪式。揭牌仪式由副校长王健主持。

郑天锡国际法与郑斌航空法图书馆藏书由著名航空法学家郑斌先生捐赠，主要包括郑斌先生及其父亲郑天锡收藏的经典国际法和外空法著作、著名国际法院判例、重要国际条约谈判资料和知名国际法学术刊物等近3000余册。

王瀚介绍了郑斌先生的学术背景和地位，强调郑天锡国际法与郑斌航空法图书馆资料的重要价值，并感谢程家瑞对此次图书资料获赠的大力支持，以及郑斌先生和程家瑞先生对西北政法大学航空法人才的培养和学科建设的支持。

程家瑞先生代表郑斌先生发言，感谢西北政法大学在航空法人才培养方面的贡献，并希望赠书成为西北政法大学航空法研究的重要助力。特别是党的十九大报告中提出要坚持文化自信，落实在学者身上就是要坚持学术自信、坚持国际法研究自信、坚持航空法研究自信，坚信中国在未来一二十年里一定能成为第一民航大国。让更多的中国航空法学者和专家参与国际航空规则的制定，掌握国际规则制定的话语权。因此，寄希望于西北政法大学国际法学院和航空法研究团队培养更多、更出色的国际法人才和航空法人才，并服务于各类国际组织。

黄解放先生讲道，郑天锡国际法与郑斌航空法图书馆的揭牌不仅是西北政法大学和航空法研究团队的喜事，也是国际法和航空法在中国的大事。郑斌先生是国际法的先驱,学而不傲,著述字字珠玑,先生的著作和论文是航空法研究人的必读文献。黄解放先生对郑斌先生的为学与为人给予了高度的评价,表达了对郑斌先生的崇高敬意。希望国际法学者承继历代先辈的志向,继续致力于国际法的研究。揭牌仪式后,各位嘉宾与学生进行了主题为“航空强国建设与航空法治现代化座谈会”。

25. 深圳大学法学院尹玉海教授在我院举行专题讲座

2017 年 11 月 7 日在西北政法大学雁塔校区研究生综合楼丝绸之路区域合作与发展法律研究院图书馆,深圳大学法学院教授、外层空间法专家、法学博士尹玉海教授为我院师生举行了题为“外层空间法理论与实践的新发展”专题讲座,本次讲座由我院院长刘亚军院长主持,我校副校长、国际法研究中心主任、郑斌航空与空间法研究所所长王瀚教授出席并致辞,我院王秀梅教授、周亚光博士、张超汉博士、刘学文博士、时杜鹃博士及 2016 级国际法专业研究生参加了讲座。

讲座开始之前,王瀚副校长宣布聘请尹玉海教授为郑斌航空与空间法研究所特聘研究员并向其颁发聘书。随后尹玉海教授为大家进行了精彩纷呈的报告,从国际与各国空间立法体系,空间碎片减缓指南、外空自卫权等理论与实践热点以及我国与外空法相关的部门等几个方面,深入分析并系统介绍了目前外层空间法理论与实践的发展情况。

最后,讲座进入互动环节,与会师生就外空军事用途,外空条约中有关人类共同财产问题与美国国内法规定等方面踊跃提问,尹玉海教授一一给予耐心解答,并就学科整合等问题进行了进一步的延伸性探讨。

26. 张望平博士等赴厦门参加中国航空法学研究会 2017 年年会

2017 年 11 月 18 日郑斌航空与空间法研究所张望平博士、张超汉博士、博士生时杜娟、硕士生刘恬赴厦门参加中国航空法学研究会 2017 年年会。本届年会由中国法学会航空法学研究会和中国民用航空局国际合作服务中心主办,厦门市法学会承办,厦门航空公司、厦门翔业集团、厦门远大联盟律师所协办。本次会议的主题是“‘一带一路’民航法治实践与创新”,来自全国各地的近200位航空法领域的专家学者和实务精英参加了会议。

会议开幕式在厦门罗约酒店会议中心举行，开幕式由中国航空法研究会会长、东航集团总法律顾问郭俊秀主持。中国民航局政策法规司副司长郭仁刚、厦门市法学会副会长吴少鹰、厦门仲裁委员会主任钟兴国分别致辞，对此次年会的召开纷纷表示祝贺。

此次年会设有四个讨论单元，参会代表分别围绕“一带一路”航空法治、“一带一路”航空国际经营法律问题与争议解决、“一带一路”民航法制建设法律问题、“一带一路”中国航空制造与服务法律问题这四个专题进行了主题发言。深入分析了“一带一路”与民航法的修订和完善、“一带一路”航线开设法律问题、政府引领民航法治创新思路、中国民航企业创立标准法律问题、无人机国际销售法律问题、航空器权利登记与航空器交易多功能平台建设、“一带一路”航空器融资租赁登记制度、“一带一路”国际货物多式联运经营人责任、“一带一路”国产飞机销售法律问题、“一带一路”机场建设投资法律挑战、“一带一路”航空跨境融资租赁风险防范、“一带一路”航空运输中实际承运人法律责任、“一带一路”国际航空仲裁、“一带一路”航空运输纠纷解决机制、航空业国际反垄断监管法律问题等民航专业法律问题。这些议题受到了航空法学界和航空实务界学者和专家的广泛共鸣和积极讨论，对今后民航立法完善、民航服务创新、民航产业管理等方面产生了重大的影响，受到了与会人员的高度关注和积极讨论。

张望平博士、张超汉博士、时杜娟博士生、刘恬硕士生在分组讨论环节分别就“一带一路”航空法律争议解决、航空产品责任的风险控制、机场投资模式、航空安保等问题发表了自己的看法，和其他与会专家充分交流了思想。

27. 张超汉博士就两岸航空运输法律冲突及解决思路作专题讲座

2017年12月6日由西北政法大学国际法学院、国际法研究中心、丝绸之路区域合作与发展法律研究院联合主办的以“两岸航空运输法律冲突及解决思路”为主题的学术讲座在我校雁塔区研究生综合大楼国际法学术报告厅举行。本次讲座由郑斌航空与空间法研究所副所长张超汉博士主讲。2016级和2017级国际法硕士研究生参加了讲座。

首先,张超汉博士从海峡两岸航空运输法律冲突产生的背景入手,指出两岸“三通”以来,航空运输日益频繁,一旦发生航空事故,将涉及受害人损害赔偿问题,但由于两岸航空法律制度不同,适用不同法律将直接影响受害人的利益。其次,张超汉博士从四个方面分析了两岸航空运输法律冲突的成因。最后,张超汉博士重点介绍了解决两岸航空运输法律冲突的三种模式:一是统一实体法模式;二是冲突法模式;三是民间机构协商模式。张超汉博士认为三种模式各有利弊,存在内在逻辑联系,将三种方法优势互补、有序并进,可作为解决两岸航空运输法律冲突的一种新思路。

讲座最后,结合讲座内容,张超汉博士讲解了学术论文的写作技巧、创新以及研究方法等,重点从观点新、视角新、材料新和方法新四个方面阐述了学术创新的路径,并对研究生学习规划、阅读计划、资料收集及就业方向提供了指导建议。

28. 欧盟航空法协会主席帕布罗教授在我校作“国际航空运输承运人责任”专题讲座

2017年12月7日欧盟航空法协会主席、荷兰莱顿大学航空与空间法国际研究所所长帕布罗·门德斯·戴莱昂(Pablo Mendes de Leon)教授来我校访问,进行了题为“国际航空运输承运人责任”的学术讲座。讲座于我校雁塔校区研究生综合楼三楼国际法学术报告厅举行,西北政法大学副校长王瀚教授为讲座致辞,西北政法大学国际法学院院长刘亚军教授担任主持。《法律科学》杂志的编辑孙尚鸿教授,西北政法大学国际法学院的青年教师张光副教授、师怡副教授、张望平博士、张超汉博士、周亚光博士以及我校2015级、2016级和2017级国际法专业研究生参加了本次讲座。

王瀚教授首先隆重介绍了帕布罗教授在航空法领域的贡献,对帕布罗教授第二次访问我校并分享其学术成果表达了诚挚的谢意。王瀚教授代表,西北政法大学航空与空间法研究所向帕布罗教授赠送了研究所于今年撰写完成并由法律出版社出版的6本航空法学专著,帕布罗教授对研究所在该领域取得的丰硕成果表示祝贺。

讲座围绕国际航空运输责任展开，帕布罗教授首先探讨了契约自由在航空运输合同中的限制问题。帕布罗教授认为，承运人的合同义务应结合当事人的约定及《华沙公约》与《蒙特利尔公约》的规定，综合考虑。他指出，尽管合同当事人有缔约自由，但此种自由受诸多因素的影响，如一般的法律原则的影响（诚实信用原则和有约必守原则），并且不得违反公共秩序。而判定国际航空运输合同中的承运人责任，还应考虑法律适用和管辖权问题。国际航空运输合同的一方当事人是航空公司，另一方当事人是旅客或者航空货物运输合同中的托运人。这两方当事人所订立的运输合同，不仅应当遵循契约自由原则，还应当受制于国际航空运输公约对于承运人责任的规定。承运人的合同义务由诸多因素决定，包括国际航空运输公约的规定、区域性安排（如欧盟）、国内立法、国际航协所规定的航空运输条件、承运人之间的协议及双方当事人的约定等。

帕布罗教授还与大家探讨了1929年《华沙公约》和1999年《蒙特利尔公约》关于航空运输责任和管辖权的规定。主要内容有：国际航空运输公约的适用、航空运输单证（客票及航空运单）、承运人承担赔偿责任的条件、损害赔偿及管辖权问题等。国际航空运输公约不调整的法律问题，如国内运输、损害赔偿的计算、精神损害赔偿、当事人的诉权、程序法问题及诉讼时效的计算等，留待国内法解决。

29. 张超汉博士应邀参加2017年海峡两岸国际私法学术研讨会

2017年12月8日至12日，2017年海峡两岸国际私法学术研讨会在台湾东华大学召开。本次会议由中国国际私法学会与我国台湾地区国际私法研究会共同主办，台湾东华大学财经法律研究所承办。来自海峡两岸的相关高校、科研单位和法律实务部门的60多位专家、学者参加了研讨。西北政法大学国际法学院青年教师，郑斌航空与空间法研究所副所长张超汉博士应邀参加了此次会议。

此次会议主要围绕“两岸国际私法的立法与司法实务”“海牙国际私法

会议的功能与展望”“人际、区际与时际法律冲突法”三大主题展开研讨。在2017年12月9日第四场“海牙国际私法会议的发展”主题研讨中,张超汉博士对台湾文化大学法律学系副教授吴盈德博士作的《涉外有价证券准据法之探讨——以海牙证券公约为例》的主题发言作了与谈。在12月10日第五场“区际法律冲突法”主题研讨中,张超汉博士发表了题为《两岸航空运输领域若干法律冲突及其解决思路》的演讲。张超汉博士对两岸航空运输法律冲突的定性及其影响、两岸航空运输法律冲突的产生原因及其表现、两岸航空运输法律冲突的解决模式及存在的问题作了重点分析与反思,并认为当前解决两岸航空运输法律冲突的方法除了传统的统一实体法和冲突法方法之外,还应当考虑民间机构相互协议模式,即通过海协会和海基会以及航空承运人之间的协议模式规定当事人之间的权利与义务以及发生航空运输争议时可适用的法律,并指出这一民间机构协议模式应当作为协调两岸航空运输法律冲突优先考虑的方法。根据会议安排,张超汉博士还对东海大学法律学院林恩玮教授关于“两岸产品责任法律适用问题之研究”的发言作了点评与交流。

张超汉博士的演讲与表现,受到两岸学者的好评。此外,张超汉博士还就我校国际航空法特色研究方向向台湾地区学者作了介绍。无疑,通过此次研讨,进一步加强了两岸国际私法学者的学术交流,向世界展示了大中华区国际私法的研究成果。

30. 王瀚教授等访问河南财经政法大学和郑州航空港经济综合实验区

2017年12月21日西北政法大学郑斌航空与空间法研究所所长王瀚教授、国际法学院院长刘亚军教授、郑斌航空与空间法研究所研究人员师怡副教授、张望平副教授、周亚光博士应邀访问了河南财经政法大学和郑州航空港经济综合实验区。

在河南财经政法大学,王瀚教授一行与该校副校长刘荣增教授和研究院院长李金铠教授进行了座谈。刘荣增教授对王瀚教授一行的到访表示欢迎,随后介绍了河南财经政法大学的办学历史、招生规模以及学科发展的情况;李金铠教授则重点介绍了研究院的人员组成、研究实力和已有成果。王瀚教授在座谈中向河南财经政法大学的热情邀请表示了感谢，并期待两个学校未来能够在诸多领域进行合作，尤其是临空经济区的合作研究。最后，王瀚教授向河南财经政法大学赠送了“中国航空法学术文库”的系列丛书和西北政法大学法律文化系列丛书。

结束了对河南财经政法大学的访问，王瀚教授一行又造访了郑州航空港经济综合实验区，该实验区是我国第一个以航空经济为引领的国家级新区。在实验区访问期间，王瀚教授等对实验区的整体布局、产业规模、发展历程、政策优势等情况进行了了解，并参观了实验区的物流仓储中心和河南电子口岸数据中心。王瀚教授指出，在“一带一路”倡议下，各地的空港建设都迎来了良好的发展机遇；郑州航空港经济综合实验区的物流服务已经处于国内领先地位，下一步应当打造更加全面的航空综合服务体系，包括飞机的融资租赁中心、维修中心和飞行体验中心等。郑州航空港经济综合实验区党工委书记马健对王瀚教授的提议表示感谢，并邀请我校的航空法团队再次访问该实验区，以便双方开展更为深入的合作。

《中国航空法评论》稿约

《中国航空法评论》是由陕西省哲学社会科学重点研究基地——西北政法大学国际法研究中心和西北政法大学郑斌航空与空间法研究所主办,由法律出版社出版的文集。

本文集秉承弘扬学术,探究法理,注重国际国内立法与司法实践的特色,力求收录海内外与航空法律、航空政策相关的一切研究成果。本文集涉及航空法热点问题评析、航空公约述评、国际国内航空法立法动态、航空案例研究、资料信息、译文摘录、学位论文等内容。

本文集面向国内外征集稿件,热忱欢迎国内外专家、学者、学界同人及同学不吝赐稿。稿件要求如下:

一、本文集欢迎选题新颖、有独到见解和学术价值的航空法中英文论文或资料信息。

二、来稿形式不限,学术专论、评论、判解研究、译作等均可,篇幅长短不拘。

三、来稿须同一语言下未曾在任何纸质和电子媒介上发表,请勿一稿多投。

四、来稿应附有作者简介(姓名、学位、工作单位、工作单位及职务、职称、研究领域和通信方式及 E-mail 地址等)。基金资助的论文应对基金项目名称、项目编号予以注明。

五、译作请附寄原文,并附作者或出版者的翻译书面授权许可。译者需保证该译本未侵犯作者或出版者的任何权利,并在可能的损害产生时自行承担损害赔偿责任。本文集主编及编委会不承担由此产生的任何责任。

六、本文集注释使用脚注,每页重新编号,不使用尾注注释规范。具体注释规范请参考文集样刊格式。

七、本文集实行文责自负原则。

八、本文集欢迎对收录的文章、案例和相关资料信息予以转载、摘登、翻译和结集出版,但应尊重原作者依照《著作权法》所享有的权利,在实施转载时请注明“转自《中国航空法评论》20××年第×卷”,以及原作者、译校者署名,同时书面通知执行主编。

九、凡向本文集投稿,即视为接受本稿约。

执行主编:张超汉

投稿邮箱:aviationlawreview@126. com

图书在版编目(CIP)数据

中国航空法评论. 第三卷 / 王瀚主编. -- 北京：法律出版社, 2018
ISBN 978-7-5197-2925-7

Ⅰ. ①中… Ⅱ. ①王… Ⅲ. ①航空法-研究-中国 Ⅳ. ①D922.296.4

中国版本图书馆CIP数据核字(2018)第281661号

中国航空法评论(第三卷)
ZHONGGUO HANGKONGFA PINGLUN (DI SAN JUAN)

王 瀚 主编

策划编辑 沈小英
责任编辑 沈小英 张泽华
装帧设计 李 瞻

出版 法律出版社
总发行 中国法律图书有限公司
经销 新华书店
印刷 北京虎彩文化传播有限公司
责任校对 郭艳萍
责任印制 吕亚莉

编辑统筹 财经法治出版分社
开本 710毫米×1000毫米 1/16
印张 20
字数 350千
版本 2018年12月第1版
印次 2018年12月第1次印刷

法律出版社/北京市丰台区莲花池西里7号(100073)
网址/www.lawpress.com.cn
投稿邮箱/info@lawpress.com.cn
举报维权邮箱/jbwq@lawpress.com.cn
销售热线/010-83938336
咨询电话/010-63939796

中国法律图书有限公司/北京市丰台区莲花池西里7号(100073)
全国各地中法图分、子公司销售电话：
统一销售客服/400-660-6393
第一法律书店/010-83938334/8335
西安分公司/029-85330678
重庆分公司/023-67453036
上海分公司/021-62071639/1636
深圳分公司/0755-83072995

书号：ISBN 978-7-5197-2925-7
定价：160.00元